THE COLOR OF CITIZENSHIP

The Color of Citizenship

RACE, MODERNITY AND LATIN AMERICAN/HISPANIC
POLITICAL THOUGHT

By Diego A. von Vacano

OXFORD
UNIVERSITY PRESS

Oxford University Press is a department of the University of Oxford.
It furthers the University's objective of excellence in research, scholarship,
and education by publishing worldwide.

Oxford   New York
Auckland   Cape Town   Dar es Salaam   Hong Kong   Karachi
Kuala Lumpur   Madrid   Melbourne   Mexico City   Nairobi
New Delhi   Shanghai   Taipei   Toronto

With offices in
Argentina   Austria   Brazil   Chile   Czech Republic   France   Greece
Guatemala   Hungary   Italy   Japan   Poland   Portugal   Singapore
South Korea   Switzerland   Thailand   Turkey   Ukraine   Vietnam

Oxford is a registered trade mark of Oxford University Press
in the UK and certain other countries.

Published in the United States of America by
Oxford University Press
198 Madison Avenue, New York, NY 10016

© Oxford University Press 2012

First issued as an Oxford University Press paperback, 2014.

Library of Congress Cataloging-in-Publication Data
Von Vacano, Diego A., 1970–
The color of citizenship : race, modernity and Latin American/Hispanic political thought / Diego A. von Vacano.
    p. cm.
Includes bibliographical references and index.
ISBN 978-0-19-974666-8 (hardback : alk. paper); 978-0-19-936888-4 (paperback)
1. Citizenship—Latin America—Philosophy—History.
2. Race—Philosophy. 3. Latin America—Race relations—Philosophy. 4. Philosophy, Latin American. I. Title.
JL967.A2V65   2011
305.80098—dc22   2011013921

To my parents, Arturo and Marcela

Contents

Preface ix

Introduction 3

1. *Paradox of Empire: Las Casas and the Birth of Race* 26
2. *Mixed into Unity: Race and Republic in the Thought of Simón Bolívar* 56
3. *Race and Nation: The Democratic Caesarism of Vallenilla Lanz* 83
4. *The Citizenship of Beauty: José Vasconcelos's Aesthetic Synthesis of Race* 112

Conclusion: Making Race Visible to Political Theory 141

Notes 165
Bibliography 207
Index 219

Preface

A RECENT BOLIVIAN film by the director Juan Carlos Valdivia, *Zona Sur*, encapsulates the complex politics of race in some parts of Latin America. In it, a wealthy, "white" family is entangled psychologically with its indigenous domestic servants. Growing up in La Paz, Bolivia, I always felt this kind of racial politics very close. While my family was lower-middle class, I attended a private French school in Achumani, in "la Zona Sur," one of the wealthier suburbs of the capital. Most of my classmates were "white," and the few who were not were sometimes treated as outcasts. Racial jokes about *indios* and *cholos* were not uncommon, and we—like most middle- and upper-class Bolivians— had *empleadas*, indigenous live-in maids who worked long, hard hours. The color line that separated Bolivians along racial lines was trenchant and deep. It created a *de facto* apartheid system that enshrined white privilege.

We eventually emigrated to the United States as political refugees owing to political turmoil in Bolivia in the 1980s. We left behind the racial politics of la Zona Sur, but I found a different kind of racial politics as a young Latino immigrant living in Queens, New York. The better classrooms and teachers were reserved for the white students, while mostly Latino and Asian immigrants were left to their own devices in what were supposed to be English as Second Language classes. I eventually realized that one's color, appearance, and way of speaking matter a lot in defining the meaning of being a "citizen," whether in Bolivia, the United States, or elsewhere.

These experiences led me to think about ways that we can theorize the intricate relationship of race to citizenship. This book is the product, and it argues that the Latin American experience—while it does indeed have many negative aspects when it comes to racial politics (as was and is the case in la Zona Sur)—can teach us a lot about the way in which race has been used to delineate a citizenry. We can trace the political uses of race in Latin American intellectual history, but we can also derive a normatively useful account of racial admixture that will serve us well as we proceed into the new century. This is because the rest of the world, including the United States, is slowly discovering what Latin America has known for centuries: miscegenation is not only not immoral, but it is inevitable and perhaps even necessary. Debates in the United States about multiracial identity, the possibility of a postracial world in the aftermath of Barack Obama, and demographic changes owed to the age of mass migration will ineluctably have to confront the intellectual tradition related to racial admixture that comes to us from Latin America.

This tradition's complexities are evident in *casta* paintings, such as the one that is this book's cover. Casta paintings, characteristic of the seventeenth and eighteenth centuries in parts of Latin America, were depictions by artists such as Miguel Cabrera and Andrés de Islas of the various *castas* or categories of mixed-race peoples that emerged out of the confluence of Amerindian, African, and Iberian groups. They are emblematic of the Spanish Enlightenment's use of aesthetic forms to enact social control, exercise power, and classify subaltern groups. Yet their inherent absurdity is evident from the bizarre names given to mixed-race individuals: for example, *Lobo, salta atrás, tente en el aire, torna atrás, Albarazado, Calpamulato, Chamizo, Coyote, Zambuigua, Cambujo,* and *Barcino*. Perhaps the most apt casta name was "No te entiendo" ("I do not understand you"), for it shows us that the attempt to delimit and classify discrete mixed-race identities leads to a *reductio ad absurdum*.

This book argues implicitly against the thinking behind casta paintings. It developed through roughly five stages. The initial concept came from teaching Latin American political thought at various institutions. For this reason, I have to thank my undergraduate students at Williams, Vassar, and Hunter colleges for helping me see the leitmotif of race throughout the history of Ibero-American ideas. I also thank the political science faculties of those colleges for providing a fecund environment for the growth of the project.

The second stage coincided with my first years as an assistant professor of political science at Texas A&M University. First and foremost, I have to thank Cary Nederman for having faith in me by asking me to apply for the position. Throughout my first three years there, I benefited from the immense support of the Department of Political Science as well as the university in general. In particular, Lisa Ellis provided me with encouragement and intellectual engagement. I benefited greatly from the suggestions of Judy Baer and Ed Portis. I also thank the graduate students in my Latin American political philosophy seminar at A&M. I am grateful to the Melbern G. Glasscock Center for Humanities Research for their generous support, as well as to the Mexican American / Latino Research Center.

While at the Institute for Advanced Study at Princeton and the Center for Advanced Study in the Behavioral Sciences at Stanford, I carried out the principal research for this book. I spent the two most productive (and idyllic) academic years of my life at these two incomparable institutions. The Woods and the Hill allowed me to wander the world of ideas to try to make sense of a seemingly endless stream of books and pages. In particular, I appreciate the intellectual and friendly support of Danielle Allen and Michael Walzer. Their suggestions were very useful in my attempt to build a structure out of books instead of bricks. I thank the faculty of the School of Social Science, including Eric Maskin and Joan Scott, as well as fellow Members, especially Aurelian Craiutu, Darrel Moellendorf, and Zouhair Ghazzal. I also thank Steve Macedo, George Kateb, Maurizio Viroli, Edward Telles, Miguel Centeno, Anthony Grafton, Deborah Yashar, Jeremy Adelman, Jonathan Israel, and Regina Graf for their advice and Yuval Jobani for our hours of conversation on Nietzsche, race, and politics. I must admit that I felt tempted to dedicate this book to the chef of the IAS, for his culinary masterpieces.

At Stanford, all the staff and fellows of the class of 2010 at CASBS were invaluable as I reached the midpoint of my intellectual explorations during the fourth stage. Iris Litt and Linda Jack were especially able in fostering intellectual engagement and fun lunchtime conversations. I am especially grateful to the participants of the Identity Table. I also thank the political theory community at Stanford, including Josh Ober, Josh Cohen, Rob Reich, and Debra Satz, as well as Tamar Herzog and Herbert Klein. I thank Larry Rosen, Konstantin Pollok, Saba Mahmood, Peter Struck, Lawrence Cohen, Barbara Fried, Sander Koole, Peggy Somers, Kanchan Chandra, and Dingxin Zhao for specific comments on my work.

The final stage of this project took place back in Texas. Again, I benefited from the extensive institutional support of Texas A&M University and the Department of Political Science. I must thank Pat Hurley and Jim Rogers as well as Ken Meier for their constant encouragement. My colleagues in all the subfields of political science provided a welcoming milieu for my return to A&M. I must also thank Jim Rosenheim, Charlie Johnson, Larry Oliver, and the Office of Latin American Programs. Christie Maloyed and Brad Goodine provided excellent research assistance. Jason Maloy's expertise in political theory and English football helped me as the project drew to a close. I benefited greatly from the BCS Soccer League and the Benson Latin American Collection of the University of Texas, Austin. I also thank the staff of the Archivo de Indias in Seville, the Vallenilla Archive held by Nikita Harwich in Saint-Germain-en-Laye, and the librarians at UNAM in Mexico City.

I am grateful to the Woodrow Wilson National Fellowship Foundation and the Mellon Foundation for funding. Outside of Princeton and Stanford, I must thank Will Kymlicka, Eduardo Bonilla-Silva, Eduardo Posada-Carbó, Iván Jaksic, Ofelia Schutte, Robert Gooding-Williams, Mark Bevir, Sarah Song, Paulina Ochoa, Michael Frazer, John McCormick, Lawrie Balfour, Mark Sawyer, José Antonio Aguilar, Joe Feagin, Lawrence Hamilton, Henry Louis Gates, Jr., and especially Jorge Gracia for years of support.

Friends and family helped me to reach the completion of this project. My parents, Arturo and Marcela, as well as my sisters, Marcela and Claudia, always provided warm encouragement. I am also grateful to María Antonieta Cámara, Mario Dorado, Alejandra Dorado, as well as to María Luisa and Pepe Cámara. Among friends and colleagues that I must thank are Ari Adut for being a fellow traveler of ideas in Texas, as well as Mario Álvarez, Otto Bottger, Séverine Boumati, Vivek Chadaga, Jorge Coronado, Silvana Cosulich, Robert Greene, Sebastián Hoyos, Christian Inchauste, Arang Keshavarzian, Samir Lone, Oliver Lu, Ashok Parameswaran, Morgann Paraskevas, Tamás Peterfalvy, Rouzbeh Pirouz, Jesse Upton, Patricio Villa, and Adam Webb. I also want to mention the name of Julia, the *empleada* who worked for my family for many years before we left Bolivia. She was a person who taught us a lot about the rich ethnic makeup of the place where I was born and raised. I would also like to thank Kazuko Suzuki for being the principal intellectual interlocutor throughout this project.

Finally, I must thank Angela Chnapko for her superlative work as the editor of this book. She guided the process with consummate efficiency and professionalism. It was a pleasure to work with the entire Oxford University Press team involved in this project.

THE COLOR OF CITIZENSHIP

INTRODUCTION

WHILE REFERRING TO the emergence of pecuniary activity as morally acceptable in the West, Hirschman's statement could very well be used to comment on the modern appearance of race on the political and social landscape around the time of the discovery of the Americas. Just as the profit motive is a complex passion, the rise of race and racial thinking in the human imaginary is something that, to this day, remains difficult to decipher. Having origins in the premodern world, "race" grew quickly once its seeds were scattered in the New World.

Why is race a persistent social problem when it is merely a superficial human characteristic, if it exists at all?[2] If we are all morally equal in spite of epiphenomenal differences, why has race been used to such great effect in politics? These questions have perdured, but few answers have been given to them until recently in the field of political philosophy. In this book, I address these questions with a narrative. It is a story that emerges from the history of ideas. I posit that these questions cannot be fully addressed with our current intellectual repertoires, which we have inherited from the Old World. I seek to show that when race does appear, it takes different forms in different places. One of the least studied of such places is Latin America.

I argue for a new framework for understanding race in light of Latin American intellectual history. Rather than discard or reject the idea of race, we should reconceptualize it, because it is a powerful social reality in the lives of most, if not all, modern people in some way or another. I show how, through a particular intellectual tradition, we can come to see the notion of race as essentially mixed, fluid, and dynamic, rather than static, fixed, or rigid. As such, admixture is inherent to the phenomenon of race. I proffer that

3

this reconceptualization of race is both analytically and normatively useful for under-standing the political role of race.

The view that races are essentially pure has had a strong hold on many minds through-out modernity. Perhaps the most emblematic of the stances against racial mixing is that of Arthur de Gobineau, who published his *Essay on the Inequality of Human Races* be-tween 1853 and 1855. Gobineau argued that there are three races (white, black, and yel-low), whose characteristics and interactions dictate history, including the rise and fall of civilizations. For him, any mixing of races was anathema, for it produced "degenerate" types and degraded the white race when it came into contact with other races.

Alexis de Tocqueville, who was—surprisingly—a close friend of Gobineau, com-mented on this book in his personal letters to him. On October 11, 1853, he wrote to tell Gobineau that he disapproved of what he considered to be the fatalism or determinism of Gobineau's racial theory.[3] He would go on to say that he was on the "opposite side of such doctrines." He did, however, offer some praise for the book, telling Gobineau that it was his best work "by far, the most remarkable of your writings, a work of great erudition . . . [and] rare perspicacity." The author of *Democracy in America* would write further that it was a book that was "well constructed," and could be read "with great pleasure owing to its intelligence." Lest we think that the commendation was not hon-est, he closes the missive by saying, "I have proven my sincerity through my criticisms; please believe also in my sincere praise."[4] Given that Tocqueville was highly critical of the thesis of Gobineau's work, it is quite remarkable that he would praise it in any manner.[5] And in a way, he did agree with Gobineau. For Tocqueville, "Those who hope that the Negroes [in the United States] will one day blend in with the Europeans are nursing a chimera. Reason does not persuade me that this will ever come to pass, and I see no evidence for it in the facts."[6]

Ten years after the letter written by Tocqueville to his friend Gobineau, in 1863, the term "miscegenation" was coined in the United States, in a falsified pamphlet entitled *Miscegenation: The Theory of the Blending of the Races, Applied to the American White Man and Negro*. This text purported to support racial intermarriage, claiming that this was the objective of the Republican Party. In reality, the pamphlet was written by a man called David Goodman Croly to sway popular opinion toward the Democrats. It was intended to inflame the sentiments of most white people, even those who supported the abolition of slavery, by drawing on their fears of racial mixing. Opposition to in-termarriage between blacks and whites in the United States was widespread, and it was expressed in this incendiary pamphlet.[7]

Some decades later, however, the Cuban patriot José Martí wrote one of his ma-jor essays entitled "The Truth about the United States." Writing in 1894 for *Patria*, a New York publication, he would state—in terms that sharply contrast with those of Gobineau and Croly—that "there are no races."[8] For him, there is an essential likeness among all so-called racial groups, as he wrote in his essay "Our America" in 1895. These statements are representative of what I call in this book the synthetic paradigm of race that can be found in Latin American intellectual history. It is a paradigm that stands in clear contradistinction to prevalent discourses of race in European and American intellectual history which promoted fixed and rigid boundaries and opposed intermixing in matters of race.

These sharp contrasts in intellectual history highlight the need to examine more closely the place of race in the course of political thought. In the field of contemporary political theory, important contributions to the construction of new frameworks have appeared in recent years.[9] Within a longer purview in the field of the history of political thought, however, the issue of race has not been adequately addressed. Canonical perspectives on this issue in European thought, while varied, have been hampered by a set of problems. Moreover, while the American tradition in political thought is a vast step forward in grasping the centrality of race in political life, it also has important limits that we need to transcend. For these reasons, I describe one particular paradigm of race found in Latin American political thought that can be useful not only to ascertain with greater clarity the nature of the idea of race but also to provide a normative framework that will allow us to retain the use of the term but with a newly reconceptualized formulation. This is because the idea of race, as much as many would like to jettison or ignore it so as not to give it validity, is a central social category of the modern period, and as such it is part and parcel of daily life and personal identity.[10]

We must look beyond Western paradigms if we are to understand race properly. In this book, I examine racial identity in relation to citizenship in the arc of the development of a particular paradigm of race outside the traditional occidental canon. By tracing the gestation, growth, and maturation of what I call the synthetic paradigm of race, we can recognize how race is a modern problem and what generated its appearance. For this, an approach by means of comparative political theory is necessary, since canonical political thought rooted in the European tradition does not tell us much about this issue.

This work is in the discipline of political theory, even though it has dimensions that touch on other fields.[11] The reason this work is grounded in political theory is that this discipline bridges the philosophical and the actual, political realms, in a way that I believe can help to elucidate the meaning of race. In this manner we can address its normative dimension as well, for race cannot be treated merely as a logical or abstract problem. It is rooted in practices and dynamics of power—sometimes political, sometimes intersubjective. But I want to argue that the discipline should confront more directly the problem of race rather than treat it as something ancillary or marginal to politics. Race is indeed a central political category in the manufacturing of political identity and the regulation of political membership.[12] Importantly, it is a dynamic political category; in other words, it changes over time and in particular historical contexts. In order to observe these changes, we must look back in time. For this reason, this book is an exercise in the history of political thought.

Canonical political theory (that is to say, the group of central Western texts dealing with matters of politics and justice from Plato to Nietzsche) has largely neglected race, even as it has gone through periods of great upheaval and creativity in dealing with other major social categories, such as class and gender. The Marxist schools of the nineteenth and twentieth centuries placed class at the center of their intellectual enterprise. Feminist perspectives have illuminated the problem of sexual oppression by placing sex and gender under the microscope at least as far back as the nineteenth century. Slowly, these two traditions became part of the political theory canon. It is now inconceivable to teach political theory without due attention to class or gender.

Only recently has there been a "third wave" questioning the canon, one in which race has emerged as theoretically salient.[13] To be sure, race remains an issue for serious (and sometimes not so serious) discussion in academic and scholarly circles.[14] But only after World War II did it emerge as an object of analysis in political theory. Still, a few names within mainstream political theory have addressed this issue, such as Hannah Arendt and Frantz Fanon (who is generally not treated as a major figure in the field).[15] But the discipline of history of political thought has generally not had much to say about it.[16] Even recent major figures in political thought are not known for engaging with race, say, John Rawls or Jürgen Habermas. There is reason to be concerned about this, since intellectual history informs contemporary normative political theory. This lacuna is all the more disturbing since it is something that can be traced back to the founding figures of Western political thought. From Aristotle to Rousseau and even to progressive thinkers such as Mill and Marx, the issues around race are either left unattended or addressed in a problematic manner. Discussions of foreigners, strangers, barbarians, and empires are there, but none gives full attention to what we understand by "race." Only in recent times has the problem of race been confronted directly by academics, but this is mostly in disciplines outside of political theory. Sociology, anthropology, cultural studies, history, comparative literature, and philosophy have paid more attention to the issue of race than political theory in recent years. There is a small but growing number of works dealing with race in political theory, yet they tend to be rooted in Western paradigms of race that can lead to limited conclusions.[17]

Yet at the same time, for the average person race is an important social reality. The commonsense view of race is that it is defined by the color of skin and the physiological characteristics of a person, which can be used to distinguish people among various groups within the human species. But, as with some other issues, political theory has been stunningly detached from the average-person perspective on race.[18] Since it is so fundamental to the lives of most people, it should be addressed more pointedly by political theorizing. In sum, historically, race has not been deemed worthy of much attention. A reconsideration of this history that looks outside traditional canons is necessary at the present moment. It is not that the idea of the canon is unjustified. Far from it. The canon of political philosophy is an important record of political wisdom and must be safeguarded. However, when a new and important political category emerges as central to political life and we find that it is inadequately treated in canonical texts, we must seek to expand our purview.

To properly understand the role of race in politics, we must locate it in its proper framework: that of modernity. In this project, we will see that race is integral to the making of the modern. It is not a vestige of premodern times, nor merely a reflection of modern phenomena. In the story of race in Latin American thought, we can trace this dynamic dimension over three principal periods of the modern era. In this way we find that race appears and becomes transformed *pari passu* with the rise of intricate processes in modern societies. We will observe how the makings of race appear quite suddenly—as Hirschman envisions the appearance of the profit motive—when the Americas are unveiled to the European imaginary. This early-modern period of discovery is followed by the height of modernity, which coincides with the construction of the nation-state. Disillusionment with the workings of the state as well as with the idea of rationality rises in the late-modern era. A focus remains on the future, but with a concomitant cosmopolitan utopianism. In all three phases, we examine how the ideas that help construct the concept of race arise and congeal with great political efficacy and utility. We find that the modern, seen in this light, is not something that appears solely in the European mind as a result of epistemological transformations originating in the thought of those such as Descartes and Bacon. It is the result of a confrontation between the West and the New World, which produces an entirely new universe of social and political realities and ideas.[19] The problem of race, generally lurking in the shadows of traditional political theory, comes to the fore when we focus our gaze on this confrontation between the past and the present. Modernity is the offspring of the encounter between the Old and the New Worlds.

Empire, Race, and European Political Thought: The Domination Paradigm

A brief overview of the development of the notion of race in some of the key figures in the history of modern political thought is necessary to think about how the canon has viewed this idea. Both the European and the American traditions are important, and both manifest diverse, multifarious accounts of how race functions in the political sphere.

European political thought's perspective on race was built on the platform of religion and putative science. Before the eighteenth century, European thought evinced a strong association between blackness and evil and sin. Yet there was no conception of race as a physical category within European thinking before the 1700s. We do not find anything similar to our conception of the term in either ancient Greek or Roman political thought. There are, nonetheless, ideas that feed into the later burgeoning of the term in Europe.[20] It is possible to find proto-racial ideas in Plato's *Republic*.[21] Breeding a master race, or a eugenic project, is a topic of chapter 5 of this capital text in the history of political philosophy. For Aristotle, philosophy is a practice that characterizes the Greek world, and thus excludes those outside it.[22] The complicated term "barbarian" gains prominence in the disciple of Plato. Standing outside the realm of the polis, the barbarian is ruled by necessity, not reason. The lack of verbal ability and political participation makes some human beings inferior to those of the Greek polis. Hence, some are slaves by nature and can be legitimately held under bondage. The doctrines of the barbarian and natural slavery in the Philosopher's writings can be interpreted as contributing to a racialist tradition.[23] As Hannah Arendt tells us, the Greeks saw themselves as a group superior to all others owing to their excellence (*aretē*). In Roman political thought, we find an iteration of the civilized-uncivilized distinction in Polybius's understanding of brutal men, who "can no longer be called human beings."[24] Cicero, however, believed that virtue could be reached by any person of any race or people (*gens*); yet this achievement by necessity would have to take place in the *civitas*, or the Roman community.[25]

The term "race" has an opaque etymology, but is often thought to originate in the Romance languages of the Middle Ages, where it referred to the breeding of animals.[26] When it was eventually applied to humans, there was a strong religious foundation to its conceptualization. The Bible was used to explain human variation, and two basic schools of thought appeared: monogenesis and polygenesis.[27] The former asserted that there was a single source of creation of all humans, and the latter posited that human groups were created separately.

Polygenesis was propounded by important figures in European thought during the Renaissance. Paracelsus, a Swiss physician and chemist, proposed in 1520 that the children of Adam were located in only a small part of the earth, while black and other nonwhite people had origins of a different nature.[28] He used biblical reasons for this argument. In 1591 Giordano Bruno, the Italian philosopher, claimed that it was not possible to conceive that the Ethiopians (black Africans) descended from the same roots as Jews. Indeed, Jews were often seen as the first "Others" in early-modern racial discourse in Europe.[29] Bruno concluded that God must have created various Adams, or that Africans came from so-called pre-Adamite groups. It is important to note that he wrote during a time when African slaves were common in his hometown of Naples.[30]

Early-modern political thought in the canonical European tradition for the most part contains a lacuna on race and its tributaries, much like the silence on the topic in medieval thought. Niccolò Machiavelli's seminal work *The Prince* does not deal with matters of purity of blood, which were beginning to appear both in the Spanish peninsula and northern Europe.[31] He ignores the racial dimensions of the discovery of the Americas, which were nonetheless the buttress of one of his favored princes, King Ferdinand of Aragon.[32] In Thomas Hobbes we find very few references to the New World as well. As Quentin Skinner has recently argued, however, Hobbes depicted the North American natives as representing fear, insecurity, and complete freedom in the iconography of the frontispiece of some of his works.[33] Thus, he associates the natives' liberty with lack of authority and security.[34] When we arrive at John Locke we encounter a more direct confrontation with the New World. In his oeuvre we find a tension between his espousal of liberty and toleration on the one hand, and a possible justification for the displacement of Native Americans.[35] Locke's regard of Native Americans on the other is encapsulated by his description of their land as "the vacant place of America."[36]

It is only when we come to the Enlightenment that we find a truly rich period in European intellectual history in terms of Western assessments of non-European peoples.[37] By the mid-eighteenth century, science took the stage in the effort to understand human variation. Carolus Linnaeus, a Swedish botanist, published *Natural System* in 1735. In it, he devised a system of human classification.[38] But it described Europeans as gentle and inventive, while Africans were crafty, indolent, and ruled by whim. In *Natural History*, written in 1749 by Georges de Buffon, the white race was presented as the touchstone.[39] Whiteness, in his view, was the original color of humanity. Johann Blumenbach wrote *On the Natural Varieties of Mankind* in 1775, advancing a theory of five human races.[40] He ranked them in terms of distance from the civilized European group. He employed the term "Caucasian," using aesthetic criteria to argue that the women of the Caucasus region were the most beautiful.

The most important characteristic of the Enlightenment for race is the initial skepticism about empire shown by some leading thinkers, which, in the course of about fifty years, was supplanted by a largely uncritical defense of colonial policies by the European intelligentsia.[41] We find an idealization of the character of indigenous peoples in Rousseau's doctrine of the "noble savage," for which he found purported evidence among the Caribs of northern Venezuela, and in Montaigne's discussion of cannibals.[42] While benevolent in spirit, the idea also betrays a certain condescension toward native American peoples. This tension is found in many other prominent thinkers of this era. Some railed against imperial policies, yet still held racialist or racist views. Such is the case of Kant. While he decried the injustice of imperialism and promoted a strong view of monogenesis, Kant had a severely myopic view of non-European peoples. For instance, he claimed, in his *Of the Different Human Races* (1775), that "the Negro . . . is indolent, lazy, and dawdling" and, using false science, that "the evaporation of phosphoric acid . . . explains why all Negroes stink."[43] Thus, while some of the anti-imperial writings of thinkers of this period are commendable in promoting principles of equality, explicitly racist statements such as Kant's tarnish this particular tradition. Similarly, Hume would write, "I am apt to suspect the Negroes, and in general all the other species of men (for there are four or five different kinds) to be naturally inferior to whites."[44] It is a position that contrasts profoundly with the intercultural egalitarianism of some other European Enlightenment thinkers, such as Montesquieu,[45] Adam Smith, Edmund Burke,[46] and also Herder.[47]

The domination paradigm, which sees a significant gulf between Europeans and non-Europeans, is also evident when we address British utilitarianism. John Stuart Mill, a principal founder of modern liberal political theory, also possessed along with Kant a similar tension in his thought, albeit reversed.[48] On the one hand he denounced racism as irrational and unjust, but he defended imperial policies on the grounds that non-European areas of the world needed them in order to progress.[49] Mill would state that despotism "is a legitimate mode of government in dealing with barbarians."[50] Thus, we find the obverse problem present in Kant: a critical view of racial thinking, but with a well-thought-out justification for colonialism, unaware that this creates a deep friction that in fact promotes a paradigm of domination toward non-Western groups.[51]

The last major component of modern canonical European thought with regard to race is found in German intellectual history. In it we find the long legacy of Hegel. This preeminent philosopher of modernity shared with Kant a disdain for most non-European cultures. He finds that, unlike Asian traditions, those of Africa and of the natives of America provided no contribution to world history. "Negroes are to be regarded as a race of children" and "the natives of America are . . . not in a position to maintain themselves in the face of the Europeans. The latter will begin a new culture over there on the soil they have conquered from the natives," he would write in *Anthropology* in 1830.[52] The first statement is simplistic and racist, while the second is patently false. What took shape in areas formerly dominated by the Inca, Maya, and Aztec, for instance, created a mixed, rich culture that was by no means a simple reproduction of European ways of life. A similar problem is found in that quintessentially radical thinker, Karl Marx. Implicit in his understanding of world history is the notion that a global proletariat should be created out of similar capitalist labor conditions throughout the world. This expectation carries with it the notion that a European-style dynamic of class conflict should be repeated throughout the world.[53] Marx is unaware of or uninterested in the fact that this would mean a displacement not only of oppressive economic conditions but also of indigenous forms of culture. As he states, "England has to fulfill a double mission in India: one destructive, the other regenerating—the annihilation of old Asiatic society, and the laying of the material foundations of Western society in Asia."[54] Finally, we arrive at who is perhaps the most complicated European author when it comes to race, Friedrich Nietzsche. Nietzsche was one of the few European thinkers of the late-modern period who did discuss race explicitly. Notwithstanding the illegitimate Nazi appropriation of phrases related to race in Nietzsche's writings, it must be said that there is no clear coherence in the totality of Nietzsche's use of the term. Still, much of what he said lent itself to either association with German nationalism[55] or was so complicated that its use and abuse by racists was no surprise. This is especially the case since his stance on Jewish people was also ambiguous, for sometimes he praised them and sometimes he deprecated them.[56] It is only late in the twentieth century that European thought began to engage seriously with matters of race, and we find this in *The Origins of Totalitarianism* by Hannah Arendt, published in 1951, where she proffers a critique of the racist ideas immanent in imperialism.[57]

Thus, in the course of European thinking about issues related to race, we find a common motif. While there are some thinkers who rejected racism, and others who were critical of racial thinking, the general tendency was to view the issues around race within the context of empire. Universalist Enlightenment ideals clashed with colonialist projects. In other words, this paradigm was fraught with internal contradictions. As European powers encountered nonwhite groups through colonial expansion and imperial administration, they tended to view the indigenous peoples as generally inferior to Western peoples. In some cases, such as that of Hegel, this was expressed in virulent, crass racism at odds with the spirit of equality inherent in the Enlightenment. In others, there is a deep contradiction between a commitment to this spirit and simple, hierarchical views of race, such as those of Kant. In what I call a domination paradigm of race, most European thinkers who dealt with the issues around race or with the term proper saw the inhabitants outside of western Europe, and especially those in far-off colonies, as either inferior *simpliciter* or as underdeveloped and thus fit for tutelage. In this paradigm, it is difficult to think of race in a cogent manner, for rigid, fixed ideas of racial hierarchy are entrenched in the political imaginary.

The Color Line and American Political Thought: The Dualistic Paradigm

The figure that perhaps most clearly acts as a bridge between European and American political thought on matters of race is Alexis de Tocqueville. A Frenchman, his contributions can be considered part of the canon of American political thought owing to their profound meditations on U.S. democracy. In his best-known work, *Democracy in America*, he does indeed depart from most of his fellow European thinkers by writing explicitly about the problematic issue of race in the country he visited.[58] He is, however, the transitional figure from a domination paradigm to one that is dualistic.[59] He advocated imperialism as some of his fellow European thinkers did, and he also pointed the way toward North America, where he found that racial issues were among the most important in society. Throughout the text of this cardinal work, he uses the terms "Anglo Americans" or the "English race in America" to define Americanness. He regards African Americans and Native Americans as distinct from the "American race," and believes there is a deep incompatibility between them and the "English race" in the United States. This coexistence of three major racial groups, far from being a source of strength (or perhaps of a subsequent rich and valuable miscegenation), represents the "dangers that threaten the confederation."[60] Thus, Tocqueville retains a condescending approach to non-European races, but at the same time affirms a categorical distinction between the three racial classifications. It is this rigid categorization that develops further in American political thought.[61] From Tocqueville's racial triad, there is a rapid move toward a dyadic understanding of race.

In this tradition of American thought, however, we find a much richer-hued understanding of the political problems associated with race relative to European intellectual history.[62] The arrival of Europeans to the Americas, both North and South, started the most significant process of the construction of race. As Omi and Winant aver in their now-classic work *Racial Formation in the United States*, "The emergence of a modern conception of race does not occur until the rise of Europe and the arrival of Europeans in the Americas."[63] While this statement has greater relevance for Spanish America because it was Spain that first landed in the New World, it also applies to the encounters of various ethnic groups in North America upon the advent of Europeans. Importantly, while the construction of whiteness was initially shaped by European contact with Native Americans,[64] the bulk of thinking about race in the United States has to do with the enslavement of Africans and their importation to the nascent republic. In effect, most major figures in American political thought refer to race, as we can see in the brief sketch that follows.[65]

Although a champion of liberal rights and "self-evident truths," Thomas Jefferson's treatment of race and slavery reveals a deep ambivalence in his political thought.[66] The issue of race is treated "scientifically" in his only book, *Notes on the State of Virginia*, where he discusses both the indigenous people of America and also black slaves. When discussing the natives, Jefferson notes that physical differences exist between the natives and whites, such as differences in physical strength and hair. He dismisses the argument that there are differences between the two in mental capacity, arguing that the absence of sophisticated culture is the consequence of not having a written language. Once this difference is considered, he argues that the natives will be "on the same module with the 'Homo sapiens Europæus.'"[67]

His treatment of black slaves follows a similar line of analysis, though he arrives at markedly different conclusions. Again, he discusses the differences between the white and black races, noting that whites have more hair, but also that they are more aesthetically pleasing. Most of his characterizations of blacks are less than complimentary. For example, he notes that blacks are as brave as and more adventuresome than whites, but also that these traits may be the consequence of a lack of forethought. He also directly compares the natives with black slaves, noting that although the natives have had no liberal education, they nevertheless demonstrate "astonishing" oratory skills, reason, and imagination. In contrast, he argues that despite their exposure to white culture, with its advanced education, black slaves display no inclination toward such cultural advancement, with the exception of music. Based upon his survey of the evidence, Jefferson tentatively concludes that "blacks . . . are inferior to the whites in the endowments both of body and mind."[68] When he is later presented with evidence of the academic and cultural achievements of some blacks, he expresses his desire to have his conclusion about the black race proven wrong. Though certainly opposed to slavery, he did little politically or privately to fight for abolition.[69]

During most of his life, Benjamin Franklin never questioned the institution of slavery or the inferiority of blacks. He owned two slaves who aided him in publishing his newspaper, the *Pennsylvania Gazette*, which also published advertisements for the slave trade.[70] Franklin first began to question the utility of the institution of slavery during the 1750s when he began working with a group that promoted the education of slaves.

As with most of Franklin's writings, his first criticisms of slavery were strictly economic. Because slavery encouraged whites to rely on others to do their work, it created a culture of indolence among slave-owning families. Furthermore, he speculated that maintaining slaves actually cost more than employing free men to do the same labor. Taking these factors together, Franklin suspected that slavery actually caused great harm to whites, but it was not until the 1760s that he began to consider the effects slavery had on blacks. Upon visiting a school for black children in Philadelphia, Franklin was quite surprised to discover how well the children were doing in the school: "I was on the whole much pleased, and from what I then saw, have conceived a higher opinion of the natural capacities of the black race, than I had ever before entertained. Their apprehension seems as quick, their memory as strong, and their docility in every respect equal to that of white children."[71]

Scholars of Abraham Lincoln vary widely when analyzing his views on race. Some have claimed that he was a great champion of racial equality, while others have argued that he was little more than a typical white supremacist. The difficulty in determining his true position comes from distinguishing between his personal convictions and his political actions.[72] Certainly Lincoln was constrained by public opinion in his ability to bring about racial equality, but it is debatable how much his own beliefs coincided with general public opinion. It is clear that Lincoln, beginning very early in his political career as an Illinois state legislator, denounced slavery as a morally depraved institution. He further argued in favor of the basic humanity of black slaves, a point that was still in wide contention. He was not a radical in his views on race, however, and often spoke out against the work of abolitionist groups. Furthermore, he supported a rather controversial plan to emancipate slaves and return them to free-slave colonies in Africa.[73] He feared that the passion surrounding this issue would make it impossible to achieve either peace or equality, and that colonization would provide the only opportunity to reconcile this problem. This was not a popular opinion among Americans given the high cost of returning freed slaves to Africa, and Lincoln did not widely promote his plan during his senatorial or presidential campaigns.

Born into slavery, Frederick Douglass never knew his father and was separated from his mother at an early age.[74] The wife of one of his masters taught him how to read and write, which, in part, inspired his desire to escape from slavery. In 1837 he managed to escape and fled to Massachusetts, where he joined the abolition movement and the Massachusetts Anti-Slavery Society. Influenced by William Lloyd Garrison, a prominent abolitionist, Douglass denounced the Constitution and expressed his willingness to "destroy the Union" in order to abolish slavery. During the 1850s, however, Douglass began to break from Garrison, arguing that the Union and the Constitution could be preserved because they did not inherently support slavery; rather, he declared that the Constitution supported justice and liberty such that it could not at the same time support the system of slavery. This guarantee of liberty extends to slaves, who should enjoy not only citizenship but also all the political and civil rights entailed by that status.

Booker T. Washington was born a slave in Virginia in 1856.[75] He emphasized the need for blacks to start at the bottom of the social ladder and to work their way up. Instead of fighting segregation and second-class citizenship, he argued that blacks needed to concentrate on learning useful skills and trades. He also called upon whites to encourage blacks in their endeavors to improve their lives, arguing that such improvement would benefit not only blacks but also whites. Indeed, he believed that once blacks bettered themselves through education and industry, they would in turn gain civil rights. Although the ideals of equality and freedom contained within the Declaration of Independence were important to Washington, he did not believe abstract principles could secure such a reality. Rather, he believed that blacks could demonstrate to whites that they were free and equal by engaging in the toils of labor that bring about home- and property-ownership in addition to education. His success lay in his ability to win over both blacks and whites by emphasizing the need for blacks to address their obligations before their rights, and by encouraging a friendship between the two races.

W. E. B. Du Bois was the first black American to earn a Ph.D. from Harvard, and his research into the historical and social condition of black Americans placed him among the most influential intellectuals of his time.[76] His work *The Philadelphia Negro* (1899) on the social and economic conditions of urban blacks in Philadelphia was the first sociological study of black communities of its kind. His subsequent work *Souls of Black Folk*, a collection of essays, focuses on the "double-consciousness" of black America: "One ever feels his two-ness,—an American, a Negro; two warring ideals in one dark body whose dogged strength alone keeps it from being torn asunder." Understanding this double self, Du Bois argues, allows the black American to merge "his double self into a better and truer self." In order to accomplish this merging of selves, however, black Americans must receive an appropriate education.

Thus, we can observe that eminent figures such as Jefferson did write about race, but often in terms that denigrate nonwhites (Jefferson would state: "I advance . . . that . . . blacks are inferior to . . . whites.")[77] We have to look to eminent African American thinkers such as W. E. B. Du Bois and Frederick Douglass to find a more in-depth engagement with the political dimensions of race. In both sides of the tradition of U.S. political thought, however, we tend to find a binary perspective on race that focuses on the "black-white" antinomy.[78] Du Bois stated that "we have at least two, perhaps three, great families of human beings—The whites and Negroes, possibly the yellow race" (*The Conservation of Races*, 1897). Thus, this "dualistic paradigm," while of immense value, has limits when we want to address problems in more diverse and mixed societies. The principal leitmotif of American political thought in relation to race is the problematic relationship between white, European descendents and those of black African slaves. At the inception of this tradition, some thinkers conceived of the Native American population as one of the three major ethnoracial groups. This conception is evident even in the nineteenth century in someone such as Tocqueville. The role of Native Americans is diminished quite rapidly, however, as the economic phenomenon of slavery becomes more salient. The slaves happened to be of black, African descent (as opposed to North African Arab origin, for instance). This lineage established the paradigmatic racial relationship in the United States, which I term dualistic because it centers on the white-black antinomy. In this schema, Native Americans cease to play much of a role in racial construction, and other groups, such as Hispanics who were in the American Southwest, for example,[79] do not figure prominently. The tragic tale of race in the United States has two prominent actors, and race itself becomes largely identified with a dichromatic paradigm.[80]

Rationale for a Synthetic Paradigm of Race

If indeed there is a domination paradigm of race that permeates most of European political thought and a dualistic paradigm in American political thought, why should we seek to find a new approach to race? The domination paradigm is limited because it is entrenched in a hierarchical, subjugation-oriented schema. It is not cogent analytically, because it clashes with the fact that there is no scientific evidence to the effect that different "racial" groups are inferior to others. It is also normatively inefficacious, for it cannot be rescued in a way that reconceptualizes the idea of race. To think of racial groups as inherently (or even provisionally) inferior is to deny the principle of human equality that is the bedrock of an egalitarian ethics. In short, there is no positive evidence, of a scientific or sociological nature, to support the fundamental claim of the domination paradigm, which is to affirm the leading role of white, European groups in either biological or civilizational terms.

A different set of limitations faces the American dualistic paradigm. To be sure, this paradigm is qualitatively different from the European one. Some central thinkers, such as Jefferson, do share with the European domination paradigm a failure to fully apply Enlightenment principles of equality, liberty, dignity, and fraternity to nonwhite groups. But other major thinkers, those in the African American tradition, engage with racial issues more deeply. While this engagement was pivotal for the construction of equality and civil rights for African Americans, it generally neglects those of other races, such as those of Hispanic or Asian origin.[81] At the same time, many of these preeminent black thinkers conceived of race as mostly fixed. They were aware of the porous boundaries between races, but still thought in terms of categorical conceptions of race. The case of Du Bois is emblematic of this tendency.[82] This categorization is problematic, because the persistent attention given to the color line affirms rather than questions racial categories. If indeed race is socially constructed, we must move away from lenses that tend to yield generally fixed and static notions of race, even if they are socially emancipatory.

An alternative to the above paradigms appears in the Latin American tradition. In this book, I trace the development of race as a dynamic political category in one particular strand of thought in the modern Ibero-American world. It is a quintessentially modern one because the discovery of the New World is itself a foundational act of modernity. The entirely new, in terms of new lands and newly found peoples in the eyes of the West, is characteristic of the events of 1492 surrounding the arrival of Columbus in Hispaniola, and this newness is at once expansively liberating and violently oppressive. It is a modernity that does not have a roseate view of progress and sees the dark dimensions of subjugation that come along with reason and development.

In the Latin American field of racial thinking, there are many varieties. The paradigm that I want to recover, which I call synthetic, is only one of many. It is a mode of thinking about the phenomenon of race and its tributaries in a way that eludes fixed, rigid notions and tends to incorporate those which are mixed and fluid. This occurs not in a limpid, perfect manner, but it is a pattern of thinking that recurs, in slightly different forms, throughout the modern history of Latin America. It stands in contradistinction with other major paradigms, such as the racialism of *indigenista* thought, which exalted "Indian" culture and races (sometimes to the point of idealization or caricature), as espoused by the Mexican thinkers Caso, Gamio, and Aguirre Beltrán.[83] And it also stands in opposition to the crypto-racism of preeminent liberals such as Argentina's Domingo Sarmiento and Juan Bautista Alberdi[84] as well as to the Latin American proponents of eugenics such as Renato Kehl, Fortuno Hernández, and Victor Delfino.[85] It is also distinct from the more recent accounts of hybridity, such as those of Nestor García Canclini and Walter Mignolo.[86]

The alternative paradigm that I explore in this book takes the notion of synthesis seriously. It is the philosophical comprehension—and transcendence—of the idea of *mestizaje*, which I take to be predominantly a politico-nationalist project with a heavy ideological charge.[87] The synthetic paradigm allows us to see that not only is race socially constructed, but it also has mixture at its core. There is no "race" that is pure or untouched by interaction with other so-called racial groups. To be sure, race is related to ethnicity, but it cannot be reduced to it. Ethnicity is necessary but not sufficient to understand common meanings of race. This is because, while the two terms are intimately related, the idea of ethnicity has closer ties to culture, while the idea of race implies—to most modern minds—some physical, somatic dimension. If this is how most people think of the idea of race, we must confront it as such. The synthetic paradigm, as we will see in the course of this work, is connected to both ethnic and phenotypical processes. These change over time, giving greater weight to one over the other at different periods; and this flux is visible in the three stages of modernity that I examine through an analysis of the ideas of four authors: Bartolomé de Las Casas, Simón Bolívar, Laureano Vallenilla Lanz, and José Vasconcelos. These are the colonial (early modern), republican (high modern), and cosmopolitan (late modern) periods of Latin American history.

In tracing critically these authors' complicated engagement with the problem of human diversity, I seek to show the development or unfolding of the ideas that eventually come together to shape what we understand as "race." Thus, race is not the same thing in all periods; it becomes constructed and redefined over time. I also argue that we must move beyond the still-pervasive understanding of race as something immutable and categorical. These authors, to be sure, do not offer translucent, incontrovertible accounts of race. What they do is engage with the *problématique* of race in such a way as to help us move beyond ossified categories, and toward a more modern view of race as inherently variegated and compatible with our current understanding of it as a social construct.

I take the multiple layers of the notion of "synthesis" seriously to elucidate the nature of race. This term refers first to the fact that "race" is something made up of separate parts combined into one entity. Thus, no race is pure, but each possesses a distinct identity of fused components. Second, the term also refers to the artificial or nonnatural essence of race. Race is not a natural phenomenon, but is socially constructed. The synthetic paradigm of race allows us to examine how this construction occurred in three different periods of Latin American intellectual history. Third, the term "synthetic" connotes a factitious notion that stands in place of something real. Thus, race is an illusion that stands in lieu of invisible relations of power, identity, membership, and citizenship. In some accounts, the term "synthetic" denotes that which requires observation if it is to be confirmed.[88] I examine this facet by positing the utility of observable aesthetic categories (such as color, shape, texture, and form) to the modern process of racialization.[89]

Last, this is a synthetic process in a neo-Hegelian sense on the plane of the philosophy of history. It is one where the first period can be seen as a thesis (the universalism of empire); the second as antithesis (the particularism of the nation); and the culminating period as a synthesis of the previous two (regional cosmopolitanism). I argue that in moving from one period to the next, we can use a Hegelian understanding of the development of ideas as constituting history, in this case, with regard to the idea of race. Hegel's postulation that history begins with unity is here expressed in the first, universalist period, when the human race is conceived of as singular. The second period expresses the introduction of the splitting of the unity into particular races. And the third is the overcoming or historical reconciliation of the first moments into a fundamental redefinition of the term "race."

Importantly, this narrative tells us that in each period, nonliberal theorizing about race provided key insights. The ideas in this story map onto the three historical periods, the colonial, the republican, and the cosmopolitan. In the first, Catholic imperialism was essential for the emergence of the synthesis of ethnicity and race; in the second, republican concepts of citizenship allowed for the idea of panracial unity at the level of the nation; and in the third, twentieth-century cosmopolitan thinkers used aesthetico-political ideas to show the common features of Latin American racial identity. Hence, this book acts as a corrective to the idea that liberalism is the only or best approach in political theory's account of ethnoracial issues. Ultimately, it aims to show that modern multicultural societies, such as the United States, can benefit from a reconceptualization of race, one that redefines it as something inherently synthetic, dynamic, mixed, and fluid, to break free from rigid categories such as those established by the legacy of the one-drop rule and laws such as the Naturalization Act of 1790, which limited naturalization to "free white persons."[90]

Taking the principle of synthesis seriously and as a complex of facets, we can avoid the criticism that this project is merely an attempt to restore the idea of *mestizaje*. Recent work in history and comparative literature has been invaluable in uncovering the subjugation that underlies much of discourse related to *mestizaje*.[91] The concept generally stands for a political project that razes difference, often carrying an essence of whiteness under a mantle of intermixing. The synthetic paradigm serves to question the stability of any racial category, be it a dominant white or a subordinated black or brown. In this manner, even indigenous Amerindian or Afro-Latino groups must be seen as inherently mixed and fluid in terms of racial identity. This project shows the multiple iterations of miscegenation that take place at various historical junctures in the political life of Latin America.[92]

These junctures are located in three modern periods. In the first, I show the birth of race *avant la lettre* in the thought of Bartolomé de Las Casas. This is the early-modern ascent of race as a central political category in Spain's project of empire. Here the essence of the process is universalism, as this author constructs a catholic conception of humanity. Far from being solely a defender of the Indians, the Spanish Dominican was committed to Spain's imperial ambitions. It is because of his Catholic imperial ideas that, paradoxically, he came to establish the foundations of a universalistic conception of the human race.[93] In the second period, the high-modern construction of the nation-state is facilitated by the use of race as a way to unify identity and create a common sense of citizenship. We find this in Simón Bolívar and later in Laureano Vallenilla Lanz, both of Venezuela. Here the essence is particularism, for specific nationalities were constructed out of the process in which race was a pivotal mode of regulation of identity, membership, and citizenship. When the nation-state fails to fulfill its promise, we find ourselves in the third period, which is that of the late modernity of early twentieth-century cosmopolitanism. Thinkers such as José Vasconcelos of Mexico construct an understanding of race that reacts to the inefficacy of the state. Here the essence of this understanding is the fusion of universalism and particularism, which yields a situated or rooted regional cosmopolitan perspective.

I choose these authors because they are emblematic of ideas in each period that lead to a synthetic paradigm of race.[94] Moreover, they are part of a line of thinking about race that does not make use of biological or scientific arguments. Thus, it is a paradigm that is constructed sociopolitically in a dynamic manner. I examine critically how these thinkers perceive race and/or its attendant concepts. Bartolomé de Las Casas has been treated as many things, ranging from a defender of indigenous peoples to a liberation theologian. But not much attention has been devoted to how his ideas feed into the making of race at the dawn of the modern period. At the same time, I believe he should be considered as a founder of modern political thought, a status that has eluded him in most accounts of the canon. In the republican period, Bolívar is the major transitional figure, someone whose writings offer arguably the most sophisticated Latin American contribution to republican theory infused with the problems of race and ethnicity. He was someone who rejected the bulk of Spanish thought, with the exception of Las Casas. As we proceed to the late-republican period, we find the oft-understudied work of Bolívar's compatriot, Laureano Vallenilla Lanz. The work of this sociologist and historian is important because it offers a view of racial synthesis from what we may call the perspective of an aristocratic republicanism that can be categorized as closer to the conservative tradition in Latin America. Thus, it shows that both liberal and conservative forms of republicanism held versions of the synthetic paradigm of race. At the same time, Vallenilla's notion of *cesarismo democrático,* I argue, has ties to both a Bolivarian and a Machiavellian conception of political power and constitutionalism. In the final period, the work of Vasconcelos must be addressed because his is arguably the most important contribution to thinking about race as a synthetic process in the history of modern Latin American philosophy. In his thought we find the universalism of Catholic ideas similar to those of Las Casas, but also the regionalism of Bolívar and the patriotism of Vallenilla. Hence, his thought is a synthesis of ideas we find in the first two periods. Vasconcelos possesses a utopian aspect, which brings up the question of whether utopian thinking is necessary as a way to address the problem of race normatively.[95]

The method that I use to examine these authors combines various resources of political theory. In the first instance, this is an exercise in the history of political thought. I examine the development of conceptions of race and their attendant influences. In this sense, it is a genealogical project.[96] To undertake a genealogical analysis of the problem of "race" is to carry out a historical analysis. This analysis does not seek to valorize the content of the term "race," but rather to disentangle the various strands that go into its making. Importantly, political power is involved centrally in the historical stages that shape it over time. The formation of "race" does not have a singular origin: it is a process that goes through a variety of transformations and historical crises or breaks. Hence, it is not unilinear: it does not follow one single path toward fruition. It is one narrative, but one that is shaped by multiple influences and periods. Last, this method does not seek to provide a moral assessment of the historical processes by which the modern notion of race was given shape.[97]

I argue that the three periods of theorizing about race are related to each other; hence I posit that we find a dialectical relationship between the periods. Thus, my method is modernist, in the sense that I argue that there is a relative coherence and accretion of ideas from one period to the next. However, this does not mean that there is progress or amelioration from one stage of the notion to the following. This is the case even as I recognize the disorder of actual social history. I do not seek to carry out a conceptual history of the term "race," but rather to examine the dynamic construction of a political category that is essential for the making of political identity. As I argue that race is best understood synthetically, I thus work within political philosophy as well, for I make a case for a particular definition of race that can have validity across space and time. Finally, this synthetic paradigm, as I elaborate it, has ethical value for modern, multicultural societies. In this sense, I work within normative political theory, claiming that, looking at the past, we can define the idea of race in a way that is morally useful for the present. Thus, while each historical transformation of the term can be examined without moral assessment, the paradigm that emerges from this analysis can be normatively valuable.

The Plan of the Book

The first part of this book concentrates on the relationship between empire and race in early modernity. I argue that there is a paradoxical process at work in this period because, while the Spanish Empire devastated and annihilated peoples and cultures in the Americas, it simultaneously laid the ground for a universalistic conception of the human race through some of its prominent thinkers. I show how the seeds of race emerged before the term was widely used in the period. In chapter 1, I examine critically the works of Las Casas (1474–1566), focusing principally on his *Short Account of the Destruction of the Indies*, which I argue has great value in the history of political thought. Reading Las Casas's works in light of this text shows us the eminently rhetorical nature of his project, as opposed to one that would be quasi-scientific (for instance, as a forerunner of ethnology) or one of rigorous Scholastic methodology.

I show Las Casas to be the first thinker to conceive of the Native Americans as part of the human race but also as categorically different from Europeans. In other words, while most of his European contemporaries (especially those who were Protestant)[98] saw the "Indians" as sub- or nonhuman, Las Casas argued for their status as members of humanity owing to their human "race" (*linaje*). Yet, at the same time, he saw them as fundamentally different from Europeans in that they were innocent, benevolent, childish, and in need of tutelage. Thus, I argue, he portrayed them as of a different human type, that is, race. Hence, Las Casas is the transitional figure from the domination paradigm to the synthetic one.

The chapter starts with a description of Las Casas's youth in Seville, his early travels to Hispaniola with Columbus, and his life as a slaveholder who eventually gives up his human chattel. It critiques his views on African slavery. It also describes the intellectual context of the time, particularly with reference to the period in which Las Casas changed his views about the Indians from a typical European paradigm to a more inclusive one (and his personal transformation from a European to an *hispanoamericano*), and to the period in which he debated Juan Ginés de Sepúlveda on the status of the Indians. I then show that Las Casas begins the synthetic paradigm of race by seeking to incorporate the Indians into the Spanish fold under the universalistic moral logic of Spanish imperialism. I also make a case for seeing Las Casas as a founder of modern political thought, particularly vis-à-vis Machiavelli, because the work of the Florentine provides a clear contrast to Las Casas that helps us understand the Spaniard's brand of modernity.

In the second part of the book (chapters 2 and 3), I explore the centrality of race to the making of the nation at the height of the modern era. From the universalistic logic of imperialism, we now move to its antinomy, the particularism of the nation-state.

Chapter 2 provides an analysis of the role of race in a founder of modern Latin American republicanism, Simón Bolívar (1783–1830). I show why Bolívar was pivotal in the construction of Latin American identity as mixed or synthetic. His writings on the very nature of Hispanic America evince a profound understanding of the realities of the biological and cultural miscegenation that was taking place in Spanish America during the colonial period. Bolívar sees Latin America's ethnoracial identity as synthetic (combining elements of indigenous, European, and African backgrounds) and distinct from that of both Europe and the United States.

The significance of Bolívar to modern political thought is that his understanding of republicanism is novel and rich in ethnoracial detail. While thoroughly educated in the Western canon (and in European schools), Bolívar's own republican theory is no mere reflection of European models. He applied Western political thought to the Americas, yet found the local ethnopolitical terrain and demography to be quite distinct from anything seen in the Old World. In this chapter, I examine his admiration for Las Casas. I show that he provides a theory of republicanism that is cognizant of ethnoracial differences and diversity, while seeking to fuse it with more classical accounts of the common good and rule of law. Rather than simply sweep race aside, his republicanism takes it seriously, even if it means that it can lead to the emergence of a strong executive to achieve order. In this chapter, I argue that Bolívar's thoughts on race and the republic can best be understood through an implicit affinity with Machiavelli's martial republicanism, rather than with Montesquieu's ideas, as is usually argued.

In chapter 3, I proffer an assay of the race-related ideas of a vastly underexamined thinker, the Venezuelan Laureano Vallenilla Lanz (1870–1936). Often considered merely an ideologue and apologist for the dictator Juan Vicente Gómez, in fact Vallenilla produced important writings on race from a conservative perspective, which in some important ways carry on the legacy of Bolívar.

I examine his trenchant critique of the idea that "pure" white Venezuelans should rule their nation, and explore his understanding of Venezuelan identity as made up of a variety of ethnic influences, including indigenous, African, and European. Vallenilla also presents Latin America's history as one of continuity with, not a radical break from, Iberia. Spain itself, he argued, was made up of a mixture of ethnic groups, such that *pureza de sangre* (purity of blood) was a dangerous myth.[99] While Vallenilla argues that Venezuela (and the rest of the Americas) must consider itself as the product of a synthesis of many ethnic and racial groups, he argues that the best way to contain their inherent tension is to provide for a strong executive in a republican system. I critically examine his notions of "democratic Caesarism," "the necessary gendarme state," and "political theology," in which he defends a strong leader within republican rule.

The chapter provides a description of his life as well as the political events and context at the time of his key writings. It places Vallenilla's thought in relation to contemporary Venezuelan politics and shows that he thinks synthetically about race by denying the idea of racial purity and by affirming the admixture of racial groups within his country. I also explore the tensions between racial identity and a strong executive in a republican government, discussing some parallels and differences with the thought of Max Weber and Carl Schmitt. The chapter shows that aristocratic republicanism cognizant of racial identities is an important element of the Latin American engagement with race.

Chapter 4 studies the links between race and cosmopolitanism during late modernity. Universalism and particularism are here subsumed to create a synthesis of both, where "Latin American regional cosmopolitanism" is the product. It is a result of the crisis of both imperialism and the nation-state, as well as increased dialogue among Latin American intellectuals. Owing to its future-oriented vision, I discuss this part in terms of a utopian perspective, which I argue is a necessary normative principle for political theorizing. In this part, I show how race can be understood through the lens of aesthetic political theory, especially in light of Nietzschean thought.

In this chapter I provide a critical analysis of perhaps the single most important contributor to racial political theory in Latin America. The legacy of José Vasconcelos (1882–1959) is vast and debatable, yet it had an immense influence in his country of Mexico as well as all over Hispanic America.

Contrary to most interpretations, which explain his views on race as a product of Mexican mestizo nationalism, I provide a philosophical analysis of how his theory of aesthetics explains his understanding of race. While most accounts of Vasconcelos are in comparative literature or history, I argue that he thought of himself principally as a philosopher, and that is how we should judge him. It is in his conceptions of music, art, dance, beauty, and aesthetics in general that he develops a notion of "synthesis," which I argue he replicates in the social world by utilizing it to make sense of ethnoracial diversity. Hence, his idea of a "cosmic race," representing the Latin race as made up of a synthesis of all the other races (white, black, Asian, and Native American), is really the product of his aesthetics of synthesis, in which diverse elements come together in harmony.

The chapter provides a brief description of his life, which was rich in political, personal, and cultural experiences. He was a central figure of the postpositivist critique of the Porfiriato regime in Mexico as well as of the Mexican Revolution. At the same time, I show he was deeply influenced by Catholic thought as well as Bolívar's idea of Latin American unity. The chapter also argues that Vasconcelos derived many of his aesthetic ideas from German philosophy, especially Nietzsche. I show the parallels and differences with this author, explaining that to make sense of Vasconcelos, we must discern this link clearly. His classic work *The Cosmic Race* is emblematic of his aesthetic conceptualization of race and racial politics, much of it influenced by a Nietzschean worldview.

Throughout these four chapters, I utilize comparative political theory to elucidate Latin American ideas in relation to those of Europe. I make use of the work of Machiavelli and Nietzsche because these two thinkers can be seen as framing modernity. Machiavelli is often understood as the founder of modern political thought and Nietzsche as its last critic. Since I argue that race must be located in the context of the modern, these thinkers provide a useful comparative framework. Hence it is instructive to conceive of Las Casas as positing an alternative modernity vis-à-vis the Florentine. Moreover, both Bolívar and Vallenilla are understood better if their ties to Machiavelli are examined. Similarly, Vasconcelos's late-modern ideas share affinities with those of Nietzsche.

In the conclusion, I discuss the broad themes of the book as well as its implications. I revisit the argument that the synthetic paradigm of race runs from the imperial to the republican periods and culminates in the cosmopolitan ideas of pan–Latin American identity. I discuss the role of Catholicism, gender, and class more broadly in this section. While these three forces created vast systems of oppression, the synthetic racial paradigm emerges in spite of them through the links between the ideas of the four authors. I also discuss the particular role of Afro-Latinos, and how they were seen by these thinkers.[100]

The conclusion also explains how the synthetic paradigm of race is normatively useful—even in the face of actual inequalities, hierarchies, and conflict—in Latin American societies. Here I discuss the relative valence of class and race. I argue that, *ceteris paribus*, the synthetic paradigm of race provides a theoretical framework that reduces racial inequality. Economic interests do tend to distort the positive effects of the paradigm, but it is the optimal lens, especially vis-à-vis other paradigms. The conclusion also dissects the entanglements between gender and race, recognizing their intricate ties but arguing that they can be analyzed separately.[101] In particular, I utilize the notion of aesthetic political theory to connect gender and miscegenation.

I propound that the synthetic paradigm is useful both because it describes empirical reality (all people are of "mixed race," not just in Latin America but elsewhere) and because it is normatively useful: by abrading hard and fast racial categories, we see the humanity of all peoples. "Race" is thus a concept to be rescued, especially for modern multiracial societies where different "racial" groups live with each other. I defend the value of a synthetic paradigm as an instrument to critically question the reification of all "racial" groups, whether they are "white," "black," "indigenous," or other. In this way I address the idea that race is inherently a hierarchical system.

I argue that the synthetic paradigm is different from and more cogent than alternative perspectives on race. Namely, I posit that neither liberalism nor postmodernism can fully grasp the meaning and development of "race."[102] I advance that the Latin American story of miscegenation and its intellectual defense were not part of a broader progress of liberty. In all three periods that I discuss, race is important, but not merely as the expression of ever-expanding notions of freedom. In fact, all three periods are deeply illiberal. Catholic imperial political thought, aristocratic republicanism, and aesthetic cosmopolitanism were not in accord with liberalism, especially understood as the moral supremacy of the individual and of rights.[103] I thus provide a critique that has implications on liberal political theory and its brands of multiculturalism.[104]

At the same time, the story I tell is quintessentially modern. It is a progressive movement toward a unified conception of race. Hence modern (not postmodern) political theory is needed to understand it. I argue that we live in a world where race is socially real; race cannot be dismantled by postmodernist approaches that seek to transcend it. I provide a critique of postmodern thought's inability to deal adequately with race because it fails to get beyond it and into a postracial world. In particular, I critique the notion of "hybridity," and claim that aesthetic political theory, which is also modern, can explain the rise and prevalence of racial thinking in late modernity without recourse to postmodernity.[105]

The conclusion closes with two brief case studies for the application of the synthetic paradigm in contemporary times. I discuss how two very different societies, the United States and Bolivia, would benefit from a broad cultural incorporation of the synthetic paradigm. In the case of the United States, rigid racial categories, largely built on the one-drop rule as well as immigration laws, have created often-antagonistic racial classifications. I argue that the synthetic paradigm could be integrated into U.S. culture through the influence of Latino immigrants, who bring the Latin American idea of mixed race with them. In this view, we are all mixed rather than of one single racial group. The appropriation of this idea, I argue, would minimize U.S. racial tensions. As another case study of the prescriptive application of the synthetic paradigm, I also discuss the current Bolivian political situation. Bolivia is a country with entrenched racial barriers, particularly between indigenous masses and white/mestizo elites. Rather than emphasize ethnoracial confrontation, as President Evo Morales has sometimes done, I argue that he should underscore the long history of miscegenation of racial groups and traditions in Bolivia. This would create a deeper sense of national unity. In either case, I do not defend the idea of mestizo nationalism; rather, I argue that a synthetic paradigm undermines understandings of race that are built on notions of purity, and hence exposes the fact that no race is privileged over any other.

From the time of early Spanish exploration in the New World to recent history, Latin America has presented many puzzles to modern minds. Albert Hirschman's contributions to the scholarship on Latin America were principally in the field of political economy. But his approach to the study of the passions and the interests surrounding the ascendance of the value of financial and economic gain in Western thought showed that certain social phenomena arise suddenly but are given normative validation at different stages in intellectual history. We can apply this approach to the puzzle of race: why it appears in a nearly spontaneous manner upon the arrival of modernity, and how it changes form throughout the course of the modern era. I seek to carry out this analysis in this book, underscoring one particular line of thinking—that of a synthetic paradigm of race—in the history of the relationship between race and politics in Latin American thought.

Moving beyond black-and-white categories, and also opposed to a domination-oriented view of race rooted in occidental grounds, this paradigm helps us make sense of the past as well as understand what we mean in our everyday use of the term "race." It is the result of a journey that begins when Spaniards first set foot on Caribbean soil, reaches its apex when creole patriots try to make sense of a cauldron of racial groups in their new nations, and begins a slow descent as thinkers confront the failures of states and seek to transcend them in a cosmopolitan fashion. It is a story that looks back to see how race shifts shape in the triptych from empire to nation and then to cosmopolis, but which can also help us make sense of racial diversity and mixing in contemporary multicultural states.

Citizenship, defined as membership in a political community, can be interpreted as the central theme of political philosophy. Who is allowed to be a member of a polity and who is not is the line of demarcation prior to issues of justice within a particular state.[106] I understand citizenship in this basic sense, as the delineation of boundaries that tell us who belongs with us and who stands outside our community. Race, as I argue in this book, has been a principal element in defining citizenship. Racial categories and identities have been used to include and exclude people from polities throughout history, as evinced in Latin American intellectual developments. At the same time, the rights and responsibilities associated with citizenship have shaped definitions of race. Thus, there is a dialectical relationship between politics and race: political forces shape understandings of race at the same time that racial ideas shape conceptions of citizenship. Race is a preeminently political idea, even as it gives form to our very conception of the modern. While most accounts of citizenship in political theory have neglected this phenomenon, we ought to engage with it for analytical, historical, and normative reasons.[107]

There is no way the written word can convey the full horror of the atrocities committed throughout this region.... The wretched Spaniards actively pursued the locals, both men and women alike, using wild dogs to track them and hunt them down. One woman, who was indisposed at the time and so not able to make good her escape, determined that the dogs should not tear her to pieces as they had done her neighbours and, taking a rope, and tying her one-year-old child to her leg, hanged herself from a beam. Yet she was not in time to prevent the dogs from ripping the infant to pieces, even though a friar did arrive and baptize the infant before it died.

—*A Short Account of the Destruction of the Indies*[1]

1

PARADOX OF EMPIRE

Las Casas and the Birth of Race

BARTOLOMÉ DE LAS CASAS was indeed capable, even in excess, of conveying the totality of terror that befell the indigenous peoples of the Americas upon the arrival of the Spanish conquistadores.[2] By most accounts, Las Casas is the most famous "defender" of the "Indians" of the Americas. But something that is essential to his contribution to political thought is his discussion of the idea of "race" *avant la lettre*.

The work of Las Casas must be examined first in the arc of our survey because he was the cardinal "internal critic"[3] of the European canon in relation to the genealogy of the modern conception of race.[4] A European by birth, he died a Latin American. His life and works opened a new channel for political theory's formation of the notion we are examining, an avenue that was not available before him. He is a central figure in Hispanic thought writ large: he was the bridge between early-modern Spanish ideas and the emergence of Spanish American political thought, particularly in matters related to racialization.

There is a paradox in Las Casas's corpus. On the one hand he was committed to the idea that all human beings were equals under the grace of God; on the other hand, he was a staunch proponent of Spanish imperialism, which denied equal political status to the communities of the "Indies" relative to Spain.[5] Yet by defending the Spanish Crown, Las Casas constructed a perspective that allowed him to seek the incorporation of all non-Europeans living in the Americas into the imperial fold. This led him to view the indigenous Americans as potential subjects of the Spanish monarchy on the same plane as those living in Iberia. While his adversaries, particularly Juan Ginés de Sepúlveda, argued that the natives were homunculi, or subhuman creatures, Las Casas proposed that they were in fact members of the human race, or *linaje humano*, as he put it. Las Casas was part of the Spanish Empire's concern—in contrast to the Portuguese, French, and British empires—with the very essence of human nature that was elicited by the "discovery" of difference.[6]

It is in this debate and in other forms of adversarial and explicitly political discourse that Las Casas inaugurates the process that produced the seeds of what would later be called "race." Had it not been for his response to antagonists, he would not have been able to insist on the full humanity first of the indigenous peoples and later of the African slaves and their descendants in the Americas.[7] Rather than seen as mainly engaged in a proto-anthropological quest to understand diverse cultures, Las Casas in fact should be considered one of the central (if inadvertent) contributors to the intellectual scaffolding that allowed the early-modern construction of racialization. This is an important distinction, for through it we can distance ourselves from an interpretation of Las Casas as a proto-scientific thinker and see him as what he really was: a partisan rhetorician.[8]

Beneath the layers of theology, history, proto-anthropology, jurisprudence, and ethics that Las Casas is usually known for, his project is fundamentally rhetorical.[9] It was not only against some soldiers, friars, or Sepúlveda himself that Las Casas argued. He also sought to persuade the monarchy itself, embodied by Emperor Charles V as well as Philip II, to change the course of Spanish policies in the New World.[10] The thrust of his argument was that the incorporation of the natives into the Crown as subjects was a moral and logical imperative because they were members of the human race, not of separate or even nonhuman lineage. Persuasion is the supreme aim of Las Casas's lifetime of writing.

The primary value of Las Casas's work with respect to the question of "what is race" lies in its modernity. While many, if not most, commentators have believed that he was basically a Thomistic, Aristotelian thinker, his oeuvre in fact shows that it undermines a fundamental tenet of the ancients.[11] That is the antinomy of "the civilized" and "the barbarian." Although he employed the concept of barbarism throughout his work, as if to show that the Aristotelian schema is relevant, what he in effect does is to show the brutality and bestiality of the Europeans and exaggerate the docility and goodness of the Amerindians. In other words, Europeans are in fact more barbaric, while the natives of the Americas are civilized, closer to that of an ideal, paradisiacal Christian modernity. For Las Casas, Christianity is a modernizing force because it is civilizing, as it moves people away from violence and chaos. He shows that the categories of "barbarian" and "civilized" are archaic. To be sure, he did employ Thomistic, Aristotelian ideas, but the effect of his oeuvre is to undermine this intellectual edifice of the ancient and medieval worlds and to usher in a new way of thinking.

While there were some early-modern thinkers such as Paracelsus and Giordano Bruno, as well as Sepúlveda, who argued that there are discrete and distinct human types in the world, they did so with hierarchical gradations. It is Las Casas who is the first to recognize human variation while seeking to incorporate diverse groups into a unitary, non-hierarchical understanding of both the human species and a single political community. This process is one of synthesis, for it aggregates diversity and makes it into unity. But it is not a story of pluralism or toleration: Las Casas did not argue for respect for multiple ways of life and the need for coexistence or a modus vivendi. Neither did he propose that Spain should tolerate, accept, or view as equal the civilizations or groups that were found in the Americas.[12] He was a militant Catholic imperialist who sought the incorporation of these new groups into the Crown in the manner of synthesis: the agglomeration of diverse elements into a unitary, coherent, and *improved* whole.

More accurately, it is the universalism of both the Church and the empire that pushes him to seek the incorporation of the natives into the Spanish fold.[13] Thus, we cannot understand Las Casas as a "pacifist liberal democrat," as Edmundo O'Gorman rightly tells us.[14] We must look at the totality of his *idearium* to understand his relevance to the theoretical makings of race. Throughout his vast opus we find the seeds of race, but it is best encapsulated in the rhetorical force of the *Short Account of the Destruction of the Indies*.[15] This text has been decried as polemical and propagandistic, and even as the least representative of Las Casas's fundamental personality.[16] However, it is precisely here that we can find the key component of Las Casas's originality.[17]

The fact that Las Casas's project is fundamentally rhetorical is crucial to our analysis of the birth of "race." It shows that he conceived of the nascent processes of racialization as quintessentially political, rather than rooted in biology. Rhetoric, as the effort to persuade, is a political instrument. It attempts to change minds in order to achieve a manipulation or transformation of power. Las Casas's chief method is rhetorical (and not proto-scientific, quasi-anthropological, philosophical, or even religious) because he conceived of incipient racial ideas within the context of political contestation and argumentation in Spain's rule over the "Indies." His use of rhetoric thus tells us that "race" is at heart a *political* construct in the early-modern period. It shows us that he constructed "racial" categories in the realm of words, not using science. This means he employed artifice: rather than using biological conceptions of discrete human groups, he created, through texts, *artificial* categorizations. This entails a move away from a biological basis. In turn, it distances his work from the naturalism immanent in Aristotelian and Thomistic accounts of human differentiation. This is what makes Las Casas an early-modern thinker rather than merely a faithful follower of premodern natural law. As such, he lays the foundation for an understanding of racial identities that are constructed rather than taken as naturally fixed or given.

In what follows, I begin with a brief contextualization of the friar's life. Then I posit that the chief methodology of his entire opus was rhetorical. This places the *Short Account of the Destruction of the Indies* squarely at the center of his writings. Using this text as a lens for his entire oeuvre, we see the crucial place the Amerindians' sentience has not only in that book but in Las Casas's philosophical anthropology as a whole. The emphasis on feeling rather than reason militates against the ancients and further pushes Las Casas into a modern mind-set, owing to its implicit critique of Aristotelian thought and its use of an aesthetic, sensory basis of morality. I show that his rhetorical method is also present in his vast historiography. I then conclude the chapter by pointing to his early use of aesthetic principles to note his concern not merely with the Amerindians' culture, but with their somatic form as well, something that is integral to the making of "race." I close the chapter with a discussion of the two most important tensions in Las Casas's corpus: the late recognition of Africans' humanity, and his attempt to build an inclusive imperial political order.

Las Casas's Transatlantic Journey

Much uncertainty surrounds Las Casas's early life. Triana, the quarter in Seville known as the birthplace of many a famous matador, was the place where Las Casas is thought to have been born around 1485.[18] The intense Andalusian sun would forge the explorers and adventurers who would seek fortune in the Americas. One of them was Las Casas: a man who initially traveled to the Americas at an early age seeking gold and trying to escape poverty, something common all over Spain at the time.[19] Las Casas's own ethnic background is still disputed. Some asseverate that he was of French origin, given that he often signed his name as "Casaus." Yet others believe he may have been embroiled personally in the issue of *limpieza de sangre*, as there is speculation that he had family ties to a converso Jewish background.[20]

This conjecture regarding the possible Jewish origin of Las Casas provides a window into the nascent debates about "race" in the Iberian peninsula. Before Las Casas was born, the debate over "purity of blood" in Spain was raging. "The polemic of blood was red-hot in the sixteenth century," as Huerga tells us.[21] Was Las Casas's lineage of "new Christian" or "old Christian" descent? In other words, did he come from those who may have converted from Judaism to Christianity? There is no definitive evidence to settle this question.[22] However, it shows how, even before Las Casas would write about different human kinds in the Americas, Spain itself was gripped, at the social level, by a preoccupation with the normative implications of a physical human element, that is, blood. An invisible physical characteristic carried much moral weight, for, as Anthony Grafton has explained, the fear that Jews were essentially dangerous owing to their difference at the level of the soul was manifested by the debate over individuals' purity of blood.[23] In the trials of the Inquisition, it was inevitable to confront the question of blood lineage, or the accused person's "racial background."[24] The term *tener su raza*, around 1552, meant to come from converso (i.e., Jewish or Muslim) origins.[25] While this meaning does not have direct consequences on Las Casas's subsequent writings on the Amerindians' "race," it does show that he lived in a context where nascent racial characteristics such as blood lineage were thought to have moral implications.

Triana was the locus of the expeditionary impulse, where the echoes of expeditions in the Americas were first heard. Las Casas recalls Columbus's departure from Seville to Barcelona in 1493 after his first trip, the most important event for the city at the close of the fifteenth century. He would describe the "Indians, who were seven in number . . . since the others had died. . . . He took many green and red parrots, as well as guaizas, masks made of fish bones . . . the finest gold, and many things never before seen in Spain."[26] Las Casas's own father arrived in Seville in 1499, having participated in the second voyage to the Americas led by Columbus. In 1501–2, at the age of seventeen,[27] Las Casas made his first transatlantic voyage of discovery and self-transformation, most likely accompanying his father, Pedro de Las Casas. His initial impetus was not at all related to the desire to "convert infidels." It was a more mundane ambition to become rich.

In 1506 he traveled back to Europe, this time to Rome. We know little about this episode, which may have had a religious influence upon him.[28] He went back to the New World, and experienced what he called a "conversion" from mere colonist to man of conscience. In 1511 he heard a sermon by Friar Antonio de Montesinos, a Dominican priest, who famously asked, "Are these not men?" regarding the indigenous peoples of the Americas in the face of their brutalization by the Spaniards.[29] The sermon moved Las Casas deeply. Slowly, Las Casas started to think more about the status of the "Indians," witness more of their travails, and examine his conscience. Eventually, he renounced his property, land, and *encomiendas*, the slaves and territory granted to him by the Crown.[30] In October 1515, he returned to Spain to address himself to Cardinal Cisneros. He propounded his "Reform of the Indies."[31] In this utopian text, written months before Thomas Moore's *Utopia*, he argued for a reorganization of the administration of the Indies. He was consequently named "Universal Protector of the Indians." He professed the Dominican Order in 1523, a process that began with a three-year trial and made him part of the order until his last days.[32]

Discovering Difference: On Las Casas's Method

Las Casas first discovered the Amerindian in the spring of 1493. Christopher Columbus was returning from his first trip to the Americas back to Seville, and he brought back with him some "Indians" as human trophies. Las Casas was nine years old at the time and remembered clearly the sight of the natives near the "arco de las Imágenes."[33] His father traveled to the New World the same year and, upon his return in 1499, brought back a young Amerindian for the young Bartolomé, as if he were bringing back an exotic pet for his son's amusement.[34]

For Las Casas, the discovery of the Americas is quite literally the beginning of a New World.[35] It is a new stage for the entire globe, and it has cultural, political, religious, social, and philosophical importance. It is a break with the past. Hence, we can say that Las Casas stands at the very inception of modernity, not simply in terms of historical time, but, in his writings, also in terms of modern political thought.[36] Much ink has been spilt over whether Machiavelli or Hobbes was the first modern political thinker. Yet Las Casas has been unjustly neglected. His work, even in the concise *Short Account*, is a watershed moment in the move from medieval to modern political thought for two main reasons. It is the first time that an entirely new population is confronted by the modern state, and it is up to Las Casas to find the rhetorical, that is, the justificatory, apparatus to incorporate these new peoples into the Spanish polity.

Indeed, Las Casas stands at the crossroads of the medieval and the modern world. One of the principal meanings of modernity is newness. And for Las Casas the Americas represent the entirely new and that which cannot be grasped with old ways of thinking or seeing. "Everything that has happened since the marvelous discovery of the Americas … has been so extraordinary that the whole story remains incredible to anyone who has not experienced it firsthand."[37] The ancient world is no longer of use, for "[the New World] seems, indeed, to overshadow all the deeds of famous men of the past, no matter how heroic, and to silence all talk of other wonders of the world."[38] A new page can be turned in human history, and the fantastic as well as the horrific sights of the Americas pose wholly new problems to politics and to political thought.

In the *Short Account*, written in 1542, we find a masterpiece of rhetoric[39] suffused with moral argumentation couched in emotive, vivid descriptions.[40] Las Casas's oeuvre is voluminous, but no other part of it has the argumentative power of the *Brevísima relación de la destruición de las Indias*, reedited in 1546[41] and finally published in 1552 (without a royal license)[42] when Las Casas was around the age of sixty-seven.[43] Much like Machiavelli's *The Prince* (written in 1513 and published in 1532), its brevity belies its significance to the origins of modern political thought. Whereas Machiavelli's most infamous work carries a radical new teaching couched in the language of a short missive of advice to a prince, Las Casas's brief missive to a prince carries a reversal of standard notions in medieval thought, which coalesced ideas from ancient political thought and Christian doctrines.[44] The *Short Account* is Las Casas's chief textual contribution to canonical political thought. This argument is especially cogent if we consider the serious weaknesses of his *Historia de las Indias*, as well as the fact that he never tried to publish this long work of flawed historiography.[45]

Many readers have dismissed the *Short Account* throughout the ages by making the mistake of not seeing it as a work of humanistic rhetoric. From the Friar Motolinía, who accused Las Casas of exaggeration, to the first Flemish edition of 1578, to the views of Manuel José Quintana, who in 1833 argued that the *Short Account* was unnecessary because it was fraught with "falsehoods,"[46] readers have tried to compare what Las Casas wrote to the "reality" of what actually happened upon the Spanish conquest of the Americas. But the *Short Account* is first and foremost a work of Renaissance rhetoric. Las Casas followed all the core conventions of rhetoric when composing, revising, and reediting this text.

Humanism in the Renaissance meant the study of human affairs (*humanitates*). It entailed five different elements. These were grammar (that is, Latin), poetry, history, moral philosophy, and rhetoric. They were meant to educate a man to be able to *persuade*: to be able to use practical reason usually either in law courts or the church.[47] In fields where proofs could not easily be given, that is, the nonlogical disciplines, rhetoric was essential in the exposition of arguments. Rhetoric requires the latching on of *pathos* to *logos*, or emotions to ideas. *Ethos*, or showing the competence of the author, is also necessary. Central to effective rhetoric, as Quintilian posited, is the vividness of descriptions. One has to "see" what the author writes about.

Las Casas's *Short Account* is, in this light, a paragon of humanist rhetoric.[48] The subject is one that deals with both the juridical and the religious status of beings (the Amerindians), but is something that eludes facile proof because of alternative explanations given by others who tried to argue that the Amerindians were not fully human.[49] Las Casas thus opts for a reasoning that is not strictly logical, combining the emotional force of his descriptions of what he saw with an argument for the *distinctive* humanity of the Amerindians. Having witnessed events in the New World, Las Casas is able also to provide *ethos*. Above all, his writing is preeminently vivid; it has an aesthetic rationality that allows the reader to practically "see" the events that Las Casas describes and to draw moral conclusions from them.

To grasp the methodology of Las Casas's text, it is instructive to compare it to the first modern political tract: Machiavelli's *Prince*. The *Short Account* is, indirectly, an anti-*Prince*.[50] They are both, essentially, letters to rulers. The Dominican friar denounces the practices of his prince, just as Machiavelli did, but for the purpose of establishing a new morality, rather than to subvert the relationship between politics and morality, as the Florentine did.[51] Throughout his short book, Machiavelli feigns genuflection to Christian ideas, but in fact he proposes all manner of inhumanity and immorality in the service of political expediency.[52] Politics is autonomous, and morality is tangential to it. That was his teaching, embodied in the person of Cesare Borgia, a brutal man of Spanish origins who was made bishop of Pamplona at the age of fifteen.[53] But for Las Casas, the key issue of his times was not the political inefficacy of the rulers of his motherland. It was the *moral* crisis of the Spanish Crown caused by the atrocities it perpetrated in the New World.

Whereas Machiavelli's masterwork of rhetoric, *The Prince*, closes with a poetic denunciation of imperialism in the form of an exhortation to liberate Italy from the foreign "barbarians" (the French and the Spanish), Las Casas's short text is an imperialist defense of Spain's presence in the Americas, but is equally fervent against the "barbarians." This time, however, the barbarians are not the native "savages," but the very same Spanish troops which also occupy the Americas in the name of civilization. Machiavelli's chief work called for the appearance of a single man who would be able to overturn the woes of Florence; this man would be modeled on Borgia or perhaps Machiavelli himself. In the case of Las Casas, a fundamental transformation in the way that the conquest is seen—which may require one man to tear the scales from the emperor's eyes—is demanded. Las Casas is the person who takes it upon himself to carry out this task.

The text is organized as a geographical survey of the Americas, from Hispaniola (the current Dominican Republic) all the way down to Cuzco in Peru, carried out by recounting the atrocities committed by the Spanish.[54] The work is rife with rhetorical exaggeration. The peoples of the Americas are humble, gentle, peace-loving, and docile, as Las Casas portrays them.[55] On the one hand, this creates an image of innocence that suits his argument that the natives are near-saints, while the Spaniards are devilish. On the other hand, it treats the Amerindians as childlike, perhaps mentally challenged, and at any rate not possessing the intellectual level of adults. But the chief aim here is to persuade the king of Spain to put a stop to the evil acts of his soldiers.[56]

If the *Short Account* is to stand at the center of Las Casas's contribution to the canon of political thought, then we can interpret the rest of his work as supporting the arguments of this brief text.[57] In the history of political thought, we must pay attention to the coherence and effectiveness of particular books. Great political thinkers must also be good writers. We cannot simply take into account the entirety of someone's opus if it does not have coherence or is not readable as texts. This is what makes the *Short Account* a historically important text: it is powerful, well argued, original, and readable. The significance of the *Apologética Historia* becomes secondary; it is the description of the discovery of difference, of how Las Casas appreciates and values the culture and land of the Amerindians. It presages modern concerns with anthropological questions.[58] Its 267 chapters make for a very precise and extended encyclopedic perspective on the Amerindian cultures.[59] But even beneath its apparent objectivity, we can feel the interested "passion *por indis* that palpitates in each page."[60]

In discovering the humanity of the indigenous peoples of the Americas, Las Casas also makes a critical step for political thought. His focus on the very possibility that the natives were human stands in sharp contrast to earlier preoccupations. In broad strokes, "from a comparative perspective, we could note that the Greek philosopher . . . was concerned with physics and metaphysics,"[61] whereas modern thought is about humanity. In between, medieval political thought is largely concerned with God. Thus, the turn toward man, Renaissance humanism, is central to the advent of modernity. Las Casas is part of Renaissance humanism, but his focus is not man's inherent amorality or the autonomy of politics, as in the case of Machiavelli. It is human difference, understood as the contrast between diverse human groups. This contrast tested the very idea of what it is to be human and was the locus of the birth of race.

Persuading the Barbarian: The Rhetoric of Nascent Racialization

Reading Las Casas's oeuvre in light of his brief *Short Account of the Destruction of the Indies*, we find that, while he was an early-modern ethnographer, anthropologist, jurist, or historiographer, these contributions are outweighed by his legacy as a rhetorician of empire. The *Apologética Historia* itself is marred by sundry flaws that make it less than convincing either on purely ethnographic grounds or on the grounds of Scholastic theology.[62] The *Short Account* allows us to observe that Las Casas's chief aim was to persuade those with power to try to curb the cruelties in the Americas, so that the Christian faith could adequately expand in the New World.[63] In this light, even the *Apologética Historia* is rhetorical in nature. As Menéndez Pidal argues, the *Apologética* is "an extreme exaggeration of the virtues of the Indians, to the point of being incredible."[64]

Why can we say that Las Casas stands at the origin of the genealogy of racialization? Principally because the notion of "ethnicity" does not adequately cover the totality of the phenomenon that the idea of "race" refers to, and Las Casas is a pivotal figure in the moment when human cultural difference became transformed into discussions about human difference per se. There is no doubt that ethnicity is central to the definition of race. But race is a socially constructed notion that refers to *categorically* distinctive kinds of human beings even across ethnicities. Las Casas was not merely trying to show that different cultural groups do things similarly in many respects. His understanding of the Amerindians can be termed proto-racialist because he treats them as essentially different from Europeans, but still within the human race and not necessarily inferior (hence he is a racialist, not a racist).

Las Casas speaks of "the Indians" as if they *all* shared *fundamentally* distinctive characteristics, both psychologically and physically. A native of Florida, according to him, is as benevolent or robust as one in Guatemala or Peru.[65] One from Hispaniola can be compared to one from Upper Peru.[66] Las Casas thinks synthetically here. He seeks to comprehend diverse human populations under one single racial rubric. This is not entirely cogent. Imagine for a second that someone were to say something similar about "native Europeans." That a native from central Germany is as thrifty, let's say, as a native from southern Spain or a Greek, or a Sicilian, a Romanian or a Scot. This sort of reasoning is no longer "ethnographic." It makes categorical claims about a large, transnational group of people.[67] This sort of formulation is the root of racialization, which then grows into a more fully-fledged version as politics, aestheticization, and other processes get tied to it. The seeds are in the ancient world (the distinctions between "us" and "them," or the "civilized" and the "barbarian"), but the roots are in the early-modern period, specifically in the works of Las Casas.

It is in the course of his debates with intellectual opponents that Las Casas came to argue for a proto-racialized understanding of the characteristics of the natives. Chief among these opponents was Juan Ginés de Sepúlveda, whom Las Casas "debated" in 1550–51.[68] In this encounter between the two eminent figures, we find that Las Casas developed his views *in relation* to those of his adversaries.[69] They did not emerge *sui generis*. Thus, the ideas of Sepúlveda are important in understanding what Las Casas was up to.[70]

In the spring of 1547 Las Casas had a full agenda: he traveled to Arande de Duero in Spain to provide an account to the Council of the Indies; renounce the Chiapas bishopric; find a new home; recruit missionaries to travel to Guatemala; and debate Juan Ginés de Sepúlveda on the status of the Amerindians.[71] Las Casas heard that Sepúlveda was seeking a license to publish a new book to be called *Democrates secundus*,[72] a continuation of his first book, by the name *Democrates primus*.[73] The first book was about the legitimacy of the Spanish emperor's wars in Europe; the second was on the legitimacy of the "Indian wars" in the New World. Much like Las Casas, Sepúlveda was a rhetorician. He was not trained as a theologian, and for this lack of preparation he was derided in various quarters. He was a man of letters, a literary figure whose works aimed to achieve artistic value as well as to persuade readers.

The dispute started in halls: not those of academia, since neither of them was a scholar; or those of power, since neither had a political role. But it ignited in religious hallways, pitting the humanistic Sepúlveda against the learned and impassioned Las Casas. A man from Seville against a man from Córdoba engaged in an intellectual *mano a mano*. The argument had two phases. The first was the effort by Las Casas to prevent the publication of the manuscript. The second was an actual discussion of the various arguments presented by each person. It was not a simultaneous debate, but it did have the drama of a world-historical moment.

Las Casas admired Sepúlveda's style. His Latin was very "polished and elegant," and he followed strict rules of rhetoric.[74] Las Casas wanted to dispute his opponent's two principal theses: that the Spanish wars in the "Indies" were morally legitimate; and that the Amerindians were obligated to submit themselves to the power of the Crown. Sepúlveda asked for permission to publish the text, but the Council of the Indies rejected it, believing it would cause a furor. Eventually, through friends, Sepúlveda acquired a license to print his work. The text was then sent to the universities at Salamanca and Alcalá to be examined. Theologians and experts in jurisprudence gave their verdict: it should not be published. Sepúlveda persisted, wrote a summary of it, and sent it to a friend in Rome, under the title of *Apología*. It appears Las Casas never actually read the text of *Democrates secundus*. Still, the king of Spain deemed the issue worthy enough to call for a discussion in Valladolid to determine the validity of Sepúlveda's claims regarding Spain's presence in the Indies.

When the debate took place, Sepúlveda spoke first. A master orator, he spoke for three hours without reading. Las Casas was not present. The next day Las Casas's turn came, and for five straight days, he read his long work summarizing what the Spanish had done in the Americas, the *Apología*. The stunned audience asked Domingo de Soto to summarize the two depositions. De Soto made it clear that the two accounts were quite different in form and substance. Nonetheless, both were presented to the Council in a forensic manner, for the purpose of convincing the audience of their respective perspectives. In May 1551, the Council held a session that did not proclaim a victor in this debate, but simply granted the value of each perspective. Two Dominican priests who were members of the junta recused themselves, while de Soto sided with Las Casas and Friar Bernardino de Arévalo supported Sepúlveda. In effect, Las Casas and Sepúlveda

acted not with objectivity or dispassionately, but tried to blow the wind in their own direction.[75] Where both saw alterity, the former saw it through the idea of an equal moral
status; the latter through the dichotomy of superiority/inferiority.[76]

Through this dispute with Sepúlveda, we discern Las Casas's enterprise as a whole
as a fundamentally rhetorical one. He was never trained as a theologian, like Vitoria,[77]
nor as a scientist or explorer.[78] Neither was he educated as a historian.[79] His allegiance
was to the Catholic Church,[80] and his method was the persuasive use of language. Addressing himself to Prince Philip, Las Casas opens the *Short Account* with a prologue
reminiscent of Machiavelli's dedicatory letter to Lorenzo de Medici in *The Prince*. This
Renaissance convention is important here because it tells us that the work is not a simple
historical treatise, or a personal eyewitness account, or a moral diatribe. It is a political
work, intended to persuade the prince of Spain. In the very first sentence he tells us that
his concern in this text is the notion, however nascent, of race: "Divine Providence has
ordained that the world shall, for the benefit and proper government of the human race
[*linaje*],[81] be divided into kingdoms and peoples and that these shall be ruled by kings."[82]

The *Short Account* as Las Casas's Central Teaching

Drenched in blood, the pages of the *Short Account* tell amazing stories that leave even
jaded twenty-first-century readers aghast. The violence of the conquest is so trenchant
that Las Casas himself seems to be at a loss for words to describe the atrocities. The *Short
Account* follows rhetorical conventions very faithfully. Above all, the graphic descriptions of massacres, beheadings, and dogs eating human flesh make for vivid, visually
stimulating reading. The *Short Account* is also characterized by the use of exaggeration,
something essential to rhetoric. Historians have long disputed the numbers that Las
Casas uses for the scale of the crimes against humanity that he describes. Las Casas also
uses the technique of repetition: he reiterates the same sort of gory stories over and over,
and uses the same terms, such as "barbaric," to describe the Spaniards' actions throughout the book. Moreover, much of what he says may have been made up; this rhetorical
technique is acceptable for persuasive speeches, but certainly not for ethnographic writing. Last, the *Short Account* manipulates the emotions of the reader. One is compelled
to go in the direction of compassion for the natives, given the cruelties and sins of the
Spaniards.

Before addressing the specifics of the text of the *Short Account*, we must remark on
the *Apologética Historia*. The privileging of this text over the *Short Account* has led some
commentators to posit that Las Casas was seeking both to catalog cultural differences
and to utilize a systematic "Aristotelian-Thomist conceptual scheme."[83] But unlike an
objective anthropological catalog of particular differences, the *Apologética Historia* of
Las Casas employs inventive juxtapositions of Amerindian and ancient European cultures without empirical basis.[84] As Pagden himself notes, the reader is "left to 'read off'"

the similarities, or dissimilarities, by himself."[85] This betrays a fundamental lack of scientific method in Las Casas's work. At the same time, Las Casas abandons the Aristotelian distinction between civilized and barbarian peoples when convenient, and in fact generally claims that the term "barbarian" applies better to the Spaniards. For these reasons, it is not possible to take the *Apologética Historia* as an objective tract. We must look elsewhere to see the basic nature of Las Casas's project.

Hence, we must go back to the *Short Account*.[86] It is in this text that his transvaluation of values is most evident. It is here where he inverts the subject of the civilized-barbarian dichotomy most clearly. One of the salient rhetorical aspects of the *Short Account* is Las Casas's use of aesthetic representation.[87] In a few instances of the text, Las Casas also refers to beauty regarding the natives' form. He calls them "handsome and easy on the eye"[88] to justify their human value.[89] From Hispaniola to Florida to the River Plate, the Indians' beauty strikes Las Casas, and he believes this is important to note as something that perhaps points to God's plan in making the natives attractive.[90] As he tells us elsewhere, "The native peoples of these Indies are . . . by reason of the good composition of their bodily parts, the harmony (*convivencia*)[91] and proportion of their exterior sense organs, the beauty of their faces or gestures and their whole *vultu* (face), the shape of their heads, their manners and movements, etc., naturally of good reason and good understanding."[92] The opposite of someone who appreciates beauty or lacks sensory perception is someone who is "anaesthetized,"[93] a term that Las Casas uses also to mean those who are morally blind owing to their lack of compassion and emotion in the face of cruelties.[94]

Beyond these glimpses of aesthetic categories to make evident some characteristics of the natives, Las Casas's cardinal rhetorical method is the subversion of the meaning of certain words. Chief among them in the *Short Account*, as I said above, is the term "barbarian." Far from engaging in a logical-rational Scholastic analysis of the distinctive meanings of the term, Las Casas in the *Short Account* simply wants to generate a moral and lexical reversal of the predominant meaning of the term. The main meaning for him is the barbarian as a perpetrator of atrocities and brutality. The predominant meaning of the term in his time was the barbarian as a non-Christian.[95] In his rhetorical method, he seeks to portray the natives as categorically distinct from the Spaniards in that they are not barbarians, but generally simply the victims of atrocities, with very few instances where they rebel or resist. In other words, they have a nearly superhuman capacity to withstand immense suffering, not to cause it, as barbarians do. In the *Short Account*, there is no complex philosophical argument regarding this term.[96]

Throughout, there is a rhetorical rearticulation of the term in order to shift the prevailing categories of "barbarian-civilized."[97] But this is not merely for the purposes of description. Las Casas is intent on showing a profound, essential distinction between the two kinds of men. The Spaniards are "*inhuman* and unjust barbarians."[98] Here Las Casas wants to make the claim that at stake is not the idea of how different cultures can be seen as similar in some way; rather, it is about the categorical definitions of what counts as human. The Spaniards are like lions or tigers or wolves;[99] in other words, they are humans of a different kind than the pacific, lamblike natives. The use of animal similes and metaphors underscore that the debate that Las Casas was engaged in was not merely culturalist, but rather an effort to prove the very humanity of the Indians.[100] Their membership in the human race as such is what was debated at the time, something that overrides issues of cross-cultural understanding. Time and again, Las Casas repeats the terms "barbarian" and its cognates to show that human beings can be of two different sorts: brutal or pacific.[101] Clearly Las Casas knows that the Spaniards are members of the human race and is not trying to persuade anyone of the opposite. But he does know that many of his opponents do not consider the natives human, and his rhetorical skills are put to use to show that they are humane and indeed part of the human race.

The Importance of the Sentience of Amerindians

While much of Las Casas's accomplishment lies in providing an internal critique of the Aristotelian model of "barbarism" and "natural slavery" (using the very principle of reason that the Philosopher held as the touchstone of what makes someone human) in effect his chief contribution in showing the humanity of the Amerindians is in his ability to convey their capacity for *sentience*.[102] Las Casas often misconstrued and misinterpreted both Aristotle and Aquinas.[103] For this reason, his efforts in scholastic philosophy are undermined. He does not achieve the level of logical rigor that we find in Vitoria. Las Casas is indeed a great thinker, but his contribution lies in a field different from that of Scholastic logic: that of a humanistic historiography that is rhetorical in nature. Specifically, his demonstration of the Amerindians' capacity to feel (pain, as well as other emotions) in a way similar to that of European human beings, is the crux of his effort to show the natives as part of the human "race" (*linaje*).[104]

To be sure, animals also do have sentience. But in the *Short Account*, Las Casas attempts to provide evidence of the specifically *human* sentience of the natives. This variety lies in the self-awareness, or consciousness, of the experience of feeling and emotion. Whereas animals suffer pain *simpliciter*, human beings are cognizant of it. Moreover, this awareness leads the human being to reason about the nature, causes, and meaning of pain and suffering. In this manner, a particular emotion, pain, leads to intellectual activity in the human being, something wholly lacking in the nonhuman species. The realization, in turn, leads to moral judgments. Thus, emotion is essential to the development of moral sentiments.[105]

At the very inception of the *Short Account*, Las Casas tells us what is central to his story. The Europeans, specifically the Spaniards, had "become so *anaesthetized* to human suffering by their own greed and ambition that they had ceased to be men in any meaningful sense of the term."[106] To become anaesthetized is to lose all feeling, all capacity of sentience, which for Las Casas is cardinal in allowing morality to function.

Aesthetic experience, understood here as sensory cognition based on feelings, is thus not merely a capacity to witness something, but to be moved in a way that will connect a person to others' suffering and their condition as human. Thus, there cannot be morality without emotion preceding it. Morals remain abstract and inert without feeling. Moreover, Las Casas goes so far as to say that this is quintessentially *human*; without it, we become degenerate and inhuman.

His moral philosophy leads Las Casas to one of the main arguments of the *Short Account*: fear and terror cannot be justified morally or politically. Writing as if he were debating Machiavelli, who believed a successful political man must be able to engage in cruelty well used, Las Casas opposes the idea of staging sanguinary massacres in public. Praise of the sort that Machiavelli reserves for Cesare Borgia's display of Remirro de Orco's butchered body on a piazza is nowhere to be found in the *Short Account*. Both Machiavelli and Las Casas face a new world and a new politics, but for Las Casas cruelty cannot be sustained as a matter of policy; it is neither moral nor expedient. Las Casas also believes that there is an implicit link between ancient cruelty and the brutalities of modern Spain. With rhetorical force, Las Casas uses a poem to compare the current Spanish decadence with that of ancient Rome:

Nero watched from Tarpey's height
The flames engulf Rome's awesome might;
Children and ancients shout in pain,
He all regards with cold disdain.[107]

In other words, we must dispense with the old, and look for new ways of thinking if we are to solve our current problems.

What distinguishes the moderns from the ancients, for Las Casas, is the ability, through Christianity, to renounce terror and fear as political methods.[108] By referring to Nero, Las Casas calls into question the Roman Empire's pagan foundations, which were unable to prevent Rome's self-immolation. Terror can only be experienced through the fear that one may experience pain and suffering. Thus, human sentience is at the heart of what makes political subjects out of a people. If a newly found group of people is discovered to be as sentient and as cognizant of suffering as the people with power, then we are morally obligated to treat them as equals. Hence, the blood-soaked pages of the *Short Account* repeat the refrain that torture is unacceptable. It is inhuman because it violates a fundamental element of what makes us human. Las Casas repeats this theme over and over, much more so than the idea that the Indians are rational. It is for this reason that the central idea in this pivotal text is the salience of conscious sentience, not the centrality of reason, as what makes someone human. Compassion, or the ability to sympathize with another person's feelings, must be the cornerstone of a just political system. Las Casas recognizes that the natives look and act differently from the Spaniards, but that does not shock him. What stuns him is the lack of compassion that the Spanish soldiers display in the face of the massive suffering that is evident in the faces of fellow members of the human race.[109]

Who Are the Real Barbarians? Writing against the Ancients

One of the principal ways that many Spaniards assigned an inferior moral status to the indigenous peoples of the Americas was by pointing out some of the "inhumane" practices they performed, such as human sacrifice, infanticide, and even cannibalism.[110] Anthropophagy was the ultimate proof, for many Europeans, that the beings that existed in the New World were in fact subhuman or other than human.[111] One of the central contributions of Las Casas's work, particularly in the *Short Account,* was the overturning of this trope.[112] What distinguished Las Casas as a person from many of his contemporaries was the fact that he actually went to and lived in the Americas. In this manner he was able to witness firsthand not only the autochthonous living conditions but also the dying conditions of the natives at the hands of the Spaniards. It is this experience that led Las Casas to place great emphasis on the *sentience* of the Amerindians in his effort to show their membership in the human race. Las Casas was quite orthodox in his theology,[113] but his application of Catholic morality was the opposite of the norm of his time.

The suffering perpetrated by the Spaniards, in Las Casas's account, was nothing less than a form of anthropophagy. To be sure, the Spaniards did not practice literal cannibalism on a wide scale, but the consumption of human flesh in the process of domination and conquest of the Americas was, in Las Casas's view, morally more opprobrious than the infrequent cannibalism of a few groups found among the natives. In the friar's rhetorical descriptions, the natives were in fact generally living in a sort of Garden of Eden environment at the time of the Spanish arrival. The Amerindians were close to biblical innocence before the Fall, the serpent being the Spanish forces that led to exile from Paradise.[114]

If indeed there was cannibalism among the natives, Las Casas wants to persuade us that much of it was caused by the Spanish. In some cases it could even be justified, owing to the brutalities committed by the Europeans.[115] Las Casas thus wants to argue that Amerindian cannibalism was in fact not the fault of the natives, but was a product of Spanish oppression. In Nicaragua, Las Casas tells us that "the Christians seized all the maize the locals had grown themselves and their own families and, as a consequence, some twenty or thirty thousand natives died of hunger, some mothers even killing their own children and eating them."[116] Further, the Spanish hardly ever fed the Indian captives, which led the natives to make "human abattoir[s]"[117] where human hands and feet were cut off in order to be eaten. In this manner, Las Casas overturns the recurrent accusation against the natives that they were anthropophagic savages. If they did eat human flesh, he says, it was a situation *in extremis* caused by Spanish brutality. Hence the natives are not infra-human.

Are the natives savages, as they are portrayed by many Spaniards? Las Casas begs to differ, and ignores the facts that the Maya were decimated by internecine wars, the Aztecs practiced human sacrifice, and the Incas were a powerful military empire.[118] Las Casas focuses on the image of the small village in the tropics, where peaceful, weak, poor, nonmaterialistic natives dwell, uninterested in worldly power.[119] But Las Casas argues that they are intelligent, hence potentially able to understand and accept the Christian faith.[120] This contradiction between their childlike nature and their purported intelligence is overlooked by the friar. For his eyes it is more important to underscore the claim that the three million inhabitants of Hispaniola were annihilated, reduced in number to about two hundred.

Hispaniola is the first of the areas to be devastated by the effects of Spanish sins. The "base appetites" of the Spaniards led to rapes, including that of the wife of Chief Guarionex.[121] Here begins the trope of sexual incontinence, of lust as a sin that drove the conquistadores to violate the women of the New World.[122] This lust leads to murder, another sin: heads cut off, people disemboweled, suckling infants ripped apart, children thrown against rocks, grilling of human beings over fire coals, and the use of dogs to tear apart the survivors. This scene seems to be nothing less than a depiction of hell. In other words, whether Las Casas's account is true or not, it delineates an image of hellish practices that equate the Spanish with barbaric, profoundly immoral behavior.[123] It is hence impossible, if one believes his story, to equate the conquerors with the purveyors of civilization. For this reason, I would argue, Las Casas decided to use the terms "Spanish" and "Christian" as synonymous in many passages of the final edition of 1552.[124] Thus, we can understand that he was not merely making a "culturalist" critique of a given nationality (Spain), but seeking to make a fundamental critique of prevailing Catholic morality, which saw Europeans as *ipso facto* civilized and moral vis-à-vis other peoples. In this sense, he moves us away from medieval doctrine and makes the first step toward a modernist critique of existing religious authorities and doctrines.

Las Casas's imaginary journey throughout the Americas continues, and the main teaching is that there is one single human race, which nonetheless has been ravaged because the Spaniards do not understand that the inhabitants are members of the same species as the Europeans.[125] Las Casas's task is to insist on the humanity of the natives in spite of external differences.[126] From Puerto Rico and Jamaica, Las Casas takes us on an infernal road trip. In northern South America, he tells us, the Amerindians were faced with the *requerimiento*, an ultimatum to convert or face war, read entirely in Spanish to native populations who had never even heard of Spain.

Las Casas understands the concept of "nation" as intimately tied to the idea of "race" (*linaje*). A nation in the Americas is a group of people with sovereignty over a land, but not exactly organized politically as European nations are, with clear national boundaries. They are connected through kinship ties, something that goes back to the idea of a common birth or origin. Las Casas does not understand this organization as implying inferiority. But to his opponents, such as Sepúlveda, the "Indians" were naturally, that is, biologically, inferior. Las Casas rejects this biological definition of peoplehood understood hierarchically, for he argues that the natives were peaceful in their own lands. Hence, they did not require "pacification" or being civilized. He believes that "nation" and "race" are coterminous in the American context.[127]

The Amerindians, for Las Casas, are rational, peaceful human beings who happen to be spiritually in the wrong, for they follow inadequate gods. He is not against their political forms of rule per se. He never decries the despotism of the indigenous kings, nor does he attack their language or customs. His concern is with the idea that Catholicism is the one true universal religion, and that any other must be incorrect and misleading. He finds that the natives are "Christians in the raw." They are innocents who suffered as much as the Christians in Europe suffered at the hands of the Turkish forces. Without going into philosophical detail, Las Casas argues that human, divine, and natural law all oppose what the Spaniards did to the natives.[128] Because he himself believes in the legitimacy of Catholic universalism, he is forced to seek a way to incorporate the natives into the fold of the Church without violence, for he thinks violence is a violation of a basic tenet of Christianity, the love of one's neighbor. The most useful is the Spanish Crown, an imperial force with the institutions that would allow the Church's universalism to properly incorporate the natives qua subjects of Spain.[129] A crisis was at hand, for the Spaniards had abandoned "all Christian sense of right and wrong"[130] and had "betrayed the Lord."[131] In fact, it is the Europeans, not the natives, who are "animals."[132]

Las Casas portrays the natives as "innocent":

The simplest people in the world—unassuming, long-suffering, unassertive, and submissive—they are without malice or guile, and are utterly faithful or obedient both to their own native lords and to the Spaniards in whose service they now find themselves.[133]

One could read this charitably, as an effort to produce a benign image of the natives. To be sure, it is intended to persuade the king that the Amerindians are not intractable. The portrayal of the natives as essentially peaceful plays the rhetorical function of advancing a key tenet of Las Casas's own rhetorical principle: to convert pagans, it is imperative to do so with peaceful means, the central point as he expounds it in *De unico vocationis modo*.[134] But at the same time, Las Casas treats them as infantile, and as lacking some human attributes which could be seen as part and parcel of being human (rancor, guile, wickedness). By setting the natives apart from the common understanding of normal human psychology (which includes positive and negative traits), Las Casas lays the basis of a human classificatory scheme that we could call racial since it refers to large categories of people as distinguished from others along essential lines. This schema contradicts the universalistic aim of *De unico vocationis modo*, which assumes all men are equal.[135]

The scheme is not only based on moral psychology. Las Casas does sometimes make a connection to physical traits as well. "They are among the least *robust* of human beings;

their delicate *constitutions* make them unable to withstand hard work or suffering and render them liable to succumb to almost any illness, no matter how mild."[136] In this way, Las Casas describes all natives of the Americas as physically inferior to Europeans, a concept that has links to the somatic component of later racial classifications. The natural goodness of the natives is thus coupled to their biological weakness. When moral or mental characteristics are coupled to corporeal or natural traits, we find the origins of racialization. In an unintended way, Las Casas's work stands at the center of these origins by referring to physical characteristics in his rhetorical construction of human difference.

A History of Goodness and Violence: Las Casas's Historiography as Rhetoric

Most analyses of Las Casas's oeuvre have shied away from giving salience to the *Short Account*, as most commentators have seen it as merely inflammatory.[137] At the same time, many argue that Las Casas's masterpiece is the *Historia de Indias* (HDI).[138] Sometimes, the *Apologética Historia Sumaria* (AHS) is given ample consideration.[139] But we must be critical of these important claims, for they provide very different perspectives on the work of the friar. The HDI, however interesting, is a long, muddled, disorganized, and chaotic text.[140] The AHS, on the other hand, is equally interesting yet very well organized. What accounts for the wide disparity of the nature of these texts? The answer to this question will help us understand Las Casas's project as a whole.

Reading the HDI followed by a close reading of the AHS shows us the fundamental character and intention of Las Casas's project. That is, to persuade. Again, this is most evident when we start from the premise that his core teaching is in the *Short Account*, despite widespread criticism that this is a propagandistic work. The HDI, *contra* Hanke, is essentially not a work of history in any modern sense of the term. It recounts, in ample detail, Columbus's first voyage, even though Las Casas was not present and provides no evidence of secondary literature on the matter. It is largely an idealized and imaginative reconstruction of what Las Casas believes might have happened. In the case of the AHS, which was originally intended to be part of the HDI, according to Hanke, we are faced with a work that has the same two aims but is constructed differently. The AHS intends to show, with two general arguments, that Amerindians are part of the human race. One is centered on the material and physical characteristics of human existence, which lead to the notion that Indians possess a mind that is reasonable in nature; the other is centered on the cultural practices of Indians, showing that these practices are also reasonable. Both points contribute to the Aristotelian argument that rationality makes for full participation in the human species. Again, both the HDI and the AHS are written with the paramount objective of persuading through a variety of strategies, not simply examining a phenomenon in a detached way.[141] Thus, while historiography and proto-anthropology may be the apparent intentions of the HDI and the AHS, respectively, in fact they serve eminently rhetorical purposes.

The HDI was written in response to the work by Gonzalo Fernández de Oviedo y Valdés, *Sumario de la natural historia de las indias*. In this text, Amerindians were portrayed as bestial savages.[142] Las Casas sought to counter this image while emphasizing eight key objectives:[143] (1) to honor the glory of God; (2) to proffer happiness to the peoples of the New World; (3) to defend the honor of the king of Castille; (4) to enhance the benefit and welfare of Spain; (5) to provide a clear, exact, and "agreeable" account of ancient events; (6) to liberate his nation of the grave error of believing that the Indians of the New World were not humans but "brutal beasts"; (7) to render a true account of the virtues and sins of the Spaniards in the Indies; and (8) to describe the greatness of the accomplishments reached through the conquest of the Indies. As these points show, the foremost aim was not purely academic or scientific. Moral persuasion as to the humanity of the Indians and the political justification of the presence of Spain in the Americas were also part of his agenda.

The HDI involves a long quasi-hagiography of Columbus.[144] But this admiration for the explorer is mixed with Las Casas's horror at the events following 1492: he wants to tell of "how much damage, how many calamities, decimations [*despoblaciones*], tales of lost souls, and how many have died in the injustices of the conquest of the Indies, and how many unforgivable sins have been committed" (HDI 1:12). His is a work of a particular kind of Catholic historiography; in other words it is partisan, presented from a particular point of view. It does not share the view of Oviedo's brand of Catholicism, nor the moral bases of Muslim, Jewish, or indigenous American religions. This partisanship is fundamental to the rhetorical force of his argument.

From the onset, the HDI tells us that it is about the human race: "el linaje humano" (HDI 1:4). Las Casas believes there are many human lines of descent, all of which emanate from one single lineage. All peoples and "lineages" (*linajes*) are equally worthy of consideration when it comes to salvation by faith in Christ.[145] Like branches from one single tree, or tributaries leading to one large river, human groups differ in their traits, but are members of the same single species or race. This idea is rooted in a naturalistic understanding of "races," for Las Casas believes human groups can be compared to plants. The extent of a plant's development is determined by the soil, not by any inherent defect of virtue of the plant. Thus, cultivation is vital, not the pointing out of immanent weaknesses or strengths of each kind of plant or human group. "All men of the world, however barbaric or brutal they may be, are inevitably able to reach the use of reason through education and religious doctrine" (HDI 1:15)[146] To be sure, we can discern Las Casas's Catholic, imperial dogmatism here, but the central point is that there is no essential, underlying mark of distinction inherent in each of the branches of the human lineage.

Las Casas's rhetoric is not consistently bereft of naturalistic tropes. He employs the pregnant term *nación* to refer to different peoples. The term is also central to Las Casas's nascent construction of the idea of race because the word "nation," etymologically, involves the idea of common birth or descent. Las Casas does not explicitly underscore this, but his usage of the term forces us to examine the link of a people to nature. There is a biological, familial sense in the term "nation." The idea of a birth within a single family is expanded to a clan and its descendents. It entails a series of concentric circles that expand out of the paradigm of one single birth within one family and moves outward to include related families and others sharing genetic markers. The word "nation" in this sense cannot be understood purely as social custom or *nomos*, but must of necessity involve a sense of *physis*, or nature. In classical Latin, the word *natio* denotes a class of people distinguished by common biological descent. Ultimately, "nation" possesses a political component, as in the conception of the "nation-state," but it originally involves a biological understanding that is tied to the idea of particular classes of humans, which is not far from our colloquial usage of the term "race." For Las Casas, "All the nations of the world are men" (HDI 2:396), which means that while there are different peoples in the world, whose biological, genealogical lineages appear quite distinctive when viewed either somatically or culturally, they all belong to the same single human race ("todo el linaje humano")[147] because those differences are merely accidental.

Interestingly, Las Casas calls on Cicero to promote this notion that no nation stands outside of the human species. He argues that the proem of *Rhetorica Vetus* essentially posits the same principle that no nation, however barbarous, should be treated as less than human. Las Casas does not expatiate at length on this reference to Cicero, so it is not clear what the specific virtue of this reference is. For Cicero, coming from a rationalistic, Stoic form of cosmopolitanism, the idea of the universality of humanity emanates from the principle of universal reason. His conception is quite different from a Christian, Catholic one. The former seeks to focus on reason, not emotion, as the basis of a common sense of humanity; whereas the latter provides a cardinal place to the emotions (charity, love, and compassion). Thus, while Cicero seems to be an important point of reference for Las Casas, as Nederman shows,[148] there is also a deep tension between the ancient Roman statesman's Stoic cosmopolitanism and the ideas of the modern Catholic thinker. They share an appreciation for the value of rhetoric, but they possess different bases for their common belief that all of humanity is one.

The ancients were, for Las Casas, fundamentally barbarians because they were unbelievers. It is faith in Christ that cultivates peace and softens barbaric customs. In this, Christianity is a modernizing, civilizing force for Las Casas. The "ferocity of the Spanish people, especially in Andalusia" (HDI 1:16), was moderated by the Christian religion. The same sort of ignorance that plagued pre-Christian Spain, Las Casas believes, is what explains the apparently savage customs of the Amerindians, not any indwelling, biological defect. In effect, Las Casas idealizes the native Americans to the point of portraying them in such a benevolent light that they appear to be of a different class of human beings. "The annihilation [*aniquilación*] of these [people] *toto genere* was facilitated by the extremely docile, humble, pauper-like, harmless, and simple *nature* [emphasis added] of these people" (HDI 1:18). Somehow, Las Casas suspends his criticism of barbarous Amerindian practices (which he denounces at length in the AHS), and portrays the Indians as nearly angelic dwellers in Paradise. This imaginary of peace and submissiveness is central to Las Casas's rhetoric of nascent racialization.

The paradisiacal description of the "New World" is part of the (less than clean) break with the ancients that Las Casas carries out.[149] The "discovery" of "another world" (HDI 1:148) by Columbus, known in Spanish as Cristóbal Colón (a name that rings with tones of colonization and conquest) implies for Las Casas the advent of a new, modern era. This claim may or may not be true, but it is the way that Las Casas wants to see the events of 1492. The expulsion of the Jews and Columbus's first voyage to the Americas as described in Columbus's diaries are cited by Las Casas as pivotal. We can infer that he sees a break from the notion of "impurity" of blood that many believed was caused by the Jewish presence in Christendom. It is a chance to start anew, in a way that avoids the ugliness of the past, and idealizes the beauty of the future.

Las Casas's Early Aestheticization of Race

Descriptions such as "the goodness, humility, simplicity, hospitability, disposition, as well as the *color and beauty* of the Indians" (HDI 1:200; emphasis added) are Las Casas's early aestheticization of the politics of race.[150] It is a modern form of linking beauty to groups of people, for it deals with what were considered newly discovered "races." But the purpose is principally rhetorical and has bases in premodernity. Las Casas here follows the ancient Roman and Greek association of beauty with moral virtue. Las Casas describes Columbus as a heroic figure who reaches Hispaniola and meets people speaking the Guanahani language. It is a meeting of the old with the new, and Las Casas does not tire from underscoring the aesthetic dimension of this encounter or mutual spectacle. "The Indians that were present . . . were stunned looking at the Christians, frightened by their beards, their *whiteness*, and their clothing" while they "observed their hands and the whiteness of their faces" (HDI 1:202; emphasis added). The admiral (Columbus) viewed the Indians' simplicity with admiration and "enjoyment and pleasure . . . marveling at their docility as if they were their [the Spaniards'] own children" (HDI 1:202). The Indians were "very well-*made*, of great beauty and pretty bodies and very attractive faces" (HDI 1:204–5; emphasis added; see also 269). Some are painted in black, some have the color of Canary Island peoples, "neither black nor white" (HDI 1:204).

In this manner, Las Casas provides a vivid description with great artistry. We almost feel as if we are side by side with Columbus as he witnesses this spectacle. The role of beauty, form, color, images, body shapes, and other kinds of aestheticization becomes prominent. It is intended to underscore the attractiveness, not the repulsion, that one feels naturally upon seeing these new peoples. If they were devils or beasts, one would feel repelled by them. Las Casas wants to argue that their beauty is a sign of moral goodness. The unintended consequence of seeking to incorporate the Amerindians into the human race is that his exaggeration creates a typology where the natives' *"natural* goodness and docility" (HDI 1:229; emphasis added) makes them appear as if they have none of the flaws that come with being human.

We also find a dimension of Las Casas's thinking that does not fit easily into a classical attempt to determine rationality based on mental capacities. It deals with Las Casas's examination, early in the AHS, of the physical characteristics of Amerindians. This concern over the corporeal has relevance for our interest in his nascent conception of race, for race is generally understood to refer to somatic, biological traits. Las Casas's approach involves an interest in the aesthetic facets of the Amerindian body.[151] His perspective differs markedly from one that would focus on the mind and on the faculty of reason, and is an example of what I have called elsewhere "aesthetic political theory."[152] It is telling that Las Casas begins AHS with a sustained effort to analyze the physical rather than the mental or social or political dimensions of the Amerindian, showing the primacy of this particular facet in Las Casas's view. He does go on later to cite from history in his effort to show the rationality of the Amerindians, but only after engaging with the corporeal. In other words, what he says about reason is not that it can be found through our understanding of the mind, but rather through our study of how the physical world is experienced and how it shapes our perceptions. We again find the preeminence of sentience, and we encounter a confrontation with feeling, affect, and emotion that is consonant with the early-modern attempt to grasp political phenomena through aesthetic categories.[153]

Las Casas begins by telling us that he wants to understand the various "nations" of the Americas.[154] However, he believes that each individual, not each group or nation, can be understood as a relation between soul and body. Following Aquinas in *De Anima*,[155] he argues that each person is individually proportioned. In other words, general statements about the nature of a person can only be made individually, not for a class or "race" or people. To some extent Aquinas's argument is contradicted by Las Casas, since he proceeds to analyze the somatic characteristics of "the Amerindian," not of specific persons.[156] "Only according to the capacity of the body can we measure the capacity of the soul/mind." Thus, the body takes a salient role in our understanding of reason. He follows this revelation with the argument that the body is located in a real, material, physical, and geographic environment. Bodies interact with and depend on specific geophysical locales.

Here Las Casas enters the murky world of proto-racialization in earnest. The environmental conditions the somatic, and then the somatic affects the mental. "People that live in cold areas and in Europe . . . *naturally* are more hard-working, and more spirited/alert than in others, but they do not have the keenness and sagacity of nations that live in warm areas" (AHS 385 in OC vol. 6; emphasis added). A rare pseudo-scientific approach is evident when Las Casas argues that the pores of humans open wider in warmer areas, making them more cowardly and timid. Besides individual proportion and environmental conditioning, Las Casas proposes that there is a third element that is conducive to "good reasoning," and here is where he believes perception of the material world enters the picture.

The "organs of the exterior senses" (AHS 391) are the key to human acquisition of information that is then used to shape a person's rational capacity. Cognition through the senses, which is a meaning of the term "aesthetic," is crucial, for *sensible tacto* is what allows persons to understand the world. Yet this perception is somehow connected to another element of the aesthetic: beauty. Las Casas goes on to say that a person's "beauty, especially of the face, and the form of the sense organs" (AHS 391) is a reflection of the ability to reason well. But this beauty is not characterized by being exceptional; beauty for Las Casas means an average, familiar face, not one that has traits that are out of proportion. It is a "mediocre" beauty that appeals to us, because it tells us that a person is near the middle of a scale, and not at one extreme or the other. Here we find an Aristotelian sense of the value of the mean. Las Casas quotes him from his Latin translation: *molles carne aptos mente videmus.* The human sense of touch is the primary one, and Las Casas follows Aquinas in that, "of all animals, it is man who has the finest sense of touch, and among men, those who have the finest sense of touch are those with a very keen intelligence. Aristotle gives an indication of this when he says: 'Those whose flesh is tender have a nimble spirit.'"[157] Tactile capacity determines subtle understanding that is keen and "pure."

The beauty of the face is important for Las Casas. *Vultus*, that is, the facial expression, is in a sense, a window to the rational soul. Las Casas finds evidence for this in many ancient thinkers, from Aristotle's *Politics*, to Servius, Sallust, and Virgil (AHS 393). He also includes Euripides, Porphyry, Ambrose, Ovid, and Quintilian in this list. Thus, he appreciates the ancient pagan world's valuation of beauty, not merely in itself, but as a measurement of human reason. It is not clear why reason should be reflected in the human face, but this is what Las Casas believed based on his reading of classical non-Christian texts. Along with the thirteenth-century Bavarian theologian Albertus Magnus, he states that the shape of the head is a sign of physiognomy that shows how subtle or keen a person's intellect is (AHS 393). Imagination, common sense, and memory depend on the "external" senses, those of sight, hearing, smell, taste, and touch (AHS 394). "Human understanding" depends on "the reception of images and forms or kinds and semblances of things that have entered the person through one of the five external senses" (AHS 397).

Why does Las Casas discuss this topic in a book about the Amerindians? Principally because he sees beauty in their form, and in their beauty he finds humanity. Contrary to his opponents' views, the Amerindians are not semihuman or beastly creatures. Relying on classical, non-Christian philosophy, he forces his antagonists to accept the rationality and humanity of the natives by way of their aesthetic characteristics. Further evidence of the aesthetic in Las Casas's argument is his emphasis on the emotions of the natives. Emotion is a core category of modern aesthetics, along with representation and form. Having laid out the sensory basis of human reason, he argues that fear, sadness, and pain cloud reasoning deeply. Sadness is the passion that is most harmful to the body. Las Casas makes statements that are sometimes ludicrous to support this idea. He thinks that "sometimes, it happens to some white parents that a black child is born, and this is because the parents saw or imagined some black person during the time of conception" (AHS 404). He also believes that Africans ("los de Etiopía") being "black," have "black and dry bodies, as well as coarse and ugly hair and heads . . . which affects their minds/spirits . . . with low levels of understanding, rustic, cruel, and bestial customs . . . and overly warm complexions due to the great heat that they suffer" (AHS 410). Las Casas is equally crude about whites, however: "For the opposite reasons . . . in the very cold lands . . . of England, Scotland, and Norway . . . [people have] huge, fleshy, thick bodies . . . as well as ferocious and cruel customs" (AHS 404). The main point here is that for Las Casas all humans are deeply affected by environmental conditions, and that these can have both somatic and moral effects. This view may not seem far from some racist European views of environmental determinism, but the difference with Las Casas is that he includes whites in his criticism of moral vices shaped by surrounding ecology.

Here we find a contradiction in Las Casas that is nonetheless telling, for it shows us his positioning at the transition between the ancient and the modern worlds. On the one hand, he believes nature shapes man, with the land, plants, animals, temperature, and other ecological factors forming the particular groups that emerge in different global localities. In this, we find a premodern conception where humans are not in control of their destinies. This lack of autonomy is closer to the views held in antiquity and the medieval period. At the same time, Las Casas teases out the various classical perspectives on the link between beauty, form and other aesthetic categories and morality, which he then directs to defend the humanity of the Amerindians. In this, he moves in a modern direction, for he contributes to a nascent aesthetic political theory, as Machiavelli also did in other ways at the dawn of the modern era.[158] Like the Florentine, Las Casas straddles the medieval world, with its roots in antiquity, and the new, modern era, one that complicates the ties between reason and aesthetic experience. For Las Casas, nature shapes the human body, especially its external senses, which then forms human reason in particular ways. *Entendimiento*, or understanding, then leads to particular cultural and civilizational forms, which are not universally the same owing to ecological conditions. This concept results in the belief that different human "races," or *linajes humanos*, can arrive at rationally ordered ways of life through different paths.

Las Casas insists that these different groups can be separated from each other because of particular biological and physical characteristics. Hence, we can insist that he establishes the bases for a modern conception of "race." He tells us that "mediocridad de sangre" is ideal (AHS 435). In other words, an average, middling kind of "blood" is most desirable (using the Aristotelian language of the mean), but that we can find all sorts of variation from the mean throughout the world's peoples, who nonetheless remain within the human species (departing from a strict Aristotelian civilized/barbarian dichotomy). The Indians reflect their inner balance of blood and perhaps other humors in their external appearance: they have "*naturally beautiful and proportional bodies*" (AHS 435; emphasis added). In other words, their lineage or race shows the kind of balance that makes them part of the human species, and their physical beauty is a reflection of their rational, well-ordered souls. Las Casas employs both classical and medieval notions of the relationship of the body's beauty to moral and soul-related characteristics in order to address a modern phenomenon: the confrontation with an entirely new people.

This confrontation does not lead toward a conception in which each individual is seen as equal in physical or moral terms to any other individual. Las Casas sees the Amerindians as a unique class, and he exaggerates some of their traits: "Their external senses are admirable. They can see much farther than us; it seems they can see through into human hearts" (AHS 435). He generalizes this belief to *all* Amerindians, saying, "*Todos* los moradores destas Indias por la mayor parte . . . sean de buenos aspectos y acatamientos, de hermosas caras y proporcionados miembros y cuerpos . . . se muestra . . . nobles animas naturalmente y así ser bien razonables y de buenos entendimientos."[159] He generalizes not only in terms of their bodies, but also their behavior: they are a "happy" people who abhor sadness and pain (AHS 450). They are "sanguine" and love to dance and celebrate. Thus, while Las Casas advances the idea that Amerindians are neither beasts nor savages but in fact are part of the human species, he also—perhaps inadvertently—creates categorical distinctions along somatic and behavioral lines that separate them from Europeans.

Thus, Las Casas is not merely concerned with showing affinities between diverse cultural groups. He goes far beyond that. He seeks to show the unitary origin of the human species or race. To be sure, Las Casas does contribute, to some extent, to an early form of ethnography. His almost-scholarly studies of diverse human groups lends credence to the idea that different cultures may share structural similarities beneath epiphenomenal differences. But more importantly, he wants to argue that there is one single human race, even if it becomes subdivided into ethnic groups in different places, spaces, and periods of time. The term *linaje* is important, for it refers to human biological lineage. It does not merely reflect a culturalist understanding of human difference. Las Casas seeks to show, through rhetorical exposition, that the Amerindians are natural (that is, biological) kin of Europeans, not simply culturally similar in some ways. While his focus was on the Amerindian, he eventually also turned his gaze to the status of Africans.

Late Redress: Las Casas's Treatment of Africans

The Spanish Catholic orders did not generally question the moral legitimacy of the use of African slaves. In the early imaginary of the Las Casas, Africans were to be treated as efficient workers. Only slowly did he begin to apply to African slaves the same moral logic that he used to view the Amerindians. In a sense, African slaves in the Americas posed the limit test case for Las Casas's conceptualization of humanity, revealing an error that he corrected all too slowly. Still, there is evidence that Las Casas did question the policies of Spain and Portugal in parts of Africa. In his brief text that has come to be called *A Short Account of the Destruction of Africa*, we find a set of concerns that parallel the ideas of the

Short Account of the Destruction of the Indies.[160] Thought to have been written around 1556,[161] it is an effort to persuade the reader of the injustice of the treatment of the inhabitants of the Canary Islands and the northwest coast of Africa by the Iberians.[162] Owing to the fact that the account of Africa was inserted into his study of the history of the Indies, it is generally overlooked as a central text regarding Las Casas's stance toward Africans.[163] Las Casas ultimately did come to see humanity as comprised also of the various African peoples.

It must be underscored that Las Casas's myopia when it came to black Africans in the context of the Americas is one of the core lacunae of his thought. He did not engage in a spirited defense of blacks in the Americas as he did of Amerindians.[164] Moreover, he sometimes had negative views of Africans in aesthetic terms. He wrote about an expedition undertaken by the Portuguese in 1444, describing the Africans that were taken as prisoners and slaves:

> Among them, there were some that were reasonably white, beautiful and handsome; others that were less white, that seemed *pardo*, and others that were as black as Ethiopians, so misshapen were their faces and bodies that they seemed to be men coming from the Southern Hemisphere.[165]

Here is a narrow-minded Las Casas, in a passage that contradicts his writings describing the aesthetic merits of Amerindians. Las Casas's writings on Africa, however, also contain a clear defense of the *guanches* (Canary Island natives, originally those from Tenerife), Moors, and black Africans.

In these writings, Las Casas denounces the atrocities perpetrated by the Portuguese in the Canary Islands and Africa. To be sure, there is an implicit project here: that of promoting the legitimate authority of Castile over the Canaries in lieu of Portugal.[166] But, at the same time, Las Casas proffers a defense of indigenous peoples that parallels his stance toward the Amerindians. For him, Europeans had no "reason or cause to invade or attack" the *guanches*.[167] What the Portuguese did in the Canaries was nothing more than sheer cruelty inflicted on a peaceful people.[168] This also applied to "blacks" from Guinea.[169] Las Casas denounces the policies of Portuguese kings Juan II and Manuel that led to the enslavement of black Africans from "Benii" (Benin).[170] At the end of the day, Las Casas would declare that "the same reasons that apply to the Indians apply to black slaves," for "both have unjustly and tyrannically been enslaved."[171]

The gradual realization in Las Casas's mind that cruelties against black Africans ought to be seen on the same moral plane as those against Amerindians finds an analogue in his meditations on the treatment of the inhabitants of the Canary Islands and the west coast of Africa.[172] In the *Short Account of the Destruction of Africa*, Juan Betancour's conquest of the Canaries is seen in a similar light as the Spanish conquest of the Indies: a peaceful, benevolent, and weak people are ravaged by a more powerful and transgressive force without any legitimate reason.[173] The Canary Islands, being off the coast of Africa, are seen by Las Casas as a territory that is not part of the natural geographic unity of the European world; in other words, the Iberians have invaded an area that is not theirs. And they have done so with "blindness."[174] He goes on to say that Petrarch was wrong to consider the denizens of these islands as little more than beasts, because the islands themselves are lush and agreeable, and their people have political order.[175] Once the Iberians went past the Canaries, they proceeded to ravage the west coast of Africa, unjustly enslaving "the blacks of Jolof," near Senegal, after buying black slaves from the Moors.[176] Las Casas tells of the enslavement of hundreds of "black *persons*,"[177] thereby showing that he considered them part of humanity.

The fact that Las Casas saw nonwhites as equal members of the human species, or, in other words, that he believed that the human species was a synthesis of many different groups, is evident in his assessment of what he believes is the *rational* conclusion of examining human diversity: "Anyone with any brains [*seso*][178] must realize that no infidel, be they Moorish, *alárabe* [nomadic Arabs and Berbers], Turkish, Tatar, or Indian or of any other kind, law, or sect/religion that he may be, can suffer war legitimately from Christians, without them committing a very grave sin."[179] Still, Las Casas believes that there are three possible reasons to wage legitimate war on infidels: if they attack or wage war against Christians; if they impede the peaceful evangelization of Christianity; or if they take away the possessions or property of Christians.[180] The second reason is rather ambiguous: Las Casas does not specify what "impede" (*estorban*) entails. If one takes a broad interpretation of this term, it is conceivable his argument would legitimate an imperialist policy toward African or Amerindian infidels. In general Las Casas believes Christianity must spread peacefully; that is, it must be a pacific empire. Yet this is a utopian belief, for it is clear that empires must rely on arms to spread. Still, there is an ambiguous defense of legitimate action by Christians against infidels in the case that they find impediments to their desire to proselytize. This support is a further reason why the case for seeing Las Casas as an anti-imperialist is not tenable.

Empire and Inclusion: Synthesis out of Diversity

If Amerindians are part of the human race as a whole, but have characteristics that are essentially different from other large regional groups in the world (such as Europeans or Muslims), what is to be done? Should Las Casas let them be? Should he be concerned with their lot? Should he try to argue for or against the intervention of the Spanish Crown in matters relevant to the status and condition of the natives? It is here where Las Casas's persona as a Catholic imperialist comes to the fore.[181] It is not in spite of this persona that Las Casas argued for a defense of the Amerindians' rights. It is precisely because of it.[182] The paradox of empire is at work in this particular case. While there was widespread devastation and despoliation on the ground, at the theoretical level the fact that Catholic imperialist intellectuals debated the very humanity of the natives led to the idea that the natives should be incorporated into the Crown as subjects equal to those living in Castile.[183] Las Casas's work accepted difference and human variation, but argued for a fundamental sameness of all categories of peoples (what we would call races). His work thus argued for a synthesis of diversity into unity.

This synthesis takes place at the religious and the political levels. On the plane of religion, Las Casas was an adamant Catholic ideologue, someone whose faith in the specifically Dominican reading of the Christian faith was unshakable. He never exercised his puissant abilities of reason to question his faith; he was convinced that Catholicism was the true belief system and was superior to all others. One must wonder why such a penetrating mind never had doubts about the nature of religious faith. In any event, Las Casas's faith was so unbreakable that not even witnessing the barbarous atrocities perpetrated by Christians in the New World led him to change his views on religion. If anything, they reinforced the idea that "true" Christianity was something beyond time and space, something that did not have to be necessarily tied to the culturally specific groups that claimed to be Christians. As we saw above, his reversal of prevailing Catholic morality meant that, for him, the true Christians were the natives. They lived according to basic Christian principles such as pacifism, modesty, poverty, communal solidarity, and humility. Christian ideas being transcendental, Las Casas's witnessing of the natives' "virtues" in fact probably made him even more certain that Christian teachings were correct.[184]

Thus, Las Casas rejected the logical conclusion that, if the Spaniards were cruel, and they were also at the same time Christians, then Christianity may not be able to hinder (and in fact may even be conducive to) cruelty because of the moral reversal that we point out above. This rejection of a logical conclusion justified Las Casas's faith, and seeing the "underdevelopment" of the natives in terms of social order, he concluded that the ideal, mutually beneficial scenario would be to, in a sense, "marry" the virtues of the natives to those of the Spaniards. The virtues of the natives were those of the above-mentioned Christian-like modes of behavior, and the virtues of the Spaniards were of the higher level of political and civic organization. In this sense, he defended a reciprocal arrangement that he believed would benefit both sides through a synthesis.

The natives' virtues center on the fact that their behavior, simply put, is less sinful than that of the Spaniards. In this sense, it is not true at all, as Pagden repeatedly emphasizes, that Las Casas's main task was to show similarities across diverse cultural groups.[185] The natives (all the way from Florida to the River Plate area, a vast swath of land indeed) were clearly more morally virtuous than the Spanish. The Spaniards showed all manner of sin: "The reason the Christians have murdered on such a vast scale and killed anyone and everyone in their way is purely and simply greed."[186] The sin of greed is contrasted to the natives' lack of materialism, "natural goodness," and "poverty." In fact, they are unable to commit harm. The sins of murder, lying, and stealing are all part and parcel of the Spanish way of life according to Las Casas.[187]

If this is the case, why does not Las Casas urge an anti-imperial struggle by the natives? To be fair, he does consider it.[188] He ponders the possibility that the best course of action for the natives is to drive the Europeans into the sea "once and for all."[189] Moreover, he is opposed to *economic* imperialism: he believes the Spaniards' "appetite for money"[190] is one reason for the moral decadence of the Spanish forces in America. Here Las Casas acts both as a critic and as a theorist of some contradictions of empire. The civic virtues of having one single polis for the world are undermined by the predatory nature of pecuniary imperialism. On this score Las Casas is a strident critic of expansionary policies that are driven principally by greed and expropriation.

Still, Las Casas considers that the moral benefits of empire outweigh the concrete costs. Since the Catholic, universal religion is the true religion in his view, and the natives are fundamentally Christians in the raw (and they often *voluntarily* submit themselves to the authority of the Church), Las Casas concludes that the long-run optimal course of action is to defend the empire while urging the king to try to curb the atrocities on the ground.[191] He concludes his assessment of the legitimacy of rule by Spain over the Americas by stating that "with this sovereign, imperial, and universal principality and lordship by the kings of Castile and León over the Indies, it is granted that they have administrative and juridical right and *dominium* over the Indian peoples and their policies."[192]

The paradox of the Spanish Empire is that while, on the one hand, it devastated, butchered, and annihilated people on the ground, on the other hand its Catholic universalism allowed apologists of imperialist policy such as Las Casas to defend the idea that the natives should be incorporated into the fold of the Crown as human beings on a par with Europeans. But these grounds do not satisfy the criteria for objective ethnography or anything worthy of the name science.[193] Vast amounts of "empirical data"[194] may have been mobilized by Las Casas, but not for the purpose of founding the discipline of ethnography. He did so for the ultimate purpose of showing that the natives could and should be integrated into the Crown.

Conclusion

The concept of "race" is not simple; it is the product of a long and complex process. This process involves the perception of external characteristics of human beings as something that entails a generalized categorical distinction made among human beings across diverse ethnic groups. It artificially creates discrete human kinds. Historically, the seeds of this process can be found in premodern periods, but it takes root in the early-modern era around the early 1500s. It is basically around the time of the conquest of the Americas by Spain that racialization takes shape, for discussions about ethnic or cultural difference became transformed into discussions about fundamental or essential differences among persons.

At the same time, some contemporaries of Las Casas argued that in fact the Amerindians were not really human. "Homunculi" is the term that Sepúlveda used, something connoting subhumanity.[195] Sepúlveda argued that the natives were closer to animals such as bees and spiders than to Europeans. In other words, the debate at the time was not merely one of how to translate different cultural practices from the language of one ethnicity to another; it was to asseverate the very humanity or nonhumanity of the "humanoid" beings that had been found in the Americas. This debate about the proper zoological or biological classification of the Amerindians points to the nascent process of racialization of the time. There is a natural or biological dimension to this argument that is essential to what is race and which is lacking in ethnicity per se. Race is as much about biology as it is about ethnicity, and it is socially constructed when arguments about both are made in conjunction to generate categorical distinctions.

These distinctions are not merely scalar, but they are also cardinal. In other words, Las Casas and his contemporaries did not simply argue about the stage of development at which the natives were to be located. They argued about whether they should be measured with the same scale as Europeans. Thus, while there is a rank-ordering process at work in the thought of some of Las Casas's contemporaries that is present even in some of his own writings, Las Casas's chief concern is to show that the natives are indeed human although they are of a sort different from Europeans.

Through rhetoric, Las Casas was able to argue for a synthetic or inclusive approach to the natives. Only under the rubric of rhetoric does his corpus gain an overall coherence. His thought was addressed to a new era when humanity was seen as universal. In this sense, O'Gorman is not correct to say that Las Casas's thought was thoroughly Aristotelian, since Las Casas's intellectual universe was not delimited by the polis and he did not accept the Philosopher's emphasis on rationality or the distinction between the civilized and the barbarian.[196] A Christian city is a "quasi-mystical union of men," as Pagden avers,[197] and this union would be made more perfect by the balance of virtues of the Spanish and the natives. The Amerindians should be added to the Spanish Crown as subjects, and their incorporation would be beneficial to them as well as to Spain. They would be helped to become more civilized in terms of social organization, but they would also bring to Spain their natural goodness and benevolence, which Las Casas argued were glimmers of true Christianity in a world where supposed Christians had become butchers of human flesh. In this way, both sides would benefit and become better in their union. For Las Casas, *Indi fratres nostri sunt*.[198] A synthesis of civilizational and moral virtues would make the empire even more glorious.

Unity, unity, unity must be our motto in all things.
The blood of our citizens is varied: let it be mixed
for the sake of unity.
—BOLÍVAR, Angostura Discourse, 1819[1]

2

MIXED INTO UNITY

Race and Republic in the Thought of Simón Bolívar

IN THE EYES of Simón Bolívar, very little of the Spanish Empire in America, a three-hundred-year-old legacy, was worth rescuing.[2] It created a world of "masses . . . carried away by religious fanaticism and seduced by the lure of voracious anarchy" and men who were "corrupted by the yoke of servitude and bestialized by the doctrine of superstition."[3] *El Libertador,* as Bolívar was known for his role in liberating six Latin American countries from Spanish rule,[4] had, however, great admiration for Bartolomé de Las Casas. He would tell us, in the Angostura Discourse, that while the atrocities committed by the Spanish seem unbelievable, "the humane Bishop of Chiapas" had left a sincere record.[5] Bolívar believed that "every impartial person has admitted the zeal, sincerity, and high character of that friend of humanity, who so fervently and so steadfastly denounced to his government and to his contemporaries the most horrible acts of sanguinary frenzy."[6] Bolívar sought a radical break from an Iberian past rooted in the autocracy of the Catholic Church. But Las Casas was spared this judgment, principally because of the bishop's abhorrence for tyranny and also for his defense of the natives of the Americas. When Bolívar arrived in Peru, he showed his appreciation for the Dominican friar by writing, "I came yesterday to the classic land of the sun, of the Incas, of fable and history. Here the true sun is gold; the Incas are the viceroys or prefects; the fable is Garcilaso's history; history is the relation by Las Casas of the destruction of the Indies."[7]

The political thought of Bolívar is central to the story of the synthetic paradigm of race in Latin American intellectual history. His ideas represent a rejoinder to the imperialist theses of Las Casas, but are joined to them in engaging complexly with issues involving race. Las Casas, as we have seen, adumbrates the notion of race. With Bolívar, we find a direct confrontation with the problem of race as such, so much so that we can aver that he was profoundly preoccupied with the racial *problématique*. Throughout his writings we find the motif of race and an effort to provide pragmatic ways to deal with the racial realities of his own continent. Both Las Casas and Bolívar are cognizant that race is crucial to the delineation of state membership for individual subjects and social groups. Bolívar accepts Las Casas's symbolic legacy, but he seeks to replace the Spaniard's imperial armature with republican ideas because he does not believe empires are legitimate. His critique of empire is the second station in the genealogy of the synthetic conception of the notion of race.

In most general histories of republicanism, Bolívar is not even cited.[8] Yet Bolívar was no mere imitator of European ideas, and his conception of the modern republic merits inclusion in the canon of political thought. For him, the "American"[9] continent's political problems are distinct from those of Europe, because the social bases of a postcolonial society are unique. Throughout his career, both in his written legacy and in his own public life, he tried to grapple with this difficult fact. Like many great but tragic leaders, he ultimately failed,[10] but his efforts in dealing squarely with race make him a central figure in modern political thought.[11] Bolívar makes significant—though never systematic—references to race in many of his writings. It is important to read the entirety of his political thought in light of these remarks, as we shall see in this chapter, for he saw Gran Colombia as a region fraught with divisions and conflict, including those of the racial sort. For him, it was a "chaos of patriots, *godos*, self-seekers, *blancos*, *pardos*, Venezuelans, *Cundinamarquis*, federalists, centralists, republicans, aristocrats, the good, and the bad."[12]

Bolívar's thought in relation to race can be termed synthetic for three reasons. The first is that he saw the Latin American person (*el americano*) as someone whose very identity is mixed. That is, to the ontological question of who the American man or woman is, his response is one involving an entity in whom coalesced indigenous, European, and African lines of descent.[13] The second and most significant reason is that his own brand of republicanism was fundamentally an effort to address the political instability produced by "race mixture" in the Americas. Race mixture here has two meanings: first, the ontological fact of combinations of racial origins, and second, the fact that many of the nascent nations in Latin America were grounded in societies that were themselves made up of various ethnoracial groups distinguished by legal, class, and other social mechanisms of social differentiation in spite of the ontological admixture of individual persons.[14]

Bolívar proffered a modern republican theory intended to address the political problems associated with societies characterized by a pervasive admixture of races.[15] Neither a classical liberal[16] nor a classical republican, Bolívar was a modern thinker who borrowed from a variety of sources in order to provide a realistic solution to the problems at hand. Montesquieu and Rousseau[17] are common points of reference for Bolívar's political prescriptions, and most commentators interpret his republican ideas as related to the French tradition. But in fact a more illuminating comparison is with Niccolò Machiavelli.[18]

Examining Bolívar in light of Machiavelli elucidates a key question in Bolívar studies: whether he was a proto-democratic republican thinker or an absolutist caudillo.[19] Through Machiavelli, we find that Bolívar's brand of republicanism combined elements of both positions and was fundamentally martial.[20] But whereas Machiavelli ignored the problem of race, for Bolívar it was the greatest—sometimes unspoken—problem for modern, postcolonial societies. Bolívar was fundamentally a Machiavellian republican, for he believed in a constitutional order very similar to the Florentine tradition of the mixed republic in the context of bellicose conditions.[21]

The third reason Bolívar's conception of the politics of race is synthetic is his views on pan-American unity. Here we find that race and ethnicity are intimately tied together, and hence Bolívar urges the creation of a single, unified political community in Latin America. He reasons on this point also on realist international relations grounds, for he sees that a global equilibrium could be found if Latin America were to be united as a counterpoise to Europe and the United States. Thus, the unity of the Americas is a largely political project, yet it is also based on the idea that ethnoracial commonalities are the social basis for a stable political regime.

Life of the Liberator

A man of dark complexion[22] and Spanish origins, Bolívar was born in Caracas, present-day Venezuela, on July 24, 1783. He is believed to have been of "white" lineage, in spite of being a seventh-generation American.[23] Bolívar was orphaned at an early age. When he was two and a half years old, his father died of tuberculosis, and his mother died of the same illness when he was nine. Born to a well-bred family, he inherited his father's library and was tutored by distinguished men, chief among them Andrés Bello.[24] But Bolívar liked, as a young boy, to associate himself with people of the lower classes, as he spent many hours strolling the streets of Caracas,[25] a world that was a "mixture of races and cultures" where "race consciousness was acute."[26] Still, race-passing was common, for Canarians, *blancos de orilla*, and some *pardos*[27] were sometimes treated as creole whites.

The society in which Bolívar lived was racially mixed. The largest ethnoracial group were the *pardos*, otherwise called mulattos, including anyone with some African descent. They made up about 50 percent of the total population of around 800,000 in the late colonial period in Venezuela. They were followed by creole Canarians, who were poor whites (*blancos de orilla*) from the Canary Islands and made up about 24 percent of the population. Blacks, who were freemen, slaves, and fugitives, amounted to about 9 percent of the population, Indians about 15 percent. As for "pure" whites, Creoles of elite status were only about 0.31 percent, and peninsular Spaniards a meager 0.18 percent.[28] Thus, society was far from homogenous, showing significant levels of miscegenation, as indicated by the number of *pardos*. The term *pardo* was sometimes used to refer to the white-African mix, and sometimes to mestizos, those of white and indigenous origins. But it was an umbrella term connoting anyone with unclear racial origins or with any race mixture. These included mulattos, *zambos*, mestizos, and even some *blancos de orilla* whose background was uncertain.[29] Thus, the term stands for something close to "the masses."

Bolívar was a member of the class known as *mantuanos*, landowners who often had slaves. They were far removed from poor whites and Canarians, who were placed on the other side of a wide chasm of class. The Creoles were always wary of *gente de color*, and feared the rising claims of *pardos*: "Race was an issue in Venezuela, usually dormant, but with the potential for violence."[30] As a consequence, slave revolts were a perennial threat to whites. But it was a society where marriage laws were not strictly enforced; hence, illegitimacy and casual unions were not rare. Marriage could evince social status, especially for the upper classes, but it did not prevent interracial mixing, especially among the lower classes.[31]

At the age of fourteen, and following family tradition, Bolívar enrolled as a military cadet in the Valley of Aragua. A year later he traveled to Spain. It is there that he met and fell deeply in love with a young woman called María Teresa Rodríguez del Toro y Alayza, who was about two years older than Bolívar. She was the daughter of a Spanish mother and a Venezuelan father.[32] They eventually married, but, tragically, she died in 1803 after contracting a fulminating fever, a mere eight months after their wedding vows. This event had an immense impact on Bolívar's life; from that moment on, he decided to enter the world of politics and military life and abandon personal, private pursuits. As he wrote, "The death of my wife propelled me early on the road to politics."[33]

Europe was, for Bolívar, the cradle of his political ideas.[34] After his wife's death, he traveled to Paris, and eventually became fluent in French. He wandered the demimonde of the City of Light, moving from "grieving widower to profligate playboy, plunging into a crazed life of gambling and sex."[35] But between 1804 and 1806, his time in Europe, Bolívar was also becoming politically savvy. He saw the weakness of Spain vis-à-vis France and Britain and witnessed the rise of Napoleon. He felt both admiration and disgust for the Corsican, seeing the greatness of his military skill but also the abomination of his counterrevolutionary transformation into emperor. Eventually Bolívar traveled to Italy, where he reread the works of Machiavelli[36] and made a historic oath in Rome to liberate his fatherland.[37]

The oath of Rome is important because it is the incipient formulation of Bolívar's thought. On August 15, 1805, Bolívar wrote a vow that begins, "So then, this is the nation of Romulus and Numa, of the Gracchi and the Horaces, of Augustus and Nero, of Caesar and Brutus, of Tiberius and Trajan?"[38] We can imagine Bolívar's youthful fervor in uttering these words, mixing admiration and skepticism. He is both laudatory and critical of ancient Rome: "Here every manner of grandeur has had its type, all miseries their cradle." It is the place of "a hundred Caligulas for every Trajan." Ultimately, its legacy is deficient, for it does not raise "the cause of humanity": "The resolution of the great problem of man set free seems to have been something inconceivable" in ancient Rome, "a mystery that would only be made clear in the New World."[39] Here is Bolívar's early break, at the age of twenty-two, with the wisdom of the ancients and with the traditions of Europe. He would go back to the Americas, as someone who did not consider himself an antiquarian Creole, but rather a modern Latin American man.

Bolívar on Latin American Racial Identity

While many commentators have focused principally—if not solely—on Bolívar's political thought understood as his formal constitutionalism,[40] there is no question that for him the social, that is, racial, dimension of his continent was of the most profound importance.[41] A central contribution of Bolívar to Latin American thought is the notion that the people being forged in Spanish America had their own, unique identity. To the question of who these people were, he responded, "We are neither Indian nor European, but a species midway between the legitimate proprietors of this country and the Spanish usurpers."[42] Here we encounter a philosophical insight by the *Libertador*. In the midst of his military and political travails, he was still able to provide a fundamental notion for a proper understanding of the new culture arising on the continent. Unlike some other *criollos*, his sense of identity did not rest in the *Madre Patria* of Spain, but neither was it founded only on the pre-Columbian roots of the indigenous peoples of the region. His use of the term "species" refers to what he believes is a categorically new sort of people that emerges out of the mix of native Americans and Spaniards.

America for Bolívar is to be defined in a negative way. "We are not Europeans; we are not Indians; we are a mixed species of aborigines and Spaniards."[43] The negation of Spanish culture and of the indigenous world is carried out here in a dialectical, synthetic way. Bolívar recognizes an original culture, that of the "Indians," which is then negated by the conquering European one. But the end result is neither a simple elimination of the indigenous dimension nor simply a replication of European ways on American soil. It is a synthesis, made up of two traditions that become inextricable and produce something altogether new.[44] Of course, this is Bolívar's *theoretical* understanding of Latin American reality. He was cognizant that in reality there were vast gulfs between particular ethnoracial groups, created by socially fabricated distinctions of class, caste, and law. *Criollos, pardos*, mestizos, mulattos, *negros*, and *indios*—to mention just some racial categories of the time—were often pitted against each other, sometimes in ways that approached race wars.[45] But for Bolívar, the root of these conflicts was political, not racial, that is, not grounded on irreconcilable racial identities.[46] He saw the increasing pace of miscegenation in Venezuela, Colombia, and other nations occur in the face of political competition for scarce state resources. At the time of Bolívar's rise, Venezuela was a multiethnic but also mixed society in terms of race.[47] Mestizos were growing in numbers at the same time that mulattos were.[48] The latter had been acquiring significant social presence in manufacturing, commerce, and manual labor, but without the concomitant political power. A very small elite of *peninsulares* (Spain-born whites) were at the top of the hierarchy and occupied the highest administrative and ecclesiastical posts. *Criollos*, those whites born in the Americas, were second in line. They tended to have large landholdings and were the economically dominant group. While they could not hold the highest positions in administration, they could use their economic influence to purchase public offices. The cacao industry was important at the time, and it was led by a "cacao aristocracy" of *criollos*, often known as "gran cacaos."[49] At the lower rungs of the social hierarchy were native Amerindians. Some, such as members of the Carib group, were enslaved.[50] At the very bottom, those of black skin and African descent were not even allowed to hold currency or move freely. They were constrained and lacked civil or social rights before independence.[51] Thus, political stations were rigid in spite of sexual relations between different groups and deep social intermixing.

The specifically *racial*, as opposed to ethnic, question of identity for Bolívar is evident in his use of terms such as "species." That is, for Bolívar the social question was grounded on the implicitly "biological" understandings of categorical distinctions between groups of people, not merely cultural differences. But it is even more salient when we consider his use of the concept of the "human family." In the following passage, Bolívar shows his preoccupation with a quasi-biological problem of racial classification in his attempt to understand where to locate the new peoples that were born out of the mixture of indigenous, Spanish, and African groups:

> Permit me to call the attention of the Congress to a matter that may be of *vital importance*. We must keep in mind that our people are neither European nor North American; rather, they are a mixture of African and the American who originated in Europe. Even Spain itself has ceased to be European because of her African blood, her institutions, and her character. It is *impossible to determine with any degree of accuracy where we belong in the human family*. The greater portion of the native Indians has been annihilated; Spaniards have *mixed* with Americans and Africans, and Africans with Indians and Spaniards. While we have all been born of the same mother, our fathers, different in origin and in blood, are foreigners, and all *differ visibly as to the color of their skin: a dissimilarity which places upon us an obligation of the greatest importance*.[52]

This is a key passage for our understanding of Bolívar's thought in relation to race as a problem of identity. The term "identity," of course, ultimately goes back to the Latin word *idem*, or "the same." This is Bolívar's definition of Latin American identity: for him, the sameness or commonality of all Latin Americans is that they come from a combination of differences. They are not tied together by virtue of historical relations related to 1492 or to a series of family resemblances.[53] In Bolívar's embryonic philosophical definition, Latin American identity is essentially a paradoxical one: it is based on its opposite, difference. Thus, we might say that he understands the racial makeup of the Latin American man as a conciliation of opposites. Or, in other words, the essence of a "white" Latin American is in fact his opposite, the entity of an "Indian" or an "African," because in fact that white person is not altogether "white" either biologically or culturally.

We must note that Bolívar opens this statement as a political pronouncement, thereby positing the fundamentally political nature of the identity question in Latin America. Thus, there cannot be a purely philosophical comprehension of identity in this case.[54] It is a statement to the Congress at Angostura, so the context is important; for Bolívar, race is a political matter of the highest significance. As he says, it is of "vital importance" to the polity. He sees that admixture is at the heart not only of his own polity but also of Spain, where "African blood" has permeated all dimensions, including institutions (we may imagine he means the state, education, and commerce) and culture (what he calls "character"). Hence, Bolívar does not believe Spain possesses white privilege *ipso facto*; indeed, it has been pervasively infused with rich, non-Western, non-European sources of culture from ancient times. In this manner Bolívar introduces a conception of race that is inherently variegated. It is not that the Latin American "race" is the only one that is mixed; Spanish blood (and by extension, European) is also quite literally "impure."

Another important aspect of this statement by Bolívar is his reference to the term "accuracy" in determining the location of the Spanish American people in the world's human family. As he avers, it is not possible to ascertain in any scientific or quasi-scientific way what is the racial "status" of this people. In effect, Bolívar undermines the scientistic approach to race. Whereas many European Enlightenment thinkers, such as Linnaeus and Buffon, argued that a scientific approach to race could be effective, here Bolívar rejects this principle. He simply denies the possibility of using exact methods to place the mixed peoples of the New World into any racial taxonomy. He sides with Las Casas in arguing that a quasi genocide eliminated most of the indigenous peoples of the Americas. For most countries, with such exceptions as Bolivia and Guatemala, this statement is not inaccurate. The indigenous blood was mixed with the Spanish, and all manner of combinations ensued in Spanish America, a social result very different from that which obtained in North America. The "mother" that Bolívar refers to is *América*, and the "fathers" are the various ethnoracial mixtures that in the end produce the totality of the Latin American peoples.

The closing of Bolívar's statement about the situation of Spanish America refers to the visible differences among the peoples of Spanish America. Again, it is one rife with paradox. One would imagine that all the admixing Bolívar refers to would yield one single kind of appearance. But given the variety of mixtures, there is a high degree of diversity in terms of outward characteristics. An invisible physical element, blood, itself distinguishes most Latin Americans from putatively pure European or indigenous peoples. But at the same time, aesthetically recognizable traits such as skin color, physiognomy, and hair type make for gradual distinctions among the various inhabitants of the continent. Thus we find again the paradox of difference within sameness. Bolívar, ahead of his time, provides a definition of race that is philosophically rich even though he is by no means a philosopher. He negates the fixity of racial boundaries; he posits the possibility of historical transformation of particular racial groups; and he provides a view of race that is aware of both the visible dimensions of the phenomenon, such as phenotype, and the nonvisible dimensions, such as the idea of blood lineage. It is not an empirical or scientific account of blood biologically understood; it is a metaphor for what may explain differences in outward appearances, a cause that was not clear to Bolívar.

What is clear, however, is his response to this paradox. On the one hand there is sameness in terms of everyone being fundamentally mixed. On the other, there are differences in gradations of skin color and characteristics that can be grasped through sensory cognition. This paradox of alterity within identity can only be resolved, according to Bolívar, through political action. He does not generally offer scientific, social, cultural, or economic answers to this phenomenon.[55] His response is quintessentially civic: it produces an "obligation of the greatest importance." He calls for finding an institutional solution to the racial paradox, a paradox that can create political instability. When admixture permeates society, but does not create a single, homogenous, entirely identical group, political interests can generate conflict and inequality. The answer to these problems, according to Bolívar, is republicanism.

Modern Republicanism and the Problem of Race

It is conceivable that a man of Bolívar's intellectual caliber, well versed in the broad history of political thought, could have argued that only a monarchy or a pure democracy could solve the problems of racial tension that existed in the newly independent Latin American nations.[56] Above all, he was a military man. And this could have led him to believe in a simple autocratic model of governance based on a martial, hierarchical conception of society or in a corporatist view of social organization. But he did not reach that conclusion, because he was steeped in the European Enlightenment tradition. Educated in Europe, and an admirer of figures such as Montesquieu and Rousseau,[57] Bolívar returned from the Old World with an approach that combined moral rectitude with pragmatic realism. There is no doubt that the French Republican tradition of these two eminent thinkers had immense influence on Bolívar. But I want to argue two central points in relation to his brand of republicanism: that we must read his republican theory in light of the few but important statements that he makes about race; and that one illuminating way to understand his own unique brand of republicanism is by comparison to another modern republican thinker—Niccolò Machiavelli.

Bolívar did not hide his dislike for the Florentine thinker.[58] Nonetheless, in the field of political theory and practice, it is possible to discern greater affinities between these two admirers of ancient Rome than between Bolívar and other republican theorists. By both comparing and contrasting them, we reach a fuller, more comprehensive view of Bolívar's own republicanism, one that is, to a large extent, original owing to its construction as a way to resolve racial tensions in mixed societies, a purpose that was not at all in the mind of the Florentine or most later republicans. Thus, in spite of Bolívar's own antipathy for the author of *The Prince*,[59] we can make a case for intellectual affinity as a way to elucidate Bolívar's legacy, a republican approach to racial issues in political life.[60] Bolívar was a Machiavellian "new prince" in the complete sense of the term.[61]

Thus, in spite of some clear similarities to the thought of Montesquieu and Rousseau as well,[62] we find a greater affinity with the Florentine, as we shall explore below. Most studies of Bolívar's political thought underscore his explicit references to the French and the Swiss theorists. But while Bolívar agreed with Montesquieu that laws must reflect the customs and local conditions of a particular people,[63] he did not tend to emphasize the same sorts of considerations that the baron did.[64] To be sure, self-government and absence of domination are central to Bolívar as well, but unlike in Montesquieu we do not find a profound concern for individual freedom in the Venezuelan.[65] Neither do we find an interest in commerce as a way to safeguard liberty.[66] In fact, he saw wealth as a menace to freedom and equality.[67] Montesquieu's well-known contribution to the idea of checks and balances finds some analogue in Bolívar, but the *Libertador* was keen on allowing temporary dictatorships and maintaining the strong power of the executive. Perhaps the greatest similarity is in the belief that civic virtue is out of the reach of most modern citizens.[68]

Likewise, commentators point to the Enlightenment character of Bolívar's thought by sometimes drawing parallels with Rousseau.[69] This connection is one of the recurring leitmotifs of Bolívar analyses: the assertion that the Swiss thinker was Bolívar's intellectual godfather. Again, beyond a shared republican orientation, their theoretical affinities are tenuous. Bolívar did not believe in the moral authority of the General Will.[70] The democratic orientation of the Rousseauian doctrine of the General Will places the *people* at the center of his republicanism. It is a popular, antielite doctrine of republican self-governance and the rule of law. But for Bolívar, a unified people, however desirable, was unlikely to exist in reality.[71] Bolívar made no assumption that there is some amorphous homogeneity (of the social or cultural sort) in a given people. One of Bolívar's great virtues as a theorist was his awareness of precisely social, cultural, ethnic, and even racial fault lines within the concept of "the people." Bolívar wished that the Americas would become one single republic, but he was cognizant of the fact that a multiplicity of identities fractured the very idea of a (Spanish) American people. As he famously declared, Gran Colombia was not made up of uniform citizens; it was a "chaos"[72] of diverse groups. He believed that this diversity was not a superficial problem. It could generate deep tensions and was especially visible in matters of ethnicity and race. Therefore, a concept of a General Will made up of the preferences of individual citizens was not self-evident.[73] The authority of the *demos* or the people that we find justified in Rousseau is negated by Bolívar's preference for a much larger republic than that which Rousseau advocated, one that is guided by an intellectual and moral elite.

More pointedly, the distance between Rousseau and Bolívar can be seen when we examine the issue at hand: the place of race in politics. To be sure, Rousseau did not have an explicit theory of the "noble savage," but his writings on human nature exhibit an important contribution to philosophical anthropology. The thinker from Geneva, in his effort to show that man is born free yet everywhere is in chains, implicitly idealizes primitive man, thereby creating a gulf between an imagined premodern, precivilized world and a modern, civilized one.[74] More explicitly, Rousseau's references to the Venezuelan Carib Amerindians show us this belief that premodern men were repositories of a kind of authentic, original freedom that was lost by cultured men. In the *Social Contract*, he tells us that "the Caribs, who of all people existing today have least departed from the state of nature, are precisely the most peaceful in their loves ... despite their ... hot climate which always seems to inflame those passions."[75] Moreover, in *Émile*, he writes that "the Caribs are better off than we are. The child has hardly left the mother's womb, it has hardly begun to move and stretch its limbs, when it is deprived of its freedom" by being "wrapped in swaddling bands." This "cruel bondage" is "torture."[76] In other words, even if the primitive man enjoys a greater degree of freedom than the civilized man, the Carib is emblematic of a non-European, and specifically Amerindian desire to curtail freedom. For Rousseau, the Carib stands outside of the political imagination of the Republic.

Bolívar believed that racial admixture can create greater *but not perfect* homogeneity in the social body. Distinctions, however subtle, can remain, and these can be mobilized for political aims. For Bolívar, the fact of racial admixture, which in a sense acts with a multiplier effect owing to the increasing diversity of types that may be possible given ever-greater diversity and miscegenation, can only be resolved through a proactive egalitarian policy. The natural process of miscegenation can generate political conflicts that must be addressed artificially, that is, through constructed institutions. He would write, "The fundamental basis of our political system hinges directly and exclusively upon the establishment and practice of equality in Venezuela."[77]

Bolívar makes this statement immediately after his comment that a response to the racial problems of Venezuela is the greatest of obligations. His commitment to equality is a product of his concern for the social inequalities that arise out of racial diversity and conflict.[78] Bolívar cannot be read as a classical republican or liberal thinker because his own republicanism is modern through and through.[79] He does not imitate blindly the models of the ancients, but rather gives his own view of republican modes and orders in a way that is pragmatic and realistic and combines a variety of resources. This manipulation or combination of various elements into a new kind of (constitutional) artifact makes Bolívar's republicanism preeminently modern. And, as we shall see, he places great value in the firm hand of the executive and in moral censorship, something that is anathema to a liberal viewpoint.

If we read his words in light of the comments that he makes on race, we find that he imagines the creator of a new constitutional order to be someone who must give form to a restless, fractious mass. And he saw this mass in a racialized manner. The threat of

a *pardocracia*, or rule by *pardos* (or mulattos and those with African blood), was tanta-
mount to the power of "hordes."[80] He would go on to say that "if the principle of political equality is generally recognized, so also must be the principle of physical and moral
inequality."[81] Read through a racial lens, this statement represents his realization that
racial distinctions or inequalities are socially problematic and that they must be resolved
through forced egalitarianism. But he refers to "moral" inequality as well, meaning that
the new citizens of the Americas are not prepared to act with civic virtue within a republican order. They lack the moral education of full-fledged citizens. A liberated people
has difficulty living newly free; the yoke of empire enervates civic virtue. To remedy this
weakness, Bolívar recommends a strong educational hand as well. As he tells us, "The diversity of racial origin will require an infinitely firm hand and great tactfulness in order
to manage this heterogeneous society, whose complicated mechanism is easily damaged,
separated, and disintegrated by the slightest controversy."[82]

Social Conflict and Republican Order

The concern with the fragility of institutions is one important similarity with the
thought of Machiavelli.[83] Whereas the Florentine wanted to create "modes and orders"
to provide stability to his fractious homeland, Bolívar wanted to provide stable constitutions for the newly liberated states. For Florence's social tumults and conflict between
the elites and the masses, Machiavelli prescribed a mixed republic as an institutional
solution. For Bolívar, similarly, "Only a hybrid government can be free,"[84] meaning that
the institutions of a free state can favor neither the *demos* nor the elites. A right balance
must be achieved between the interests of the people and those of the few. Bolívar was
no radical democrat, but neither was he merely a believer in aristocracy, as some have
argued. He did not, unlike Rousseau, try to apply a universalistic sense of citizenship to
all members of a society.[85] Bolívar rejected the call by those such as the *pardo* general José
Padilla for absolute—not merely legal—equality.[86] He proposed a hereditary Senate, but
also gave the tribunes significant authority.[87] His is a mixed constitution, similar to that
of Machiavelli, but cognizant of ethnoracial social fractures. And he expressed this in his
constitution for Bolivia, "a bridge between Europe and America, between the army and
the people, between democracy and aristocracy, and between monarchy and republic."[88]
The people and the state are, ideally, in equilibrium, yet they are overseen by one single
man, a princely lifetime president. The belief in a strong executive is another central
element that ties together Bolívar's and Machiavelli's conceptions of a modern republic.

It is important to note that Bolívar's strategy to address the problem of social order
was grounded on rhetoric rather than deliberation. The principal mechanism to convey
his ideas was not abstract philosophizing or promoting the idea that a republic must
be based on the well-thought-out consent of the people. It is through rhetoric that he
sought, like Machiavelli, to argue that his account of republicanism was the most cogent.

His chief works are principally addresses to diverse audiences. The Cartagena Manifesto was in fact entitled "Memorial Addressed to the Citizens of New Granada by a Citizen from Caracas," and published as a pamphlet in 1813. The Jamaica Letter, while it appears to be an epistle to "an English Gentleman" (Henry Cullen), has the nature of public document in delineating the relationship of Spanish America to the United Kingdom. It is clear that Bolívar's intention was to bring the message to the "attention of the larger British community in Jamaica and of English speakers elsewhere."[89] The Bolivian constitution drafted by Bolívar was presented with an address to the Constituent Congress at Lima on May 25, 1826, and opens with this exhortative yet falsely modest statement: "Legislators! As I offer you this draft of a constitution for Bolivia, I am overwhelmed by confusion and trepidation, knowing that I have no talent for making laws."[90]

The address at Angostura was delivered at the inauguration of the Congress of Angostura on February 15, 1819. The address to the "Congreso Admirable" and the message to the Convention of Ocaña are likewise public orations, both addressed to "Fellow Citizens." Even some of the lesser works are rhetorical in nature. His youthful oath taken in Rome in 1805 has the emotional power of *pathos* and the moral declaration of *ethos* as it closes with verve and *repetitio:* "I swear before you, I swear by the God of my fathers, I swear on their graves, I swear by my country that I will not rest body or soul until I have broken the chains binding us to the will of Spanish might!" The Decree of War to the Death of 1813, the Manifesto to the Nations of the World of the same year, the Manifesto of Carúpano written a year later, and the Declaration of Angostura of 1818 are likewise examples of republican political rhetoric. The text "My Delirium at Chimborazo" of 1822 shows us that Bolívar possessed the talents of a graphic, almost surrealist novelist. He declares, "I was coming along, cloaked in the mantle of Iris, from the place where the torrential Orinoco [river] pays tribute to the God of waters. . . . Nothing could stop me. . . . [C]aught up in a spiritual tremor I had never before experienced, and which seemed to me . . . a kind of divine frenzy. . . . I climb as if driven by this frenzy. . . . It was the God of Colombia taking possession of me."[91]

The Princely Republican

Just as Machiavelli's prince is *uno solo,* a man alone, so was Bolívar. The Liberator's own life was one of isolation and individual responsibility.[92] He stood by himself most of the time, against conspiracies, threats to his life, and even against those who wanted him to lead for as long as possible. But even in his theoretical work, such as the constitution that he wrote for Bolivia, there is a valuation of a powerful executive, an institutional mechanism that would not be tolerated by present-day liberal democracies.[93] In his scheme, the president rules for life and is able to choose his successor. In spite of being an admirer of the British constitution, Bolívar did not believe a constitutional monarchy would work in Latin America. He wanted a much more activist executive, someone whose role was more than that of a symbol buttressing the ideology of national unity. Bolívar wanted a powerful president whose firm hand could prevent centrifugal political and social forces from eroding the polity. The pinnacle of this doctrine is his espousal of the post of Dictator and Supreme Chief of the Republic, which he accepted as a temporary but necessary position.[94] In this proposal he owed the ancient Roman constitution a significant debt; yet at the same time it laid the ground for the Latin American propensity to conceive of dictatorship as an acceptable political recourse.[95]

Above all, this commitment to a strong executive shows that both Bolívar and Machiavelli believed that a republic is intimately tied to the military and to the martial life.[96] We do not find this connection as clearly in Rousseau or Montesquieu. Bolívar was a general, and Machiavelli was secretary to the war magistracy of the Ten in Florence. For Machiavelli, a prince must always think about war: "He must, therefore, never raise his thought from this exercise of war, and in peacetime he must train himself more than in time of war."[97] This martial approach to republicanism is essential to the thought of these two theorists.[98] Ultimately, it abuts their promotion of a strong executive. But it also entails a belief that the republic is in constant danger, both from within and without. Strong arms are as important as strong laws.[99] The army is the backbone of the polity, for without it, society will collapse. Moreover, while in the last chapter of *The Prince* Machiavelli urged the liberation of Italy from the "barbarians," Bolívar's thought is suffused with a similar anti-imperialist call for the emancipation of one's *patria*. We do not discern this perpetual state of martial alert in the thought of either Rousseau or Montesquieu. In fact, the latter's belief in the virtues of commerce attenuates the fear of other states that is always awake in Machiavelli. War stands at the center of Machiavelli's intellectual enterprise, along with the idea of power.[100]

Thus, good arms, not just good laws, are the bulwark against tyranny in Bolívar's Machiavellian conception of the republic.[101] A standing army, not mercenaries, is essential for a nation according to Bolívar.[102] In the Cartagena Manifesto, Bolívar writes that a lack of professional troops is the Achilles heel of a new republican state. Bolívar assails the "firm opposition to raising seasoned, disciplined troops, prepared to take their place on the field of battle and indoctrinated with the desire to defend liberty with success and honor."[103] This critique primarily concerns international relations. If a nation lacks a disciplined army, it will succumb to external threats and invasions.[104] Thus, civic virtue is tied to martial *virtus*. The virile courage needed to defend one's motherland, risking life and limb, is no theoretical axiom.[105] For both Bolívar and Machiavelli, it is a real necessity,[106] which is especially the case vis-à-vis foreign imperial powers. In the case of Bolívar, the Spanish Empire was anathema, rearing its head again and again in Venezuelan affairs. The First Venezuelan Republic failed, facing vast Royalist opposition. It is in response to this demise that Bolívar wrote the Cartagena Manifesto in 1812. Just as Bolívar wanted to liberate his country from foreign invaders, so did Machiavelli urge the unity of Florence—as well as Italy—against the French and the Spanish.[107] The anticolonial and anti-imperial thought in Bolívar's republicanism is much more similar to that of Machiavelli than to the ideas of Rousseau or Montesquieu,[108] for whom republicanism is, in a sense, threatened by an internal monarchy, not an external empire. These are thinkers who are emblematic of the French Revolution's attack on a domestic king and the rise of one particular (petit bourgeois) class, whereas Bolívar was influenced by the man who overturned much of the Revolution, Napoleon. Both were military men above all, seeking to establish form through force and the creation or imposition of new laws.[109]

The military not only protects one's state against foreign encroachers. It can itself be a liberating force. Those blacks and *pardos* who joined Bolívar's hierarchical army were emancipated through it. "The inclusion of colored and black troops in the independence movement shattered the old colonial social order. *Pardos* literally came of age as a result of their involvement in the hierarchy of Bolívar's military organization."[110] Their membership in a revolutionary force did not lead to their domination, but rather to their eventual manumission and acquisition of citizenship.[111] Thus, the idea that any form of subjection to another man's will is *ipso facto* domination is not accurate. Participation in an army such as that of Bolívar, which was hierarchical and led by one supreme commander, was an instrument for the forging of a new—and freer—civic life. For theorists who believe that dependence and domination inevitably entail loss of freedom, the martial republicanism of Bolívar is a rejoinder.[112] A definition of domination (the opposite of republican liberty) by agents as occurring "if and only if they have a certain power over that other; in particular a power of interference on an arbitrary basis"[113] is not entirely useful. The definition is restricted to a precise conditional ("if and only if"), but that precision is undermined by the vague phrase "a certain power." This power could refer to any kind of leverage: psychological, emotional, political, social, cultural, economic, and so on. The definition specifies this power as interference that is arbitrary. While the term "arbitrary" would seem to include forms of interference that are not based on a law,[114] it is clear that those in legal positions of power can indeed exercise their authority in arbitrary ways. Bureaucrats often behave in this fashion. And military commanders certainly have "power over another." Further, they sometimes exercise such power arbitrarily, in the sense that they are the arbiters of decisions that are made on the battlefield. They do not follow any specific law of war or battle. This is especially the case for constitutional dictators (such as Bolívar). The very term "dictator" contains a sense of arbitrariness, since he is allowed to use his position to transform into legal fiat his personal judgment (*arbitrium*) about the public good.

At the same time, in the case of Venezuela's independence movement, the very participation and involvement in a situation of dependence (following orders from superiors) is what allowed nonwhites to acquire equality and liberty.[115] While there may be a temporary loss of individual freedom as a result of being under the command of someone else, the gains in civic freedom are much greater. This notion is part of the justification of Bolívar's own martial or militaristic republicanism.

Republics against Empires

However, there are limits to Bolívar's affinity with Machiavelli in the martial realm. Here Bolívar's thought can be seen as a corrective to one of the major problems in the thought of Machiavelli. For the Florentine, it is possible, and often natural, for a republic to become imperial. The term *imperio* meant for Machiavelli simply "power."[116] And in a world of constant competition, in which one must proceed proactively or be assaulted,[117] an ever-increasing expansion of power and territory makes sense. For this reason, Machiavelli aimed to transform his beloved Florence into a new Rome, at least in his vision. It was to be the rebirth of an empire on the Italian peninsula, and perhaps beyond it. The distinction between republic and empire is thus elided by Machiavelli because his chief intellectual concern is power. Bolívar's chief intellectual concern, however, is freedom.[118] The single most important reason that he repudiated Machiavelli was that Bolívar did not agree that a republic could be imperial. To become so would mean to take away the freedom of others, which is self-contradictory if liberty is the core of the common good. For this reason, Bolívar repudiated the entire Machiavellian corpus, thereby losing a vast resource that he could have used to provide pragmatic solutions for his country's problems. However, he does provide an insightful critique of imperialist republicanism:

> The principles that should preserve the government are disregarded [when republics become expansionary] and finally it degenerates into despotism. The distinctive feature of small republics is permanence: that of large republics varies, but always with a tendency towards empire. Almost all small republics have long lives. Among the larger republics, only Rome lasted several centuries, for its capital was a republic. The rest of her dominions were governed by divers laws and institutions.[119]

If a republic becomes expansionary, it crosses a line that puts it in monarchical territory, according to Bolívar, because there the logic of the king becomes salient: The monarch has a "constant desire to increase his possessions, wealth, and authority."[120] Thus, while some thinkers, such as Rousseau, argue that popular sovereignty can check the executive, and others, such as Montesquieu, believe that commerce can attenuate imperial desires, Bolívar finds a logical contradiction in the very idea of an expansive republic. And this contradiction is harmful to the republic itself, for it transforms it into its opposite, however slowly the process occurs.[121]

Still, as in the case of Machiavelli, we find a perennial fear of conspiracies and instability throughout the writings of Bolívar. He does not think republics are safe from the depredations of other states, be they empires or other republics. Nor does he think that internal class conflict can ever be eliminated. Just as Machiavelli believes the *grandi* (elites) seek to dominate while the *popolari* (people) simply wish to be left alone, Bolívar finds that certain leaders of various ethnoracial political groups, especially the *pardos* (mulattos), seek complete domination, while others,[122] such as the Indians, simply want to be left in peace. The class conflict that is part and parcel of Machiavelli's thought is equally present in that of Bolívar; in both cases, social distinctions (not necessarily made by wealth) are the source of conflict. For the Florentine, natural humors tend to make some people seek domination, while others want to remain tranquil. Bolívar is time and again concerned by the rise of distinctions based on racial identifications. His greatest fear is that of *pardocracia*, the idea that only *pardos* should rule Venezuela and turn it into a sort of Haiti.[123] This fear of partisanship, as opposed to thinking about the common good, is what Machiavelli also had in mind when he feared corruption (that is, self-seeking action at the expense of the public good).

It is widely accepted that Bolívar "saw racial 'diversity' as an impediment to 'perfect' democracy."[124] However, this statement is misleading, since Bolívar was no believer in widespread popular democracy along the lines of Rousseau's General Will.[125] He did not believe a perfect democracy could ever be achieved. He did indeed fear some of the political and social consequences of racial diversity, and in this sense he contributes to the effort of trying to understand how to deal with racial pluralism in a postcolonial society. At the same time, some commentators have correctly pointed out his fear of *pardocracia*, but incorrectly assign it to an antirepublican bias.[126] Bolívar did fear *pardo* rule, but mainly because he believed that it would not take into account the totality of interests and different groups within Venezuelan society. It was not a fear based on antipathy or prejudice.[127] It was grounded on a simple belief that *pardos* would favor their own kind and ignore the needs of other groups. Only a mixed constitution keenly aware of social conflict and with a strong central authority could enforce political equality and protect it from foreign powers. Here lies the core of the Machiavellian republican tradition, to which Bolívar adds greater depth and texture through his understanding of ethnic and racial diversity.

Civic Virtue

It could be argued that Bolívar rejected any Machiavellian influence principally owing to the nefarious moral implications of such an outlook. To be sure, it is possible to see Bolívar as a man of great rectitude. But while he disliked Machiavelli's call for the separation of morality from politics, in fact there are ways in which they are similar on the moral plane. One element is that Bolívar was quick to reject the idea that capital punishment for treason was unacceptable. He tells us that instability and corruption ensue if those who offend the interests of the state are not punished by death. This policy effectively validates a perspective not too distant from the morality of the state or *raison d'état*, for Bolívar is willing to commit a serious moral transgression in retaliation for a purely political one. As he tells us in the Cartagena Manifesto, the rebels of the city of Coro should have been put to death because they did not accept the legitimacy of the new independent government. The junta did not act with enough force, and "thence was born an impunity against the state."[128]

Bolívar consequently qualifies as a realist in his republican outlook rather than an idealist who did not want to break moral codes, especially those of Christianity.[129] Here arises the second commonality with Machiavelli: Bolívar was not Christian in any discernible sense.[130] In fact, his loyal Irish aide, Daniel O'Leary, believed he was a "complete atheist."[131] Bolívar thoroughly rejected the influence of the Catholic Church and wanted a complete separation from it in matters of state.[132] Just as Machiavelli was fundamentally inimical to the role and values of Christianity (see *Discourses* II.2.2) and against the political power of the Catholic Church in Rome, so did Bolívar seek to promote an essentially secular state.[133] "Ignorant and superstitious"[134] people were fooled by priests, in his view. He did not mince words when it came to the clergy:

> It is probable that following the downfall of the Peninsula, there will be a tremendous migration of men of all classes, particularly of cardinals, archbishops, bishops, canons, and revolutionary clerics, all capable not only of subverting our incipient, faltering states, but of encompassing the entire new world in frightful anarchy.[135]

Likewise, immediately after the earthquake of 1812 that brought the end of the First Republic, he accused the clerical supporters of Miyares and Monteverde of being "ignorant and corrupt."[136] To be sure, Machiavelli saw the expediency of appearing religious, something that Bolívar also saw. In the place of religious education, Bolívar sought to provide the state with the capacity to educate its citizens through civic morality. Yet he tried to appear pious in some instances, such as his decision to ban the legislative works of Jeremy Bentham, which were hated by the Church (even though Bolívar himself admired utilitarianism),[137] and also to include the teachings of religion in his ideal model of early education.[138] In effect, Bolívar was a realist, not someone who placed admirable yet unrealizable principles above all else.[139] His solution to the deleterious influence of the clerics was to use force "to pacify our rebellious provinces," as he euphemistically portrayed his actions.[140]

These two admirers of ancient Rome were alike in their conception of virtue. For both, virtue has principally two aspects: one is the willingness to act with valor and force for the motherland, and the other is to respect and love its laws, the meaning of Machiavellian *virtù*. Its roots are in the Latin term *vir*, or male, which implies an archetypal masculinity that embraces danger, force, courage, and violence when necessary.[141] But it also means a desire to follow the civic order of one's land. It is a respect for the law that makes everyone subjects of it. This project of civil education was a difficult task for both Machiavelli and Bolívar, for the citizens that they wanted to work with as raw civic material were prone to corruption and self-regard. Only if led by the strong hand of a virtuous leader, invested with the constitutional powers of longevity, they believed, can stability be found in conflict-ridden societies. Far from being a liberal who believed in the moral primacy of the individual and his or her right to free speech, Bolívar prized the establishment of institutions that would oversee morality and public education. This task was the function of the Areopagus, "an irreproachable and holy tribunal" (Article XII).[142] It was modeled after the ancient Athenian supreme council and was to be made up of forty members in full control of morality, custom, and educational matters. Its purpose was to constitutionally oversee matters related to corruption. To understand how far from modern liberalism (understood as sanctifying the ethical centrality of the individual) Bolívar was, we must note that the Areopagus he proposed was made up of two houses, one of which, the moral chamber, was to be in control of all morality, whether individual, familial, departmental, provincial, or other. It would go so far as to publish lists of virtuous men, ranking each person in terms of public virtue and public vice. In addition, a second house, a chamber of education, would tightly regulate pedagogy. While Bolívar was a staunch defender of freedom and secularism, this attachment was derived from his republicanism, not from a liberalism in which individuals are given moral priority.[143]

Constitution Making in Diverse Societies

An expression of Bolívar's political thought is the constitution he wrote for Bolivia, the country named after him and created in 1825 out of what was formerly known as Upper Peru.[144] Bolivia was to be the most racially divided of all the new nations in South America. To be sure, it is a country of great racial diversity, measured by the number of ethnic groups that have existed there since its founding. Aymara, Quechua, Callahuaya, Guaraní, and other indigenous groups, as well as Afro-Bolivians, mestizos, and *criollos* occupied the land when the country was established, and continue to live there to this day. But here is where Bolívar's greatest political error is visible: while he was cognizant of the racial problems and divisions in Latin America as a whole, he did not reflect this preoccupation in his theoretical model of a perfect state as drawn up in the Bolivian constitution.[145] Herein lies the most jarring of all contrasts in the thought of Bolívar, a keen awareness of the depth and complexity of race at the social level, without a concomitant reflection of this understanding at the level of his explicit constitutionalism.

Bolívar was well aware of the cultural and political richness of the indigenous American peoples. For this reason he sided with Las Casas's description of what the Spanish did to the native peoples. He praises the Chilean Araucanians,[146] as well as Montezuma of the Aztecs and Atahualpa of the Incas.[147] While not showing great depth of knowledge of the indigenous cultures, he mentions them with respect and admiration, decrying the "vilest of treatment" that these native rulers had to endure at the hands of the Spanish. Similarly, he denounces the humiliation of the "ruler of Michoacán [and] the *zipa* of Bogotá, and all the other *toquis, imas, ulmenes, caciques* and other Indian dignitaries who succumbed before Spain's might."[148] In the same tone as Las Casas, he rails against the wars of extermination of the Indians.[149] His discussion of Quetzalcoatl is more politically astute, for he sees that Mexican patriots made use of the myth of the divine lawgiver as a way to mobilize religion for the sake of liberty.[150]

The constitution he wrote for Bolivia, however, lacks reference to any indigenous, pre-Columbian influences or sources. For a country as heavily indigenous as Bolivia, the omission was a fatal mistake. Most Bolivians at the time of the founding were neither *criollos* nor mestizos, but were termed *indios* and *cholos* (urban "Indians"). Most did not even speak Spanish as their primary language. It is here where Bolívar failed to adapt his political thought to his realism. The Bolivian constitution does appear *prima facie* to be a document that would help provide stability to a multiracial, multiethnic state.[151] Yet we can fault Bolívar for not incorporating explicit references to the actual racial and ethnic groups that inhabited the nation and to ways of creating a single national identity. In this omission we find that he was fundamentally not—in spite of what he says to the contrary—a thinker following Montesquieu, for he neglected to create constitutions suitable for a particular people under specific conditions.[152] This fact is especially salient when we consider that his favored model for a modern republic was the British one. He considered it a republican system in spite of having a monarch, for he believed its legitimacy rested on popular sovereignty. It also had division and balance of powers, and civil liberties. But it is not evident how the British model could have been the answer for the complex ethnoracial case of Bolivia.

Bolivia's constitution created a single, unitary state. It is centralized, which Bolívar saw as a good idea for a weak, poor, nascent nation.[153] Moreover, centralization would enable the state to forge a national identity out of a variety of racial and ethnic groups. But these ideas are not specified in Bolívar's model. While he admired federalism, he believed it was too "perfect" for a new, diverse state, and would lead to greater instability and even anarchy.[154] He feared factionalism, and he proposed a lifelong president as a way to provide continuity of policies over a long period of time. Certainly this prescription is not a liberal one, but it was aimed at coalescing the state in a Machiavellian sense. There is no evidence that Bolívar was concerned with Bolivia's deep racial cleavages, but a unitary state, for a small and fragmented society, would appear to be a good idea. The lifelong president would have, however, limited powers, such as appointing some officials as well as his successor, subject to a vote by Congress. This "democratic Caesarism," a mark of Bolivarian thought, shows that Bolívar was neither a demagogue nor an aristocrat in political matters. Bolívar did not anticipate the political party system that would plague Bolivia for a hundred years, battling over natural resources and state coffers. But his deepest failure was in not recognizing the vital importance of creating a sense of national unity out of a variety of ethnoracial groups in the new country.

Another dimension of the Bolivian constitution that has indirect relevance to ethnoracial concerns is Bolívar's understanding of the moral power of the Censors.[155] Bolívar ardently believed that a people newly liberated can lose its freedom because it lacks civic education and virtue. He believed that Latin Americans had not even had local tyrants:

their rulers had always been foreigners.[156] Bolívar's history is not altogether precise, for most of the pre-Columbian political systems were not republics, but rather monarchical regimes. The Inca ruled a vast South American territory without any democratic account-ability. But Bolívar does not mention this past, and he merely posits that the vast Indian masses of the continent are unprepared to become full-fledged citizens because they had never tasted freedom. He does not seek to impress upon the native peoples the fact that a creole republican system is superior to an indigenous, autochthonous tyranny such as that of the Inca. For this reason, he believes the Censors must be institutionally guaranteed the power to dictate moral and educational conduct for a society that is nascent in its civil life. Bolívar fails to incorporate Inca principles or customs into his Bolivian model, unlike the case of Francisco de Miranda, who did believe it was important to employ indigenous terms and ideas in the newly constituted republican systems as a way to create continuity and a sense of national unity.[157] It is a tragic fact of history that we do not have a combina-tion of Bolívar's and Miranda's constitutional ideas, since Bolívar turned over Miranda to Spain for his role in what was considered a treacherous surrender to Spanish forces in 1816.

To fully understand Bolívar's mode of republicanism, we must note his staunch op-position to slavery.[158] A basic principle behind the ideal form of government for Ven-ezuela, as he declares in the Angostura Discourse, is the elimination of this institution. There are three reasons for his opposition to slavery, one moral, the others pragmatic. For Bolívar it was a moral affront to the universal dignity of humanity. As he declared, "Slavery is the negation of all law."[159] But more importantly, it had real effects on a polity. The inhabitants of a country with a sizable and long-lasting system of slavery are unable to act as proper citizens once freedom has been achieved. In addition, Bolívar needed able-bodied men to join the revolutionary forces to combat the Spanish. These two prag-matic reasons led him to manumit his own slaves, as well as to urge the emancipation of all slaves, even if his proposal was not met with positive responses by *hacendados*.[160] However, his ideas have the effect of militating against all slavery, not maintaining it even in a republican system, as did Thomas Jefferson, for instance.[161]

Bolívar's republican understanding of race shows his eminently political and dynamic construction of racial identity. To be sure, the *Libertador* was not driven by deontolog-ical morality when it came to slavery and citizenship. As much as he agreed with Mon-tesquieu on the immorality of slavery, he also found it expedient to liberate slaves for the practical reason of gaining soldier-citizens.[162] In his life-and-death struggle against both Spanish royalists and domestic enemies, Bolívar simply needed well-armed men. As a consequence of this military imperative, which is closely tied to his martial under-standing of republicanism, he came to the conclusion that racial differences are mere "accidents of skin."[163] His reasoning was instrumentalist, not the product of a sense of universal duty, and certainly not of a Christian morality.

Bolívar makes this patently clear in a letter to General Francisco de Paula Santander writ-ten on April 18, 1820. We need to quote his words at length in order to discern how clearly his political philosophy of martial republicanism led him to the utility of racial equality:

The military and political reasons for ordering the recruitment of slaves are quite obvious. We need strong, hardy men who are accustomed to inclement weather and fatigue, men who will embrace the cause and the career of arms with enthusiasm, men who will identify their own cause with the public interest and who value their lives only slightly more than their deaths.[164]

Similarly, Bolívar saw Spaniards who fought for the liberation of the Americas as "Americans." He would say that "Spaniards who render distinguished service to the state will be regarded and treated as Americans."[165] Thus, he had a flexible, artificial conception of ethnoracial identity: to the extent that a European acted in the political service of American independence, he would become magically transformed, as it were, into a Latin American. There was nothing essential about being European, and ethnoracial identity was malleable depending on political choices and circumstances. But Bolívar tried to force this choice, using language reminiscent of the great Florentine: "Spaniards and Canarians, even if you profess neutrality, know that you will die unless you work actively to bring about the freedom of America."[166]

One could fault Bolívar's reasoning as merely cold-hearted Machiavellian realism. And we could even say that he manipulated nonwhite groups in order to achieve a political end. For instance, in his decree for the emancipation of slaves he remarked, "Considering that justice, policy, and the country imperiously demand the inalienable rights of nature, I have decided to formally decree absolute freedom for the slaves who have groaned under the Spanish yoke during the previous three centuries." But this freedom is conditional: all able-bodied men must enlist under the flag of Venezuela, and "the new citizen who refuses to bear arms in fulfillment of the sacred duty to defend his freedom shall be subject to servitude, not only for himself, but also for his children."[167]

But while he was Machiavellian in both the strict civic-martial republican sense and the more pedestrian sense of having a keen understanding of cynical political expediency,[168] he also possessed a strong notion of moral rectitude. Out of admiration for Montesquieu's understanding of equality and freedom he would write:

The political reasons [for emancipation] are even more powerful. The liberation of the slaves has been instituted by law and by fact. The congress has considered the words of Montesquieu: *in moderate governments political freedom makes civil freedom precious, and anyone deprived of the latter still lacks the former: he sees a happy society in which he has no part; he finds security guaranteed for others but not for him. Nothing so lowers us to the condition of beasts as seeing free men but not being one. Such people are enemies of society and they become dangerous in numbers. It is not surprising that in moderate governments the state has been brought into turmoil by the rebellion of slaves or that this rarely happens in despotic states.*[169]

Likewise, Bolívar acted out of moral motivations when he dealt with indigenous groups. We cannot discern ulterior motives of political expedience when we examine his decrees related to "Indians." In the Decree on Indian Lands of May 20, 1820, Bolívar orders the return of all communal lands to the Indians, as well as their redistribution to Indian families.[170] He does this because he wishes to

> correct the abuses practiced in Cundinamarca [Colombia] in most of the native villages, against their persons as well as their communal lands and their freedom, and considering that this segment of the population of the republic deserves the most paternal attention from the government because they were the most aggrieved, oppressed, and humiliated during the period of Spanish despotism.[171]

Bolívar orders that Indians be considered "like other free men in the Republic."[172] He would later proclaim in Cuzco the equality of Indians and reject the exploitation of their labor. He argues that "equality among all citizens is the basis of the constitution in the Republic."[173] He is aware that abuse of Indian workers is rife, and consequently bans any demand for Indian labor without free contracts. This included the prohibition of *faenas*, *séptimas*, *mitas*, and *pongueajes*.

Bolívar was a man of praxis, a thinker-practitioner, someone who valued political theory but saw wickedness as inherent to the human condition. As he asks in the Manifesto of Carúpano: "How could the simple theory of political philosophy, based only on truth and nature, prevail over vice[?]" He goes on to remark that Christianity is not only a weak doctrine, but a debilitating one; he doubts that "vice armed with unfettered license limited only by one's appetite" will be "suddenly transformed by the prestigious veneer of religion into a political virtue and a form of Christian charity." Against Machiavelli's *tristizia* he juxtaposes *codicia*: "No, it is impossible for ordinary men to appreciate the high value of the realm of freedom or to choose it over blind ambition and vile greed." In fact, chance has a greater role in human affairs than free will: "The primitive cause of all misfortune [is] the frailty of the human race and the power of chance to determine events," because "man is the plaything of fortune." Just as Machiavelli alludes in his poem *The Golden Ass* to the loss of human volition, Bolívar warns that "to expect politics and war to move to the rhythm of plans we formulate in darkness guided only by the purity of our intentions and aided by the limited means at our disposal is to strive for the effects of a divine power through merely human agency."[174]

Toward Pan-American Unity

The Bolivarian dream of a united Latin America was not the product of roseate idealism. Quite to the contrary, Bolívar had two pragmatic reasons to urge the creation of a single republic made up of various territories. These territories eventually did break from continental unity and formed new nations. But ethnoracial identity as well as a realist view of international relations perspective led Bolívar to believe it was in the best interest of the Latin American peoples to form one large union, commencing with the unity of Colombia, the country made up of Venezuela and New Granada (present-day Colombia). From this base, he envisioned a united South America through an Andean Union.[175] The act of founding a new state, like Romulus, necessitates "creative genius."[176]

His main reason for the promotion of this unity was global equilibrium. Bolívar saw that Europe and the United States were to become hegemonic powers in world affairs.[177] He believed Britain stood outside of this dyad of the North as a third power. But he believed that greater peace and stability could be achieved if Latin America became a true counterpoise to the power of Europe and the expansion of the United States. This consideration was a pragmatic one, unrelated to any principle of racial or ethnic commonality. Thus he believed that even Britain could be admitted to a union of the Americas. The Congress of Panama would create a common front against European and U.S. encroachment in the region, with Britain acting as a "constituent member."[178] This proposal emerges out of a pragmatic concern, but seems to be naïve in not seeing that Britain would only accede to such a plan if its own interests were to stand above those of its Spanish American partners.

There is a somewhat innocent pragmatism in Bolívar's writings on foreign relations. In a letter to Sir Richard Wellesley written on May 27, 1815, Bolívar seeks the support of Britain for the Spanish American cause. Bolívar appeals to "generous souls" who know the "value of freedom" and who "defend justice."[179] While Bolívar may have been trying to use rhetoric to seek support against the Spanish, it is possible to fault him for actually believing that Britain would act out of pure beneficence. An invitation to enter the Spanish American lands would have perhaps led to imperial ambitions on the part of Britain. There is a confusion in Bolívar between pragmatic and idealistic motivations. He writes that the "balance of world power and the interests of Great Britain are perfectly in accord with the salvation of America" and continues by opening up America to the British: "My land offers vast opportunities to her defenders and friends."[180] Showing no intimation of the possibility that Britain might use Bolívar's overture to expand its global empire into Spanish America, Bolívar goes so far as to say that there would eventually be a coincidence of civic status, commercial interests, and even customs between the two regions.[181]

But Bolívar's myopic perspective on this matter is counteracted by another consideration. There is in Bolívar's thought—albeit implicitly—a belief that over time the peoples of Latin America would lose particularistic attachments and become increasingly homogeneous, leading toward "a single government to infuse life into the New World,"[182] facilitating the union of the continent. This union would be built on political grounds. However, it would rest on the social ties forged by miscegenation. General Tomás Cipriano de Mosquera, who was Bolívar's secretary and later president of Gran Colombia, paraphrased the words of the Liberator: "Neither we nor the generation following us will see the glory of the republic which we are founding. I believe Spanish America to be in a chrysalis: there will be a metamorphosis of the physical existence of its inhabitants. At the end, there will be a new caste composed of an amalgamation of all races, which will produce a homogeneous people."[183] According to Mosquera, Bolívar urged, "Let us not stop the march of the human race with exotic institutions . . . in the virgin lands of America."[184]

Bolívar envisions first a political federation of like American nations. He rejects inclusion of the United States and Haiti.[185] We can surmise that this rejection is attributable to ethnic reasons, for he says that Buenos Aires would also not be a good choice for inclusion (after initial rejection for geopolitical reasons), whereas Mexico, Guatemala, and Colombia, as well as Peru, Chile, and Upper Peru (later Bolivia) would be good allies. The federation would be "homogenous, compact, and solid." He explains that the "Americans from the North and those from Haiti, simply because they are foreigners, are too heterogeneous in character to fit in."[186] That is to say, they are too different in ethnoracial terms from the rest of the Americas, the United States being too Anglo-Saxon,[187] and Haiti being too African, with both showing little of what Spanish America has, which is miscegenation.[188]

Over time, "Differences of origin and color would lose their influence and power,"[189] he would declare to the Congress of Panama, where he believed a continental capital could be founded because of the central location of the isthmus. These differences of origin and color, we can surmise, could only come about through greater racial intermixing.[190] Thus, there is an intimation that Bolívar favors, even if without an attendant public policy, an accelerated miscegenation[191] in the continent, as opposed to simply having multiracial or multiethnic states. In the long run, Bolívar does not endorse a pluralist state that seeks a *modus vivendi* for a variety of distinct ethnoracial groups. He envisions instead the unplanned generation of a single people brought about by the synthesis of intermixing. A consequence of this line of thought is the idea that it could be extended throughout the world through greater commerce and cultural exchange—leading to a single cosmopolitan state. "In the course of the centuries, there might, perhaps, come to exist one single nation throughout the world—a federal nation."[192] The federalism that he was so critical of in relation to South America comes back as the most cogent theoretical possibility for the future, *if* this future involves the emergence of one single social body made up of racial intermixture. If this homogeneity does not occur, then federalism, for Bolívar, is a chimera.

In the face of mounting nationalist, regionalist, and elite-interest pressures, Gran Colombia found itself in a centrifugal situation. Nationalism in Venezuela was on the rise, as it was in Peru. On August 27, 1828, Bolívar became dictator as a way to counteract this dissolution of a united America. The initial impetus for this decision was the popular will, for the *cabildo abierto* of Bogotá chose to empower the *Libertador*. Military discipline became a central concern, and Bolívar expanded the army. He sought to prevent a completely arbitrary dictatorship by relying on predetermined rules.[193] By this time, the staunchly anticlerical Bolívar had decided to seek the support of the clergy for political reasons. Nonetheless, these political maneuvers did not succeed in creating order and unity. In November 1830, the canton of Valencia erupted in rebellion, seeking the separation of Venezuela from New Granada (present-day Colombia).

Conclusion

Toward the end of his life, Bolívar was too much of a realist to imagine that his ambition of a united America could ever be achieved. Civil strife, internal divisions, and weak constitutions could not hold the Latin American countries together even if they shared ethnoracial characteristics. And in spite of common geopolitical interests, the synthesis of the Americas was ultimately unworkable:

> It is a grandiose idea to think of consolidating the New World into a single nation, united by pacts into a single bond. It is reasoned that, as these parts have a common origin, language, customs, and religion, they ought to have a single government to permit the newly formed states to unite in a confederation. *But this is not possible.*[194]

Bolívar came to believe that the geographic and demographic differences among the peoples of the Americas would be insurmountable. Perhaps, in a distant future, "in some happier period of our regeneration,"[195] such an ideal might reach fruition. The term "regeneration" denotes natural or biological reconstitution. If the word is read in light of Bolívar's many references to Latin America's unique racial composition, we might imagine that he envisions a future where greater miscegenation would create the social homogeneity that might allow a single, large, united republic.

It is true that republican patriotism in the European tradition "recognizes no political or moral value in the unity and ethnic homogeneity of a people."[196] But when it chooses to remain blind to race and ethnicity, it becomes abstract and almost utopian. Among Bolívar's greatest achievements was placing race at the heart of republican theory to elude extreme abstraction. He grappled with the tensions and contradictions of societies made up of real humanity in all its hues.

In a quasi-Hegelian fashion, Bolívar believed that the future of Latin America would bring with it world-historical import. Progress would come from Asia, move to Europe, and finally arrive in "Colombia," as he was wont to call Latin America:

> As soon as we are ... under the guidance of a liberal nation, we will achieve accord in cultivating the virtues and talents that lead to glory. Then will we march majestically toward that great prosperity for which South America is destined. Then will those sciences and arts, which, born in the East, have enlightened Europe, wing

their way to a free Colombia [i.e., Latin America], which will cordially bid them welcome.[197]

Culture would move in a progressive manner from East to West, coming to full development only when it reached Latin America. This vision, perhaps utopian, shows Bolívar as a modernist, not as someone looking back to an ancient past, whether of European or indigenous American roots. Latin America thus assumes a central place in world history. This is a theme that is taken up by late-modern thinkers.

Addressing soldiers upon the execution, for conspiracy and desertion, of General Manuel Piar, Bolívar promotes the idea that, through republican and martial action, racial divisions can be erased: "Have our arms not destroyed the chains of slaves? Have not the odious differences between classes and colors been abolished forever?"[198] He believes that only a republican mode of government can eliminate racial distinctions and create citizens out of a synthesis of ethnoracial groups. He rejects being compared to Napoleon, for, while he admired the latter's military prowess, he did not value his authoritarianism.[199] If a Napoleonic system were implemented in Gran Colombia, eventually "equality would be destroyed, and the people of color would see all their rights stripped away by a new aristocracy."[200]

While he was a man of great practical importance to the history of Latin America, Bolívar was also its preeminent republican theorist. At the core of his modern republicanism is a balance between pragmatism and idealism. In this equilibrium we also find the centrality of race to his understanding of the American continent's political reality. It is through the lens of martial republicanism, best grasped from a Machiavellian angle, that we can see the nature of the Bolivarian republic. In this framework we find the salience of racial categories in Bolívar's thought, in which the "starting point was the multiracial character of society."[201] Bolívar did not believe an internal monarchy was the greatest danger to the American republics. The real dangers are external imperial powers and internal racial strife. Neither commercial republics, in the sense of Montesquieu, nor a democratic notion of the General Will, in the sense of Rousseau, was a proper answer. At the same time, Bolívar rejected federalism of the sort advocated by, for instance, the *Federalist Papers*. Only through a martial conception of republican citizenship, one which posits the state as perpetually threatened by external enemies and in constant need of able-bodied citizen-soldiers led by a strong executive, did Bolívar come to the idea of the racial equality of men. This model provides us with an important example of the dynamic, specifically *political* construction of racial identities at the same time that it shows us the role of race in the making of political identities.

Still, in the waning days of his life Bolívar became cognizant of the tragedy of Latin America. His realism prevailed over his idealism. While he strove all his life to achieve a republican form of unity for the continent's multiple racial and ethnic groups, he ultimately came to believe that his efforts had been for naught. External threats from larger powers as well as internal factionalism would weigh down weak states; and his dream of a united Spanish America came to seem a mere chimera.[202] His conclusions, just one month before his death, were ominous.

Bolívar wrote to General Juan José Flores, "I have ruled for twenty years, and I have derived . . . only a few conclusions." These are that America cannot be governed; that "those who serve revolutions plough the sea"; that the only thing to be done is to emigrate out of the continent; that America would eventually be the place of primitive chaos; and last that the continent would soon fall "into the hands of the unrestrained multitudes and then into the hands of tyrants . . . of all colors and races."[203] With these words, Bolívar surrenders his dream of creating a single, unified Latin American race, for he envisions an anarchic state of variegated groups. He ultimately moved toward the idea that America can only be ruled by an able despotism because, as modern Americans,

we are far from the beautiful times of Athens and Rome, and we must not be compared with anything European. The origin of our being is most impure: everything that precedes us is wrapped in the dark veil of crime. We are the abominable synthesis of those wild tigers that came to America to spill blood and breed and of the victims they sacrificed, to then mix illegitimate offspring with slaves ripped out of Africa. With such physical admixtures and moral elements, how can we afford to place laws above leaders, and principles above men?[204]

El Libertador, was thus a thinker whose republicanism was closer to that of the Italian Renaissance than to his own era of the Enlightenment. Rather than relying on reason, he critiqued the ancients to produce something new. More specifically, he sought, like Machiavelli, to strike a balance between elite and popular interests. He corrected and supplemented the Florentine in many aspects, primarily in one blind spot for European republicanism: the importance of race as a problem for republics, especially those that are postcolonial. He also sought to create an extended republic firmly bolstered not just by laws, but by arms. His concern over race wars in Venezuela was not the result of either an antipathy to *pardos* or pride as a *criollo*, but rather a Machiavellian worry about the danger of instability in a socially fractured state. In such a context he was concerned with stable institutions, not with introducing moralism into politics. To the extent that he thought about morality, it was primarily about the concept of republican, civic virtue. Ultimately, his effort to find a balance between democracy and aristocracy in an ethnically diverse and racially mixed state failed within a republican conception of politics.[205] But it would be taken up a few decades later—in a new, and more authoritarian form of "democratic Caesarism" within a nationalistic conception of politics—by his compatriot, Laureano Vallenilla Lanz.

3

RACE AND NATION

The Democratic Caesarism of Vallenilla Lanz

AS THE NINETEENTH century waned, republican theory in Latin America reached a critical point. Simón Bolívar's republicanism was in a sense modular, for it was intended to fit states as different as Venezuela, Peru, or Bolivia. But its application to differing states was not always successful. The need to examine the specific conditions of particular countries became pressing, bringing the problem of nationality to the fore.[1] European republican models were proffered as a way to find political order, in spite of social, cultural, and ethnic differences, through the ideas of the rule of law and the common good allied against monarchical authority. These models were not adequate, however, for the burgeoning Latin American states, characterized as they were by racial heterogeneity and mixing. Bolívar's model reached its limits when confronted by modern problems such as mass society and the rise of industrialization. The Bolivarian dream of one united Latin American state failed as a practical blueprint. Could the same be said about its theoretical legacy?

Here we must consider the intellectual contribution of Laureano Vallenilla Lanz. In his works Vallenilla makes an effort to sustain Bolivarian political philosophy in the twentieth century. We also sense the spirit of Machiavellian republicanism, inflected by a broad array of French intellectual influences.[2] Vallenilla would tell us that his principal aim was to contribute to the formation of national identity in Venezuela, responding to the writings (and shortcomings) of Bolívar and Machiavelli.[3] His purpose was "to contribute to the elaboration of our national sentiment," to instill a love of *patria* in a "distinctive nation that should be able to establish its own constitution based on the effective social and historical facts."[4] His view is inspired by "the political principles of the *Libertador*"[5] and those of Machiavelli. Vallenilla notes that "some critics have given me the great honor of comparing my modest little book [*Cesarismo Democrático*] to Machiavelli's *The Prince*. I have no way of showing my gratitude for this comparison!"[6]

While Simón Bolívar is often classed as a liberal owing to some of his ideas, such as the separation of church and state, Vallenilla, we are told, represents a more conservative brand of Latin American political thought, exposed by his defense of dictatorship. But as I will show in this chapter, the line between these two labels is not limpid. Political thought in Latin America forms a complex tradition, for which a simple nomenclature of "right" and "left" inherited from the French Revolution is not entirely apt. This inadequacy is evident in relation to the role of race in republicanism, as we saw with Bolívar, and takes a different shape in the understanding of race in the context of nationality in the thought of Vallenilla. Moving away from Bolívar's continental conception of early republicanism and into a purely national account, Vallenilla represents the latter part of the second stage in the genealogy of the synthetic understanding of race in the Latin American tradition.

Largely unknown outside of Latin America, and often linked primarily to the dictatorship of Juan Vicente Gómez inside Venezuela,[7] Vallenilla provides an intriguing case of thinking about race in a nonhierarchical manner from what appears to be the traditional political Right. While racism is generally tied to right-wing thought, here we find a profound "conservative" thinker who examines the social reality of his country's racial complexity and connects it to a theory of political constitutionalism.[8] It is a theory that seeks to account for Venezuela's ethnoracial diversity and to provide for it a system based on the rule of law and the common good—republican bulwarks—with an emphasis on a strong executive. It is progressive because it does not remain rooted to antiquated biological or hierarchical views of race. In this sense, it is closer to a "liberal" view of racial equality that sees admixture as valuable. Yet it is also conservative in its defense of a strong executive as a way to deal with the sociopolitical problems related to racial heterogeneity. At the same time, it shows that a popular republicanism could only be possible if headed by one strong leader coming from the *demos*, something that strains the core republican notion of antiauthoritarianism.

In the ideas related to race admixture in Vallenilla there is an iteration of the synthetic paradigm of race in Latin American thought. Vallenilla saw race not as fixed or natural, but as something fluid and inherently mercurial that shaped social categories and determined political phenomena. He underscores the importance of social foundations in the making of political institutions. While racism was in the ascendant in the early decades of the twentieth century in the United States and especially in parts of Europe, we find in Vallenilla a thinker engaged with the problems of mass society as he seeks to address the question of racial mixture and diversity in a (mostly) nonracist manner. Vallenilla shows, in spite of some internal tensions and inconsistencies, how nationality and the modern state are built upon racial phenomena.[9]

Vallenilla was a *pensador bolivariano,* a broadly trained thinker who was deeply influ-enced by and admired the work of Simón Bolívar.[10] In the work of Vallenilla, we also find the crisis of republicanism as it grapples with the demands of nation-making. Val-lenilla writes about a Venezuela no longer seeking independence but rather trying to find for itself an optimal constitutional order within a specific socioracial context. We move from a Machiavellian martial republicanism, as expressed in the thought of Bolívar, to a more focused concern with the balance between the executive and the *demos* in Val-lenilla's effort to understand the specific phenomenon of Venezuelan *nationality.* This system does not entail a defense of nationalism dependent on a particular ethnoracial identity (hence the wide gulf between his ideas and those of fascism); but it means that understanding a polity requires a comprehension of the development of its cultural and social identity.

Against near-sighted critiques by contemporaries claiming that Bolívar was in fact in favor of monarchy, Vallenilla showed that nothing could be further from the truth. Such charges were leveled by thinkers such as Carlos A. Villanueva, and Vallenilla re-futed them comprehensively.[11] Not only did Vallenilla defend Bolívar against accusa-tions of links to monarchical ideas, but he also saw that the great general was the first thinker to asseverate that the social bases of Latin America were of utmost importance to its political order.[12] Racial heterogeneity and the need for balance between elites and masses, as we shall see, were crucial facts of Latin American reality, according to Valle-nilla's assessment of Bolívar's ideas. "Diversity and the visible differences of epidermis"[13] were preeminent factors all over Latin American societies, but especially in Venezuela. Whereas Bolívar's republicanism was not specifically national, there is a more direct engagement with the idea of a common birth of a people, or nationality, in the works of Vallenilla.[14]

Intellectual and Historical Context of Vallenilla's Ideas

Vallenilla did not live a life of quiet contemplation. He was a sociologist and historian, but he was also involved in journalism and the national politics of his time. He rep-resents the intellectual spirit found in the space between Bolívar's republicanism and José Vasconcelos's postnationalist critique of positivism—in other words, the space of the making of the nation, understood in this case as the self-understanding of citizens based on underlying social bases. His views deepen the specificity of republicanism by articulating a particular conception of nationality, and come before the crisis of the nation-state that led to the regional cosmopolitanism of Vasconcelos.

Vallenilla was born in the small town of Barcelona, Venezuela, in 1870. He grew up in a milieu of political instability, demagoguery, and *caudillismo,* or strongman politics. His father was a medical doctor who owned an impressive library.[15] It is there that young Laureano discovered many of the European thinkers that would influence his thought.

From Darwin to Spencer to John Stuart Mill, and especially Auguste Comte, he acquired a broad European-inflected education.

After a period of "frivolity and dandyism"[16] during his university studies in engineering, Vallenilla eventually came under the intellectual spell of political and social studies. His journalistic career began with *La Nueva Era* in Barcelona, continued at *El Imparcial*, and eventually led him to *El Cojo Ilustrado*, a journal that was a magnet to many important positivist thinkers in Venezuela.[17] These included José Gil Fortoul,[18] Luis Razetti, and Emilio Coll.[19] For them, countering the prevalence of violence was a key concern. At a time when the Andean caudillo Cipriano Castro took power, this preoccupation with violence was at the core of national politics. In 1901–1902 a *revolución liberadora* took place against Castro, and Vallenilla was arrested. Eventually he was released and decided to travel to Europe in October 1904 at the age of thirty-four.

Europe was, in many ways, Vallenilla's intellectual cradle.[20] Unlike Bolívar, who believed Latin America could make a clean break from Europe—and especially Spain—Vallenilla believed that Latin America's fate was intimately tied to its Iberian past. In belle époque Paris, Vallenilla found a nourishing environment where he met many Venezuelan, Colombian, and Mexican thinkers. He also became friends with the great modernist poet Rubén Darío of Nicaragua. As an auditor at the Sorbonne and the Collège de France, he became increasingly interested in positivism as a solution to societies fraught with chaos and violence. It was there where he absorbed the ideas of Charles Langlois and Charles Seignobos, who promoted a factual, analytic form of historiography opposed to the "great man" view of history and of the notion that each nation has a specific "spirit."[21] He also came into contact with the ideas of Ernest Renan and Hippolyte Taine, which see society as a totality made of social forces, not produced by individuals.

Through his stay in Europe, European ideas in Vallenilla's nascent approach to race grew more significant. Lesser-known thinkers come to the fore when we examine Vallenilla's developing effort to understand "race" and its role in society. While eager to produce something theoretical of value to the specific nationality of Venezuela, he was deeply marked by Francophone sociological works about race at the turn of the century. Vallenilla initially believed in the permanence of racial traits for the three main races[22] and also in polygenesis, which he acquired from Ludwig Gumplowicz's *La lutte des races* (1883). But Vallenilla did not remain adamant about these ideas; in fact his thought about race changed drastically over the years, moving toward a social-constructivist approach by the time he wrote his major works.

Race was, for Vallenilla, one of the major social forces in a modern, organic society. He maintained that its complexity was closely connected to the level of violence in a society. Furthering his worries about violence, he found in Sorel a source of insight.[23] With regards to the idea of society as an organic entity or whole, he was influenced by René Worms, Felix le Dantec, Georg Jellinek, Leon Duguit, and Edouard Laboulaye. Within this society that is a holistic complex, the state plays a pivotal role in mediating and mobilizing social forces. Two important influences on Vallenilla's view of the state must be underscored: the *César démocratique* in the work of Laboulaye, and Hippolyte Taine's notion of the *gendarme nécessaire*. As we will see, Vallenilla incorporated and transformed these concepts to produce a theory suited to the Latin American context, and more specifically to his own country.

One important result of his key works *Cesarismo Democrático* (1919) and *Disgregación e Integración* (1930), which were critical of liberal democracy and which advocated a form of dictatorial politics, was his association with the autocrat Juan Vicente Gómez, who held on to power for twenty-seven years.[24] Many called Vallenilla an apologist and philosopher of dictatorship. But it must be remembered that the notes that led to these two works were mostly written between 1905 and 1909, before Gómez's ascent to power.[25] His essay "Gendarme Necesario" appeared in 1911, also before the dictator's rise. Thus, while Vallenilla does provide a theoretical defense of a form of dictatorship, he did not do so for the purpose of defending Gómez.[26] He was no mere apologist for tyranny. Romulo Betancourt called Vallenilla a "tropical Machiavelli,"[27] seeking to brand him a defender of despotism. But Vallenilla was proud to be associated with the Florentine republican who advocated a strong princely executive within a republican order. As he wrote in "Por qué escribí '*Cesarismo Democrático*,'" Vallenilla felt the greatest admiration for Machiavelli. In response to attacks on his influence, Vallenilla replied, "They have tried to offend me, but they have actually given me the highest praise I could aspire to as a writer! Only the ignorant have yet to understand that Machiavelli was the least *Machiavellian* of all."[28]

At the time Vallenilla's work on democratic Caesarism appeared, many intellectuals denied that democracy could be reconciled with an autocratic form of rule as emblematized by Caesarism. Eduardo Santos, a Colombian liberal, called Vallenilla "a philosopher of the dictatorship" associated with Juan Vicente Gómez. Vallenilla would reply that the idea of democracy meant, for Colombia, only a reference to the one hundred most important families in the nation, not "su pueblo, es decir, la masa" ("the people, that is, the masses"). This perspective was, to Vallenilla's eyes, a "Panglossian" one that did not recognize the elitism of contemporary Latin American democracies, be it that of Colombia or neighboring Venezuela.[29] Thus, Vallenilla was critical of the roseate view of liberal democracy, for it did not express the totality of the *demos* or people. Vallenilla would declare that "while there is a privileged class in society and the upper echelons are not accessible to the sons of the lower classes [*pueblo*], democracy, that is, true social democracy, is completely utopian."[30]

Colonial social relations, before independence, formed the relatively rigid social classes that Colombia or Venezuela faced, according to Vallenilla. The conditions of pauperism, both absolute and relative, led Vallenilla to reject "liberal-bourgeois" opponents of Gómez, for he believed civil liberties and formal equality before the law were not enough to dismantle real social inequalities. In *El sentido americano de la democracia* ("The Latin American Meaning of Democracy") he would write, "The existence of classes in misery has led to the failure of democracy. This is because there cannot be equality where misery corrodes the great majority of the population."[31] Hence, far from being a defender of the ruling classes or a staunch reactionary insensitive to the ills of the lower ranks of the people, Vallenilla came to his critique of liberal-bourgeois ideology from an appreciation of the depth and magnitude of poverty in Venezuelan society. He did not defend privilege as such, nor did he blame the poor for their travails. For him, capitalism undermined the democratic promise, and it led to the ferment of the pauperized classes.

If indeed Vallenilla was seeking to defend the interests of the popular classes, why would he defend a dictator like Gómez? His answer was that the Gómez regime was establishing the protective structure that would provide a safeguard to the lowest ranks in society, and thereby to eventually make for a "more effective democracy."[32] This assessment may not have been entirely accurate, for the *latifundios gomeros*, or industrial rubber plantations, were the dominant forms of production at the time, something far from state-owned enterprises. In effect, while Vallenilla's sympathies toward the lower classes may have been in the right place, he erred in believing that the petroleum-based autocracy of Gómez was fundamentally a nationalist regime.[33]

However, Vallenilla was principally a sociologist, historian, and journalist; he was not an ideologue. He did not provide a wholesale defense of Gómez, because he saw his rule as a "necessary evil"[34] that would assist Venezuela's progress toward material development.[35] Here Vallenilla's two principal intellectual pillars coalesce: a Machiavellian conception of political expediency as superseding moral considerations ("necessary evil") and a positivist, Comtean belief in the need for material progress. It is on these two pillars that Vallenilla built the concept of the *gendarme necesario*, or the "necessary gendarme" state. Only such a state could distinguish between moral and political needs and lay the grounds for material progress in a country riven by poverty.[36] It is a theory that emanates from the legacy of Bolívar, where a strong executive safeguards popular sovereignty in a system of the rule of law for the common good. Moreover, it is tied to a political conception that is both patriotic and revolutionary, seeking to defend a motherland while establishing a new mode of rule.

In this schema, the ethnoracial dimension plays a pivotal role. The conceptions of the *patria* and of popular sovereignty are intimately connected to a particular ethnoracial identity. We saw this same relation in Bolívar's account of martial, revolutionary republicanism, in which race is central to the political order. For Vallenilla, the popular masses are not faceless, colorless, or abstract entities. Even more so than for Bolívar, they are the particular ethnoracial groups that emerge out of Venezuelan soil.[37] Bolívar's Angostura Discourse of 1819 is a proclamation of the democratic institutions necessary for "Indo-Hispanic-African societies."[38] As the Venezuelan Marxist Carlos Irazábal wrote in the 1930s, Bolívar "propounded a theory of a strong and lifetime executive" in order to respond to the particular problems associated with the ethnoracial mix of his *patria*. Bolívar shaped his republican theory under the influence of the Enlightenment, the French Revolution, and the model of the United Kingdom. But, as we saw in the previous chapter, the core principle of the Bolivarian brand of republicanism is a martial one. It is shaped by the wartime conditions of a battle for independence, where military legality takes precedence over civil legality. And it is characterized by the *Libertador*'s leadership of his troops. More precisely, the troops "had some whites in them, but were predominantly from the *castas viles: mulatos, zambos, mestizos, negros libres, indios.*" In other words, they were of the population of color in general.[39]

In this tradition established by Bolívar, not all dictatorships are of the same kind. Dictatorship is not synonymous with tyranny. Some dictatorships favor the powerful elites; some favor the national, popular masses.[40] Some seek to find a balance. Bolívar recognized this idea. He saw a fundamentally antielitist drive in the concatenation of civil equality, absolute equality, and *pardocracia* that was the natural negation of privilege. He feared *pardocracia* yet understood the basic motivation for equality that it contained.[41] Summarizing the basic thesis of Vallenilla's democratic Caesarism, his son would write:

> Only an enlightened despotism can carry out the revolution that is destined to triumph over ignorance and backwardness, to stabilize institutions, and to form citizens. Liberty is an attribute of citizenship, and citizenship is *incompatible with misery*. Dictatorship is a transitory evil, the treatment of an endemic illness.[42]

While Bolívar introduced the issue of race to give substance to his republicanism, Vallenilla is concerned with mass poverty. This essentially late-modern problem, which was not as widespread in Bolívar's time, becomes cardinal to Vallenilla's political and social theory.[43] It is in a sense paradoxical that the largely lionized Bolívar in fact held a more elite-centered conception of republicanism, whereas Vallenilla, generally demonized because of his support for Gómez, supported a system in which the popular masses were central, albeit led by a (mixed-race) dictator.

Method and Positivist Philosophy

Positivism, at the turn of the century, was seen by a wide gamut of Latin American intellectuals as the lens through which to find ways to modernize societies and deal with their specifically modern problems. This idea meant moving past the upheavals of the independence movement and seeking order and progress through scientific and empirical approaches. Economic advancement and political stability were to replace the vestiges of feudalism and religiosity as norms. In many cases, positivism was allied to conservative perspectives, due to the belief that technocratic elites were more knowledgeable about, and capable of bringing, development.[44]

An important element of Vallenilla's contribution to the synthetic paradigm of race in Latin American thought is his eclectic positivist method.[45] He was an admirer of Auguste Comte[46] as one of Venezuela's positivist triumvirate, along with José Gil Fortoul and Pedro Manuel Arcaya.[47] He was also a student of the two founders of French positivist historiography, the aforementioned Langlois and Seignobos. He was deeply influenced by French thinkers such as Celestin Bouglé and Lucien Febvre. From Bouglé, a student of Emile Durkheim, Vallenilla was led to the centrality of democracy and secularism[48] as well as the specific concept of *césarisme démocratique*, which was related to Laboulaye's *César démocratique*. For Taine, history is a psychological problem. What goes on in the mind of men and women is of utmost significance to historical developments. This concept is of interest in understanding Vallenilla since Taine saw climate, race, and historical moments or junctures as determining factors in historical periods.[49] While a psychological understanding of race *qua* identity is not explicit in Vallenilla, Taine's linkage of race and psychology adumbrates later empirical work.

Unlike Bolívar, Vallenilla was a scholar (though a self-taught one), and saw his enterprise as that of a sociologist and historian, for whom the historical process and context of a phenomenon is of the highest importance. His positivism, however, did not adhere strictly to any one particular school. Comte was acknowledged to be the founder of this perspective, and from the French sociologist Vallenilla derived a systematic, holistic, and fact-based approach. But Vallenilla did not believe that he had to follow a classical account of positivism,[50] for he also acted as a journalist and political activist. He did not want merely to understand societies, but also to influence the direction of Venezuelan politics.[51]

When he applied this method to the understanding of racial identity in Venezuela, he pointed out immediately that the Caracas nobility was able to purchase its titles. In other words, noble status was principally based on social, not natural, order. Importantly, he saw social phenomena as part of a continuity of events, not as isolated facts. For Vallenilla, the significance of continuity leads to his valuation of interdisciplinarity, for to understand a phenomenon, one had to comprehend it in the totality of its contexts. History, sociology, biology, anthropology, psychology, and economics were, for Vallenilla, intertwined.

As much as Vallenilla was committed to a positivist worldview, he believed religion was fundamental to the proper workings of a society. This idea is not far from what Auguste Comte believed. In *Notas sobre la Religión*, Vallenilla would state:

> I am a free thinker, a determinist, a positivist. However, I am the first person to condemn indifference to religion in our society, because nothing is more attuned to human nature than the religious instinct, and no one should underestimate its importance as a social tie and moral restraint for the masses.[52]

Religion is thus seen by Vallenilla as something functional, rather than innately moral, in a way that recalls Renan. For Vallenilla, social phenomena are the product of long, complex, overdetermined processes. Nothing appears *ex nihilo*, and nothing can be a complete break from the past, hence Vallenilla's denial of revolutions as radical points of no return. In this sense, he is far from Bolívar, who believed a clean break from Spain could be made through wars of independence and revolution.

This historicist methodology meant that each nation received its political system through its particular historical development. As Vallenilla declared, "I start from the premise that each people gets the government that it produces out of its own idiosyncrasy and degree of culture, rather than the government it deserves."[53] Yet Vallenilla was not free from some Eurocentric bias. Cognizant as he was that Latin American identity was made of an admixture of influences, he still believed that immigration from Europe would help to improve local "culture."[54] From this method, Vallenilla would produce his chief work, *Cesarismo Democrático*, which treads a fine line between an explication of dictatorship and a justification for it. To some admirers, such as Maldonado, the book could explain what occurred not just in Venezuela but in other parts of Latin America as well, such as Argentina, Bolivia, Peru, and Mexico, and in European states of the early twentieth century such as France, Italy, Germany, and Spain. As such, it was a book "not just for Venezuela, but for all of Hispanic America; and a book not just for the present, but for an entire epoch."[55]

Vallenilla's brand of positivism did not emanate from the cloisters of academia. It was a theoretical instrument that he found useful to address the pressing historical, social, and political problems of Venezuela. The scientistic ideas of organicism and evolution were essentially metaphorical for Vallenilla; he did not carry out quantitative research or data gathering, but rather saw them as ways to enlighten our understanding of the past. His was a positivism principally aimed at explaining *la longue durée*. Venezuela's problems of his day, in Vallenilla's view, could not be examined without a wide historical assay. Evolution meant historical development, not a concept specifically derived from Spencer or Darwin.[56] The organic analogy provided a periodization of history into gestation, birth, growth, decay, and death of particular societies.[57] It was not strictly related to Durkheim's distinction between mechanical and organic solidarity, since Vallenilla did not pay great attention to institutions but rather to historical forces. Vallenilla's method was interdisciplinary, based on praxis (understood as knowledge oriented to effect change upon the world), qualitative, and focused on the social as opposed to the institutional bases of politics.

The Ties between Spain and *Hispanoamérica*

For Vallenilla, races and racial admixture are the key positive facts in postcolonial societies like those of Latin America. Vallenilla believed races are what comprise the population of society. He also thought that Latin America's racial diversity allowed observers to see political problems more clearly.[58] Citing Humboldt, he argued that political reality was easier to grasp in Havana or Caracas than in Europe, especially north of the Pyrenees, because "the more *mestizaje*, the easier the incorporation of ideas."[59] This claim was supported, he believed, by Gabriel Tarde's conception of increased inventiveness in conditions of racial mixture. In Vallenilla's view, racial complexity results in more complex, intellectually open minds. Out of this openness, he believed, Latin Americans and Spaniards could forge a common *raza*, a collective ethos. It would lead to progress, liberty, and democracy. This optimism is the reason for the title of his essay, "La Fiesta de la Raza." Adumbrating Vasconcelos, he sees a common mission as a result of a common language and common historical development.

From his conception of "raza," Vallenilla moved to the task of understanding the politico-cultural dimensions of the "Hispanic American" people. He moved away from Bolívar's rejection of all things Spanish in order to advocate closer ties between the former colonies and the *madre patria*. He promoted this connection not for a moral reason, but rather because, sociologically and historically, Latin American nations had not really made a clean break from Spain.[60] The wars of independence, in Vallenilla's view, were fundamentally *civil wars*. Creoles divided their support between republicanism and the Royalist cause.[61] Far from a simple rupture[62] of the Spanish yoke, the wars were fought between Creoles who were *godos* (Royalists) and the minority, which favored republicanism.[63] This idea, that there was no real break from Spain, was almost sacrilegious in the eyes of most Latin American historians of the time, since it claimed that a vast segment of the creole elite was in fact not on the side of patriotic republicanism. Moreover, Vallenilla argued that the Royalists were not exclusively from the lower rungs in society.

A "fraternity" of peoples could be forged, following the spirit of Solórzano, who in the sixteenth century defended Americans from the charge of being irrational.[64] But Vallenilla points out "Americans" meant the sons and daughters of the Spaniards who had mixed with the natives, not the indigenous peoples per se. He recognizes opposition in the peninsula as well, as some at the Cortes de Cádiz in 1812 asked whether Americans were irrational, and the writer Pío Baroja called Americans "monkeys." With a mocking tone, Vallenilla decries the lack of culture in Spain and France as a response to such racialist views. Forging an alliance between Latin America and Spain, thus, would not be easy. Instead of Baroja, he finds value in more universalist and modernist Spanish thinkers like Unamuno, Valle Inclán, Altamira, and Carrere.

This union of the Latins, eventually leading to a political community, could be possible if grounded on the proper norms. Against the provincialism of Baroja, universalism is crucial for Vallenilla. He believes that it is a universalism that must go back to the Romans. This basis leads to a concept of race that is immanently social. "When Hispanic Americans speak of the Latin race, we understand the term to represent a mentality, psychology, soul, spirit, and culture." He goes on to say that "no one can deny the influence of Rome over peoples of diverse races."[65] We must recall that Bolívar's tutor Andrés Bello saw in Spain Rome's most important inheritor because of its language, institutions, and colonial outlook.[66]

Still, Vallenilla's view of racial diversity is not utopian. While he appreciates the depth that racial intermixing provides individuals, he also thinks that contact among various "racial" groups can be conflictive. In other words, while there is more racial mixing in

Latin America than in Europe, this intermixing is never complete. There are distinct ethnoracial groups that persist, leading to "peoples which are nothing but the product of the social chemistry of race struggle."[67] Thus, while Latin America has roots that go back all the way to its Iberian past and its pre-Columbian civilizations, the national identities of *modern* Latin American states are *sui generis*. They cannot be classified as either "Hispanic" or "Indian."

Vallenilla recalls the words of another thinker who was highly critical of the idea of race but believed it was necessary to understand the core of Spanish America. For José Martí, no amount of European or Anglo-Saxon ideology could comprehend the Spanish American reality. Vallenilla reminds us of his words in *Nuestra América*:

> A decree by Hamilton will not stop the thrust of the *llanero*'s colt. A sentence by Sieyès will not move the still blood of the Indian race. The good man of government in [Latin] America is not the one who knows how to govern a German or a Frenchman, but rather, he who knows what elements make up his country.[68]

While able to discern the continuities between his nation and Spain, and to be open-minded enough to learn from European thinkers, Vallenilla heeds Martí's call to produce ideas that will fit the autochthonous American soil.[69] It is in this light that he came to defend a constitutional order with a strong executive who both expressed and controlled democratic forces.

The Concept of "Race" in Vallenilla

At the center of Vallenilla's intellectual enterprise is the effort to understand the sociopolitical reality of his homeland, Venezuela. He is a social and cultural critic, not merely a specialized scholar. Vallenilla wrote his major works in the early decades of the twentieth century, long after Venezuela had achieved Bolívar's ambition of independence from Spain. The problem at hand was to develop a constitution and national self-understanding that would be stable and lead to growth and development. For Vallenilla a starting point of this analysis of Venezuelan national reality was, significantly, race.

Behind the present social reality, he argued, was a long historical process, which he called *evolución*. This does not mean "evolution" in the biological sense, but rather the social development that occurs over a long period. For Vallenilla, the concept of *raza* was central to Venezuela's historical process. Examining Venezuela's racial composition and history also meant two important, more general contributions. One was the refutation of racism, and the other the negation of the idea that miscegenation leads to decadence.[70] While he was not always entirely consistent, his ideas eventually result in a social-constructivist approach that is ahead of its time. He thought critically about race at a time when most of his contemporaries were apologists for racism or had myopic views on the topic.

In a speech he gave at Teatro Calcaño on August 1, 1914, in Caracas, he provided a description of his understanding of the role of race. His starting premise was that while he was an objective "scientist" in the broad sense, he carried out his analyses for the benefit of the glory of his *patria*. Thus, he was no disinterested objectivist, but rather a partisan, partial observer who valued the interests of his motherland in a republican fashion.[71]

For Vallenilla, the specifically *racial* character of Venezuela should be the first topic in understanding its social reality. One must carry out a "scientific study of the primordial traits that give the Venezuelan people a unique physiognomy vis-à-vis other Latin American peoples."[72] With a critical approach, Vallenilla asks what makes a nation. Unlike many of his European contemporaries, he does not believe a common ethnic origin is the answer. Neither is a common language or the occupation of a territory over a long period of time. He gives Spain as an example that negates these possibilities, for it is a country of many ethnic groups and of many languages as well.[73] What makes a nation is the long process of *evolución*, especially as it involves the historical and social intertwining of ethnoracial groups. Vallenilla gives the example of Latin American nations in general:

All the peoples of Latin America come from Spain. The Spaniards mixed [*se mezclaron*] to a certain degree with the indigenous people, and then with blacks. Hence we can agree with Murillo Toro that "In Hispanic America we are all *café con leche*, some with more coffee, some with more milk." But this mixture itself came from Spain, where it took place for centuries when Carthaginians, Greeks, Romans, Goths, Visigoths, Asiatic Arabs, Berbers, and blacks from Africa combined to produce a peninsular disposition towards mixing that was continued in America. This must worry the old and worn theories of some anthropo-psychologists who hold dear the idea of Spanish racial purity [*pureza de raza*], and who do define or understand what a race is.[74]

Thus, Vallenilla extends the Bolivarian notion that Latin American identity is unique because it is preeminently mixed. He pushes it further to show that Spanish identity itself, which was thought to be "pure" by some academics, was itself the product of ethnoracial admixture. Using a Latin American lens crafted by Bolívar, Vallenilla examines European identity and sees a similar mixing, at least in the Iberian peninsula.

While he himself was mostly of Spanish extraction and from the upper echelons of society, Vallenilla assailed racist and racialist theories that were often used to defend white, upper-class privilege. He was staunchly opposed to the legacy of Gobineau, which held that some races are innately inferior.[75] He declared:

It seems incredible that—in our polychromatic Venezuela, in this great mosaic where all the European men of wisdom could come to study all the representations of the ethnological continuum living in an absolute social and political community, in this classical land of democratic leveling—there are still those who, perhaps unconsciously, and under the guise of historical research, argue for the psychological inequality of the races.[76]

Writing in 1914, the use of terms such as "polychromatic" and "mosaic" with reference to the racial makeup of a nation is indeed ahead of its time. Ethnoracial differences were centrifugal forces in the United States and Europe then, but for Vallenilla, even if he was perhaps too optimistic about racial democracy in Venezuela, such differences were in fact forces to congeal national unity.[77] Vallenilla decries those who argue for the idea of racial inequality, pointing out that they are generally called "liberals" but follow Gobineau's principles.

Continuing his critique of racialism, Vallenilla targets Gobineau's legacy. He finds it "absurd"[78] to believe that "white blood" determines nobility of spirit. He also mocks those who think they attacked Bolívar for possibly having some African blood through his ancestor Don Francisco Marín Narváez and his mulatta servant Josefina Marín. He criticizes the ideas of the Dutch-Italian physiologist Jacob Moleschott, a liberal, who believed, in the late nineteenth century, that political parties can be explained through "purely encephalic causes," making a reference to the often racialized idea of phrenology. For Moleschott, different families tended to have different kinds of brains, which secreted ideas just as the liver secretes bile. In Vallenilla's view, such theories, and those of Gobineau, were absurd. The idea that "the white race is intellectually superior" was anathema to Vallenilla.[79]

Vallenilla was opposed not only to the idea that the white race is biologically superior, but also the belief that race has a direct link to cultural or political domination. "Ethnic origins," he would write, "have no explanatory power."[80] Neither nations nor individuals are superior owing to "racial causes." Vallenilla points to the Japanese as an example of a highly civilized group that is nonwhite and that puzzles sociological apologists for racialism.[81] Science has shown, according to Vallenilla, that race does not determine social superiority.[82] In effect, he believes Bolívar instead of Gobineau: "Fortunately for humanity, experience and history destroy Gobineau's theory completely. The famous sentence by Bolívar referring to Latin America, 'We do not know to which race we belong,' is perfectly applicable to humanity as a whole."[83] Anticipating the ethos of Vasconcelos and Gilberto Freyre, he also remarks somewhat facetiously, "I have already said elsewhere that, just as in comedies, bloody histories end up in matrimony. Sexual love takes care of resolving the greatest conflicts of humanity."[84]

Lest we misunderstand what he means by "race," Vallenilla tells us that he merely uses the term in order to facilitate social classification. In other words, there is no essentialist definition of each particular "race." There is such admixture that miscegenation is present everywhere, but nowhere as much as in Latin America. Vallenilla defends the mestizo character of Latin American identity, attacking not just Gobineau, but also other prominent European thinkers of the time. He rejects Otto Ammon, a German anthropologist who, writing in the early 1900s, believed that a high proportion of people of Germanic ancestry are found within European aristocracies.[85] Ammon would write that "people of mixed race are physiologically and psychologically inferior to the component races."[86] Vallenilla also assailed Georges Vacher de Lapouge, the French racialist anthropologist and proponent of eugenics whose main works were written at the turn of the century and who argued that *métissage* creates physiological regression and infertility.[87] Vallenilla also finds flaws in Charles Darwin for his statement that mixed races lead to a savage disposition.[88] Vallenilla denounced the racialist ideas of David Livingstone and Gustave Le Bon.[89] According to Le Bon, racial mixture in Latin America was the cause of its anarchic nature.[90] Vallenilla responds by pointing to the cases of Brazil and Argentina, which show significant admixture yet still have a high degree of order.[91] Vallenilla argues that it was not high European immigration that led to these two countries' progress; rather it was race admixture.[92] This claim contravened José Ingenieros, the Italian-born Comtean philosopher from Argentina. In Vallenilla's view, the term "European" was itself arbitrary, pointing out the vast cultural distance between Italians and Poles, for instance.

Contrary to European eugenics, Vallenilla's perspective is antiracialist. He denies that sociology can be reduced to "the so-called philosophy of races."[93] However, his thinking is not entirely indigenous to Latin America, as it is partially influenced by European views. He points to the work of the French sociologist Gabriel Tarde, who opposed most of his contemporaries by arguing in *L'Action Instrumentale* that European admixture was in fact increasing and was a positive phenomenon.[94] "Panmixtia," or race admixture, did not cause degeneration. Following Théodule-Armand Ribot's *L'heredité psychologique*, Vallenilla argued that racial admixture can create men of great intellectual ability, such as those in Venezuela, leading him to reject the biological conception of race as applied to social relations. "Let us not speak of race, then; it is a vague, imprecise term that does not correspond to any sociological reality and cannot explain anything when applied to trying to understand the development [*evolución*] of peoples."[95]

This assessment came after recognizing that he himself had previously used racial ideas in sociological analysis. Ideas, for Vallenilla, are transmitted not through race but through sociopsychological processes. "Seeking to establish an absolute analogy between skin color and intellectual agility is anti-scientific."[96] While he admired Ernest Renan, he rejected his hierarchical understanding of humanity as divided into unequal races. For Latin America, this meant one should instead try to understand the interactions of three equal races (indigenous, black, and white). But Vallenilla sometimes devolved into quasi-scientific language, as when he described this task as similar to that of the "chemist," trying to determine the particular interactions of diverse races. Still, such declarations are rare, and they do not undermine the overall force of his critique of European racialism. His scholarly definition of race is understood socially: "The true scientific [that is, objective] concept of race is one of culture, mentality, psychological affinity, and similarity of values of people of diverse [ethnic] origins brought together by a collective sensibility."[97]

By 1930, when he published his study of Venezuelan nationality, *Disgregación e Integración*, Vallenilla had made both advances and errors in his effort to account for race. He paradoxically moved closer to a social-constructivist approach to race at the same time that he was mired in untenable claims about racial traits and conditions. He was enlightened in his agreement with Georges Palante, who pushed a social, as opposed to biological, conception of race:

> The social forms that some believe are the product of ethnic differences are in fact the causes of these differences. A people shows intellectual or moral differences vis-à-vis other peoples. Yet these distinctive traits are rather the product of processes that a people has gone through, and of the social forms that it has experienced; in other words they are the product of sociological development, rather than anatomical phenomena.[98]

Yet one problematic notion found in this important text is the idea that the *medio* (environment) can affect or trump racial formations. On the one hand, Vallenilla sometimes means by the term *medio* the *social* environment, but sometimes he means the *natural* environment, such as geography and climate. In his effort to develop a scientific approach to race, he believed, more insight could be found in physical, as opposed to ideal, conditions. It is important to underscore that he rejected racial essentialism, saying, "There are many powerful causes that determine the deep differences between peoples with a common ethnic ancestry."[99]

Still, he returns to the *medio* to claim that there is a link between racial identity or characteristics and natural circumstances. In what amounts to an unscientific mistake, Vallenilla claims that the "climate" of a given region can "bring about the formation of a new race."[100] He points to the United States as a place where the white race has moved significantly away from its European roots due to the natural environment, which brings whites closer to the "natives." It is not due to racial intermixing, for Englishmen did not mix with the Indians. He claims that Latin American variety in terms of geography and climate also affected the racial heterogeneity of Latin Americans. *El medio físico y telúrico* is the expression that Vallenilla uses to refer to the influence of geography and the land on ethnoracial groups.

Vallenilla underscores this idea by saying that "race is the expression of the environment."[101] He believes, without precise scientific evidence, that geography can alter the makeup of human kind. Although this assertion is on the whole untenable, we may infer that it has something to do with the way that the environment affects the genetic composition of a given ethnic group over hundreds of years. Vallenilla calls on Montesquieu and Buckle as well as John Stuart Mill to defend the idea of *etología política*. He wants to posit it as a counterpoint to the belief that a particular race has an immutable ethos or spiritual essence, what he calls *genio*. Coming to the fore is his progressive effort to move away from essentialism and toward the idea, as he puts it, that groups that come from the same race can develop differently given distinct *medios*. He finds further support for this thesis in another giant of Latin American thought, Domingo Sarmiento.[102]

While Sarmiento cannot be rescued for a contribution to a proper understanding of racial ideas because he advocated the extermination of nonwhite peoples in Argentina,[103] what we find in common with Vallenilla is the belief that natural environment can trump purported racial essences. The similarities continue in Vallenilla's emphasis on the common conditions of the Venezuelan *llanos* and the Argentine *pampas*. The fact that Indians, whites, and Africans mixed in both areas is not the end-all of the racial discussion. The physical environment engendered a *particular* and new racial group in each locale. Vallenilla remarks that "we would make a great mistake if we believed that the Venezuelan *llanero* is merely the result of the white, Indian, and black mixture. The psychological heritage of the three mother races disappears altogether owing to the physio-psychological effect that is imposed by the environment."[104] Thus, race is not fundamentally or only a combination of other races, but it also involves the factor of natural environmental influences.

This fact, moreover, has sociopolitical consequences.[105] Just as the gaucho was born on the Argentine pampas out of a racial mix of diverse groups in the account of Sarmiento's *Life in the Argentine Republic in the Days of the Tyrants*, so is the Venezuelan *llanero* forged in empty, vast steppes. And it is man's relation to an animal, the horse, which produces a particular sociopolitical structure. The horse, both for Sarmiento and for Vallenilla, is the ultimate source of *caudillismo*. The man who can break in a horse, control it, ride it well, and look down on those who are not horsemen, gains instant charisma and authority.[106] José Tomás Boves, the Venezuelan *llanero* bandit,[107] is not far from Juan Manuel de Rosas or even Facundo Quiroga in Sarmiento's historical tale.[108] A man who is prone to violence, has authority over weaker men, and is admired for his courage and prowess over nature can become a caudillo who rises above others. In countries where mountains rather than plains exist, Vallenilla tells us, these men are not born. Such is the case of Bolivia and Peru.[109] But the horseman is not only a man of authority; he is a man closely tied to violence and criminality,[110] ultimately altering the largely elusive quest for political stability.

Although this pseudoscientific approach is flawed because it does not have precise methodology or irrefutable evidence, Vallenilla was trying to get to a nonbiological and nonessentialist definition of race. If the natural telluric environment could alter racial traits, then no race was immutable. Moreover, it was not defined only by its internal blood-related or somatic characteristics. The dissolution of the idea of fixed, permanent races is what Vallenilla means by the term *disgregación*. The putative three main races (white, black, and red) could be disaggregated in the course of intermixing and existence in new natural and social environments. And while Latin America evinced general miscegenation, it was not uniform, because each region of the continent had different kinds and levels of social and ethnic intermixing. Going against the prevalent idea of the time that most "Indians" were savages, Vallenilla writes that "the indigenous population of America could be found in diverse degrees of civilization: from perfectly constituted societies to primitive hordes."[111] For this reason, the Conquest took on a different form in each part of the Americas.

From this uneven intermixing, different groups emerged, producing a "great somatic and social differentiation." Vallenilla saw these differences occurring between the social psychology of the mulatto and that of the mestizo. The feeling of inferiority in the mulatto was deeper, not because of any inherent characteristic, but for socioeconomic reasons. Being connected to a formerly enslaved population created this sense of injury. Whites had "taken over" the land and slaves, and bought titles of whiteness. Even particular clothes marked them as superior to the formerly enslaved.[112] Vallenilla opposes the simple, racist view, commonly expressed at the time with the words *Quien ha visto un indio, ha visto a todos* ("If you have seen one Indian, you've seen them all").[113] Vallenilla recognizes that the indigenous peoples were justifiably wary of whites, for Europeans had every intention of exterminating them.

Here arises another crucial shortcoming in Vallenilla. In this key text which studies the origins of Venezuelan nationality, he only examines the "Indian" and "black" races. He does not cast a critical gaze upon "whites."[114] There is no reason why he should focus on the "other" races, as if the white race were the principal or dominant one in Venezuela. If anything, the *pardos* were dominant as a race. Vallenilla falls into the same error that many European thinkers did, which is to assume that the "white" race is somehow the "neutral" one. Ignoring a possible critique of the social conditions of white hegemony, Vallenilla goes on to examine the social traits of Indians and blacks. He finds, above all, a history of tribalism. Not only were the Venezuelan Indians basically small groups of ruthless warriors, but they lacked the civilization of the Inca, Aztecs, or Maya. According to Vallenilla, tribalism and *caciquismo,* that is, the deference to a single personalistic authority, came to be part of the national psyche of Venezuela by way of its Indian origins. A similar phenomenon could be found among the descendants of Africans: a multitude of tribal groups were uprooted from their homeland and thrown upon American land. In the case of Venezuela, no great pre-Columbian civilization was there to feed into a nascent political culture.

This line of argumentation does not seem cogent. It is not clear in what direct way tribalism and *caciquismo* entered Venezuelan national identity,[115] or, in what way they affected its *political* development. This account is especially problematic because Vallenilla does not examine the relations of exploitation and oppression between whites and "Indians." He simply examines the Indian groups and their supposed legacy abstracted from social relations with the dominant white groups. Moreover, we can compare these less-developed Indian groups such as the Caribs to tribes in the United States. The fact that similar warrior tribes that did not have advanced civilizations existed in North America did not prevent the United States from becoming a stable democratic state.

Still, Vallenilla could answer with his insistent idea that miscegenation was conse-quential. In the United States, the vast majority of Native Americans were extermi-nated. But he asserts that this was far from the case in Venezuela. Again positing an idea that was anathema to many of his contemporaries, he claims that all persons, even whites, in Venezuela had Indian blood. "It was indigenous blood that was predominant in the makeup of the Venezuelan people; not just among the so-called 'people of color,' but also in the immense majority of whites and even among the *mantuanos*, who con-sidered themselves to be pure descendants of the Conquistadores."[116] In effect, Vallenilla claims that *all* people in his country are of mixed blood, even those who claimed a right to rule as a result of their ties to putatively pure Iberian roots. In this manner Vallenilla undermines the claim, made commonly by many of his contemporaries, that there is a natural hierarchy or implicit nobility in Latin American peoples that is determined by the amount of "pure" Spanish or European blood in a person or family.

Importantly, this argument has other ramifications in Vallenilla's concept of race. In spite of arguing that Indian and African tribalism slowed down the political develop-ment of the Venezuelan nation, Vallenilla goes on to say that intelligence has nothing to do with one's race. This contradictory or paradoxical way of thinking, which on the one hand posits an arrested development caused by nonwhite cultures, and, on the other, the belief that race does not determine intelligence, is found in key passages of Vallenilla's writings on race. Fundamentally, it can be explained by his idea that racial heterogeneity does not produce degeneration or inferiority, but socially complex and problematic polit-ical orders.[117] A *población policroma*, or polychromatic people, yields social disintegration and possible political anarchy. Vallenilla insists that his theory is not racist, for "ethnic or-igins explain nothing by themselves; they are merely one factor in the development [*evo-lución*] of our peoples. No nation, no individual is more or less intelligent, or more or less courageous, or more or less apt for civilization because they belong to this or that race."[118]

In spite of his fundamentally antiracist view of race and identity, Vallenilla made the serious mistake of advocating European immigration as one possible solution to the prob-lems of racial heterogeneity. He consistently critiqued Spanish maltreatment of native Americans; he pointed to the political role of African influences; and he favored the view that racial miscegenation is admirable rather than execrable. But in his position of influ-ence, Vallenilla urged more European migration to Venezuela to attenuate social instabil-ity.[119] Pushing aside his more enlightened contributions, he implicitly posits a cultural (not racial) superiority of white, European culture over that of Indians and blacks. This error is egregious and cannot be reconciled with his critical writings on race and his advocacy of racial admixture.[120] However, we cannot assert that Vallenilla advocated the whitening or "bleaching" of Venezuelan society (especially considering that he believed the Indian influence on Venezuelan blood was most powerful). He ultimately wanted to promote greater miscegenation. This policy directive of increasing European migration, though, did not meet with great success. The policy that he did advocate more strongly, however, in order to promote political and social stability was that of democratic Caesarism.

Democratic Caesarism as a Response to Racial Heterogeneity

Despite important errors, Vallenilla's views on race were progressive in nature, recognizing its social construction, promoting racial mixture during a time of deep racialism, and recognizing subsequent political complications. Racial diversity and mixing were to be admired, but had a problematic dimension. The concept of *cesarismo democrático* is itself paradoxical and is an example of syncretic political thinking.[121] It is paradoxical, for it combines two principles that are usually opposed to each other, just as the mixing of white and black people was considered negative by most of Vallenilla's contemporaries. It is a hybrid concept that Vallenilla uses to explain social reality in Venezuela and the rest of Latin America. It also becomes normative hand in hand with its theoretical formulation. For Vallenilla, it is the response to racial heterogeneity and mixture, for it is the pragmatic way to control the tensions that appear from highly mixed societies. Vallenilla does not believe that harmony easily arises from increased intermixing. Democracy *tout court* is not possible; it requires the strong arm of a powerful executive.

The hybrid notion of *cesarismo democrático* is not untenable. It is a cogent conceptualization of a modern form of politics. Far from being an apology for tyranny or crude dictatorship, it is an extension of Bolívar's republicanism into the field of twentieth-century politics. In the section "The Constitutional Principles of the Liberator," Vallenilla argues that the social bases (that is, heterogeneous and mixed racial composition) of Latin America led Bolívar to argue for a *presidente vitalicio* (lifetime president), something that falls squarely into a Caesarist conception of democracy. He saw the same phenomenon in Paraguay, Argentina, Ecuador, Mexico, and Colombia, with the example of the Bolivian constitution written by Bolívar as the "natural" form of government for the mixed societies of Spanish America.[122]

This idea fits into the Machiavellian line of thinking (one of many in the republican tradition) because it corresponds to the relationship that exists between the two primary works by the Florentine, *The Discourses on Livy* and *The Prince*. Rather than simply looking at the former text as proto-democratic and ignoring the second, or focusing on the latter as a handbook for tyrants and ignoring the first, any proper understanding of Machiavelli's oeuvre must take both into account. It is a perspective that is aware of the centrality of the *popolari*, or average citizens, but also of the *grandi*, the leadership of a state. It is true that Machiavelli favored the people[123] over elites, as opposed to Guicciardini, for instance, but it is also true that in *The Prince* Machiavelli emphasizes the importance of a strong executive and, in particular, of a strong individual leader. The many and the one must find balance. We must also recall that Machiavelli finds value in the institutionalization of dictatorship in the ancient Roman Republic. The heading of chapter 34 of Book One of the *Discourses* is "The dictatorial authority did good and not harm to the Roman republic; and that the authority which citizens take away, not those are given them by free suffrage, are pernicious to civil society." It tells us that "it is seen that the Dictatorship while it was given according to public orders and not by individual authority, always did good to the City" because "it was not the name or the rank of Dictator that placed Rome in servitude, but it was the authority taken by the Citizens to perpetuate themselves in the Empire (government): and if the title of Dictator did not exist in Rome, they would have taken another."[124]

A similar institutional defense of a strong executive is encapsulated by the tenet of *cesarismo democrático*. A nascent state that is weak and divided requires the strong leadership of one person who will act for the common good and under the rule of law.[125] Republicanism in the Machiavellian tradition is a "theory of political liberty that considers citizens' participation in sovereign deliberation necessary *only* when it remains within well-defined boundaries,"[126] not in every form or instance of legislation. The constitutionally bound dictator cannot modify existing laws, abrogate or alter the constitution, or change the organization of political institutions, which differentiates him from a tyrant. At the same time, we must underscore an important contribution that Vallenilla made regarding the concept of democracy. He did not believe that it was a principle that could be universally applied in the same fashion in different cultural, social, and historical circumstances. Each nation-state has its own characteristics, and democracy means a different thing for each, if anything at all. Vallenilla argued that democracy had a very distinctive meaning in the Americas vis-à-vis Europe. He was thinking primarily of Spanish America, but also of the United States.

Essentially, Vallenilla believed that a strong executive with broad powers was consonant with democracy under certain conditions. The idea of a General Will, or the will of the people, was a chimera. A single leader is necessary for the interests of the *demos* to be realized. He saw this effect in the Latin American tradition of *caudillismo*, but also in the United States' presidential system of democracy, where the executive is central to the workings of politics. He found evidence for this in Woodrow Wilson, and it is something that we can trace to the legacy of Andrew Jackson. More specifically, Vallenilla believed that throughout the Americas democracy was buttressed by the concept and reality of equality. Unlike European democracies, where equality was largely formal and abstract, American (both North and South) notions of democracy were conceived on real egalitarianism. In the United States this took form in the erasure of rigid social distinctions. In Latin America, for Vallenilla, this was principally evident in the facts of racial heterogeneity (the existence of many races) and of racial miscegenation (mixing among the various races),[127] creating, in his view, a literal egalitarianism at the level of social ontology. The People gain an identity: that is, the population becomes the same owing to racial intermixing over a long period of time. For Vallenilla, the national leader should reflect this mixing personally.

Purely formalistic understandings of democracy are inadequate in this view. Reducing democracy to regular elections does not yield true equality.[128] In the Latin American context, it only produces struggles for political power that become petty and substance-free. Using the English terms, Vallenilla calls it a struggle between "the *ins* and the *outs*,"[129] that is, those in power versus those seeking power. The result is a vacuous and often corrupting competition based solely on self-interest, using political parties as vehicles for self-gain.[130] But Vallenilla finds that the Latin American tradition of accepting a caudillo or leader can break this chain of corruption. A "prestigious personality"[131] is thus necessary to diminish the negative effects of party politicking. In addition, Vallenilla repeats the point that mass poverty is a recurring ill in most Latin American societies. Economic inequality usually becomes aggravated under liberal-democratic regimes, for parties are controlled by leading families and elites that use them to entrench their economic dominance. Class distinctions become exacerbated, and misery becomes widespread. Hardly a Marxian thinker,[132] Vallenilla did believe that classes were buttressed by liberal democratic electoral systems.

In the text *Democratic Caesarism*, written in 1919, four years after his early thoughts on the concept of race, Vallenilla employs this conception of democracy. He seeks to find the *effective* social bases of Venezuela's constitution.[133] The use of the term "effective" shows a deeply Machiavellian conception of order. For the Florentine, a surface of appearances covers a true reality that he calls *"la verità effetuale della cosa"* in chapter 15 of *The Prince*: the effective truth of things. Vallenilla, much like Bolívar, is a profoundly Machiavellian thinker. While references to Machiavelli are not omnipresent, the fact is that Vallenilla admired the Italian statesman highly. In response to the accusation that his thought was Machiavellian, he declared that he was proud to be called by such a term. He himself used the phrase "el Maquiavelo de América" consciously, seeking to defend a view of politics not principally grounded on ethical norms but on social facts.[134]

Vallenilla takes his cue from Bolívar's Angostura Discourse. It is there, as we saw in the last chapter, that we find a synthetic conception of Latin American identity in general. Now Vallenilla wants to apply this conception to a particular, Venezuelan setting. As he would write later in *Disgregación e Integración*, "We will not fall into the error that some foreign and Latin American writers have made of grouping together all Hispanic nations into one category, since we have a particular ethnic composition, which is our own mix of Spaniards, Indians, and blacks."[135] Thus, Vallenilla sees that while most Latin American nations evince miscegenation, each particular area and nation in the region possesses a particular composition of racial admixture.

Venezuela, being the *Libertador's* homeland, has a special position in this Machiavellian-Bolivarian tradition that Vallenilla continues.[136] It is in this nation that Bolívar developed his conception of the racial republic. Vallenilla extends the Bolivarian insight about mixed-race identity.[137] Neither Vallenilla nor Bolívar, though, advocates a particular racial identity as a prerequisite for republican order. But republican order must be cognizant of the particular culture and ethnoracial realities that exist in the land where they seek to install a political regime. In addition, Vallenilla follows some theoretical defenses of a strong executive. For Bolívar, *tiranía* contains a "paradox."[138] Sometimes it is entirely negative when a people are subjected to the whims of a foreign tyrant. But it is an "active tyranny"—with a somewhat positive effect—when a domestic tyrant emerges, allowing the people to learn from the experience of his rule. While Vallenilla does not endorse the classical concept of tyranny, he does agree with Bolívar that a domestic dictator can in fact act to the benefit of a people. Bolívar's belief that Spanish-American ethnoracial mixing could be the source of political tensions was also influential in Vallenilla's belief that a dictator could mitigate them.[139]

Vallenilla begins his key text by declaring that the admixture of races and ethnicities is not only found in Spanish America, but in the Iberian peninsula as well. Moreover, this claim means that there is no natural nobility that derives its authority from "pure" white blood. He affirms that *mantuanismo*, the colonial nobility to which Bolívar himself belonged, inevitably possessed "a great quantity of Indian and black blood," and that Spaniards too, "even those of the highest nobility, were mixed with Moors and Jews."[140] He obviates the widespread Hispanic American prejudice, he says, which views Spaniards as a "pure race" (*raza pura*); the fact is that Phoenicians, Carthaginians, Greeks, Romans, and Arabs mixed with the local populations in Spain. Thus, the *madre patria* was a crossroads of racial and ethnic mixture. Much like Vasconcelos and Freyre later on, Vallenilla would emphasize the erotic dimensions of Peninsular attitudes to nonwhites: "It is indubitable that Spaniards mixed with black Africans, knowing the scruples of Mediterranean Europeans with regard to mixing with anthropologically distinct races."[141]

A propensity to have erotic relations with the natives distinguished the Spanish from the English, according to Vallenilla. It led to different colonial relations, and different form of social development (*evolución*). Vallenilla refers to Tocqueville's remarks that the English were also much less inclined toward miscegenation than the French.[142] Spanish kings, such as Phillip II, had relations with African slaves brought to him as gifts. The Inquisition tried to ascertain *pureza de sangre*, or purity of blood, and this led to *estatutos de limpieza de sangre*, which were in effect in Venezuela up until the wars of independence. But these inquiries into purity of blood often found the opposite: Fray Agustín Salucio would discern that even the most eminent among the Spanish nobility had Jewish or Moorish origins, what was then considered "what is most vile in the world."[143]

Religion, in a sense, outweighed race in Europe. That is to say, religious heterogeneity was not acceptable, for Christian values were to be dominant over Jewish or Muslim ideas. This was the case in Spain and in France, according to Vallenilla. A similar emphasis on religious homogeneity could be found among Muslims: in spite of great racial diversity and mixing, monotheistic religions tend to demand uniformity of belief. But in Latin America such was not the case, according to Vallenilla. Social relations were not determined by religious affiliation, but rather by the "color of the skin" owing to racial heterogeneity.[144] Two opposing forces met each other: dicta related to finding *pureza de sangre*, and the social reality of miscegenation. In effect, what these inquiries found is that "the older the family in question, the more likely the existence of African blood in its origins."[145] In Venezuelan society, the term "white" was a purely formalistic and legal one, not one based on social fact. It was a term of legal status, which whites used to distinguish themselves from mestizo persons. But in fact, Vallenilla tells us, citing Pedro

Manuel Arcaya, most people formally declared "white" in the late colonial censuses were in truth mestizos. The confusions over purity of race were such that, as Gil Fortoul would argue, some peninsular Spaniards were darker than American mestizos.[146]

The paradox that took place in Venezuela was that racial prejudice became deeply entrenched precisely *because* of the high degree of miscegenation. In particular, *pardos* born of Spanish and black intermixing became a very sizable population, threatening the interests of elite Creoles. Hence, as the vast majority of the masses were *pardos* broadly understood, elites feared their ascendancy. Vallenilla reminds us that, for Tocqueville, preoccupation over racial status and identity was strongest amongst the states in the United States that had abolished slavery. For Vallenilla, "There has never been, historically, a pure race anywhere in the world."[147] Nevertheless, this fact was resisted everywhere racial mixing took place. Vallenilla denounces the "defeated science" of Gobineau for its erroneous belief in the negative aspects of increased European racial promiscuity with non-Europeans.[148] Following Topinard,[149] Vallenilla tried, through theoretical contributions, to show that races are merely "conceptions" and not biological realities.

The political consequence of this is pithily summarized in Vallenilla's declaration that "entre raza y nación no existe hoy ninguna relación."[150] That is, there is no relationship between races and nations; a state cannot be justified or legitimated on fundamentally racial grounds.[151] Against the conception of Gobineau and other Europeans who considered race the dominant principle for political organization, growth, and possible decay, Vallenilla wants to underscore the racial "heterogeneity" that is the very fiber of Venezuelan society. This heterogeneity, found in colonial times, persists in independent Venezuela. In order to prevent it from becoming anarchic or leading to racial conflict, a "necessary gendarme" state must be constructed.

In *Cesarismo Democrático*, Vallenilla wants to analyze objectively the causes and uses of *caudillismo*. In this tradition, leaders are not chosen, they impose themselves. This conception of leadership is Machiavellian and finds its roots in *The Prince*. The figure of Cesare Borgia as a Spanish caudillo is most apt. Through *virtù* and Fortune, Borgia pacified and controlled the Romagna. This move entailed force, fraud, foresight, and flexibility, forming in the process the basis of order in a state that is created out of anarchic conditions. "It is the typical character of a martial state," as Vallenilla avers.[152] As we saw in analyzing Bolívar's Machiavellian perspective, it is a situation where the army is society mobilized, and society is the army in repose. For Vallenilla, a leader must be the head or capital force of a mass. Just as Machiavelli's Prince must impose form on a fractious entity, the necessary gendarme state must be wrought out of brute conditions.[153] According to Taine, Vallenilla argues, the herd must be tamed by one man. From this struggle, one leader, the caudillo, emerges, and he is usually a military man, an "executioner."[154]

What distinguishes Vallenilla's account of the princely, extraordinary man from that of Bolívar or Machiavelli is the social context from which he emerges. Not only is it one of anarchic conditions, as for the Florentine, or one of racial diversity, as with the *Libertador*, but it is one where widespread economic poverty is a dominant phenomenon. "Misery" is a recurring theme in the writings of Vallenilla. Here we find that political theory cannot remain formalistic, that is, concerned with the institutions that can be fashioned for a state. The context of economic disparity is such that it must come to the fore when an ideal constitution or regime is developed. Vallenilla reminds us that misery was endemic from the early years of the nineteenth century.[155] Fraud and corruption in the economic sense were also pervasive.[156] Vallenilla does not carry out a class analysis of the Marxian kind to explicate this inequality, because he believes inequality is fundamentally social rather than economic, and that it ultimately goes back to racial diversity and distinctions. Poverty matters, but only as a context for the playing-out of ethnoracial tensions. Still, Vallenilla moves us forward to a more contemporary setting where we recognize the significance of widespread economic inequality in the first years of the twentieth century.

Thus, given this social context of poverty and racial distinctions in spite of pervasive ethnoracial intermixing, finding institutional solutions was a difficult challenge. Vallenilla goes back to Bolívar's Machiavellism: "The *Libertador* was convinced that it was necessary to unleash a 'cruel energy in order to attune the state.'"[157] Under conditions of war and misery, there was no time for reformist institution-building. A man capable of swift, brutal repression was needed; a man like Bolívar. Vallenilla reminds us of Bolívar's darker, Machiavellian side, able to perform "well-used cruelties": "I have given the order to execute all rebels. I have ordered capital punishment for all crimes against the State."[158]

Bolívar, as Vallenilla was rightly aware, was fearful of *pardocracia*, because the mulatto, another term for *pardo*, was seen as fractious. Vallenilla agrees with Domingo Sarmiento's caricaturish description of the mulatto: a man of "burning imagination; an individualist and leveler, social-climber and anarchic, a 'servile but ambitious race.'"[159] Thus, the basis of Bolívar's constitutional order, according to Vallenilla, was formed by racial dynamics. Vallenilla does not disagree with this premise, for he finds it apt for most of Latin America. After 1824, according to Vallenilla, Bolívar became chiefly concerned with social reorganization, not independence. Once freedom from Spain was achieved, domestic order became a national necessity. The increasingly mixed masses became larger as time progressed throughout the nineteenth century and into the twentieth. This mass was disordered, better described as "anarcho-pardia," as it were. And for Vallenilla, this is the *demos* that Venezuela inherited. The Machiavellian, strong, sometimes cruel leader was needed to control this *demos*, and thus a modern Caesarism was proposed by Vallenilla.

Rather than seeing Vallenilla as an apologist of tyranny, as many have seen him over time,[160] we should interpret his ideas as a particularly Latin American brand of (conservative) republicanism. Critics have judged him to be merely a defender of autocracy. But in fact we must understand his thought, especially in relation to the idea of *cesarismo democrático* and his views on race, as a conservative reaction to the more "liberal" republicanism of Bolívar. Moreover, Vallenilla's ideas are not close to fascism, something that was also claimed given Vallenilla's admiration for Mussolini.

There are various reasons for a republican understanding of *cesarismo democrático*. Above all, he sought to underscore the principles of the common good and the rule of law. To be sure, he was deeply skeptical of liberal thought, but he did not develop a defense or justification for arbitrary power. Vallenilla sought to define an institutionally delimited form of government to locate the authority of the executive. He did favor a strong leader, but nowhere did he advocate autocracy or the supremacy of the president outside of the boundaries of state mechanisms. He believed that a strong executive with a long term of office would be the best solution to the social turbulence that emerges in a racially mixed society. Throughout his writings, Vallenilla shows his patriotic concern, which reflects his belief in the common good. He does not argue for *cesarismo democrático* for the purpose of the enrichment or benefit of the president. What may be considered problematic is the degree of representation that the people may have in his system. But representation and participation are not the most fundamental components of a republican form of government.[161] More critical are the elements of the common good and the rule of law, as applied to a particular culture within a nation. Vallenilla attempted a culturally nuanced understanding of the specific social conditions of his *patria*, along with the institutional mechanism that would produce stability given diverse collective social actors. Unlike liberalism, republicanism conceives of social order as a balance of collective group interests, not individuals. The same can be said for Vallenilla's perspective.

But this system is still far from fascistic politics. Vallenilla's thought lacks the basic components of fascist ideology: chauvinistic nationalism, militarism, corporatism, personalistic rule, and totalitarianism. Vallenilla was patriotic without being chauvinistic;[162] he never argued that Venezuela was the most advanced among Latin American nations. Moreover, he did not urge the militarization of the state, especially for the purpose of war with neighboring states. While he believed Venezuela had a distinctive national character, he also believed it shared much in common with other Latin American nations. In addition, while he believed society should be understood organically, he did not advocate a corporatist view of government made up of estates. Most of his major writings were composed before the rise of Gómez, and he never pronounced this dictator the embodiment of the Venezuelan nation. Last, he did not advocate the complete control of society by a centralized state. Thus, he was far from totalitarian, fascistic politics in spite of his misguided admiration for Benito Mussolini.

The Problems of Late-Modern Mass Society in Comparative Perspective

Vallenilla's writings anticipate some of the central theoretical problems of the politics of late modernity. Besides his discussion of the relevance of racial social foundations to a polity—which shows the importance of social theory to political theory—Vallenilla also pointed to critical issues in modern mass societies that find resonance in the German social and political theorists Max Weber and Carl Schmitt.[163] These involve the unsustainability of liberal democratic regimes, and the related emergence of dictatorial politics, discussed under the rubrics of *Cäsarismus* by Weber and *Diktatur* by Schmitt. In Vallenilla's writings, links to the thought of these German theorists appear. While Vallenilla was most closely associated to French social thought, especially in the development of his synthetic conception of race, his ideas of democratic Caesarism and the "necessary gendarme" connect to German social thought as well. However, given Vallenilla's repudiation of racist and racialist ideas in which race is seen as a fixed and hierarchical category, he never endorsed a theory of nationalism or fascism. Vallenilla was indeed concerned with developing a particular sense of Venezuelan nationality, but it never devolved into a crude nationalism that would slide into the militarism, totalitarian politics, antirationalism, or an (anti-Semitic) emphasis on racial purity that were emblematic of German fascism in the form of National Socialism, with which Schmitt was closely associated as a member of the Nazi Party.

Like Vallenilla, Schmitt endorsed dictatorship.[164] But they support this form of rule for different reasons. Vallenilla emphasized the specifically republican conception of dictatorship. He trod a fine line between republicanism and a more authoritarian form of rule in his *Cesarismo Democrático* of 1919. Two years later, Schmitt crossed this line in his work *On Dictatorship*. The theoretical factors for Vallenilla are again located in the fact of Latin America's racial heterogeneity, whereas Schmitt was concerned with the legal and juridical idea of sovereignty, in which he understood the power of the executive or the dictator as a state of exception that is prolonged. For Schmitt, the problem of liberalism is that it is an extension of the logic of technological rationality into the sphere of politics. The "technical character of dictatorship" that Machiavelli emphasizes is part of Schmitt's own critique.[165]

The problem of modern Caesarism is ultimately Machiavellian.[166] Schmitt points out that, in the *Discourses*, Machiavelli admires the way dictatorship was institutionalized by the Roman Republic.[167] The dictator was appointed by the consuls on petition by the Senate. "He was not bound by law and acted as a kind of king with unlimited authority over life or death."[168] At the same time, Schmitt sees that the Machiavellian understanding of the dictator differs from the "tyrant, and dictatorship is not some form of absolute domination but rather a republican constitution's proper means of protecting liberty."[169] While Vallenilla followed Bolívar's martial Machiavellian republicanism into the twentieth century, he tried to remain within a republican constitutional structure. In this sense, Schmitt's underscoring of the purely technical (as opposed to ethical) approach of Machiavellian views of dictatorship resemble Vallenilla's concerns with a stable political order suitable for a society that is (racially and economically) fragmented.[170]

At the same time, we must underscore the fact that Vallenilla also preceded Schmitt on the issue of "political theology." In 1920 Vallenilla wrote a critique of Colombia's excessive clerical power and its effect on the polity.[171] Schmitt's famous essay on political theology appeared in 1922. The commonalities are not evident, but it is important to note the related terminology. At the core, their projects are similar: to justify "sovereign dictatorial powers" for the executive.[172] Again, this similarity derived from the fact that both saw liberal democracy as inadequate for the governance of late-modern societies. For Schmitt, a quasi-religious redemption exists when liberal political order is rescued by the state of exception and dictatorial action.[173] Thus, the modern state is a product of secularized theological concepts. In Vallenilla's view, a society that is unable to establish sovereignty on purely secular grounds, as he saw the case in Colombia, should be characterized as dominated by "political theology."

Schmitt's *Nomos of the Earth* (*Nomos der Erde*) dates the emergence of a Eurocentric world order to the period of the Americas' discovery. He shares with Vallenilla an appreciation of the historico-theoretical importance of the New World to global politics. However, Vallenilla rejects the idea that theoretical models developed in Europe can be easily applied to postcolonial societies such as those of Latin America. Moreover, in "The Concept of the Political" (1927) Schmitt develops a negative conception of the political community: the state is defined against an enemy.[174] In the work of Vallenilla that community is positive: it is an expression of a national character developed over time and rooted in specific autochthonous conditions, without the need for external enemies— one reason that Vallenilla's concept of Venezuelan nationality does not emerge into a militant nationalism. In Vallenilla's eyes, the populations of Venezuela and its neighbors (Colombia above all) and the rest of Latin America are all related closely in terms of racial and ethnic identity. This fact prevented him from articulating an agonistic conception of international relations within the austral Americas. Thus, Vallenilla's work is a critique of liberal democracy that does not fall into the sense of *agon* that permeated some critics of liberalism in Europe. For this reason it did not involve any mystification or mythology of racial identity, but rather an effort to use quasi-scientific positivism to undermine racialist views.

Max Weber, like Vallenilla, believed mass democracy was "democracy in name only."[175] He saw Caesarism as a way to deal with the excessive power of modern bureaucracies. Thus, their concerns with the same issue came from very different origins. For Weber, Caesarism represented the defects of Bismarckian rule. At the same time, it showed the possible proactive powers of leadership, and exists in relation to charisma.[176] What is important at this juncture is to show that, from very different perspectives, the idea of Caesarism as both a problem and a solution in modern states appeared roughly around the same time in Europe and in South America. Liberal democracy was seen as an inadequate institutional mechanism to create real, as opposed to formal, equality in Venezuela, and as unable to rein in the power of bureaucratic machineries in Germany. Both Weber and Vallenilla saw Caesarism (in objective sociological terms) as a way out of the modern impasse of the liberal democratic state in mass societies. Both saw Caesarism as a product of the ineffectual leadership of both the bourgeois and the proletarian social classes of their respective countries.[177] And both saw Caesarism as reconcilable with the rule of law (Bolivarian republican constitutionalism for Vallenilla, and a parliamentary system for Weber).[178]

In Vallenilla's eyes, the attempt to develop liberalism in Venezuela was an all-around failure. Economic liberalism, federalism, political parties, and liberal constitutions all contributed to this failed attempt.[179] Laissez-faire economic policies were inadequate, given that mercantilism was the dominant economic form before 1830. Regional oligarchies developed throughout Venezuela, entrenching their economic and social power, which devolved into political power, especially in the form of regional caudillos. This development was another reason for the rejection of a free-market model, since it would not benefit the ruling classes. Vallenilla points to the specifically racial reasons for the push toward a federal constitution: the desire to maintain a separation of racial groups in a heterogeneous population. Vallenilla believed decentralization, for this reason, was a tendency in most of Latin America, but it was a mistake given the weak states that prevailed. For Vallenilla a more centralized state grounded by a strong executive, as Bolívar desired, was a better idea. Federalism only aided the political ambitions of local caudillos. The historical political parties represented entrenched rather than open constituencies. For instance the *Partido Conservador de Caracas* was made up of middle-class interests, according to Vallenilla. This *godo* party was in fact liberal, not *mantuano*. In other words it supported liberal causes such as laissez-faire economic policies.[180] But for Vallenilla, such parties were artificial obstacles to the progress toward natural equality that was taking place at the social level. These parties also battled local caudillos, whom Vallenilla considered to be the natural leaders of social groups in Venezuela. For Vallenilla, caudillos like Páez, Monagas, Guzmán Blanco, Crespo, Castro, Gómez, and so on were representative of popular interests, whereas political parties aligned to liberal ideas were chiefly elitist. The "natural" egalitarianism that Vallenilla referred to was due to the "admixture of races" that was effectively taking place at the grassroots level of Venezuelan society.[181]

While Vallenilla shares with Weber and Schmitt a critical perspective on liberal democracy, he was able to avoid some traps that hindered the two late-modern German critics. He eluded the sometimes "imperialistic" language of Weber,[182] and he did not engage in the fascistic logic that Schmitt found alluring. Owing to his awareness of the racial diversity, heterogeneity, and mixing inherent in Venezuelan society and its historical roots, Vallenilla was averse to forms of nationalism dependent on the assumptions of purity of blood, contained in concepts such as *Volk* or *Herrenvolk*. At no point in his intellectual life did Vallenilla advocate a sense of nationhood in Venezuela that would be comparatively superior to that of Colombia or Spain, for example. Neither did he believe in any particular link between racial or blood ties and the need for expansionary, imperialistic foreign relations.

Conclusion

Let us not speak, then, of "race." It is an anthropological term that does not have any sociological reality and which cannot explain anything when one tries to apply it to the development of a people. Let us speak of Society, People, Nation. Studying scientifically each of these terms, we will come to the conclusion that, whatever our ethnic origin, Venezuela is above all a social entity, defined psychologically and politically, even when compared to other Latin American nations.

These words, written in 1930 in *Disgregación e Integración*, get to the essence of Vallenilla's project. He found race to be a central issue of political modernity.[183] But he did not believe it was possible to reduce it to a biological or natural-scientific definition. It is, above all, a socially constructed term. It is intimately tied to the political; hence, he examined the state as a central institution in a modern nation like Venezuela. And his own country's specificity had to be examined per se, not as a simple iteration of the Latin American condition.

Vallenilla shows us, at the same time, that not all European thinkers at the turn of the century were mired in the generally hegemonic domination paradigm of race. His intellectual development is a result of the interactions of European, mainly French, ideas in sociology and history, with the Latin American forms of republican theory. The interaction of these two intellectual lineages was applied to the situation of his own country but also of Latin America in general. From thinkers such as Jacques Novicow he would incorporate nonessentialist views of race. "Happily, for humanity, countless facts show conclusively that there is no link between some ideas and some anthropological types [races]. Whites have had, throughout the centuries, ideas that differ little from those of blacks."[184] In Venezuela, he believed, it was decisive to understand the interaction and complications of the social composition created by miscegenation between Indians, Africans, and Europeans. But this, against Renan, did not mean that there were "superior or inferior races, or noble or ignoble races."[185]

Even as he did not want to perpetuate the use of the term "race," Vallenilla believed it was an ineluctable concept of modernity. No full account of a nation's reality could do without an analysis, both historical and sociological, of race. For this reason he preferred to refer to "social race," since, in his view, race did not have biological meaning.[186] In his analysis of Venezuela, he used a synthetic conception of race, one in which diverse elements came together to form a new entity. Vallenilla made errors of judgment in dealing with some cardinal issues, such as the role of climate and immigration, and he failed to critically analyze the "white" race. But he promoted the idea that there is no such thing as a pure race, and that political thought cannot dispense with a critical perspective on this issue. As a positivist, he believed his role was to provide the intellectual bases for building a stable, ordered society. Such was his faith in reason and the state, pillars of the height of modernity. This faith, however, would not go unchallenged in the waning days of the modern era, as we shall see in the next chapter's analysis of the work of José Vasconcelos, a thinker who—while associated intimately with his nation of Mexico—posed a puissant challenge to nationalism.

4

THE CITIZENSHIP OF BEAUTY

José Vasconcelos's Aesthetic Synthesis of Race

FAR FROM BEING merely a nationalist convulsion, the Mexican Revolution was a profoundly transnational affair. The eminent historian Friedrich Katz tells us that it did not take place in isolation but involved a transformation of the northern frontier into the border, a hybrid area of Latin American, European, and U.S. influences.[2] Through its upheavals and displacement of people, as well as its beckoning of foreigners to Mexico during the long period that it covered, the Revolution made of Mexico a veritable cauldron of ideas and intertwined lives. It created legends out of men, both in the political and in the cultural spheres. From Madero to Villa to Zapata, as well as icons such as the photographers Tina Modotti and Edward Weston or the Cuban Communist Julio Antonio Mella, the Revolution allowed people with creative energy to flourish in the midst of social and political tumults.

One such person on the intellectual plane was José Vasconcelos. Arguably the leading figure of Latin American philosophy of the first half of the twentieth century,[3] Vasconcelos's career as a lawyer, philosopher, *letrado*, and public figure spanned a vast swath of the long Mexican Revolution, which began in 1910.[4] Upon his death in 1959, the year of the Cuban Revolution, Vasconcelos had created a profound cultural transformation not only in the Mexican but also the Latin American landscape. In his person ideas that burgeoned in the colonial period coalesce with concerns that were central in the republican period of Latin American history. Vasconcelos's staunch Catholicism, especially at the end of his life, fused with his lifelong passion for his motherland, but in the end this blend produced a new and original set of ideas about the import of Latin America that transcended those two influences, even if those ideas were surrounded by muddled, sometimes incoherent paradoxes.[5] And he was someone whose plans never fully came to fruition, someone whose name was lauded and cursed by history at different times.

Vasconcelos provides us, in his penetrating though sometimes baroque writings, a vision of synthesis that encapsulates the movement of the idea of race from its germination in the thought of Las Casas, to the republican ambitions of Bolívar[6] and the nationalist aims of Vallenilla Lanz, to a late-modern, cosmopolitan period. In a sense, Vasconcelos was responding indirectly to Vallenilla, for the Mexican thinker believed the nationalist period showed that "caesarism is the scourge of the Latin race."[7]

For Vasconcelos, synthesis was a fundamental response to previous intellectual developments in Latin America.[8] Not content with the haphazard nature—in his view—of much of Latin American philosophy, he sought a philosophical system that was coherent and built from complementary parts. Whether he succeeded or not is debatable, for his philosophical and literary output had mixed results. Yet when it comes to the problem of race in the history of Latin American thought, it is impossible to elude Vasconcelos's oeuvre. In Vasconcelos, we find the synthesis of two strains we have encountered in previous chapters. The particularism of nation-states, which was a central component in republicanism, is present. Moreover, the universalism of Roman Catholic political theology of the colonial era is there as well. Vasconcelos joins these two strains together. In this fusion we find his account of race in late modernity. It is the fourth and last stage in the genealogy of the modern synthetic conceptualization of race in the Spanish American tradition.

In this chapter, I argue that in Vasconcelos's works culminates the synthetic approach to racial identity. I posit that, while most interpretations of Vasconcelos's account of race have understood it as a product of Mexican mestizo nationalism, in fact his understanding of race originates in his philosophy.[9] More specifically, it is a consequence of his philosophical aesthetics, or how he views the nature of art and beauty. In focusing on his philosophical project, I also examine one particular influence on his philosophical aesthetics, Friedrich Nietzsche, whom Vasconcelos mentions in a number of central passages. Thus, this chapter explores Vasconcelos's account of race through the prism of his aesthetics as influenced by the German philosopher. It seeks to see Vasconcelos's notion of race as a product of having Nietzsche as an implicit interlocutor, and how Vasconcelos conceives of synthesis.

This exploration does not claim that there is identity between all of the ideas of these thinkers. What it does is to tease out the implications of thinking about race along aesthetic lines, which is what I believe Vasconcelos does. Nietzsche and Vasconcelos do not coincide on all matters racial or aesthetic, yet reading Vasconcelos in light of one of his most significant influences shows that the synthetic paradigm of race in Latin American thought came to rely on a particular conception of aesthetics as a way to define the "Latin" or "cosmic" race, once the discourse of empire (in early modernity) and that of the nation (at the apex of the modern) were no longer cogent on a wide scale. In a sense, art, beauty, and form (and more broadly, cultural production) came to sustain the idea of race when imperialism and nationalism were no longer tenable.

From Revolution to Reaction: Vasconcelos's Personal Trajectory

Born in Oaxaca, Mexico, in 1882 of mostly European blood, Vasconcelos spent much of his early life on the border, the area between the United States and his home country. Through this experience, he witnessed the tensions and antagonism between the two cultures, something that would mark him forever.

In his years as a student, he focused mainly on law. The predominant intellectual atmosphere of the time was Comtean positivism, a philosophy of social science that was pervasive throughout Latin America at the turn of the century, as we saw in the work of Vallenilla. It was the dominant ideology of the Porfiriato: the autocratic rule of Porfirio Díaz, which would eventually fall under the pressures of the Revolution of 1910. In this long period of authoritarian rule, Vasconcelos worked tirelessly for democracy, joining the ranks of those opposing the reelection of Díaz. For this, he was exiled, and spent much of his time in the United States.

The exiled Vasconcelos began to study philosophy and the thought of India at the New York Public Library. Immersed in ideas, he eventually resurfaced to political life when Francisco Madero deposed Díaz, and the exile returned to his homeland to become an *engagé* intellectual. But the tumultuous events of the Revolution did not allow for stability: Madero was assassinated, and Vasconcelos, as his supporter, had to flee to Europe—where he visited France, Spain, Italy, and England. He returned home when Carranza came to power in 1914, but a year later Vasconcelos broke with Carranza and returned to New York.

In New York he wrote specifically philosophical works, and began to explore ideas in aesthetics. Soon after, however, the peripatetic thinker was on the move again, this time to Lima, Peru, where he worked for a while,[10] and eventually back to the United States, where he opened a small law firm in San Diego. Upon Obregón's overthrow of Carranza, whom Vasconcelos despised, the philosopher once again went back to Mexico, where he was named rector of the National University (UNAM), and eventually minister of education in 1921. It is thus with education that his name is often associated to this day.

In this position, he was able to combine his grand public ambitions with his own personal philosophy. His aesthetic bent led him to commission the gargantuan murals of the UNAM, an important artistic legacy which went side by side with his reform of the national educational system, which allowed for the promotion of both humanistic and technical training.

The Calles regime took power in 1925 and eventually brought forth the *Cristero* revolt, a Catholic movement that was crushed by the anticlerical Calles. Vasconcelos, increasingly Catholic in his thought, opposed Calles and eventually had to flee to Europe again. That same year his most famous work, *La Raza Cósmica*, was published in Spain. At this juncture, Vasconcelos was an almost perennial exile even though he was a deeply committed nationalist. He was to return to Mexico to run for president. And while he was popular, he lost. This dramatic and traumatic defeat was indelible. He left Mexico, only to return in 1940, rife with resentment and incredulous that a man of his caliber could not be elected to the highest office.

The disillusionment after this defeat led to a long period in which he avoided political life and became more entrenched in matters philosophical and literary. His own personal migration toward Catholicism was accentuated by Jesuit friends. At the end of his life, he remained a marginal man, sequestered as head of the national library.

Increasingly fervent about Catholicism, he would write about the positive dimensions of the Church in an excessively uncritical manner. "The Church is always right,"[11] he would say without any care for critical rationality, and forgetting his earlier critiques of the Church's property holdings.[12] He defended the "civilizational" projects of the Church during the colonial period, seemingly unaware, as Las Casas was, of the ravages and atrocities perpetrated by the Spanish conquistadores, whom Vasconcelos admired almost in hero-worship.[13] His explanation was that the ultimate truth rested in the ideas of Catholicism: the pre-Columbian societies were for him barbarous and unworthy of persistence. They lacked, in his view, the idea of *caritas* and the sense of love that, to him, was central to Catholic teachings.

Paradoxically, while these rigid and myopic ideas became more prominent in his personality, they are in some key ways contradicted by his best-known work, *La Raza Cósmica*. In it, he argues that the Latin American peoples are in fact a fusion of a variety of ethnic and racial backgrounds, rather than simply the product of a civilizational mission by Spaniards over the indigenous or the African populations of the Americas. Thus, while he personally became an immured conservative ideologue, theoretically he presented a perspective that would be of great consequence for the idea that race is mixed and fluid, rather than fixed and discrete.

Reading the Import of *La Raza Cósmica*

In the early part of the twentieth century, Latin American intellectuals became increasingly interested in the idea of "the future." José Enrique Rodó's *Ariel* (1900) and Vasconcelos's *La Raza Cósmica* (1925) are the best exemplars. This modernism was of an antipositivist sort. It was a reaction to the Comtean and Spencerian ideas that were so prominent at the turn of the century, especially among liberal members of the local intelligentsia. Both Rodó and Vasconcelos found a response in the idea of the aesthetic. But for them, the aesthetic wasn't simply the experimentation with *l'art pour l'art*; it was, at base, a spiritual phenomenon.

In Rodó's eyes, this aesthetic dimension was one of perfectionism: human beings, of any historical period, could and should develop holistically, in a way that would enhance their artistic abilities and sensibilities.[14] But for Vasconcelos the aesthetic has a temporal dimension: he envisioned a time when persons would eventually be able to be fully aesthetic beings, which was their essence to begin with. For both men, materialism and individualism, of the kind they found common in the United States and the United Kingdom, were anathema.

One of the central ideas of *La Raza Cósmica* is that progress is possible, but it is not one toward greater technological capacity. It is toward what we might consider a quasi-utopian ideal, where socially enforced norms need not to exist. Actions are based on feeling; the *pathos* of aesthetic emotion dictates action; and the principal norm is that of a joy felt when perceiving beauty. This way of life can only be possible in the "Aesthetic or Spiritual era," which Vasconcelos describes in *La Raza Cósmica*. Creative imagination, fantasy, and taste, not rationality, are what humans crave and are destined to develop. The age of reason, initiated in the Enlightenment, would slowly come to an end.

It is difficult to accept the totality of Vasconcelos's utopian vision. It entails an end of "necessity": the end of marriages entered into out of need, the end of social norms, the end of barriers to feeling. It is difficult to believe that a society could exist without some sort of coercive apparatus for the regulation of peace, at the very least. But for our purposes, this vision does have relevant implications for race. For Vasconcelos, this future would erode ethnic barriers, and individuals of diverse races would eventually be able to liberate themselves from social pressures and follow their instincts for beauty, regardless of the race of the person they loved. As a consequence, greater admixture and miscegenation would ensue.

Why does Vasconcelos call this new group the "cosmic" race? It would seem he believes that a new kind of order would prevail in the future if indeed love and affect are the central "norms" (if they can be called that). The notion, in fact, has an anarchic strain, for we can imagine that individuals whose preferences are shaped by desire and affect may in some cases act in ways that do not respect the preferences of others. The equilibrium that Vasconcelos seems to expect appears unwarranted. One way he might support this idea would be to believe most people in the future would agree that this way of life (one guided by love and affect) is indeed the best for all humans. But this is not very plausible. It is likely that a variety of individuals will have conflicting preferences, and these may change over time. It is not at all clear that most would converge on the belief that an aesthetic way of life is unequivocally best for all. People who wish to pursue scientific endeavors, or who want to follow monastic or antiaesthetic preferences, would continue to do so, unless compelled by an "aesthetic majority" to follow the mainstream. But Vasconcelos is curiously quiet about the structural conditions that would lead to the historical stage that would allow for a widespread aesthetically oriented *Weltanschauung*.

It also seems that Vasconcelos calls it the "cosmic" race because it has a cosmopolitan dimension. That is, it transcends nationalistic boundaries. Not only does he expect there to be order in the future "Aesthetic Period," but he expects relations to be those of individuals of any nationality, race, ethnicity, religion, or region of the world. An individual emblematic of his future vision is one who feels free, feels at home wherever he or she goes, and is able to appreciate the local culture (especially the art forms) that he or she encounters. Vasconcelos also argues that that person will actually engage in personal relationships with local people as a consequence of his or her appreciation of the local aesthetic. This elision of nationalistic boundaries allows a cosmopolitan ethos, even if he grants that there are particular regions of the world characterized by regional cultures. It is a grounded cosmopolitanism, rooted in regional cultures rather than specific nationalities.

What appears prescient above all in his analysis is his insistence on the greater prevalence of miscegenation over time. Rodó was silent about this, but Vasconcelos hits the mark when he presages the movement of modernity toward greater intermixing of "racial" types.[15] In addition, he provides a useful conceptualization of race as linked to ethnicity: in other words, race is not merely a biological category, as many early scientific thinkers such as Linnaeus and Blumenbach believed. Rather, it is not possible to speak of race without reference to cultural practices and differences between cultures: this is an idea that we find in Las Casas and which is here recovered by Vasconcelos.

Utopian as they were, Vasconcelos's images of the future make two important contributions. One is the implicit critique of social Darwinism and Spencerianism. While Vasconcelos uses their model of evolutionism, which is then made more philosophical with his three stages (a form of Hegelianism), he moves toward the significance of ethnicity as defining race. This move allows him to incorporate "spiritual" and even moral characteristics into his definition of race. Thus, we are liberated from biological determinism, and can engage in social philosophy in trying to understand what "race" is. Moreover, it allows a critique of the denigration of the "mongrel" human being, which was seen by many European thinkers, such as Gobineau, as inferior to any "pure" race.

Second, this move allows us to put the scientific dimension of race aside while we explore its philosophical aspect. To be sure, Vasconcelos tried to provide both a positive and a normative account of how the third, aesthetic period follows the "materialistic" and the "political" eras. He does not succeed in the former, for he does not delineate the conditions that lead toward the decay of the political era and the emergence of the aesthetic period. Nonetheless, he intimates that racial identity can be linked to the aesthetic. He thereby opens up the possibility that—beyond a possible culture that prizes beauty and art in the future—we may be able to understand the phenomenon of racial identity aesthetically, that is, using notions borrowed from the philosophy of art.

Following Vasconcelos's lead, then, we can explore this linkage between race and art. We can do so by mining Vasconcelos's writings on race to see what precisely their philosophical basis is. In doing so, we can elucidate his project and connect it to the larger history of modern philosophy.

Vasconcelos's Racial Harmony

In explaining why Brazilians should be thought of as part of the "Latin" world, José Vasconcelos tells a vignette that for him carries much substance in our effort to understand race. The story is in his short essay "El problema del Brasil" (The Brazil Problem).

He tells us of his visit to Lima, where one evening he attends a dance performance by a female Brazilian artist.

Recalling Nietzsche's fascination with Bizet's *Carmen*, Vasconcelos recounts that the sight of the dancer holds a deep meaning:

> The spontaneous and intense art of the dancer produced in us a certain joy, like that experienced by someone returning to something of their own but which had been ignored or distant; or as if, from the depths of our ethnic conscience, new emotions were born which held a happiness never felt before. It was strange but not discordant.[16]

Vasconcelos believes Kant would agree that aesthetic reason shows us that this experience has a philosophical meaning.[17] In fact, it is not Kant who can support Vasconcelos's claim. Underneath this particular assertion, and infusing his entire approach to the problem of race, we find an important affinity with the ideas of Friedrich Nietzsche. This affinity elucidates the philosophical bases of Vasconcelos's account of race writ large.[18] Moreover, while there are important differences between the two thinkers on key principles, relating them to each other yields a fruitful area of study for the purpose of seeing how race and racialization are part and parcel of modernity.

There are important nodes of commonality between the thinkers. They both argued against the abstract reason of Kant and Hegel; they saw the centrality of agonism in life; they had similar concerns about providing a cogent view of joyous pessimism; they admired Indian thought; they argued for a regional, continental sense of identity against nationalism; they underscored the place of emotion and the body in philosophy; they wrote rhetorically; and—not insignificantly—they had an enlarged sense of their own importance. What distinguishes them most clearly is a divergence in religion and politics. Nietzsche was a preeminent critic of Christianity, whereas Vasconcelos was a devout Catholic, especially at the end of his life. This led to Vasconcelos's emphasis on "Providence" and the order of the world, whereas Nietzsche argued against order and *telos*. In the political field, Vasconcelos was an *engagé* intellectual, whereas Nietzsche shied away from actual politics. Both, importantly, had things to say about race.

Race is a major issue in contemporary societies, yet political philosophy, especially in the canonical European tradition, has surprisingly little to say about it.[19] Latin American philosophy, *par contre*, has grappled with the issue since its inception. Within this tradition, José Vasconcelos is a central figure.[20] His writings on race are of paramount importance, yet some remain obscure. Within them, we find various influences, from Aquinas to Bergson. I want to argue that some appear to resonate with Nietzschean themes if not direct influences.[21] It is this resonance that we explore here to determine what undergirds Vasconcelos's ideas on race and to open a dialogue between European and Latin American political thought.

While Nietzsche is often considered one of the most opaque of modern philosophers, I want to turn the tables around and use his work (which is usually the object of analysis) to elucidate the obscure origins of Vasconcelos's account of race. I want to examine the ways in which Vasconcelos's key work on race, *La Raza Cósmica*, as well as other, lesser-known writings by Vasconcelos, can be read as Nietzschean-inflected texts. My claim is not that Vasconcelos followed Nietzsche *al pie de la letra* (word by word), nor that they agreed on most philosophical principles. To be sure, Vasconcelos is a (perhaps *the*) leading light in Latin American modernism's confrontation with race on the philosophical plane. However, it is still unclear what undergirds his vast architectonic, and further philosophical analysis is needed.[22] Nietzsche is a contested figure, yet I want to posit that to understand Vasconcelos's account of race, we need to observe through two lenses of the German thinker's ideas: one is his method of moral genealogy, which we can apply to the political morality of race, and the other is his view on the centrality of aesthetics.

Although the ties of Vasconcelos to Nietzsche have been alluded to before, no extensive analysis of them has been carried out heretofore. This question is important not just for the meaning of race, but also for aesthetics. As Kathleen Higgins states, "The view that aesthetic experience has epistemological significance has been defended by . . . Vasconcelos." She goes on to ask, "How similar, we might ask, are these views to those theories about art's epistemological role advanced in the West" by thinkers such as Nietzsche?[23]

Excursus: Nietzsche, Aesthetics, and Race

Before we embark on an account of Vasconcelos's ideas on race through a Nietzschean lens, we must first construct this particular lens. To be sure, Nietzsche is one of the most contested of philosophers, as we find an abundance of perspectives on this perspectivist thinker. In order to link him to Vasconcelos, we must examine whether there is any fit between the two philosophers besides the aforementioned general common themes.

The place of Nietzsche in the course of modern thought is what must first be determined.[24] Is Nietzsche a radical new thinker who does away with all previous modes of philosophy? Is he the last modern thinker? Or perhaps the dynamite that destroys modernity? From Lukács to Heidegger to Deleuze, we have different takes on these questions. What I want to point to is the coherence of themes that recur in Nietzsche. It may be true that his works are disparate and sometimes internally incoherent, lacking much positive evidence, even when they claim to make statements about the historical development of values. But Nietzsche's central concern was to develop a set of values, an ethics, which would stand in spite of the realization that foundational metaphysics is impossible in the modern era. Nietzsche's lifelong task was to provide *the* most cogent perspective on human experience in late modernity. It was not to deny that values were possible.

Nietzsche was critical of the metaphysics of Plato, Kant, and Hegel, *inter alia*, but he did not entirely do away with their methodology. Specifically, we can find instances of dialectical thinking in Nietzsche, something that owes much to the idealist tradition that he attacked.[25] The clash of opposites engaged in a productive agon is evident throughout Nietzsche's oeuvre. From the Dionysian/Apollonian tension in *Birth of Tragedy*, to the symbiotic relationship between slave and master morality in *Genealogy of Morals*, to Zarathustra's encounters throughout his journey, to his understanding of music in *Will to Power*, we find an effort to reconcile antinomies. These antinomies are not merely underscored to make salient the prevalence of difference in Nietzsche, as Deleuze argues, but they are the target of critical analysis that seeks to resolve them. Viewed in this light, the distance between Hegel and Nietzsche is not that great, as Rampley argues.[26]

We can find an encapsulation of this affinity in Nietzsche's account of aesthetics. This account is not entirely consistent, nor can we trace clearly its development throughout Nietzsche's life.[27] However, the aesthetic for Nietzsche is indeed central. The aesthetic is the justification of the world because it is the way that human beings can fight the principal problem of modernity, nihilism. And this fight is not merely one of celebration of incoherent moments of resistance. It is one where antinomies coalesce and are resolved. In a statement whose significance cannot be underestimated in spite of the fact that it occurs in one of his notes, he tells us in *Will to Power* that "'Beauty' is for the artist something outside all orders of rank, because in beauty opposites are tamed; the highest sign of power, namely, power over opposites" (803). Thus, Nietzsche's much-celebrated valuation of the *pathos* of distance and hierarchies vanishes in his account of aesthetics. Nietzsche finds in the aesthetic a way to resolve the tensions and antagonisms that he finds are inevitable in other realms of life. In this manner, art affirms life (*Will to Power*, 821), especially when it is beautiful (*Will to Power*, 809).

We must read Nietzsche's account of art as a way to synthesize two different drives in human beings. We find this theory in *The Birth of Tragedy*, and it is something that is reformulated, after his skepticism about art in *Human, All too Human*, in the *Gay Science*. Nietzsche was never fully clear when it came to his aesthetics, but we find an engagement with the coupling of the ideas of Apollonian form and Dionysian *Rausch* (frenzy) in *The Birth of Tragedy*. In *Human, All Too Human*, he moved away from art and toward science, but returns to the centrality of art as a way to affirm life (that is, to be antinihilistic) in *Gay Science*. There, we find that *gaya scienza* fuses two drives: the childish, joyful, light-hearted spirit of southern Europe (Provençal troubadours, or sometimes Bizet's music, or Machiavelli's style of writing) with a Germano-Hellenistic concern with knowledge, *Wissenschaft*, the sort of wisdom that avoids the dangerous hyperrationality of Socratic thinking. This fusion or synthesis of the drive to know and the drive toward frenzy, expressed in artistic form (especially in beauty), is what Nietzsche finds necessary in late modernity, and it circles back to *The Birth of Tragedy*.[28] As Young writes, "From this initial understanding of the dichotomy between Apollonian and Dionysian art it seems to follow that according to the birth of tragedy thesis great art must consist in some kind of *synthesis* . . . between the beautiful representation of phenomenal reality and music."[29]

In the realm of art, and especially of music, Nietzsche believes, the artist can finally find a way to reconcile opposites. In an art form such as painting, a painter can use both lines and shapes in one single work; in poetry, the poet can make the ugly gain a certain beauty through diction and rhythm; and in opera, opposites such as language and action can be fused under music to create what Nietzsche thought for a while was possible, a *Gesamtkunstwerk*. The centrality of art (particularly music) is such that it fundamentally replaces religion, as it helps to connect individuals who are no longer able to connect with each other on purely religious grounds, giving art and music a nearly totalistic character in the Nietzschean framework.[30]

Wagner's use of the term *Gesamtkunstwerk* in his 1849 essay "Art and Revolution" is critical to understanding Nietzsche's account of art. For the great German composer, it meant the *synthesis* of the three performative arts with the three plastic arts. Thus, music, poetry, and dance could be coalesced with architecture, painting, and sculpture, to create a totalistic work of art. This holistic understanding of the ideal work of art was never fully repudiated by Nietzsche. To be sure, Nietzsche broke with Wagner in 1876, but not over this concept. Rather, he found the content (not the form) of Wagner's operas to be excessively infused with Christian and romanticized, nationalistic themes.[31] Nietzsche assails the composer in *The Case of Wagner,* but mainly to blame him for misunderstanding the whole, the totality, not for seeking to grasp it: decadence means that "life no longer resides in the *whole*. The word becomes sovereign and leaps out of the sentence . . . the whole is no longer the whole" (7; emphasis added). Thus, Nietzsche attacks Wagner's particular expression of his "argument," but not its substance, which advocates an integrative sense of art. The idea of a synthetic work of art that manages to combine disparate opposites into a whole that is not merely coherent but also beautiful was never abandoned by Nietzsche. As he tells us in *The Will to Power*, "The exaggeration, the disproportion, the *non-harmony* of normal phenomena constitute the pathological state" (Book I, Section 47, p.29; emphasis added) that he so abhorred. Nietzsche later moved away from tragic opera and closer to music as a way to resolve these tensions, but still with the ambition to find resolution, or harmony, as he claims, even if only within music.

What this tells us is that Nietzsche was committed, throughout his life, to providing an account of how art could itself be synthetic and resolve the conflicting tensions and drives in human existence. In this sense, he was integrative, even if he did not seek to build a system, as Hegel did.[32] It may be true that there is only "a perspective seeing, only a perspective knowing," as Nietzsche claims in *The Genealogy of Morals*, but he goes on to say in this passage that each new perspective adds to the totality of knowledge that each person can garner: "The more affects we allow to speak about an object, the more eyes, different eyes we know to employ for the same thing, the more *complete* will our 'concept' of this thing, our 'objectivity,' be."[33] Thus, it is up to the self to integrate a variety of interpretations for a fuller, richer account of the world or of life. It is not the case that any interpretation is as valid or rich as any other. While his account of art is integrative, it is not totalistic, for he recognized the need to set limits to artistic expressions, in order to make good art: "The good poet of the future will depict *only reality* . . . but by no means every reality" (*Human, All Too Human*, II.114).

This perspective allows us to determine that his account of art is *synthetic*, whether it is in his admiration of Attic tragedy (where the Dionysian and the Apollonian are married together), or in his love for Wagner's operas during a period of his life; or in his own sense of self, in the way that he believed the self and its various tendencies could be managed under one sense of style and one dominant drive. Hence, the capacity to select one powerful drive and allow it to control all other subordinate drives is a reflection of the harmony that exists when opposites are reconciled. The selection of one drive, the Will to Power, is the ordering principle that allows this reconciliation. It ceases to be all-dominant when the drives are made harmonious and beauty is thus found, in an artwork or in a person.[34]

The harmonization of a person's characteristics is what we are after when we seek to apply Nietzschean aesthetics to racial identity. Here is where we must be creative with Nietzsche's writings, and depart from a purely textual analysis. Whereas Nietzsche's account of aesthetics places him in a late-modernist camp where synthesis and integration are critical and are carried out through a dialectical process, his account of race is more complicated and murky. We can only make something out of it if we discard conventional approaches and point to new angles of understanding it.

Surprisingly, not much research exists on Nietzsche and race.[35] That which exists focuses either on his actual uses of the term "race" and related concepts, such as peoples and nations, or on his treatment of the Jewish people.[36] Focusing on these two aspects is understandable, but it generally only yields evidence of Nietzsche's own stance within what I have called the European domination paradigm of race. I want to posit a novel claim: that Nietzsche is useful for our better understanding of race, rather, through his genealogical method in morality as it is tied to his aesthetics.

By putting aside his particular remarks on races and nations (which do indeed show him to be culturally tied to Germanocentrism, as Conway demonstrates),[37] we can think about how he could have applied his historical-materialistic approach in moral genealogy to racial identity. As Robert Gooding-Williams tells us, even if we find noxious evidence in Nietzsche's racial thinking, we can make use of his methodology and elements of his thought in order to better understand race.[38] Nietzsche never directly applied his moral genealogy to racialization, but this is precisely where a Nietzschean approach can be useful. I call his method historical-materialistic because, even if it lacks details and specificity, his account of morality in *Genealogy of Morals* points to the emergence of moral valuations within particular historical periods or moments. At the same time, Nietzsche makes frequent reference to somatic, physical, and physiological human characteristics.[39] He is a philosopher for whom the body is the central lens of cognition: we acquire knowledge as information is passed through the senses. For Nietzsche, we cannot make synthetic a priori statements. The somatic is fundamental to our acquisition of knowledge, and this helps him to undermine the grand metaphysical claims of other philosophical perspectives.[40] Hence, the body in Nietzsche plays two functions: one is to deny a basic metaphysical reality that is beyond experience. The other is to supply metaphors for the way that human cognition develops. In other words, he uses bodily metaphors as a way to represent "scientific" (that is, knowledge-oriented) claims, which for him lack exactitude and precision.

If this is the case, we can think of how he could have applied his historical-materialistic genealogy of morals to somatic characteristics that are tied to processes of racialization. The key passage for this purpose is in *Genealogy of Morals*, First Essay, Section 5, where he does not "endorse" a racist view, but rather seeks to trace the premodern roots of racial thinking based on appearances and morphology. It appears in the context of Nietzsche's philological discussion of values.

> In the Latin *malus* (which I place side by side with μελας) the vulgar man can be distinguished as the dark-coloured, and above all as the black-haired (*"hic niger est"*), as the pre-Aryan inhabitants of the Italian soil, whose complexion formed the clearest feature of distinction from the dominant blondes, namely, the Aryan conquering race: . . . good, noble, clean, but originally the blonde-haired man in contrast to the dark black-haired aboriginals.[41]

What Nietzsche seeks to tell us here is that at some point in the history of words, physical appearances, somatic form, and phenotypical differences became associated with *moral* characteristics. It is not that these characteristics are innate, but rather that they came to be tied to particular groups using physical criteria.[42] Nietzsche is incorrect in placing this moment in history in a premodern time, for we know now that racialization is modern. Yet his insight into the link between a historically located ascription of moral values according to physical characteristics provides us with an aesthetic basis for understanding racialization.

Thus, while the bulk of references to the body in Nietzsche tend to focus on invisible processes—such as digestion (*Beyond Good and Evil*, 141), *névrose* (*The Case of Wagner*, 5), or chemistry (*Human, All Too Human*, I.1)—we may suggest that this framework could be equally valuable for critiquing the way that visible (that is, aesthetically perceived),[43] phenotypical characteristics are tied to moral values. For Nietzsche, the term *malus* (bad or evil), in this passage, came to refer to dark-colored or dark-haired peoples at a given point in time. This assignation of moral values along somatic characteristics was political because it was power-related. It comes in contradistinction to the "conquering" or powerful group, which is "fair" (understood as both light-skinned and as just). It is moral in that it ascribes an inferior status to the aboriginals, conquered by an imperial power. Just as Las Casas describes the way in which most Spaniards denigrated the natives of the Americas, we see how, for Nietzsche, power relations lead to assignations of moral value according to both ethnic and racial (i.e., cultural and somatic) lines.

What does this foray into Nietzsche's aesthetics and an interpretation of his genealogy for racialization tell us in relation to Vasconcelos? First, that Nietzsche can be interpreted as a late-modernist thinker. To be sure, he stood against foundational metaphysics, yet his writings aim at the construction of what he thought was *the most* cogent perspective, not merely one of many. This places him closer to Hegel than is generally acknowledged. And it places him nearer Vasconcelos, who also sought to provide a cogent moral theory of race at a time when values were on the whole untenable. Second, it tells us that, for both, the aesthetic serves as a way to resolve such tensions. And third, Nietzsche's concerns with both aesthetics and the somatic, which occur separately in his work, can be combined to provide an account of racialization and racial identity, something that Vasconcelos does, as we will see. In this sense, we can say that Vasconcelos was a Nietzschean *pensador* who built on the premises of the German thinker on matters aesthetic as applied to racial phenomena. By doing this, we also extricate Nietzsche's relevance to racial ideas from the mine field of the German historico-cultural context,[44] and place him in a different (Latin American) context to determine how his thought can be of use to thinking about race.

Vasconcelos's Essays: An Overture to the Problem of Race

If we look more closely than we usually do, we find that there is clear evidence of a direct line of influence from Nietzsche to Vasconcelos, and we can aver that both ground their philosophical projects on aesthetic bases.[45] Vasconcelos makes references to Nietzsche that are sometimes critical. For example, in *Indología* he expresses his belief that the race of the future will be worthy not because it will create a few "Nietzschean" *Übermenschen*, but rather a "Totinem" (from *totus* and *inem*, Latin for "all" and "man") of a universal, synthetic humanity.[46] Yet beyond these disagreements, there is a basic concordance between Nietzsche and Vasconcelos on the value of the aesthetic experience not just in providing humans a link to the workings of the universe, but also in giving ethical value to man's existence.[47] Even more to the point, the two share notions of harmony, rhythm, and music. As Martha Robles tells us, "As soon as [Vasconcelos] began his autobiographical symphony, he gave himself the task of trying to persuade in the highest operatic German style: the music of Wagner, mythical invocations . . . and the historical voluntarism that from Schopenhauer and Nietzsche led to the paragon of Mexican *mestizaje*."[48]

In one of his key works, *Monismo Estético*, where Vasconcelos explains the unity of his cosmology and his theory of art and music, there is an explicit indebtedness to Nietzsche. Vasconcelos tells us that his essay on auditive mysticism, integral to this work, came from "an idea from a certain paragraph, in that fount of books, which is called *The Birth of Tragedy,* written by Nietzsche."[49] Vasconcelos goes on to say that his theory of dance, also of great important to his aesthetics, comes from reading Nietzsche's first book.[50]

While much has been made of Nietzsche's lack of a system, the opposite must be said of Vasconcelos: perhaps under the influence of Aristotle, Augustine, and Aquinas, Vasconcelos aimed to construct a vast philosophical edifice where all elements fit together. It is in this light that we can make sense of the two movements in Vasconcelos's racial harmony. The first can be found in some of his short essays, and the second in his well-known work *La Raza Cósmica.* Moving from apparent discord to harmony: this is Vasconcelos's project in his dealing with all phenomena, including racial ideas.

Perhaps more than any other social concept, race is preeminently modern. There is ample historical evidence that the notions around race emerge only in times we consider modern, that is, at the beginning of the 1500s immediately after the conquest of the Americas by Spain.[51] There is some evidence of premodern roots of race and racism.[52] But a coherent notion of race only appears *pari passu* with the rise of modernity. Thus, the notion of modernity is useful for our purposes of understanding what race is and how Nietzsche and Vasconcelos perceive it.

The fact that race is historically contingent on the rise of modernity opens up the possibility of carrying out a genealogy of its emergence. Against the idea that morality is an eternal, fixed, and universal set of dicta, or that it is simply the application of rationally derived obligations, a Nietzschean approach to morality tells us that what we receive as morally valid arguments in fact tend to be the product of historically located and evolving power relations. This is useful for our understanding of race for two reasons. One is that the prevailing views on racial morality at the time of Nietzsche's and Vasconcelos's writing were simply the predominant, not the only possible, views on race. And second, a critical genealogy of the rise of these views can help generate a deconstruction of their validity.

In the 1920s, arguably more so than at any other time, Latin American intellectuals were in constant dialogue with each other even across vast distances. The nascent idea of a single "Latin America" was the topic of debate for thinkers as disparate as José Carlos Mariátegui and Laureano Vallenilla Lanz. Vasconcelos was an *éminence grise* of this school: before the publication of *La Raza Cósmica,* Vasconcelos was already a well-known figure across Latin America. In some of his short and understudied essays we find elements of a philosophical perspective that can explain why race and the aesthetic are cardinal to the Mexican thinker's intellectual project. He thought of himself in the way that Nietzsche conceived of Zarathustra: a heroic, titanically striving individual with the capacity to shape an entire cultural arena.

Writing letters to "Peruvian Youth," to "students in Colombia," and "the children of Mexico," Vasconcelos's short essays point to a concern with the future, something quite fundamental to the modernist project. Just as José Enrique Rodó's Próspero was an old teacher imparting his lessons in the form of a swan song to the younger generations of Latin Americans in *Ariel*, Vasconcelos also thinks of himself as a great teacher who must be concerned with the shaping of young minds in order to create a better future. And this is a Latin American future, not one bounded by particular nationalities. Vasconcelos saw himself as a Nietzschean agent, a leading actor shaping the culture of his people through the power of his literary art. As Martha Robles tells us, "More than his Mexican contemporaries, Vasconcelos draws a Nietzschean figure through his writings, as someone who urges the creation of a culture of greatness."[53]

This preoccupation with transcending national boundaries is part of a larger cultural project which Vasconcelos sees as essential in striving for the ideal of a future society guided by the aesthetic principle rather than by pragmatism or materialism. The teleology of his project is one where aesthetic life is the aim, that is, living according to the dictates of beauty, the appreciation of art, creativity, spirituality, and the impulses of emotion and sympathy. All else is secondary, including his racial doctrines.

We can see this as we examine the short essays in his *Ideario de Acción*, published in Lima, Peru, in 1924. The Mexican Revolution was the context of Vasconcelos's life and works, but he never became bounded by it. Rather than remain a Mexican nationalist, Vasconcelos urged the creation of a common Latin American civilization with a higher purpose.[54] Thus, we can understand why he writes letters to the youth of the Americas. The harmony that he did not witness in (post-)Revolutionary Mexico, he believed, could be forged at a higher scale, on the plane of all of Latin America.

In a speech given in Santiago de Chile, Vasconcelos shows his fundamental opposition to nationalism as something too limited and grounded on coercion.[55] At the university's School of the Humanities, he declared,

> I believe that nationality is an expired idea, and in fact above and beyond the motherlands of today—which hardly move me anymore—I can see the flags of new *ethnic federations* that will work together for the future of the world. I can envision the Iberoamerican flag as one, floating over Brazil, Mexico, Peru, Argentina, Chile, Ecuador . . .[56]

Why would a leading figure of the Mexican Revolution, a head of the UNAM (the largest national university). and a potential president of the Mexican Republic, speak against nationalism in the aftermath of one of the most tumultuous moments of nationalist fervor the world has ever seen? One could easily imagine that given his institutional and historical roles, he would be one of the staunchest nationalists and anticosmopolitans of his time.

Yet he was not; and the explanation lies in the fact that he was a philosopher who valued the aesthetic principle—specifically the idea of harmony—above all else. Vasconcelos was able to dissociate himself from his roles as a public official and to declare, without prejudice, his deeper values. As he tells us in a speech delivered in Mexico on October

12, 1920, in commemoration of the "Día de la Raza," or the discovery of America: "I will speak today having thrown off my mantle of a public servant."[57] While asserting that he speaks as a "Mexican teacher," his main message that day is the idea that Latin American unity will and must prevail over narrow nationalism. In this process, the idea of *nuestra raza* (our race) is central. He understands this idea not merely as a biological term, as the English word "race" is often construed.[58] He means "people" and "civilization"; and this people is the Latin American people, not just Mexicans.

It is within this schema that we must locate his understanding of race. It is not that race is the central idea of his philosophy, but that it is the fulcrum on which the aesthetic category of harmony turns, insofar as his philosophy applies to the human world. Harmony for him is not only a metaphysical principle but also a social one. Vasconcelos rails against the Porfiriato (and indirectly against Vallenilla), but he also believes that autocracy is the bane of the Latin peoples: "Tyranny is the principal cause of underdevelopment for the peoples of Spanish America."[59] Vasconcelos wants social harmony in his ideal state, and for this he seeks the abolition of all sorts of dictatorships because they force social order and prevent freely chosen social bonds that lead, in his view, to harmonious relations.[60]

Vasconcelos links tyranny and dictatorship—which causes social discord—to the backward tendencies of the Latin *raza*, or people/civilization. Vasconcelos is thus a progressive or modernist thinker, someone who is quite radical in the sense that he wants to get to the root of what is necessary for the human species—free association. For Vasconcelos, dictators like Venezuela's Juan Vicente Gómez, for whom Vallenilla Lanz worked, are "human pig[s]"[61] that delay the progress of the Latin "race" toward a harmonious future. Hence, while contemporary racialist thinking in Europe was moving toward fascism, and racism was part of a reactionary program in the United States, the racial thinking of Vasconcelos was in fact progressive if not revolutionary.[62]

Rather than focusing on a primitive or primordialist conception of race, Vasconcelos understands it in terms of cultural affinity or, as he often puts it, "sympathy." For this reason Brazil is part of the Latin world as well. Not only does Vasconcelos feel an aesthetic bond when he sees the Brazilian dancer we note above—showing a common note or wavelength on which the Brazilian and Mexican ethos rests—but he also believes there is also a common historical dimension.[63]

In a speech delivered on the occasion of presenting a statue of the Aztec warrior Cuauhtémoc to the republic of Brazil in Rio de Janeiro, Vasconcelos underscores the historical ties that link the two nations. For him, the figure of the "Indian" past of the Americas must be recovered. Cuauhtémoc, for Vasconcelos, is a hero, albeit a defeated one. Yet he is also the "creative spell that brings forth a new race, strong and glorious."[64] The glory behind the Aztec leader was his unyielding resistance against the "Sons of the Sun," the Spanish conquistadores. Vasconcelos understands the birth of the Latin American race or peoples as one that emerges from a tense *agon*, that between the Spaniard and the

Amerindian. It is not the product of a happy marriage, an encounter, or even a violation.[65] Vasconcelos sees *América* as born out of a struggle between equal forces. A Nietzschean sense of agonism is at work here: neither side is clearly superior to the other, and the wrestling between the two cultures yields a more powerful third civilization.[66]

For Cortés, according to Vasconcelos, the resistance offered by Cuauhtémoc must have been formidable. The conquistador

> must have felt like a brother of his great enemy, a brother for his greatness and pain, and also because from that moment on, it was written on the lands of Anáhuac that there would not be just one race as victorious, but two races in perpetual conflict, until the Republic would put an end to this struggle, declaring that Mexican soil would not be the property of one single skin color, or of two separate races, but of all the races populating the earth, as long as they adjust their form to the Indian-Spanish *rhythm*.[67]

For Vasconcelos, the harmony and rhythm of the Latin world was produced by an initial stage that was discordant and full of conflict and agonism.[68] In *La Raza Cósmica*, he tells us that "opposition and fight, particularly when transposed to the field of the spirit, serve to better define the contenders."[69] Just as Nietzsche admired Heraclitus, we find in Vasconcelos a certain awe in the face of two bitter enemies whose power produces a new way of life. And this new way of life is the basis on which all others must rest.[70]

The reason for Brazil's inclusion in the Latin world is that it shares with the rest of Ibero-America the same appreciation for this sense of harmony and rhythm. To be sure, it is not merely musical. It is a rhythm of life, a way of living, a valuation of certain customs and attitudes that differ from others.[71] As Latin Americans, Vasconcelos states, "We will invent the new *form* [of life] according to our own *taste*, and we will *create* a universal way of life, which will nevertheless have the imprint of our soul's *rhythm*."[72] Here is an evidently aesthetic conceptualization of social order, one modeled after aesthetic ideas which Vasconcelos believed to be the solution to a modern world of flux, change, and frequent discord—a modern world that was otherwise losing its grasp of beauty.

Adumbrating his philosophy of history in *La Raza Cósmica*, Vasconcelos writes of three historical stages in his essay "Nueva Ley de los Tres Estados" (New Law of the Three States). In it, he presents a three-tier vision of historical progress in which an aesthetic era supplants a first stage that he calls materialist and a second stage that he calls intellectual. Thus, while being critical of the central tenet of modernity, reason, Vasconcelos nonetheless believes in progress, something that is quite modern. Yet this progress is toward a social order that is grounded on people behaving according to an aesthetic logic. This philosophy is still modernist, since the aesthetic *qua* independent activity is a modern phenomenon, but one that is guided by a dynamic different from that of competing modernities.

For Vasconcelos, the vehicle the moves us toward this panacea is the racial harmonization that comes from the unification of Latin America both at the political and at the social levels. He wants to abrade national boundaries in order to create "ethnic federations" of nations that share ethnic roots and practices. At the social level, he wants to strive toward another modern ideal, equality, by pushing greater racial miscegenation.[73] And this mixing is the result of people heeding the norms of taste and "sympathy," not reason or the law.[74]

On the political plane, Vasconcelos associates the first stage with imperialism. "Brute force" unifies disparate peoples but does not achieve true, free association. The second stage is more reasonable and is connected to the rise of nation-states. It is a step forward from the first stage, for it aims at greater homogeneity. However, it is still founded on force and self-interest, rather than free, uncoerced activity and interaction. It is only in the third stage, located principally in Latin America, that Vasconcelos sees a solution.

It is here where "relations between peoples are ruled freely by sympathy and taste. Taste is the supreme law of the inner life, which manifests itself outwardly as sympathy and beauty, and it will become the undisputed norm of public order and relations between states."[75] This utopian vision responds to the very modern problem of why desire, or the longing for something deep, has disappeared from life. It is a problem that Nietzsche knows too well, as we find in his account of the "last man": modern man as destitute of any deep desire, and satisfied only by simple consumption. Vasconcelos sees the same problem, and believes that it can be addressed by the recovery of an instinctive sense of beauty that lies deep in the heart of man himself. Hence the emphasis on desire and miscegenation.

Unlike *La Raza Cósmica*, this essay does have practical suggestions to hasten the arrival of the third stage. Vasconcelos urges greater economic equality; he wants states to carry out modern, functional projects such as the construction of bridges, railways, ships, and other things that will tighten the bonds between nations seen as ethnically related. He also wants the termination of apish imitation of others, especially European (particularly French) and American ways of doing things.[76] He advocates free trade and the institution of a Zollverein system that would "be the salvation of our race."[77] Vasconcelos tells us he understands the anti-Americanism of some of his contemporaries, but argues that the unity of Latin America should not be negative: it should be aimed at a creative, positive affirmation born out of common cultural and racial ties. Still, there does not seem to be any guarantee that work in infrastructure will lead to greater social interaction between diverse groups.

From disparate texts, we find common threads in the works of Vasconcelos preceding his major study, *La Raza Cósmica*.[78] Biological conceptualizations of race are not as prominent as they would become in his most famous book. Here are the buttresses of a philosophical position. The central one is the notion of the aesthetic, which permeates the essays and shows Vasconcelos to be centrally concerned with the problem of bringing beauty back in, against the modernist current going in the opposite direction.[79] Just as Nietzsche sought to provide a justification for life on aesthetic grounds, Vasconcelos struggles with the idea that the waves of modernity tend to do away with beauty. Vasconcelos wants to recover beauty and find a way to make it a social norm. It is under this schema that his racial ideas develop, not the other way around.

While Nietzsche urged a sort of new renaissance of fundamental European values for a transnational cultural project, Vasconcelos similarly wanted a regional integration of his own continent. Latin America would be the place for a rebirth, not just of Latin values, but of humanity as a whole. In this project, racial miscegenation understood now more as a natural or biological concept would merge with the metaphysical and the political imperatives that we find in his short essays.

La Raza Cósmica in Nietzschean Tones

As he tells us in the prologue to the 1948 edition of *La Raza Cósmica*, Vasconcelos's aim in this text is to show that "the various races of the earth tend to intermix at a gradually increasing pace, and eventually will give rise to a new human type, composed of selections from each of the races already in existence."[80] This thesis is part of a project combining different methodologies. Didier Jaén rightly states that while "others wrote literature or created art, Vasconcelos tried to construct systems. His aim was that of encompassing within a complete philosophical system, such as Saint Thomas'[,] the glimpses of a Nietzsche or a Schopenhauer, as well as the visions of science."[81]

Nietzsche claimed to be a thinker opposed to systematic, structural philosophy. Yet, as I noted earlier, the overall effect of his whole corpus provides a general architectonic and recurrence of motifs that in fact does create legitimacy for the notion of something that is "Nietzschean." *Pace* postmodernism, there are doctrines, methodologies, concerns, metaphors, revaluation of terms, and overall purpose in the opus of Nietzsche that lend it coherence and a degree of systematicity. Nietzsche was a modern thinker: a critic of modernity who found it important to point to the defects and crises of the modern world, albeit with a particular perspective intended to be proposed as a better alternative to other philosophical views. His work is not a congeries of dissociated, aimless ideas. Thus, the relevance of this thought for modern concerns.

One of these concerns is race. Against inadequate interpretations of Nietzsche as a forerunner of fascism, in fact his ideas support the very notion of miscegenation. This is a miscegenation of ideas, cultures, and, indeed, races. While the ancient Greeks thought of themselves as a breed of masters superior to "barbarians," Nietzsche believed that race admixture favors the acquisition of culture in both nations and individuals.[82] He often emphasized that his last name showed his Polish origin, hence his own mixed breeding. He yearned for the "mixed race, that of the European man."[83] Against the view that he was anti-Semitic, he proposed that the Jewish culture was an invaluable contributor to this admixture in Europe.[84] As Kaufmann tells us, "To draw the conclusion that Nietzsche . . . abominated mixed races is . . . to miss the very gist of his philosophy."[85] Nietzsche would tell us that "one cannot erase out of the soul of a man what his ancestors have done most eagerly and often. . . . It is not at all possible that a man should not have in his body the qualities and preferences of his parents and ancestors—whatever appearances may say against this. This is the problem of race" (*Beyond Good and Evil*, 264). In other words, the problem of race is not a *moral* problem at base. One's race is not a chosen, willed creation made by oneself. As Nietzsche understands it, race is something beyond subjective control. It is socially constructed, and—more specifically—the product of aesthetic, artistic, and cultural affinities.

We must recall that the "aesthetic" is a modern construct. Prior to 1785, when the German author Alexander Baumgarten coined the term, the idea of thinking about art for art's sake, and of the philosophical meanings of beauty per se, did not exist. The other meaning of the aesthetic for our purposes is cognition through the senses. Thus, the aesthetic, as a modern concept, refers to art, beauty, and sensory perception. Ideas of art before the Enlightenment did not make artistic contemplation independent of other sorts of thinking. Art was not an object of analysis, but rather an integral part of social, cultural, and even political life. This was especially true of antiquity, something that is evident in Heidegger's discussions of art.

Before as well as after his concern with race, Vasconcelos was arguably more interested in the problems associated with an aesthetic conceptualization of metaphysics, as he wrote *Monismo Estético* in 1919 and *Estética* in 1936.[86]

How does Vasconcelos understand the aesthetic? For him, it is *the* single most important facet of human existence.[87] In other words, he believes it is the essence of what it is to be human. It is logically and ontologically prior to the category of the racial.[88] More than being rational, practical, or social, aestheticism is what makes us truly distinct from other kinds of beings. By aesthetic Vasconcelos means four interrelated things: being creative, appreciating beauty, being in touch with emotions, and being spiritual. The entire history of humankind, for Vasconcelos, has moved teleologically toward the epoch in which humans will finally be able to be aesthetic beings, freed from practical demands and utilitarian concerns. The aesthetic spirit will reflect itself in real life: "Spiral constructions will be raised in useless ostentation of beauty, because the new aesthetics will try to adapt itself to the endless curve of the spiral, which represents freedom of desire and the triumph of being in the conquest of infinity."[89]

This teleological approach—shown in the symbol of the spiral—is similar to that of Hegel.[90] Here there is a departure from Nietzsche, for Nietzsche never wrote a philosophy of history akin to that of Hegel. Indeed Nietzsche reacts against Hegel, but, like Marx, he appropriates key elements of the Hegelian approach. However, in terms of a philosophy of history, Vasconcelos uses a fundamentally Hegelian structure to define the three key periods of human history in *La Raza Cósmica*: the material, the intellectual, and the aesthetic.[91]

For Vasconcelos, unlike Hegel, the culminating historical period is not one of other-worldly spirituality; it is one where concrete, organic human beings exist in an aesthetic culture. In other words, Vasconcelos's vision of the future is very much like something Nietzsche might have sketched had he been able to achieve his goal, expressed on his deathbed, of writing a more explicitly political text. Not only did Nietzsche wish to write a more political tract as he approached the end of his life, but he also intimated an interest in a more global, cosmopolitan view of politics which he termed the question of the "good European," in other words, concerns beyond the nation-state and nationalism.[92]

The parallel with Vasconcelos is quite clear. The Mexican thinker writes *La Raza Cósmica* as a response to *pensadores*, such as Vallenilla, who were concerned with national identity and state-making, and Vasconcelos proposes a larger, more cosmopolitan (or "cosmic") view of Latin American cultural identity, similar to Nietzsche's pan-European identity. Unlike Sarmiento or Martí, Vasconcelos does not write for a given, particular national group, especially in his key text. While Vasconcelos was very much a key figure of the Mexican nationalist intelligentsia, *La Raza Cósmica* is not a Mexicanist text at all. It does not share with Sarmiento's *Civilization or Barbarism* a defense of "the national" in Argentina or with Martí's Cuban republicanism a desire to construct a specific nationality.

In all three cases, race is a central concern, but whereas Sarmiento uses race as a divisive element (except for this idealization of the gaucho image) and Martí uses race to construct a common Cuban sense of citizenship, Vasconcelos uses race to build a postnational political order in the service of a larger aesthetic purpose for humankind. Hence we can speak of *La Raza Cósmica* as a text of rooted cosmopolitanism: it is grounded in the Latin American experience, but it holds a world-historical mission.[93]

Throughout *La Raza Cósmica*, Vasconcelos conceives the *emotional* aspect of the aesthetic as tied to the biological basis that will drive the vehicle of race toward his teleological aim of a postnational and postrational world social order. The central emotions are those of love and desire. With a distinctively rhetorical as opposed to scientific approach that evokes Nietzsche's style, Vasconcelos argues (rather hyperbolically) that the Latin race or people is more attuned to emotions, and that this will allow its members to form sexual and matrimonial unions with those of any race, unlike Anglos, for example, who are unable to see the beauty in a Japanese person (again Vasconcelos uses hyperbole).[94] This is not far from what Nietzsche argues when he says that at the root of the aesthetic sentiment lies the sexual impulse.[95] In other words, sexual desire and its form are what generate the instinct for the creativity and judgment of the aesthetic.

Creativity, for both Vasconcelos and Nietzsche, is cardinal to the aesthetic essence of man. Nietzsche shied away from terms such as essence or "noumenon," but he effectively constructed a conception of human nature that privileged the aesthetic. For Nietzsche the aesthetic has a twofold value: one is as the most adequate response to the philosophical problem of nihilism. An aesthetic approach to life is the most fully life-affirming. This contravenes the negation of life by various forms of nihilism. At the same time,

Nietzsche thought of art, and especially music, as a form of connection between man and the world and nature. While never calling it a metaphysics, Nietzsche places art and music on the highest pedestal of human responses to nihilism, from the age of Attic tragedy all the way to his own times. Hence, the aesthetic is no mere secondary concern for him. Moreover, the aesthetic does not merely refer to art. An aesthetic approach to life can take many forms, including that of politics.[96]

While Vasconcelos often refers to the creative role of the Latin race in the movement toward a fifth or cosmic race, it is here where Nietzsche actually appears less abstract. It is not clear how the Latin race "creates" a new future, beyond the idea of racial miscegenation, which is a more biological, unconscious act. A more convincing account of creativity is one where there is a conscious agent who seeks to produce something new, not someone who generates something against her will. For this reason the Nietzschean incorporation of a Machiavellian notion of *virtù* in political creativity is cogent.[97] Here Vasconcelos lacks the particular political actors that will be the creative force in leading and shaping the new cultural arena defined by Latin patterns and norms. In this respect, Vasconcelos's vision seems significantly incomplete, for the process he advocates lacks guidance and direction. Perhaps this absence produces one fatal flaw in Vasconcelos's cosmic vision.

Vasconcelos's understanding of beauty is more cogent than Nietzsche's because it is more thoroughly cosmopolitan. For Vasconcelos, the positive fact that Latins incorporate all existing ethnic types means that differing views of what is beautiful will coalesce into the fifth race.[98] The criteria for beauty are thus not limited to a particular cultural tradition; they are derived from the mixing of all understandings of beauty.[99] Beauty is central to Nietzsche and to Vasconcelos, but a Eurocentric basis prevents Nietzsche from understanding that different cultures have different notions of beauty (e.g., asymmetry is central to Japanese aesthetics). By combining miscegenation with the ethnocultural mixing of ideas of beauty, Vasconcelos provides a truly cosmopolitan, global vision of a movement toward a universalist sense of beauty produced not by abstract reason, as in Kant, but by real, biological, historical, and social processes in the progress of "miscegenation."[100]

Last, and most significantly, the aesthetic has a spiritual dimension. It is here where Vasconcelos most evidently departs from Nietzsche. There is no doubt that for Nietzsche the aesthetic also has a spiritual plane. Human beings are a combination of plant and spirit,[101] in other words, organic beings with a spiritual facet. Yet, owing to his radical atheism, Nietzsche is unable to provide a cogent account of secular spirituality. His rejection of Judeo-Christian values is not replaced by a positive contribution that is clearly as spiritual as a religious tradition. He attempts to do so, for this is the purpose of *Thus Spoke Zarathustra*. But the fundamentally rational ideas behind metaphors in this text obviate a direct spirituality that is present, for instance, in Catholic mysticism.

Vasconcelos, inversely, argues that the Latin race's leading role in the movement to the fifth race is to a significant extent the result of its Catholic roots. Like Rodó, Vasconcelos rejects Nietzsche's repudiation of Christianity.[102] In Vasconcelos's model, spirituality is fundamental, but it cannot be a secular spirituality like that of Mariátegui.[103] There is no substitute for religious spirituality. For Vasconcelos, the biological process of the mixing of the races must occur out of love; and love, for Vasconcelos, must be understood as a Christian idea of love of one's neighbor as well as love of one's enemies (that is, of one's racial "Others").[104] For him, a Protestant notion of sectarianism, a Judaic notion of the Chosen, or an Islamic notion of the infidel, are simply not able to capture the universalism of the Christian Catholic doctrine of love. Not only did Vasconcelos praise the Catholic Church explicitly for its role in establishing the universalist basis of a Latin American ethos, but the mystical style that appears in some of his writings can be seen as part of the Catholic rational-mystical tradition that goes back all the way to Sor Juana Inés de la Cruz. Nietzsche attempts to construct a mystical, secular spirituality in *Zarathustra*, but the absence of common myths, the negative nature of the Nietzschean "faith" (i.e., it is written *against* Christianity), and the ultimately philosophical (as opposed to nonrational) bases of the text make it unable to supplant the Christian ethos.

Vasconcelos writes: "The history of North America is like the uninterrupted and vigorous allegro of a triumphal march.... How different the sounds of the Ibero-American development! They resemble the profound scherzo of a deep and infinite symphony."[105] Recalling Nietzsche's description of Machiavelli's writing in musical terms,[106] Vasconcelos wants to show that beneath this metaphor of music lies a metaphysics of the inner harmony of the cosmos, to which man can be privy through history.

We must recall that for Vasconcelos, all of his doctrines were to be harmonized into his meta-theory, that of aesthetic monism. Man can only know the world by comprehending its rhythms, as Vasconcelos explained in his essay on Pythagorism. Not only is the aesthetic the central category of ontological understanding, but more specifically— as Nietzsche also asserted—music, rhythm, and harmony are at the core of this process.

To fully understand what underlies Vasconcelos's views on race, we must examine how he sees the aesthetic *qua* fundamental metaphysics. This explains why Vasconcelos believes an increasing level of miscegenation will be conducive to a more beneficent social future. In effect, his conception of the idea of *synthesis* is what ties together his aesthetic and his racial miscegenation views.

When discussing the nature of aesthetics, Vasconcelos tells us that

> to connect the plastic arts to poetry in general, in the field of synthetic aesthetics, it is required to have a system that can unite diverse and even opposite elements, in a whole that will transcend its parts. ... [A]esthetics ties together heterogeneous systems, something that is evident in musical form, melody, sound, and plasticity; rhythm is what dominates poetry and all arts that involve composition.[107]

In this light we can better understand Vasconcelos's vignette about the Brazilian dancer who impressed him so much in Lima. Rhythm is not something purely out in the world; it is something that can be "tuned into" by the human body. Indeed, even the human cell is subject to rhythm: "The cell, in biology, is also shaken by the confused rhythms of its needs and desires."[108] A pleasant rhythm is that which corresponds to "cardiac diastolic and systolic functions."[109] Thus, the human body itself is governed by this fundamental rhythmic nature of life. If this is the case, there is a biological basis for particular attitudes to the aesthetic; and different cultures have different ways of cultivating them. In this juncture of biology and culture we find what Vasconcelos means by "race."

The incorporation of diverse elements into a harmonious whole is the main aim of Vasconcelos's philosophy in general. What he states about the nature of aesthetics, we may infer, can be translated into the field of the social. For him, aesthetics is "an organized system of heterogeneous elements."[110] And this, for human beings, is perceived through sensory cognition. He calls "image" the totality of sensory perceptions that we have, such that we should not privilege abstract reasoning; rather, humans experience the world through their senses and thereby attune themselves to the order of the world. Color, sound, taste, touch, and smell are the ways in which we perceive the world and arrange it for aesthetic purposes and make sense of it, according to Vasconcelos.[111]

Through harmony, the individual becomes part of a larger, ordered whole. Music is not "out there" as an object; it is linked to the very rhythmic nature of humans. Thus, rhythm is the nexus between human biology and the external world. Harmony "brings the individual beyond his or her own possibilities and into the *citizenship of beauty*, where he or she develops in an improved manner."[112] As citizens of the realm of the beautiful, humans, according to Vasconcelos, can achieve greater approximation to the perfect, just as the Aristotelian notion of man *qua* social animal is aimed at the *telos* of perfection.

Vasconcelos never explicitly tied his philosophy of aesthetics to his philosophy of racial identity. For this reason, much misreading has occurred, in the sense of interpreting his writings on race as merely reflecting cultural biases, or literary whims, or even political imperatives (the oft-repeated "construction of the nation" through racial narratives). But in fact, it is the specifically philosophical premises of his understanding of the aesthetic that can explain his incorporation of a "racial doctrine" into his holistic philosophical apparatus. If for aesthetics "the secret is in the composition of its elements. . . . the art of arranging heterogeneous parts,"[113] then we can infer that his ideal social order is also one where diverse, heterogeneous ethnic and racial groups are freely incorporated and synthesized into a whole, by virtue of the aesthetic principle.

"Beyond good and evil, in a world of aesthetic *pathos*, the only thing that will matter will be that the act, being beautiful, shall produce joy."[114] In these unequivocally Nietzschean terms Vasconcelos describes his utopian society of the third, aesthetic stage of human history. And for the Mexican philosopher, it is race that is the vehicle to this future social harmony. "Will is power," he maintains, a blind power that is liberated in the third stage of history, when all races mix together and become one. "It expands into harmony and ascends into the creative mystery of melody. It satisfies itself and dissolves into emotion, fusing itself with the joy of the universe: it becomes passion of beauty."[115] Just as Nietzsche sought to philosophize with a hammer (a tuning fork) to find a harmonious link between man and nature, so too does Vasconcelos want to attune man and history.

For Nietzsche, the term "race" represents groups of people defined by biological *and* cultural ties.[116] This same meaning is assigned to race by Vasconcelos. Both thinkers exalted miscegenation rather than racial "purity."[117] Neither believes, as late twentieth-century conventional wisdom holds, that race is *merely* "socially constructed." At root, for them, there is indeed a biological basis of race that explains the distinctive characteristics of the main "racial" groups in the world. Writing before the emergence of advances in genetics, which show the absence of a genetic definition of race, the two thinkers believe race is a group of people with a common biological descent and a common cultural history. In other words, they abrade the distinction between the terms "race" and "ethnicity," in a manner that recalls Alain Locke's notion of "ethnic race."

Nothing is more dangerous than amateurish attempts to use science for political purposes. It is perhaps for this reason that neither Nietzsche nor Vasconcelos attempted to square their ideas of race with the prevailing "scientific" accounts of race. Nietzsche never gave credence to phrenology or eugenics; he rejected Spencerian evolutionary theory and the idea of the survival of the fittest.[118] In fact, many misconceptions about his understanding of race are due to a belief that he endorsed evolution or was anti-Semitic.[119]

Vasconcelos in effect wrote a tract geared at racial inclusiveness at a time of rising racism in Germany and segregation in the United States. Thus, both have to be commended for trying to find philosophical approaches to race, rather than acting as amateur scientists in seeking to define race through science. For both, "race" is a cultural affair, but one that is premised on the fact that human beings in fact look different along general lines.

This question of appearance, of how people look, points to the fundamentally aesthetic nature of the race problem. Rather than a matter of science, genetics, or biology, or a religious issue of monogenesis or polygenesis, or as merely a matter of social construction, the aesthetic lens that both Nietzsche and Vasconcelos use to think of race tells us that human beings for some reason—especially in the modern era—pay special attention to how things look, appear, feel, and are shaped. The primacy of sensory cognition and experience in making us human is what Nietzsche sought to underscore. This human orientation is perennial, but becomes more salient during the modern era with its rapid dislocations and transformations. Vasconcelos carries this thought through, arguing that human beings indeed follow their aesthetic sense more than other capacities, and that this preference will be reflected in the future through the mixing of "racial" types.

This Nietzschean idea of the importance of aesthetic or sensory cognition to humans is, I believe, more valuable to our understanding of race and to what Vasconcelos meant by race than Nietzsche's explicit references to the term "race." Vasconcelos's use of the term "race" is fairly traditional; it is not dissimilar to Nietzsche's use of the term as representing human groups bound together by common descent, cultural history, and geographic location.

In Vasconcelos's somewhat fecetious view of the future, we "would feel no repugnance at all if [we saw] the union of a black Apollo and a blond Venus, which goes to prove that everything is sanctified by beauty. On the other hand it is repugnant to see those married couples that come out of the judge's offices or the temples."[120] Vasconcelos is thus deeply troubled by the retreat of beauty from the modern world, and wants to bring it back in through a vehicle he knows well is a modern creation: race. By reading his words in a Nietzschean light,[121] we are led to the view that race and racialization are fundamentally aesthetic phenomena, products of the human anxiety over the loss of beauty in times of accelerated modern rhythms.

Conclusion: Legacy of a Philosophical *Enfant Terrible*

What does it mean to say that "race" can be understood aesthetically? Given what we have learned from Nietzsche and Vasconcelos, we can say that one way to understand the phenomena of "race" and racialization is to conceive them as part of the late-modernist emergence of aesthetic categories in the social world. Race and racialization are coeval with modernity, and they are tied to the gradual incorporation of an aesthetic lens to make sense of the world which comes *pari passu* with the advent of modernity. In other words, as modern flux, change, uncertainty, and disorder appear out of the discovery of new ways of living, new technologies, and new peoples (such as the discovery of the New World), as well as the disconcerting displacing of old modes, humans make sense of this new landscape by resorting to the basic principles of aesthetic theory: color, appearance, texture, shape, form, and sounds. This holds for the very nature of politics as such.[122] But it also helps to explain that, at root, racialization is an aesthetic process. Individuals fixate on another person's outward appearance: on her skin color, hair texture, shape of the eyes or nose, and other morphological or phenotypical features. And this is often associated with another aesthetic phenomenon: emotion. Emotions often accompany the visualization of a person of a different "race"; these include fear, awe, trust, or attraction. Emotion is a central part of the aesthetic, and it cannot be easily reduced to logical or rational explications. In this manner, the changes and disorder that are produced by modernization are explained, at a basic mental or psychological level, by the use of aesthetic ordering of the world, sometimes tied to emotions and to moral valuations of individuals based on their putative "racial" identification.

Race and racialization did not feature as prominent social phenomena before modernity. To be sure, the ancient Greeks and Romans, as well as the Incas, Aztecs, and Maya, had a sense of ethnic difference, but their civilization did not make race important, as moderns do. It is with the rise of modernity, understood as beginning with the discovery of the New World, that new peoples (the "Indians" of Latin America) were examined as being part of the human species. This process has different phases in the modern period, but it cannot be understood properly without modernist political philosophy. Race is not merely a product of social construction, nor of religion alone, nor solely of science. It is a complex process, rather than a fixed, immutable factor. But to make sense of it in the modern world, we should try to understand it as one manifestation of the relevance of aesthetic classifications in the political world.

Late in his life, the older Vasconcelos was not necessarily wiser. He would go on to contradict some of his earlier, enlightening aesthetic approaches to race by retreating into a carapace of religious dogma. By 1957, when he wrote the essays for *En el ocaso de mi vida* (At the Twilight of My Life), his ideas became muddled, a congeries of inconsistent pronouncements that were supposed to cohere owing to their Catholic armature.

Nonetheless, some insights can still be drawn from these latter writings, which have not received much attention. Vasconcelos still believed, two years before his death, that race was indeed a central (if not *the* central) social category of identity and analysis. Moreover, in his virulent critique of Marxism, at the time on the ascendant in Mexico as well as all over Latin America, he did have some substantive points. For him, "class consciousness" was an empty slogan, something to which "racial identity" was infinitely superior.[123] As he declared: "Class consciousness! To understand better the vacuity, the sterility of this term, it is enough to respond with two words ... Race Consciousness!"[124] We can almost hear his curmudgeonly remonstration, as he bemoans the fact that Marxism is spreading all over Latin America. But behind this outburst, there are important points in Vasconcelos's critique of Marxism.

It is an important juncture in the history of Latin American political thought: the rise of Marxism being resisted by one of the last influential postpositivists. But Vasconcelos makes the insightful remark that a simple dichotomy of "bourgeois or proletarian" leaves too much out of the social world; it reduces complex phenomena to an all-too-simple duality. And this duality may, in itself, be inadequate. As Vasconcelos says, why would someone wish to remain a proletarian forever? The thrust of modernity is to progress, to have more, and to acquire prosperity. So the idea that "class consciousness" of the proletarian sort is attractive is misleading. Moreover, he argues that as soon as a proletarian acquires private property, she no longer is technically part of the class. This generates a sort of hypocrisy, Vasconcelos argues, among adherents to Marxism. They personally want greater prosperity, but politically they are wedded to their putative class identity.

Race, on the other hand, has a more lasting imprint on identity, according to Vasconcelos. At the end of his life he speaks about race in an inconsistent manner: as a reactionary nationalist but also as a proponent of a new Latin American "race." These two positions are not tenable simultaneously. This contradiction in Vasconcelos's later thought is glaring, for he speaks of the "nationalism of race and language" that made great countries into world powers. English nationalism, he says, was fundamentally a "racial pride" rooted in ancestor worship.[125] Such utterances are incompatible with his earlier position, in *La Raza Cósmica*, which argued for the transcending of nationalism through racial miscegenation. They are akin to those conservative thinkers who find greatness in the past, not in the future, as Vasconcelos did in his *La Raza Cósmica*. He failed to realize that there is no clear, necessary link between a purported nation's ethnic past and its present; and he failed to see how his own proposal for more miscegenation would in fact do away with crude nationalisms. He devolves into crude ethnocentrism as he praises Latin over Nahuatl, the Cross over "barbarian idols."[126] He is unable to provide a definitive, logical proof of the supremacy of the Christian God over other deities, particularly on empirical grounds. Vasconcelos decried abstract idealism in philosophy,[127] but here he fails to provide a concrete approach to show how, in his view, Catholicism is by necessity a superior religion.

Even as Vasconcelos slowly entered a clouded sphere of judgment as he reacted to Marxism toward the end of his life, and expressed nationalistic ideas that are similar to a crude racial paradigm found in Hegel, he still occasionally showed glimpses of his key contributions in terms of understanding race as something mixed and fluid. The Latin peoples, he would say, are characterized not by a simple domination of European over Indian, but rather by a "mestizaje that, before aspiring to be universal, must first recognize itself as a form of what is Hispanic, in which the indigenous dimension is not an opposition, but . . . a vein of copper that, as it enters our souls, solidifies our character."[128] Here there is still some preference given to the Spanish or "Hispanic" component of the Latin race, but he was able to propose a definition of the race as a synthesis of European and indigenous influences. More pointedly, he could describe the shield of the National University of Mexico (UNAM) as an emblem of the Latin American race as "a mix with a Latin base, Spanish and Italian, but which does not exclude any of man's varieties; not the black of Brazil, not the Chinese of the Peruvian coasts. It is a composite race, which will be even more so in the future."[129]

Just as he provided some important critiques of Marxism, Vasconcelos must also be seen as a valuable critic of liberalism. His claim that materialism and a mediocre character are associated with advanced liberal-democratic states such as the United States and the United Kingdom, should not be dismissed as nationalist rants. The fast pace of the modern world, its breakup of traditional ways of life, and its premium on liberal individualism do seem to promote a utilitarian, results-oriented culture over one that prizes aesthetic contemplation. If one values the latter, then it is not fully cogent to view uncritically the link between a liberal democratic society with the aesthetic flourishing of individuals. Perhaps these are indeed diametrically opposed, as Vasconcelos argued.

Additionally, Vasconcelos provides an interesting critique of liberalism by way of an assay of the abstractions of the Enlightenment. He argues that the fundamental principles of liberalism, which go back to the era of the French Revolution, are generally empty slogans. "Liberty . . . reason . . . fraternity" are "tired myths" that simply cannot replace the living, personal God of Catholicism or its saints, actual, flesh-and-blood persons who embodied particular ideals. As a consequence, he believes that the modern will is weakened, for behind it lies a desire for power. Again echoing the teachings of Nietzsche, he sees ambition behind abstract ideals. "Such has been this ambition for power," he tells us, "that it has constituted the mask of liberalism, manifested in the British Empire."[130]

The Mexican philosopher redeems himself in the last words of his essays in "In the Twilight of My Life." Having provided a series of uncritical defenses of the Catholic Church, primordialist nationalism, and the European essence of civilization, Vasconcelos concludes by going back to the relationship between race and art. In these words we find a refined reasoning about the nature of race *qua* aesthetic phenomenon.

At the very essence of Latin American identity, race is to be found. He tells us that "we, in [Latin] America have something much more serious than all the racial conflicts of Europe; it is the very necessity of the coexistence of the Indian, the white, and the black inside the same nationality."[131] He goes on to argue that Catholic doctrine helped establish the moral equality of all races; but that the black race stands as the most problematic for its exclusion and marginalization. But Vasconcelos wants to include it in the cosmic, synthetic race. And while Argentina and Uruguay do not need to do so, the rest of Latin America must confront its racial diversity.[132]

His answer lies in art: "Thus, we say that art, properly understood, is a form of superhuman love that solves through *harmony* all conflicts, in a way that economic and sociological analyses cannot." He writes in his last days that the problem of racial conflict cannot be resolved rationally. *Logos* is incapable of resolving racial tensions. To be sure, a Christian, specifically Catholic notion of the Word is needed; but beyond this, it is an "aesthetic instinct" that may allow a coordination of coexistence among all races. He admits: "I cannot find a way to resolve, through reason, the conflict white-black-Indian," but witnessing Indians dancing *sandungas tehuanas* or listening to the spirituals of Marian Anderson, "I have resolved it many times in my heart." "The most powerful, highest, and most original art of the New World: that is what the Negro spiritual is," he tells us.[133]

If, at its core, race in late-modernity is an aesthetic phenomenon that becomes problematic when individuals assign moral value according to somatic and phenotypical characteristics, then the solution to this differentiation, Vasconcelos argues, must also be artistic. But we cannot "unlearn" to fixate on others' hair texture, skin color, and morphology. What we can do is erase the moral valence of these external features by understanding and appreciating the art forms of different ethnic and "racial" groups. This sort of valuation will erase hierarchies, in Vasconcelos's view. Not only will it do that, but we will learn from the art what the spiritual and emotional experiences of other groups mean. In this manner, Vasconcelos provides a novel exit from the racial labyrinth.

CONCLUSION

Making Race Visible to Political Theory

A Return to *Theoria*

Sometimes a word is worth a thousand images. This is the case with the word "theory," which has rich ocular origins. The fourth-century BCE Greek term *theoria* is pregnant with implications of visual perception. The word itself goes back to the term *theoros*, a man who would witness a spectacle or festival, confronting foreign people or places, in order to report it back to a community.[2] *Theoria* thus contains the elements of vision, perception, aesthetic appreciation, foreignness, and a social understanding of shared meanings of spectatorship. This tells us that the roots of contemplation are in the comprehension of events and phenomena perceived through the senses. Political theory is an instantiation of this process.[3] One such phenomenon immediately amenable to this perspective is race. The Western conception of this term, initially found in beliefs related to nonvisible somatic traits such as blood and lineage—as in the case of the Jewish communities in medieval and Renaissance Europe[4]—became increasingly attached to visible, aesthetically discernible human characteristics as the occidental colonialist enterprise set sail across oceans. Faced with humans who appeared to Europeans as fundamentally different, this enterprise held on to visual markers of somatic and phenotypical difference as a way to instantiate power differentials. The story of Europe's conquest of Latin America and the unfolding of Latin American intellectual history shows us how race was born in the modern era. It is on this stage that a variety of actors shaped our initial meanings of race as a visible somatic category. As we observe the drama that unfolded, we see that the notion developed in different and complex ways at different stages in political history. It helps us see that the visually fraught "race" itself hides a thousand complex words.

The purview of political philosophy ought to include, as a central focus, race. For hundreds of years now, the principal paradigms in political theory have been largely color-blind in their attempt to understand the meaning of justice and citizenship. Premodern political thought did not have to deal with the notion of race, as it did not yet exist. But in the modern era, some of the preeminent schools of political theory have attempted to deal with the relationship of race to justice and citizenship in a way that has relied on color-blindness. These schools of political theory, including republicanism, liberalism, and Marxism, have not been able to provide an adequate apparatus to get a purchase on the complex relationship of race to political power.

The republican tradition has historically emphasized an abstract conception of citizenship detached from particular cultural or ethnic identity categories. The common good, the rule of law, as well as antimonarchical and antidomination principles have been its guiding lights since Machiavelli and Rousseau. In this tradition, civic virtue has not been connected to specific ethnoracial phenomena, since its very aim is to find a normatively and rhetorically defensible conception of political membership that applies to all citizens of the polity equally. As a consequence, the republican perspective has generally chosen not to address issues of ethnoracial distinctions for fear that it would lead to greater inequality.[5] The long history of this tradition, up to the present day, has preferred to sidestep race as if it were nonexistent or a minor issue for contemporary politics. But this is clearly not the case. As the current debate over the wearing of the hijab or the burka in France and other European republics tells us, race and ethnicity are at the center of definitions of citizenship. To seek to recover a conception of republicanism built on rhetoric,[6] or to construct an account of normative deliberation within a republican schema,[7] without addressing directly the multiracial and multiethnic composition of modern republics (even those in Europe) is bound to be a problematic project. Perhaps—although highly unlikely—there was a time when race and ethnicity did not matter to early republics. In the contemporary period it clearly does matter owing to the massive migration of people from former colonies to republics that were once colonial powers. With them they bring ethnoracial difference to the heart of the metropole. Contemporary industrialized states are now themselves "postcolonial."

Similarly, the story of liberalism's approach to race is not without problems. From Hobbes's denigration of American Indians as symbols of the absence of civic freedom, to Locke's complicated account of North American natives, to Kant's inconsistent philosophical anthropology and Mill's involvement in the colonial enterprise, the philosophical bases of liberalism have not helped to build solid towers from which to observe the politics of race. Closer to the contemporary era, Rawls's monumental *chef d'oeuvre* entitled simply *A Theory of Justice* reinvigorated a neo-Kantian liberalism, without solving the problem of liberal myopia regarding race. The veil of ignorance prevents us from knowing our own racial identities, and an analytical perspective excludes historical explanations for racial dynamics, for example such as those of the post–Civil War United States. The difference principle may work to help ethnic and racial minorities improve their lot relative to a status *ex ante*, but it does not allow us to critically examine the gradual historical development of racial discrimination or a possible emancipation from race. The work of Will Kymlicka is perhaps the most significant attempt to reconcile liberalism and multicultural politics.[8] Yet it does not generally reach beyond reified ethnic social categories that seem relatively immutable and given.[9] Kymlicka proffers a valuable effort to find normative bases for justice in nonhomogenous societies, but he does not carry out an extensive critical analysis of the way that ethnic groups themselves are shaped by the politics of contestation, defined by power relations, and engaged with specifically *racialized* identity repertoires.[10]

The third central pillar of modernity in political philosophy, Marxism, has also fared inconsistently with regard to race. At its base, it seeks to explain the world through the prism of class and economic struggle. This orientation either marginalizes race or incorporates it under the umbrella of class as a secondary category. Again, as with Rawlsian liberalism, this may incidentally help those in the bottom rungs who happen to be nonwhite, but this result is left up to chance and is an indirect possible consequence. The emphasis on class in Marxism buried ethnoracial dynamics in a way that was ultimately catastrophic for Eastern Europe and the Balkans, and was highly inadequate in Latin America. Latin American Marxism did recognize the centrality of race, as in the work of José Carlos Mariátegui, but even then it was seen as a fundamentally *economic* issue.[11] For Mariátegui, a thinker on the same level as Antonio Gramsci, "el problema del indio"[12] was a class problem. For Guillermo Lora and other more orthodox Latin American Marxists, the proletariat was the vehicle through which social transformation could be achieved, independently of Amerindian culture. Race and ethnicity were seen as part of the superstructure and leading to a kind of false consciousness that could detract from revolutionary consciousness. Only now is Latin American neo-Marxian thought beginning to engage seriously with indigenous Amerindian political thought, as in some of the work of Álvaro García Linera.[13]

Thus, throughout the history of political thought, the preeminent accounts of justice have been flawed in their dealing with the pervasive problems related to race, racial identity, and racial inequality. Citizenship and membership, as well as notions of equality, are in reality shaped by racial distinctions, such that race ought to be seen as a cardinal component of the political theory lexicon. In order to expand our ability to see race and how it relates to political power, we need to reconceptualize the meaning of race to move away from domination- or dualism-centered approaches, as I describe in the introduction. If the canonical tradition of Western political thought does not help us address race adequately, we must look beyond it.[14] This is why we ought to refer to the method of comparative political theory, and through it to observe Latin American political thought, in which race has played a pivotal role from the beginning of the encounter between Amerindian and European peoples. This tradition is not wholly independent, as it has deep roots in European ideas. But the issues and problems in the Spanish Americas elicited particular debates that can help us, in comparative perspective, to reconceptualize race.

This reconceptualization of what creates race and how race shapes citizenship requires a multifaceted understanding of political theory. In a sense, it needs an interdisciplinary approach to political theory itself. It involves the way in which normative issues, political philosophy, and the history of political thought interact. Race has normative dimensions in that it helps to regulate citizenship, but this process can only be understood after a careful assay of the history of political thought, and also while thinking philosophically about what "race" is. A one-dimensional approach to race will yield only limited results and will not be fully useful at the level of normative analysis, political philosophy, and the history of ideas. While the study of the history of political thought may appear to be objective in a sense, it is in fact centrally driven by normative preferences and aims that explain which concepts and problems are studied and which are not. It is important to provide a cogent account of the history of political thought related to race if it is to have relevance to both a philosophical understanding of race and a normative take on how we should understand race in contemporary times.

Race as a River: The History of Political Thought and Racial Identity

In the preceding chapters, I have attempted to show how various thinkers have conceptualized political issues around the notion of race and cognate ideas throughout the history of Latin American political thought. As such, it has been a survey of race and race-related ideas in intellectual history. But the thinkers selected are not a random group or an exhaustive list of thinkers in the Hispanic tradition that dealt with race. They were selected because I believe they elucidate the problematic relationship between race and citizenship. Thus, there is an aim behind this selection: it is the normative desire to provide a reconceptualization of race that is useful analytically, normatively, philosophically, and methodologically. The result is what I call the synthetic paradigm of race that emerges through a reading of these particular thinkers, as I will explain below.

In analytical terms, these thinkers help us understand what race actually is. Thus, they help us analyze a social phenomenon. They are useful in seeing that race is a changing, dynamic construct that must be understood in particular historical contexts and is largely shaped by political factors. Their analyses of the politics of racialization in their own particular environments lead us to the conclusion that racialization is a complex phenomenon that can be approached from a variety of methodological perspectives. Normatively, these thinkers help us to develop a concept of race that is not fixed or categorical, but fluid and mercurial. If all "races" and racial identities are fluid, then there is no one single racial group that ought to be considered normatively superior over others. Last, these thinkers help us construct a philosophical definition of race as a nonessentialist synthetic entity, made up of various elements that interact with each other.

This new paradigm, built from a selective reading of some ideas in a few thinkers in the history of Latin American political thought, can help us distance ourselves from paradigms of race that are not as analytically accurate, philosophically robust, or normatively desirable, such as the European domination paradigm and the (North) American dualistic paradigm.[15] In this manner, we do not have to reject the notion of race, which some have argued is erroneous or misleading. Some philosophers have argued that not only is the term "race" deluding since it does not refer to anything real, but the very use of it contributes to a racialist or racist worldview.[16] But the fact remains that it does exist at the level of social discourse, even if it is artificial and socially constructed. It is used at the colloquial level, at the level of political discussion, and even at the intrapersonal level in individuals' self-understandings. To marginalize the term "race" would be to ignore these levels of its existence. What is necessary is a reconceptualization of it that does not promote either color-blindness or racism.

One philosophical foundation for this reconceptualization project is in the scope of aesthetic political theory. The Greek term *theoria* takes us to the somatic and appearance-level dimensions of human experience. The way that we perceive others in the modern world is laden with information that we garner consciously and subconsciously about the appearance of others. This includes the color of the skin, the texture of hair, the form of bodily features, and the sound of others' speech. These pieces of information have been used to define the "racial." Race is thus part of the modern process by which human beings order their world by focusing on the external physical appearance of others. Thus, while race is socially constructed, it is constructed out of interpretations of visible physical characteristics that can be apprehended aesthetically. Racism emerges when this aestheticization results in reification of other humans. When others are seen as merely objects that are apprehended visually, without concern for moral dimensions, we have the basis of racism. Thus, it is akin to the isolation of art objects as things separate from social or moral relations in the history of modern aesthetic theory. Racialization appears where the axes of aesthetic reification of others and the era of modern imperialism cross.

But this ordering of the world along aesthetic lines is ridden with complications and contradictions. The thinkers that we have examined do not proffer hermetically consistent accounts of the way that race is or should be understood. They are fraught thinkers. In examining closely their key texts, the historian of ideas must make sense of them and determine how analytically cogent they are and to what extent they are useful normatively. This can be said of specific thinkers in particular historical contexts, or of larger traditions in which certain concepts are of particular relevance. In our present account, we have considered the tradition of Latin American political thought and concerned ourselves with the primary objective of examining and elucidating the roles of one concept and its related notions: race.

In this story of the way that four central thinkers examined ideas related to what we understand as race, we find, *ex post*, a logic or structure. Each episode of the narrative can be taken separately to illuminate a given historical period's formulations of racial politics, but at the end of the day there is a relative succession of concatenated projects, concepts, and heuristics from one thinker to the other. This relatedness shows us that the idea of race does not rear its head arbitrarily or in a contingent manner. As Hirschman tells us about the passions related to economic enterprise, such modern phenomena emerge rather suddenly upon the stage of human behavior. The same can be said about the appearance of race as a heuristic device to help humans deal with rapid modern transformations. Upon the "discovery" of the Americas, racialization *avant la lettre* took place as the Spanish encountered somatically distinct peoples. The modern account of race thus begins a cataclysmic moment of confrontation, which was followed by relatively well-delineated historical periods in which "race" was articulated and re-articulated to fit particular political objectives. The colonial moment was followed by the republican period (which contained the nationalist moment), and the narrative was concluded by the cosmopolitan stage in Latin American intellectual history.

How can we postulate the existence of such patterns? As historians of ideas, we prag-matically postulate particular traditions. We show how thinkers transform these tradi-tions in response to specific, localized dilemmas.[17] In practical terms, most would agree that there is such a thing as "Latin America," and that its history of thought makes a particular tradition different from that of Europe, Asia, Africa, or North America. One reason for this is that the intellectual history of the area focuses on some issues more than others in ways that are different from those other parts of the world. Thus, the intellectual tradition itself shapes what we understand as "Latin America."[18]

Within this Latin American tradition, there is a Hispanic (non-Portuguese)[19] perspec-tive, and it is there that I claim that a pointed concern with race, racialization, and related problems emerged from the very inception of the period that we understand as founda-tional to the Hispanic tradition.[20] These concepts and their tributaries (that is, ideas that *led* to their formulation) were born out of specific critical moments that required some sort of heuristic device to make sense of problems associated with them. The often bloody encounters that characterized the meeting of European and Amerindian peoples, and the horrific violence that was visited upon the indigenous peoples of the Americas by the more technologically advanced Spaniards, created social, political, and moral *crises* that challenged the Latin American intellectual tradition.[21] While devastation ensued on the ground, at the very least some thinkers such as Las Casas became aware of the moral and intellectual urgency of dealing with interracial conflict and tensions.

These dilemmas revolving around race were sundry in the Latin American tradition. For Las Casas, a commitment to the imperial Crown and the universal Catholic Church clashed with his moral defense of the humanity of the Amerindians. For Bolívar, his highly Eurocentric education created friction with his realization that Spanish Ameri-cans were wholly different from the peoples of Europe. For Vallenilla Lanz, a profound valorization of the Bolivarian republican tradition was in tension with its internal de-fense of a strong executive for racially diverse societies. And for Vasconcelos, a personal commitment to the Mexican nation was put under pressure by a more cosmopolitan, transnational conception of identity that he saw emerging out of a positive increase in miscegenation in the Americas. All of these thinkers' works are fraught with such ten-sions and dilemmas, but they help us more clearly perceive the centrality of race to po-litical life.

Hence, a certain logic exists in this narrative. It is not a linear progression, but neither is it random. The colonial period in which Las Casas wrote was followed by the early republican era of Bolívar. Within this republican period, a later republicanism emerged in which nationality was crucial. This was the moment of Vallenilla Lanz. Finally, a third period can be seen in the postnationalist, postpositivist era of Vasconcelos. In this third period coalesced the universalism of the colonial era and the particularism of the second, republican period, generating a rooted cosmopolitanism grounded on the Latin American experience. This is not a strictly Hegelian dialectic, for it does not hold the Idea as the underlying logic of history, but it does share with Hegelian historiography the concatenation of ideas as they relate to lived experience. In that sense, we can borrow the analog of synthesis, for the third, cosmopolitan period can be seen as consolidating some aspects of the previous two. Moreover, the second period reacts to the first in a manner analogous to the thesis-antithesis dialectic in Hegelian thought.

In the narrative that I have constructed, there is a relationship between the thinkers that I highlight. It is not an apparent relationship that emerges by itself without drawing out the connections. This arc also tells us that the early theorists of "racial" processes, such as Bartolomé de Las Casas, struggled with these processes even though the word "race" had not yet fully developed. One is that previous to the arrival of the Spaniards in the Americas, there was no equivalent concept. Different indigenous ethnic groups existed and saw themselves as distinct, but there is no evidence, either archeological or intellectual, that they possessed an idea of race analogous to ours. In fact, one could even point to a reverse phenomenon. Rather than visible physical/somatic differences being seen as markers or inferiority or superiority, many indigenous groups in the pre-Columbian Americas modified their own bodies according to hierarchical power relations.[22] Only with the arrival of the Europeans did notions of race emerge. In other words, race is a modern phenomenon. This arc also tells us that the early theorists of "racial" processes, such as Bartolomé de Las Casas, struggled with these processes even though the word "race" did not yet exist. Las Casas was no crude anthropologist trying to explain merely cultural differences. He struggled between his universalistic conception of humanity and the conflict that pervaded Spanish-Amerindian relations. At the same time, he felt the need to posit a political morality that would incorporate the Amerindians under the Spanish imperial Crown in the face of denigrating, dehumanizing perspectives such as those of Sepúlveda. The language of theology and morality was an essential component to Las Casas's fundamentally rhetorical attempt to find a political solution to the nascent racial question.

This language of theology and morality was absent from the central moment of the second phase in the history of Latin American thought's encounter with race. Simón Bolívar, far from being a republican in the vein of Rousseau or Montesquieu, as most accounts of his ideas argue, took a mostly amoral tack in breaking from the Spanish past and seeking to build a form of republicanism that would reflect the multiracial and racially mixed nature of Spanish American societies. This amoralism can be seen as a rejection of the Spanish Scholastic tradition, but it is fundamentally a product of Bolívar's implicit, unconscious Machiavellianism. A military man concerned with increasing the ranks of his troops in order to fight Spanish imperialism, Bolívar wrote texts that evince his awareness of the racial question but that do so without the moralism of the one Spaniard he admired, Las Casas. To understand this, we must understand his republicanism not as liberalism or as conservatism, but as a Latin American version of Machiavelli's martial concept of civic virtue. Bolívar, like the Florentine's ideal prince, was always concerned with war, and always feared foreign encroachments. He was not particularly concerned with nationality, for he thought of Latin America as one single state, much as Machiavelli thought of the Italian peninsula, without a concept of nationalism. More central to Bolívar's thought was the awareness that racial intermixing was so pervasive in South America that a new kind or race of humanity was being forged. This new group was thoroughly different from previous historical periods and required new political schemas to address its problems, one of which was the potential conflict between *pardos* and *criollos*.

Out of this potential problem, and efforts to understand it, we get to the second moment of the republican phase of Latin American political theory. The late republicanism of Laureano Vallenilla Lanz is inspired to a significant extent by the Bolivarian perspective in its Machiavellianism and its emphasis on centralization and the power of the executive. But here a new concern emerges, that is, the need for nationality as a way to glue together disparate ethnoracial groups. Venezuela's particular racial composition was, at the dawn of the twentieth century, distinct from that of Colombia, Ecuador, or Bolivia. Vallenilla saw it as a potential centrifugal force in spite of widespread racial mixing and though no race is superior to any other. Vallenilla's rejection of all biological explanations of race, as well as his acerbic critiques of thinkers such as Gobineau, are fundamental to understanding the rejection of essentialist accounts of race that did take place in some Latin American intellectual circles. For Vallenilla, Gobineau's valuation of the white race and denigration of *métissage* was nonsense upon stilts. Not only was there no positive scientific evidence for Gobineau's claims, but in fact racial admixture could be seen at all times. The idea of a "pure" Spanish race was itself a chimera, for as Vallenilla often emphasized, the Spanish were made up of a variety of intermixed groups such as the Romans, Celts, Jews, and Moors. If anything, Vallenilla tells us, racial intermixture leads to a broader sense of culture, even in times of widespread poverty, something that Vallenilla saw as symptomatic of late modernity.

The nation-state was positivism's choice vehicle to bring prosperity, order, and progress to Latin America. Vallenilla shared in this project. But as the twentieth century moved forward and the problems of poverty, inequality and entrenched, unenlightened dictatorship persisted (for example, Juan Vicente Gómez in Venezuela and Porfirio Díaz in Mexico), a wave of disillusionment emerged. It is there that we find the regional cosmopolitanism of José Vasconcelos. Born and raised in the borderlands of northern Mexico, educated in the rigorous European philosophical traditions, and a onetime candidate for the Mexican presidency, Vasconcelos's work should be seen as a rejection of the nation-state and the ideals of rationalism. It rejects the aspirations of those, such as Vallenilla and Sarmiento, who saw in positivism and the nation a way to bring forth progress. Thus, Vasconcelos should not be seen as an apologist or ideologue of Mexican state-sponsored *mestizaje* discourse, but rather as a philosopher who grappled with the emergence of a postnational moment driven by extensive racial admixture. He chose to address the phenomenon of racial intermixing by valorizing it, rather than denouncing it as many of his contemporaries did at home and abroad. Miscegenation, in Vasconcelos, finally sloughs off its pejorative connotations. To be sure, he was a thinker with many contradictions, from his ignorance about pre-Columbian Mexico to his late-life Catholic reawakening, but he is of significance because he provides a philosophical understanding of the positive fact and the normative desirability of miscegenation at a time of global racism. It is a philosophical apparatus that rests on aesthetic principles. These principles take us back to the intimations of somatic form and beauty given by Las Casas, but they are mostly a product of a profound influence by the work of Nietzsche.

Thus, while it is not possible for us to subscribe to the Hegelian idea that objective reason or *Geist* directly shapes the development of events or ideas in history since there is no evidence of a spiritual force guiding historical processes, a look back at the way that race has been examined by Latin American intellectuals reveals a moderate order and concatenation that shapes a particular intellectual tradition.[23] The colonial period can be seen as the thesis to which the republican period responds as antithesis. Empire is the central idea behind the colonial era, while the antimonarchical, anti-imperial ethos of the republic focused on citizenship and the common good. The colonial era in Latin America was built on the universalism of the Catholic Church, with its belief that the Church was the institution to bring a universalist understanding of both faith and humanity. Besides Las Casas, we can also locate Vitoria (although he never traveled to the Americas), Solórzano, and Inca Garcilaso de la Vega here. The close ties of the Church to the Spanish Empire were rejected by the republican period's central (and particularistic) idea of self-rule. But the republican idea of citizenship did not remain abstract for long, as nationality entered it through the breakup of New Granada. Particularism thus became the driving principle of late republicanism. José Martí and Domingo Sarmiento belong to this period.[24] When the nation-state was shown to be unable to bring order and prosperity in the way that positivism believed it would, the third stage, that of regional cosmopolitanism, emerged. Here the universalistic idea of transnational identity from the colonial era was retained, while the particularism of the republican period persisted as a Latin American regional identity. Thinkers like Vasconcelos, José Enrique Rodó, José Carlos Mariátegui, and Gilberto Freyre are representative of this regional cosmopolitanism, with its sense of shared identity across nationalities but demarcating Latin American identity as distinct from that of other parts of the world.

It may be objected that the use of a logical or philosophical schema to understand intellectual history (even a loose quasi-Hegelian logic of thesis-antithesis-synthesis such as the one I employ here) imposes an a priori order on historical events. Some may seek to defend the absolute priority of material or social events on the ground. However, from a postfoundationalist perspective, it is not clear what "the given facts" are. All encounters with facts are made from philosophically informed perspectives and theoretical commitments. From a postfoundationalist point of view, which I assume here, theory must of necessity enter into the historical material that we encounter.[25] A particular philosophical approach is thus required if a historian of thought is to face the materials, especially at the level of ideas. I suggest that we must rely on philosophy to make sense of the concatenation of ideas or events, and this imposes on us a need to rely on logic.[26] Building on a Wittgensteinian concept of grammar, we can explore a particular problem such as the role of race within the language schemas that were used by central thinkers in a given tradition. While there is nothing like "race" as such, there is a grammar of related concepts that was used by various thinkers in diverse settings related to each other by the historical events going back to 1492. As Jorge Gracia has argued elsewhere, this connection to the events of 1492 is the root of "Latin American" or "Spanish American" identity in a broad cultural sense.[27]

A metaphor may be apt here to understand the concept of "race" that we can get to after having examined the four thinkers that comprise this study. We can think of race as a river. This is because, while fluid, mixed, and changing, a river retains a relative shape over time and over a broad geographical region.[28]

The thinkers we have encountered are all connected to each other by the phenomenon of 1492, that is, the Spanish encounter/conquest of the Americas. They are all concerned with the process of the formation of what we would call ethnoracial identity. This is not because they had such a concept, but because they dealt with it in their own way at critical junctures in the history of political thought. Las Casas is usually called "The Defender of the Indians." But we must ask how he saw these putative "Indians." He saw them as members of the human race, even if that was an unpopular stance at the time. He explored their identity, even without recourse to the idea of race. But in the term *linaje humano* and in his rhetorical project, he is the thinker who establishes the foundation for what would later be called race. In the case of Bolívar, the very ontological uniqueness of the American person *qua* mixed entity tells us that he was also concerned with the idea of ethnoracial identity, but within an implicit-Machiavellian republican schema. It is with Vallenilla Lanz that we finally find a fuller conception of "race," one which rejects biological meanings of it prevalent at the time and still extant. Finally the idea of race seeks to transcend alterity altogether in the work of Vasconcelos.

Thus these *pensadores* show us that there is nothing essential about the idea of race. A concept of race in the colonial period is not the same as one in the republican or national or cosmopolitan periods. Each period's conception of race is shaped by a variety of factors, none of which is integral to the definition of the term. Categorical distinctions within the human species can be made, but there is no *sine qua non* of racial identity. Some elements may be present in one era and be absent in another. But, over time, they build on each other. No period is a *tabula rasa*. Thus, to understand race, we must always locate it in a given historical period but in relation to preceding periods as well. The river of race is fed not just by "other" races or ethnicities, but also by social, political, economic, and cultural factors that contribute to its shaping over *la longue durée*. Thus, race is a synthetic concept that refers to visible, aesthetically perceived somatic characteristics of humans to generate—through political dynamics—discrete, categorical groups. In other words, it is a notion that is dependent on preceding historical developments and that has no particular essence. It is artificial and is molded primarily through power relations. However, it can also involve a myriad of fields of human experience—from culture to religion, science, and social relations. The physical characteristics have no moral or intellectual value in themselves, but they have been used by a variety of agents to justify arguments in favor of and against equality, particularly in terms of citizenship (defined as membership in a political community). Race is the product of the confluence of two modern phenomena: the form of European imperialism that emerged after 1492 (which encountered the entirely "new" peoples of the Americas under the ideological rubrics of Christianity) and the appearance of aesthetic reasoning, understood as cognition through the senses. When this kind of reasoning was applied to human somatic traits in the context of imperial projects, the notion of race was born.

The Synthetic Paradigm of Race

If to understand race we ought to abandon a hierarchical, domination-based principle, which derives from canonical European political thought, and we should also move beyond the (North) American dualistic paradigm of race, we find a possible alternative in Latin American political thought. This is the synthetic paradigm of race that emerges from a reading of the four thinkers that I have explored. As I explained in the introduction, the Latin American perspectives on race are many: some are closer to the domination paradigm, some are racialist. But if we look closely into the work of a few key *pensadores*, they help us construct a theoretically useful account of race.

My use of the term "synthetic" entails two sides: one is methodological and one is substantive.[29] The latter is a first-order concept, the former a second-order concept. The method of selecting and interpreting some components of particular ideas or contributions of some thinkers is itself methodologically synthetic. It seeks to penetrate the naturalistic fallacy of seeing race as a biological fact.[30] It also attempts to address the presentist interpretation of race as centered on somatic characteristics that are socially constructed so as to have some deeper meaning. A simple conceptual history would not allow the normative deconstruction of this naturalism and presentism, because it would simply trace a series of thin facts about the meaning of the term. A dialectical reconstruction of meanings of race in particular historical junctures, which is what I have presented, is itself normative because there is a dynamic process from the first stage (the colonial) to the second stage (the republican) that culminates in the third (the cosmopolitan). This statement is predicated on what I argue above about the inherently normative logic of the history of ideas. I did not carry out a conceptual history of the term "race" because much relevant history antedates the word, which could be missed with such an approach. At the same time, the synthetic method differs from a strictly genealogical approach, for I did not look backward from the concept of race, but rather forward from a nascent set of concepts that are related to a proto-racial understanding of race *avant la lettre*. Moreover, I did not posit an inversion of meaning or "slave revolt" in matters of race in the way that Nietzsche describes the genealogy of morals. Whereas the Nietzschean method unravels the past historical components and meanings behind a surface meaning of a term to look for power relations, the synthetic method garners analytically, philosophically, and normatively useful components from various stages in the understanding of a term for a contemporary approach to an issue, in this case that of race.

However, the synthetic method has affinities with the Nietzschean project.[31] First, it seeks to uncover the hidden historical processes that result in a reified concept that contemporaries perceive as given or fixed.[32] There is great fluidity and change within the very concept, but that is not easily visible when words are used as if they had an eternal meaning. This can be said of "good," "bad" and "evil," but also of "race."[33] The synthetic method also emphasizes historical development in particular stages as they are shaped by power relations. For this reason, to understand "race" we must go back to the period before the concept even existed (e.g., in the works of Las Casas), when the idea of *linaje* was more common. Here, we find power relations between the Spaniards and the Amerindians shaping the way that intellectuals such as Las Casas conceived of proto-racial identity. The power relations themselves were replicated in the intellectual agonism between Las Casas and Sepúlveda, for example. Similarly, the republican period saw a contestation between different ideas of citizenship, and power played a key role in incorporating freed slaves as new citizens in Bolívar's anti-imperial army. Relative power differentials between particular racial groups also shaped the ideas of Vallenilla and Vasconcelos. Thus, Nietzsche's use of power as a fulcrum in his genealogical method finds a parallel in my examination of *political* power in the making of "race" in the Latin American tradition. It shows us that "race" is a preeminently political concept.

This synthetic method gleans from history components that help us make sense of our contemporary understanding of race.[34] The Hegelian conception of *Aufhebung* is useful here. From the colonial period of Las Casas, we find the basic elements of race: alterity, colonialism, incipient aestheticization of the Other, violence, power, and a tension between a universalistic conception of humanity and a sense of wonderment associated with difference. These elements were cardinal to the colonial period, but they remain with us in our notion of race. From the republican period, we can glean a clearly political manipulation of understandings of membership and exclusion in the work of Bolívar. Race is used to distinguish members from nonmembers in a polity, and is applied in an amoral manner to benefit the interests of the state. This distinction is what Bolívar's Machiavellianism shows us, and it is still with us in the use of race to delineate state borders. In the nationality-centered period of late republicanism in Vallenilla's work we find the intimate connection between race and nationalism.[35] This extends the republican project of membership, but gets closer to ethnicity as well, for particular *cultural* practices are associated with specific nationalities. Vallenilla's prescient words tell us also that race is mixed and fluid, that there is no such thing as a pure race. This is the adumbration of the late twentieth-century understanding that race is a social construct, but Vallenilla wrote his words much earlier, in a period of intense racism and fear of *mestizaje*. From Vasconcelos we gather not the idolatry of *mestizaje* as a national political project, as many have argued, but rather the attempt to understand race philosophically. Aesthetics is the lens with which to best understand the basis of racialization, and it also shows us a way into the future, when we might be able to transcend racial hierarchies while retaining the concept of race in a cosmopolitan world.

If we combine these elements, we find that race is a complex of phenomena. This is the substantive dimension of the synthetic paradigm of race. It tells us that race cannot be reduced to one single, succinct definition or essence. The method that we employ thus helps us to de-essentialize race. It tells us that race is indeed a socially constructed phenomenon predominantly driven by political power in the attempt to create specific meanings of citizenship: in other words, of who belongs with us or against us. The drawing of this line of membership is the purpose of race. The delineation draws on claims about categorical, discrete bodily distinctions among humans. Thus, it separates large groups of humans based on putative somatic or phenotypical attributes. These attributes are perceived aesthetically, and are subsequently given moral valuations. It is not that race is shaped out of thin air: aesthetic judgments of somatic characteristics are elevated or denigrated in such a way as to construct large categorizations that are useful politically to define membership (i.e., citizenship) and nonmembership. The elements that go into the making of race are sundry: they can be gleaned from religion, science, culture, art, politics, and practically any field of human life as long as they help draw this line of demarcation of citizenship.

The substance of race is thus amorphous. It does not have a preestablished or eternal meaning. Agents in given historical moments work with the particular components that make up race in a given juncture, or sometimes are able to bring in new elements to reshape meanings of race. This tells us that "race" is mixed and fluid. It does not have the rigid, categorical, and immutable borders that it appears to have. Even in contemporary times, we often believe that "races" are given, that one must belong to one race or another in a categorical sense. The synthetic paradigm of race tells us that this is a mistake: not only must we understand discourses of race along historical axes (as opposed to in abstraction), but a careful reading of history shows us that the lines between putative races shift, flow, and can be altered, especially through political power.

Another meaning of the term synthetic is "artificial." This is what emerges from our reading of the synthetic paradigm in Latin American thought. From Las Casas's transvaluation of values, in which he turns the tables around and shows (against the Aristotelian tradition) Europeans as savages and Amerindians as "civilized," to Bolívar's manipulation of racial identities to create modern citizens, to Vallenilla's rejection of the idea of the purity of race, to Vasconcelos's reliance on art and aesthetic practice in reshaping racial identities, we find that this paradigm exposes race as a human fabrication or artifice. Race is misleading, as any artifice is, but if exposed, it cannot regain its deluding power. It is true that race can be used by those in power to exclude and oppress; but a careful reading of the thinkers in the synthetic tradition helps us realize that the emperor has no clothes. The powerful may use race to exclude, but race is a thin concept that can be shed if we understand it as synthetic or artificial.

Race refers to human bodies, but the statements made about race are interpretations, or second-order claims. As such, these statements cannot be verified against reality. They are interpretations based on observable pieces of information about physical characteristics that in themselves do not possess evident sources of normativity. Thus, these claims cannot be examined analytically against concrete reality, as one could with a scientific experiment. This aspect of observation is a secondary meaning of "synthesis." Observation here merely refers to the immediacy of perception, not to sustained, elaborate contemplation. It is in this sense that the perception of "race" is a thin aesthetic experience. The aesthetic here becomes the factitious, that which is made out of particular interpretations and not incontrovertible facts.

This is where we get to the normative dimension of the synthetic paradigm of race. If we conceive of "race" as an artificial and factitious complex of elements that can be manipulated and given shape, then we ought not to think of race in any naturalistic manner. We ought to understand it as a concept with a fraught historical past, not from a presentist perspective. So, for instance, claims about President Barack Obama cannot be understood merely with a present-day lens, but rather they must be seen in light of a long historical tale that goes back at least as far back as the period of slavery in the American past. At the same time, a synthetic conception of race argues that no race is pure. Each putative race is composed of parts or elements that appear to produce a whole. In this light, we should not accept the notions of "white," "black," "Amerindian," "indigenous," "Asian," "Arab," "Hispanic," and so on, as somehow possessing clear delineations. A person who is said to be "white" will likely have in her past the genetic material of regions outside of Europe. The same could be said about a "black" person's African roots. A synthetic conception of race allows us to have a synthetic conception of personhood as well. It destabilizes the idea of race as a central point in identity. If *all* human beings are synthetic beings themselves, as opposed to grounded on some pure or immutable or impermeable core identity, then we cannot legitimately create hierarchical racial orderings. We ought to accept race as artificial and make it explicit that when we use the idea of race, we are using a factitious term. The synthetic paradigm of race is useful in deconstructing the inadequate understanding of race that persists in most modern societies, where race tends to be seen as a fixed fact of personal or group identity. It helps us to recognize the rhetorical, superficial character of the term "race" and to discard its essentializing tendencies.

Under this new normative lens of race, the idea of miscegenation loses its negative connotation. If no race is morally superior to any other, the mixing of ethnic or racial groups through intermarriage and procreation cannot be seen as immoral or corrupting as Gobineau argued. This lays the ground for a possible valorization of miscegenation as a moral good, in the sense of creating a broad, universalistic human family without racial hierarchies. This may never occur in practice, but it could be an abstract, utopian ideal in the way that Vasconcelos argued. Whether this valorization is moral or aesthetic, increased racial intermarriage becomes a potential norm under a synthetic paradigm of race. This is different from the idolatry of *mestizaje* in Latin American history, for three reasons. The first is that *mestizaje* rests on the assumption that discrete races exist which can combine through intermarriage or intercourse to produce a new human type. The synthetic paradigm rejects any naturalistic claim that races exist as things in the world. If there is no biological "white" or "Amerindian" race, then there cannot be a mestizo race from their union. Thus, it rests on philosophical foundations that are entirely distinct from *mestizaje*. Second, the term *mestizaje* historically refers to the specific combination of Spanish and Amerindian people, whereas the synthetic paradigm argues that all human beings' racial identities are variegated and nonspecific. This applies to those of African, Asian, Arab, or any other origin, and not just to the Iberian-Amerindian relationship. Moreover, *mestizaje* was used historically to hide the process of "whitening" that was entailed by the incorporation of Amerindian peoples into a *criollo* or Spanish culture.[36] But the synthetic paradigm that I describe through the four stages of Latin American intellectual history rejects the idea of whitening, which was found in racialist thinkers such as Sarmiento.[37] This points to the third reason that the synthetic paradigm is different from *mestizaje*. The notion of *mestizaje* tended to be, again historically, a political ideology. Whether in Mexico, Colombia, Chile, or Central American nations,[38] particular states propagated the idea of *mestizaje* as state ideology to unify national groups. The synthetic paradigm is a theoretical, not an ideological, apparatus. It has never been used as a term for political purposes, and I do not argue for such a use. I use it in this study as an analytical tool to observe how, in intellectual history, the idea of race first emerged in colonial times, integrating the Amerindians into the idea of a universal humanity in the work of Las Casas, and was then deconstructed politically by the martial Machiavellianism of Bolívar and the rejection of racial purity in the nationality thesis of Vallenilla, and ultimately decomposed into a cosmopolitan idea by the aesthetics of Vasconcelos. The synthetic paradigm is this arc of intellectual history, which tells a vastly different story from that of African Americans in the thought of the United States and from the colonialist understanding of race throughout European intellectual history. Under this schema, any particular "race" is shown to be intimately connected to another "race" (genetically, historically, socially, or culturally). There is no such thing as racial purity. Moreover, these putative races are themselves constructed—politically—as conceptual assemblages out of multifarious interpretations of data from the religious, cultural, scientific, social, and political fields. Indeed, no entity in the world stands outside the set of elements that could be used to define a particular "race."

With the Demise of Modernity, the Demise of Race?

Still, the question remains: if race is indeed a thin concept, why does it have so much power? The answer to this must again refer to history.

The premodern world did not have a concept of race. Modernity, as a historical concept, is what explains the power of racial identities and politics. Why did the ancient Greeks and Romans, while cognizant of physical, somatic differences, not make much of them in the way that the modern would do later? Similarly, pre-Columbian cultures had a sense of ethnic or cultural differentiation, but not of deep racial distinctions. It is on the ground of modernity that we can determine why race persists. While modernity has a variety of meanings, via the form modernity takes in Latin American history we can most clearly articulate the centrality of race to modern life. This examination of Latin American intellectual history also helps us ascertain the value of the concept of modernity, for without it, we could not understand race.

While there is much debate about the meaning and usefulness of the idea of modernity, there is a standard definition that is commonly used. It generally refers to the world in a period beyond traditional forms of life. This means a postmedieval or postfeudal society, one centered on the idea of progress. This progress is expressed in extensive markets or trade in the economic realm, individuality and greater mobility at the social level, and a system of rights based on nation-states at the political level. Thus, freedom, equality, and progress are the intellectual principles of the modern. It is tied to the rise of capitalism, industrialization, secularism, the nation-state, and the shaping of the self. Modernity, from this perspective, became congealed only in the nineteenth century. It is then when sociologists such as Max Weber focused on rationalization, Marx on industrialization, and philosophers such as Nietzsche and psychologists such as Freud considered the idea of loss of certainty.[39] Culturally, it contains the rise of mass society and the isolation of the individual, but also the emergence of aesthetics as an expression of the autonomy of art. Philosophically, the progress of Reason in the work of Hegel is emblematic of this perspective on modernity.

However, the etymology of the term "modernity" gives us a clue to what may be wrong with this traditional understanding of modernity. It goes back to the Latin adverb *modo*, or "just now."[40] The quarrel between ancients and moderns is usually defined as that between the classical world of the Greeks and Romans and the European world of the eighteenth and nineteenth centuries. However, this definition skips over a large swath of historical time that possesses important philosophical attributes. The idea of the "just now" in essence refers to "the new." And while it is true that the world of the nineteenth century in the throes of capitalism was quite new and carried with it extensive and rapid transformations, the first instance of an encounter with the entirely new is the discovery/encounter of the New World in 1492.[41]

It is only when the world of Europe encounters an *entirely new* world that one can speak of modernity as such. This is because the notion of modernity has newness as its essence. The colonialist enterprise around the year 1492 stands at the crucible of various new processes even in Europe. A proto-capitalist world market was emerging in the Italian peninsula, in which global trade was becoming more salient. Religion was ceding ground to humanism, exemplified again in the Italian Renaissance and its focus on man rather than God, as in the work of Machiavelli and Michelangelo. The seeds of the nation-state were appearing, as evinced in the call to liberate Italy from the barbarians in the last chapter of Machiavelli's *Prince*. And the realm of science was detaching itself from alchemy and moving toward greater systematicity, as in the work of Copernicus, Kepler, Giordano Bruno, and Paracelsus. All these events, along with the cultural and social transformations that were entailed by the discovery of the New World, predate Descartes's *Discourse on Method* of 1637, often mentioned as the birth of modernity.[42]

Descartes's work is of great importance for both theoretical and philosophical reasons, but it cannot be accurately described as the inception of modernity. Not only was it not accompanied by events on the ground that could be described as new and modern, but its philosophical import is subsequent to that of Machiavelli's *Prince* in ushering in a vision of the world that is systematic, detached from God, focused on humans, realistic, and able to separate politics from morality, all of which can be said to be hallmarks of modernity.[43] At the same time, as I argued in the first chapter, the work of Las Casas presents an important alternative version of the advent of modernity. In it, classical understandings based on Aristotle's notions of natural slavery and barbarism are overturned by the Dominican friar. Thus, the early sixteenth century is the site for both philosophical and on-the-ground radical ruptures that can be described as modern. Modernity cannot be fully described if circumscribed to events or ideas in the European imaginary, as by a focus on the work of Descartes or even on the later German idealist philosophical tradition of Kant and Hegel. Modernity is not the product of dissatisfactions in European (and specifically German) high culture.[44]

The encounter between the cultures of Europe and those of the Americas that shaped the epic of 1492 is the principal origination of modernity. To be sure, some cardinal elements were established in Europe before this event, such as Machiavelli's shattering of a unified conception of the world. But the first instantiation of this idea appears in the nonplussed reactions of Europeans and Amerindians facing each other. Modernity brings with it widespread and deep disruption, a sense of vertigo that accompanies a shaking of one's moral and philosophical foundations. It is in this vertiginous vortex that human beings rely on a basic ability to make sense of the world: a simple reliance on aesthetic categorization. Forms, shapes, colors, sounds, and all that is primeval in the sensory realm became the parapets to prevent a fall into unreason when this encounter took place. Human beings at the dawn of modernity came to rely on sensory cognition as a way to order the world.[45] Importantly, this is a Christian modernity. The ancient Greeks and Romans, as well as the pre-Columbian peoples of the Americas, did not conceive of race. Only with the advent of modern Christian imperialism does race appear. Race is a Christian creation.

What this leads to is the notion that modernity makes race. This means that only through the prism of newness can the radical confrontation of Europeans and Amerindians be explained. Spaniards did not view the Amerindians as "people from India" or from the East or from small islands. They saw them as inhabiting an entirely new universe, not as beings to be classified into already existing categories.[46] In this process, the dialectical relationship between Europeans and Amerindians was aestheticized. That is, to make sense of the new, Spaniards utilized ideas related to form, beauty, representation, and emotion. Las Casas, as we have seen, pointed to the apparent differences of the natives in order to minimize them, but paradoxically he also praised their beauty in a way that would draw categorical distinctions between humans. These distinctions were only erased with great difficulty by subsequent Latin American thinkers such as Bolívar, Vallenilla, and Vasconcelos. But once "race" was seen, it could not be "unseen." This is why the phenomenon of race persists even as modernity proceeds into its late stages. This process of aestheticization of difference is quintessentially modern, since it became a pervasive way of making sense of a rapidly changing world and of new forms and experiences.

At the same time, race makes modernity. For the first time in human history, an entirely "new" people was "discovered" or conquered by the subject of Europe. As Enrique Dussel tells us, there is no historical precedent for the total subjugation by a people of another, newly found people that we witness in the forging of the Latin American experience.[47] Previous waves of European travels to Asia created constant intercultural dialogues and interactions as well as violence, but they did not confront entirely new peoples nor lead to their total subordination. As I have shown in the four preceding chapters, race was pivotal in the making and reshaping of understandings of membership, identity, and citizenship at the levels of politics and culture. Thus, the modern political constructs of empire, republic, nation, and cosmopolis all hinged on various comprehensions and arguments about the role and dynamics of race. The central political ideas of modernity, freedom and equality, were articulated and fashioned according to a imperatives that engaged with race and racial groups. While this is most clearly the case in the context of Latin America, it is possible to imagine a similar story about empire, republic, nation, and cosmopolis in other parts of the world, including Europe, Africa, and Asia. The political life of modernity is coeval and codependent with the changing articulations of race through different historical periods.

The modernity-guiding character of race is thus most evident in the political realm. However, as I have shown in the story told heretofore, the social, economic, and cultural are intertwined with the political. One cannot speak about the encounter of 1492 without reference to the drive for gold that motivated the Spanish. The relations between *pardos* and *criollos* and *canarios* in Bolívar's Venezuelan society often occurred outside the bounds of the political and the state; hence the social level is also of great importance. Class structures were forged out of the experiences of colonialism, the early republican state, and the capitalist period, in which Vallenilla underscored mass poverty. Hence it is undeniable that race and class are linked fates, originating in the European colonization of Amerindians and the exploitation of African peoples. This intersectionality also involves gender, for the very idea of race involves the sexual relations of individuals and the formation of families shaped by racial intermarriage and fluid legal codes.[48] The language that aestheticizes the Other is itself pregnant with an erotics of power. Las Casas's description of the beauty of Amerindian women, Bolívar's martial *machismo* intertwined with civic *virtù,* and Vasconcelos's admiration for female Brazilian dancers are all tied to the gendered dimension of racial identities.

As we have seen in the four different stages of Latin American political modernity, race depended on various economic and cultural frameworks. It did not stand alone, floating in a vacuum. There is a dialectical relationship between race and modernity. It is for this reason that we cannot grant the idea that race would disappear if modernity were surpassed. It is true that racialization gains great velocity upon the arrival of colonialism, but the disappearance of colonialism does not mean the end of race. This is because, as we have argued, race is intertwined with the high modernism of aesthetic politics. Once visible, race cannot be made invisible. It is part of the late-modern imaginary. As long as modern processes persist, race shall persist. But since race is a central pillar of modernity, there is no possibility of unmaking a racial sense of the world. Hence, what is necessary is a new articulation of the racial idea.

If the various strains that make up modernity still linger with us, and some such as capitalism and race do so with great force, it is unlikely that we can enter a postmodern world. There is no question that capitalism and race persist, even if in shapes different from those of the nineteenth century. At the same time, the aesthetics of politics, a quintessentially modern phenomenon, gains ground as mass media such as the Internet, television, and mobile phones allow a more extensive transformation of politics into spectacle and image rather than substance. It is a mistake to confuse late modernity with a postmodern world. Just as Latin America's political modernity was transformed around the changing ideas of race in the four stages I describe, so does global modernity change from an early form to a later one. The constraints of modernity are with us, and this makes a postmodern idea of hybridity largely a chimera. Understood as delimitation and demarcation, modernity prevents a free self-fashioning of personhood in a way that follows a hybridity script.[49] If a way to transcend or unmake modern processes does emerge, such as the ability of unseeing race, it may be possible to speak of a postmodern stage. However, we are far from that possibility.

Implications of the Latin American Synthetic Paradigm

One important lesson from the tradition we have examined here is that liberalism has been a very weak intellectual influence in the region we examine. At the same time, I have argued that this Latin American synthetic paradigm can be normatively useful. Are these two facts related? Does the relative absence of a liberal strain have anything to do with the usefulness of the synthetic paradigm?

To be sure, the nineteenth-century Latin American understanding of liberalism was an important political and cultural element of the time. Simón Bolívar, Benito Juárez, José María Luis Mora, and others comprise this tradition, according to most accounts.[50] However, the canonical Western liberal tradition in political philosophy tends to concentrate on the rights of the *individual* as the core moral criterion with which to judge a political order. The Western liberal canon includes Hobbes, Locke, Kant, Mill, and more recently, Rawls. In this tradition, individual autonomy is capital. The same cannot be said of nineteenth-century Latin American liberalism. In that tradition, the political separation of church and state is important, but for reasons having to do with political accommodation more than individual rights.[51] This is what Charles Hale called the "structure of political liberalism,"[52] with an emphasis on constitutionalism and anticorporatism. Instead of a focus on individual rights, a more communitarian tradition can be seen in Latin American intellectual history. Even where there was some influence of utilitarianism, as in the case of Mora, there was no clear articulation of the philosophical bases for a normative criterion dependent on individual autonomy.[53] From Las Casas's universalism, which held onto the idea that salvation could only be achieved through the Catholic Church, to Bolívar's Machiavellian republicanism, to Vallenilla's construction of a common nationality under a Caesarist regime at odds with liberal democracy, to Vasconcelos's profound repudiation of the British liberal tradition, we encounter a robust antiliberal (that is, not based on individual rights) perspective.

What does this tell us? I would argue that grappling with the issue of race is not helped by a liberal perspective that focuses on individual autonomy. Such an approach is flawed in two ways. First, it contributes to an ahistorical understanding of race. Thus, a liberal individual may deny the importance of race, or treat it as a characteristic without a historical past, or minimize its power over individual autonomy. The second is that it may prevent our seeing the group-centered (as opposed to individually centered) construction of race. As we have seen, race is a deeply political category, and politics, in the way that the four thinkers examined understand it, is a collective, social enterprise. To focus on the individual would be to dehistoricize and to decontextualize in a way that would miss the group dynamics of racial identity. Thus, contemporary liberal multiculturalism in normative political theory uses the term "minority rights" as a given: a "minority" such as African Americans or Hispanics or Native Americans or First Peoples is seen as a clearly demarcated group that is analogous to individuals in a normative scheme. They are not critiqued as socially and politically constructed synthetic entities.[54] While we may not want follow the antiliberalism of the four thinkers examined, we can learn from thinking of race as a communal or group characteristic that is synthetically constructed and dynamic. This requires a historical understanding, not one that abstracts from the past and focuses on individual experience.

This paradigm also helps us recognize that race and ethnicity are related but distinct concepts, and that race cannot be absorbed into the term "ethnicity."[55] Both are synthetic concepts: in other words, particular ethnicities or races are made up of various combinations of social, political, cultural, economic, and historical processes. But a simple distinction is useful. Following common current usage, and against the classical Weberian conflation of "blood ties" and culture, I argue that the term "ethnicity" seems to have greater affinity to cultural frameworks, whereas the idea of race is tied to somatic ones. These may be invisible (as with blood), or they may be visible, as when physical characteristics such as skin color and hair type are aestheticized. These qualities in turn may be ascribed to particular cultural groups, but the moment of corporeal aestheticization is theoretically distinct from the identity of a cultural group. As long as physical, corporeal characteristics are alluded to, race, not ethnicity, appears central. It is for this reason that we cannot merely say that Las Casas was a proto-anthropologist or ethnographer seeking to study foreign cultures: his references to the Amerindian body and to the status of Amerindians in human classificatory schemes point to a nascent project of racialization.

The modern term "ethnicity" is theoretically subsequent to the concept of race. Ethnicity depends on arguments about racial or somatic human groups, whereas race does not depend essentially on a concept of cultural difference. Race is a first-order concept, for it distinguishes among *kinds* of humans. Often, these kinds are not considered equal, for a hierarchical ordering of races may be shaped by power relations. Ethnicity is a second-order concept, for it distinguishes different kinds of customs found among beings that are all considered equally human. While Las Casas may have appeared to be interested in explaining different ways of doing things (customs), in effect his writings sought to understand somatically different kinds of human beings as part of the same species (race). The language of ethnicity rests on assumptions and beliefs about racial identities, that is, hierarchical normative values that are grounded on beliefs about physical differences. Thus, the idea of ethnicity is conceptually subsequent to the idea of race.[56] The idea of race is necessary for the construction of the idea of ethnicity, whereas the idea of race requires centrally the notion of differential somatic aestheticization, not necessarily cultural comparisons. As race is then more fundamental, it can run across ethnicities. Thus we can speak of ethnicities such as the French in Brittany, the Irish in Northern Ireland, Germans in Bavaria, Italians in Friuli, and Hungarians as "racially" "white," for they may share, in general, some apparent yet superficial somatic characteristic of lighter skin relative to, for example, sub-Saharan Africans. These labels and boundaries are socially constructed, but they rely on beliefs that rest on claims about somatic (what I call aesthetically discernible) characteristics. Subsequently, a similar process may occur, in which those of different "races" are seen as ethnically the same owing to similar cultural practices.[57]

This distinction between the racial and the ethnic is also useful for contemporary political and normative debates. To take two present-day examples, we can view the United States and Bolivia as interesting locales for possible use of a synthetic paradigm of race as a normative criterion. Both are nations with tension-fraught histories of race, unable yet to deal with the issues associated with racial conflict. I would argue that both of these nations have had difficulties on the plane of race owing to the inappropriate paradigms that have been predominant in their culture. To be sure, they are very different from each other and there are many perspectives on race within each nation. However, I would posit that the United States has been excessively steeped in the dualistic paradigm and Bolivia in the domination paradigm that I describe in the introduction. Both are nations that, while very different historically and in terms of economic and political development, have not been characterized by widespread racial intermixing. As a result, categorical, highly demarcated concepts of race have taken hold in each, something that only seems to be slowly changing at the dawn of the twenty-first century. For both, educational policies that emphasize the synthetic nature of racial identity would be normatively desirable.[58]

In the case of Bolivia, one of Latin America's poorest nations, the first step toward a synthetic paradigm would be to examine its racial history. Founded in 1825, one of the last nations in the region to gain independence from Spain, Bolivia experienced relatively low levels of miscegenation in comparison to neighboring states like Chile and Peru. *Criollo* elites maintained a strong hold on power and carried out repressive policies toward indigenous groups such as the Aymara, Quechua, and Guaraní, believing that these Amerindian groups were racially inferior to Europeans and their descendants. The Revolution of 1952 led to formal equality among all citizens, but this did not erase racial discrimination and distinctions. A profound cleavage along ethnoracial lines could be discerned up to the 1990s, something that was not altogether different from a South African apartheid regime at the social level. The failure of neoliberal, free-market economics in the country led to the rise of the first indigenous president, Evo Morales, and his MAS (*Movimiento al Socialismo*) party. The causes of Morales's rise were fundamentally political, not racial, for the existing party apparatus comprised of the Movimiento Nacionalista Revolucionario (MNR), Movimiento de Izquierda Revolucionaria (MIR), and Acción Democrática Nacionalista (ADN) parties succumbed to extreme corruption. While Morales's government was a historical watershed event, deep resentment has emerged in some areas of Bolivia where indigenous groups are not as prevalent. This includes the eastern lowlands area of Santa Cruz, as well as pockets of the wealthier suburbs of the cities of La Paz and Cochabamba. Morales brought greater social justice to most of the Bolivians who are Amerindian. However, one significant misstep was his inability to create a sense of common national identity. It is here where a synthetic paradigm of race could be useful.

Rather than emphasize only the need to redress acts of injustice suffered by indige-nous Bolivians, Morales would also benefit from underscoring the fact that Bolivia is made up of various distinct but intermixed elements in terms of race, ethnicity, region, class, and culture.[59] Instead of fetishizing the purity of Aymara origins of Bolivia, a more accurate and useful policy would be to make explicit the synthetic nature of Bolivian identity. While at one level it may be true that *criollos* of Spanish origin and Amerin-dians of Aymara and Quechua origin are the key social groups, a synthetic paradigm in fact tells us that the *criollos* and mestizos themselves are not of a "pure" race. Even "pure" Spanish blood contains Moorish, Jewish, Celtic, and Roman influences, as Vallenilla said about Venezuelan *criollos*. At the same time, the *indígena* of Bolivia is likely to be a person of mixed Aymara-Quechua descent, groups that themselves originate ultimately in Asia. Thus, the mythology of pure races must be deconstructed on both sides: on the side of the white or mestizo group as well as the side of *indígena*.

Educational policies that teach, at a relatively young age, that races are in no way pure and are always composed of various ethnoracial influences would serve to erode the racialism and racism that have pervaded Bolivian history. Racial entrenchment and animosity might be minimized by understanding Bolivia's colonial history in light of the work of Las Casas, which emphasizes the humanity of Amerindians; its republi-can period in light of Bolívar's writings on the mixed identity of Latin Americans; its national period in the post-1952 era in light of Vallenilla's rejection of the purity of race thesis; and its contemporary, twenty-first century condition in light of Vasconcelos' pan-Americanism. In this way, *camba* groups in the east would learn to see that their fellow Bolivians in the highlands, the *collas*, are as mixed and fluid in their identity as they are. Only a conscious, national-level educational policy that makes the synthetic paradigm an explicit method of understanding racial identity and relations could achieve this. The ideology of *mestizaje*, as I argued before, is too limited in its emphasis on Spanish-indig-enous mixing, and it hides a long history of racial whitening as state policy and ideology.

A similar analysis could be made of a very different contemporary society, that of the United States. Again, as with the case of Bolivia, a historical examination of race relations would be the first step. It is for this reason that educational policies are of great importance. They would allow a critical analysis of race and ethnicity not merely at the university level, but also at earlier stages in education. Ideas such as those of Samuel Huntington's in works such as *Who Are We?* and *The Clash of Civilizations* would have to be critiqued by the synthetic paradigm of race. The synthetic approach underscores the porosity of lines that demarcate ethnic and racial categories. It undermines reified, monolithic conceptions of ethnoracial identity. To Huntington's idea that Americans are rooted in the white, Anglo-Saxon, Protestant tradition, it would point to the histori-cal fact that Spaniards arrived on the western coast of North America fifty years before the Pilgrims came to the American Northeast. The porosity of ethnoracial boundaries is evident to this day, with the massive migration of populations from Latin American to the United States. Not only are Latin American conceptions of race being brought to the

North by Latino migrants,[60] but entire intellectual repertoires are also being imported by new immigrants.[61]

The synthetic model would also point to the influence on American culture of both Native American and African American culture. However, a critical step is to deconstruct even these "minority" groups as much as one can deconstruct the majority group.[62] It is important not to fetishize subaltern groups and treat them as monolithic or racially pure themselves, be they African Americans, or Hispanics, or Asians, or any other minority group.

Reading early U.S. colonial history in light of the work of Las Casas shows us that Native Americans were treated in dehumanizing, barbarous ways. Similarly, the contributions of Americans of African descent during the Civil War, for instance, point to Bolívar's Machiavellian martial conception of republicanism, which sought to create equal citizens out of racially diverse soldiers. Early twentieth-century U.S. race relations may clearly be seen as morally problematic in light of Vallenilla's rejection of ideas of racial purity. In a more contemporary setting, the debate over immigration and its attendant racial tensions, read under the rubric of Vasconcelos, would tell us that in fact the greater intermixing of a multiplicity of ethnoracial groups in the United States is not only a demographic trend that will likely not be curtailed, but it may in fact be morally and aesthetically desirable. It would tell us that a more transnational, intercultural way of life is possible through the mixing of different people, especially in large, cosmopolitan cities such as New York, Los Angeles, and Miami. These are the cities that Huntington fears will spearhead the Balkanization of the United States. The synthetic paradigm, *par contre*, tells us that the accelerated intermixing of ethnoracial groups is morally desirable because it mitigates the moral error of patriotism and helps to create a new sense of democratic individuality that transcends rigid racial categories.

While it is true that the concept of race can have morally pernicious effects under certain circumstances, it has become, over the course of modern history, an integral part of the lexicon of group and personal identity. It has become engrained in our modern consciousness after having gone through various stages of transformation. At the same time, it helps us make sense of our selves and political interests. For these reasons, it would not be a good idea to simply jettison the term. Instead, we need a reconceptualization that shows its inherently unstable and porous nature.[63] Only a historical account can help us recognize this nature, since the alternative is simply a momentary glimpse into the idea of race. A synthetic paradigm, built from a historical reading of some cardinal thinkers from the Latin American tradition, tells us that racial identity is mixed, fluid, and dynamic, and always shaped in political contexts and by political forces. It tells us that all humans are part of one race, even if phenotypically different. It also tells us that citizenship can be forged through political projects that acknowledge the inherent admixture of human beings. Moreover, it rejects categorical, purity-centered definitions of race, and it encourages ethnoracial interactions to create a more catholic, aesthetically rich cosmopolitan future.

Notes

INTRODUCTION

1. Albert O. Hirschman, *The Passions and the Interests: Political Arguments for Capitalism before Its Triumph* (Princeton, NJ: Princeton University Press, 1977), 11.

2. Race is not "biologically real," as Ian Hacking tells us, questioning the relevance of the term ("Why *Race* Still Matters," *Daedalus* 134 [2005]: 102–116). The idea, however, has powerful political purchase in reality.

3. Alexis de Tocqueville, *Oeuvres Complètes* (Paris: Éditions Gallimard, 1952), 9:199; my translation.

4. Letter of November 17, 1853, ibid., 204.

5. A preeminent figure in democratic thought, Tocqueville maintained a long friendship with a man who is synonymous with racism and opposition to any racial mixing. They corresponded between 1843 and 1859.

6. Tocqueville, *Democracy in America*, trans. Arthur Goldhammer (New York: Library of America, 2004), 395. Tocqueville wrote these words in 1835.

7. For a detailed history of miscegenation law in the United States, see Peggy Pascoe, *What Comes Naturally: Miscegenation Law and the Making of Race in America* (New York: Oxford University Press, 2009).

8. José Martí, *Jose Marti Reader: Writings on the Americas*, eds. Deborah Shnookal and Mirta Muñi (New York: Ocean Press, 1999), 119.

9. See, for instance, Jorge J. E. Gracia, ed., *Race or Ethnicity? On Black and Latino Identity* (Ithaca, NY: Cornell University Press, 2007); Danielle S. Allen, *Talking to Strangers* (Chicago: University of Chicago Press, 2006); Robert Gooding-Williams, *Look, A Negro!* (New York: Routledge, 2005); Michael Hanchard, *Party/Politics* (New York: Oxford University Press,

2006); Linda Martín Alcoff, *Visible Identities* (New York: Oxford University Press, 2005); and Barack Obama, *Dreams from My Father* (New York: Three Rivers Press, 2004).

10. Some philosophers seek to eliminate the term altogether from any discussion of ethnicity. See, for instance, Naomi Zack, "Race and Philosophic Meaning," in *Race/Sex* (New York: Routledge, 1997). Even if logically untenable, however, the term "race" has wide social currency.

11. While I recognize the complicated and often unclean realities on the ground, this is not a work in social or political history.

12. For a rich selection of detailed case studies that express this statement in social and political history, see Nancy P. Appelbaum, Anne S. Macpherson, and Karin Alejandra Rosemblatt, eds., *Race and Nation in Modern Latin America* (Chapel Hill: University of North Carolina Press, 2003). Other historical works that deal with the role of race in making nationality are Rogers Brubaker, *Citizenship and Nationhood in France and Germany* (Cambridge, MA: Harvard University Press, 1992); Desmond King, *Making Americans: Immigration, Race, and the Origins of the Diverse Democracy* (Cambridge, MA: Harvard University Press, 2002); and Anthony Marx, *Making Race and Nation: A Comparison of the United States, South Africa, and Brazil* (New York: Cambridge University Press, 1998).

13. Much of this literature is indebted to Iris Marion Young's critique of the ideal of universal citizenship (see Young, "Polity and Group Difference," *Ethics* 99 (1989): 250–274; *Inclusion and Democracy*, New York: Oxford University Press, 2000).

14. See Philip Kitcher, "Does 'Race' Have a Future?" *Philosophy & Public Affairs* 35 (2007): 293–317.

15. Hannah Arendt in *The Origins of Totalitarianism* (New York: Schocken, 2004); and Frantz Fanon in *Black Skin, White Masks*, trans. Charles Lam Markmann (New York: Grove Press, 2008).

16. I will discuss the case of American political thought below, which tends to be treated as separate from canonical (European) political thought.

17. Important works in political theory/philosophy and race have appeared only fairly recently. These include the seminal works by Kwame Anthony Appiah and Amy Gutmann, *Color Conscious* (Princeton, NJ: Princeton University Press, 1996); Charles Mills, *The Racial Contract* (Ithaca, NY: Cornell University Press, 1997); Étienne Balibar and Immanuel Maurice Wallerstein, *Race, Nation, Class* (New York: Verso, 1991); and David Theo Goldberg, *The Racial State* (Malden, MA: Blackwell, 2002).

18. The most glaring example of the distance between political philosophy and common sense is that politics, for the former, lies in the realm of justice or morality, whereas for the latter it is largely about corruption, deception, self-interest, or immorality.

19. Following Enrique Dussel, *El Encubrimiento del Otro* (Barcelona: Antropos Editorial, 1992), Walter D. Mignolo, *The Darker Side of the Renaissance* (Ann Arbor: University of Michigan Press, 2002) and Margaret Greer, Walter Mignolo, and Maureen Quilligan, eds., *Rereading the Black Legend: The Discourses of Religious and Racial Difference in the Renaissance Empires* (Chicago: University of Chicago Press, 2008). More generally, it is akin to Alexandre Kojève's pessimistic, negative neo-Hegelianism. See *Introduction to the Reading of Hegel: Lectures on the "Phenomenology of Spirit"*, assembled by Raymond Queneau, eds. Allan Bloom, trans. James H. Nichols, Jr. (New York: Basic Books, 1969).

20. See Benjamin H. Isaac, *The Invention of Racism in Classical Antiquity* (Princeton, NJ: Princeton University Press, 2004).

21. Karl Popper and Bertrand Russell provide this line of analysis. See Ivan Hannaford, *Race: The History of an Idea in the West* (Baltimore, MD: Johns Hopkins University Press, 1996), 31.

22. See Anthony Pagden, *Lords of All the World: Ideologies of Empire in Spain, Britain and France c. 1500–c. 1800* (New Haven, CT: Yale University Press, 1995), 18.

23. Hannaford, *Race*, 45.

24. Ibid., 66.

25. See Pagden, *Lords of All the World*, 19.

26. For an etymological analysis of the term, see Audrey Smedley, *Race in North America: Origin and Evolution of a Worldview* (Boulder, CO: Westview, 1999), chap. 2.

27. See Eric Voegelin, *The History of the Race Idea* (Columbia: University of Missouri Press, 1998), 41.

28. See Joseph L. Graves, *The Emperor's New Clothes: Biological Theories of Race at the Millennium* (Piscataway, NJ: Rutgers University Press, 2002), 25.

29. See Robert Bernasconi and Tommy Lee Lott, *The Idea of Race* (Cambridge, MA: Hackett, 2000), vii. The idea that Jews possessed a fundamentally different kind of soul than did Christians can be seen as proto-racialization. I owe this insight to a conversation with Anthony Grafton.

30. Graves, *The Emperor's New Clothes*, 25.

31. This is especially peculiar, since some of Machiavelli's works were published in Spain in the sixteenth century. See Helena Puigdomenech Forcada, *Maquiavelo en España* (Madrid: Fundación Universitaria Española, 1988), 21.

32. We find silence on racial themes (of phenotype and human kinds) in Machiavelli's corpus as a whole, including in the *Discourses on Livy* and in his poetry and dramatic works. He does, however, discuss the ethnic (i.e., cultural and national) origins of his homeland in *Florentine Histories*, book 1, chaps. 1–10.

33. Quentin Skinner, *Hobbes and Republican Liberty* (New York: Cambridge University Press, 2008), 99.

34. This is what Goldberg refers to when he sees in Hobbes "the logic of fixing racially conceived 'Natives' in a prehistorical condition of pure Being naturally incapable of development and so historical progress" (*The Racial State*, 43).

35. See ibid., 43–44; Jonathan Israel, *Enlightenment Contested* (New York: Oxford University Press, 2006), 604; James Farr, "Locke, Natural Law, and New World Slavery," *Political Theory* 36 (2008): 495–522; David Armitage, "John Locke, Carolina, and the 'Two Treatises of Government,'" *Political Theory* 32 (2004): 602–627.

36. Pagden, *Lords of All the World*, 77.

37. See Israel, *Enlightenment Contested*, 590–614. The Radical Enlightenment, especially between ca. 1660 and 1750, brought with it instances of anticolonialist thought. Israel focuses more on debates on empire, rather than specifically racial discourses of differences in lineage and phenotype among world peoples.

38. See Voegelin, *Race Idea*, 50.

39. Graves, *The Emperor's New Clothes*, 40. See Voegelin, *Race Idea*, 45–50, and also Pagden, *Lords of All the World*, 165.

40. See Voegelin, *Race Idea*, 123; Graves, *The Emperor's New Clothes*, 40.

41. See Jennifer Pitts, *A Turn to Empire: The Rise of Imperial Liberalism in Britain and France* (Princeton, NJ: Princeton University Press, 2005), 1–3.

42. See Sankar Muthu, *Enlightenment against Empire* (Princeton, NJ: Princeton University Press, 2003), 14–17.

43. In Bernasconi and Lott, *The Idea of Race*, 17. Such declarations in Kant's anthropological works contradict his own critical views of colonialism (see Pitts, *A Turn to Empire*, 15).

44. Muthu, *Enlightenment against Empire*, 183. Muthu de-emphasizes Kant's racism by asseverating that his later writings show no reflection of it. However, this, even if true, does not negate what he actually did say about nonwhite races.

45. See Pagden, *Lords of All the World*, 173–174.

46. See Pitts, *A Turn to Empire*, 43, 59. In the case of Burke, it is peculiar that he stood simultaneously against the rights of man and the British maltreatment of foreign peoples.

47. See Muthu, *Enlightenment against Empire*, 210–226.

48. Mill's defense of empire stands in sharp contrast with Bentham's critique of it.

49. For an extended discussion of the problem of race in Kant and Mill, see Thomas McCarthy, *Race, Empire, and the Idea of Human Development* (New York: Cambridge University Press, 2009).

50. In Pitts, *A Turn to Empire*, 1.

51. In Mill, we find quasi-racialist language that goes against his commitment to equality (see Pitts, *A Turn to Empire*, 20).

52. In Bernasconi and Lott, *The Idea of Race*, 40, 44.

53. See Shlomo Avineri, *Karl Marx on Colonialism and Modernization* (Garden City, NY: Doubleday Anchor, 1969).

54. In Goldberg, *The Racial State*, 52.

55. As Daniel Conway shows in "'The Great Play and Fight of Forces': Nietzsche on Race," in *Philosophers on Race*, eds. Julie Ward and Tommy Lee Lott (Malden, MA: Blackwell, 2000), 167–190.

56. See Jacob Golomb and Robert S. Wistrich, eds., *Nietzsche, Godfather of Fascism?* (Princeton, NJ: Princeton University Press, 2002).

57. See, especially, part 2, chaps. 6 and 7.

58. See vol. 1, part 2, chap. 10 of *Democracy in America*.

59. The author of *Democracy in America* staunchly defended imperial control of Algeria by France (see Pitts, *A Turn to Empire*, 204).

60. Tocqueville, *Democracy in America*, 365.

61. Matthew Frye Jacobson, *Whiteness of a Different Color* (Cambridge, MA: Harvard University Press, 1998) shows the changing categorizations of the white race in U.S. history.

62. For detailed accounts, the following works are important, *inter alia*: George M. Fredrickson, *Racism: A Short History* (Princeton, NJ: Princeton University Press, 2002); Thomas F. Gossett, *Race: A History of an Idea in America* (New York: Oxford University Press, 1963); Rogers Smith, *Civic Ideals: Conflicting Visions of Citizenship in U.S. History* (New Haven, CT: Yale University Press, 1997); Joel Olson, *The Abolition of White Democracy* (Minneapolis: University of Minnesota Press, 2004); George Shulman, *American Prophecy: Race and Redemption in American Political Culture* (Minneapolis: University of Minnesota Press, 2008); Wilson Carey McWilliams, *The Idea of Fraternity in America* (Berkeley: University of California Press, 1973).

63. Michael Omi and Howard Winant, *Racial Formation in the United States* (New York: Routledge, 1994), 61.

64. See Peter Silver, *Our Savage Neighbors: How Indian War Transformed Early America* (New York: Norton, 2007).

65. Christie Maloyed provided invaluable insight for this section.

66. See Joe R. Feagin, *Systemic Racism* (New York: Routledge, 2006), 87–101.

67. Jefferson, *Notes on the State of Virginia*, ed. David Waldstreicher (New York: Palgrave Macmillan, 2002), 123.

68. Ibid., 180.

69. Jefferson freed four of his slaves, two of whom were his sons, to hide the fact that he had slaves. See Annette Gordon-Reed, *The Hemingses of Monticello* (New York: Norton, 2008).

70. David Waldstreicher, *Runaway America: Benjamin Franklin, Slavery, and the American Revolution* (New York: Hill and Wang, 2005).

71. Walter Isaacson, *Benjamin Franklin: An American Life* (New York: Simon and Schuster, 2004), 152.

72. Henry Louis Gates, Jr., ed., *Lincoln on Slavery and Race* (Princeton, NJ: Princeton University Press, 2009).

73. George M. Fredrickson, *Big Enough to be Inconsistent: Abraham Lincoln Confronts Race and Slavery* (Cambridge, MA: Harvard University Press, 2008).

74. On Douglass, see Feagin, *Systemic Racism*, 60–61, 65–66, 220.

75. See Robert Jefferson Norrell, *Up from History: The Life of Booker T. Washington* (Cambridge, MA: Belknap Press, 2009).

76. Recent literature on Du Bois includes Robert Gooding-Williams, *In the Shadow of Du Bois* (Cambridge, MA: Harvard University Press, 2009) and Lawrie Balfour, *Democracy's Reconstruction: Du Bois in the 21st Century* (New York: Oxford University Press, 2009).

77. *Notes on the State of Virginia*, 1781. Quoted in Smedley, *Race in North America*, 193.

78. The black/white divide is the product of a complicated set of processes, which include law and culture. Some important works that show this dimension are Winthrop D. Jordan, *White over Black: American Attitudes towards the Negro, 1520–1812* (Chapel Hill: University of North Carolina Press, 1968); George M. Fredrickson, *Black Image in the White Mind: The Debate on Afro-American Character and Destiny, 1817–1914* (New York: Harper and Row, 1971); Cornel West, *Prophesy Deliverance! An Afro-American Revolutionary Christianity* (Philadelphia: Westminster Press, 1982); Michael C. Dawson, *Black Visions: The Roots of Contemporary African-American Political Ideologies* (Chicago: University of Chicago Press, 2001)Tommie Shelby, *We Who Are Dark: The Philosophical Foundations of Black Solidarity* (Cambridge, MA: Belknap Press, 2007); and Henry Louis Gates, *Tradition in the Black Atlantic* (New York: Basic Civitas, 2010).

79. Descendents of Spanish settlers who arrived in the 1600s, or of Mexican citizens (after the takeover of the Southwest by the United States during the Mexican American War of 1846–1848).

80. The influx of immigrants from Latin America and Asia to the United States has not in itself altered the dichromatic model. "Honorary whites" and "collective blacks" still form a dyadic schema. See Eduardo Bonilla-Silva, "New Racism," in Bonilla-Silva and Ashley Doane, *White Out: The Continuing Significance of Racism* (London: Routledge, 2003), 282. Hence, a new reconceptualization of race is needed beyond mere changes in demographics.

81. The presence of Asians and Hispanics in the United States predates the twentieth century.

82. While biracial himself, Du Bois stated that there were two, perhaps three, races.

83. See Richard Graham, ed., *The Idea of Race in Latin America, 1870–1940* (Austin: University of Texas Press, 1990).

84. Alberdi believed that the American republics were merely appendages of European culture. See "Foundations and Points of Departure for the Political Organization of the Republic of Argentina," 203, in *Nineteenth-Century Nation-Building and the Latin American Intellectual Tradition*, eds. and trans. Janet Burke and Ted Humphrey (Indianapolis, IN: Hackett, 2007).

85. See Nancy Stepan, *The Hour of Eugenics: Race, Gender, and Nation in Latin America* (Ithaca, NY: Cornell University Press, 1991).

86. Néstor García Canclini, *Hybrid Cultures* (Minneapolis: University of Minnesota Press, 1997); Walter D. Mignolo, *The Idea of Latin America* (Malden, MA: Blackwell, 2005).

87. See, for instance, Javier Sanjinés, *El Espejismo del Mestizaje* (La Paz: IFEA, 2005); and Carrie C. Chorba, *Mexico, from Mestizo to Multicultural* (Nashville: Vanderbilt University Press, 2007).

88. As opposed to analytic (see http://www.merriam-webster.com/dictionary/synthetic).

89. See David Bindman, *Ape to Apollo: Aesthetics and the Idea of Race in the 18th Century* (London: Reaktion, 2002); Uli Linke, *Blood and Nation: The European Aesthetics of Race* (Philadelphia: University of Pennsylvania Press, 1999); Nalini Persram, eds., *Postcolonialism and Political Theory* (Lanham, MD: Lexington Books, 2007); Maxine Leeds Craig, *Ain't I a Beauty Queen?* (New York: Oxford University Press, 2002).

90. A legal analysis of the one-drop rule can be found in Ian F. Haney López, *White by Law* (New York: New York University Press, 1996).

91. These include Javier Sanjinés, *Mestizaje Upside Down* (Pittsburgh: University of Pittsburgh Press, 2004); Marilyn Grace Miller, *The Rise and Fall of the Cosmic Race: The Cult of Mestizaje in Latin America* (Austin: University of Texas Press, 2004); Estelle Tarica, *The Inner Life of Mestizo Nationalism* (Minneapolis: University of Minnesota Press, 2008), Juan de Castro, *Mestizo Nations* (Tucson: University of Arizona Press, 2002).

92. While the term "miscegenation" generally has a negative connotation given that it arose out of the U.S. Civil War period of racial strife, I seek to detach it from this pejorative association.

93. It is paradoxical because the destructive force of empire brought forth a positive and broad conception of humanity. This implication appears to contradict the logic posited initially.

94. I make some references to other thinkers in this tradition, such as Martí and Mariátegui as well.

95. Other figures also offer important contributions to the understanding of admixture, but they are better comprehended with the framework of literary and cultural studies than that of political theory. These include Pedro Henríquez Ureña, Fernando Ortíz, Ángel Rama, and Jesús Martín Barbero.

96. I concur with Raymond Geuss's understanding of Nietzschean genealogy here. It is a method of doing intellectual history that is the opposite of "pedigree." See Geuss, *Morality, Culture, and History* (New York: Cambridge University Press, 1999), 1. It is noteworthy that the concept of pedigree itself involves a biological or racial dimension.

97. See ibid., 3.

98. See Smedley, *Race in North America*, 53–65.

99. See Tamar Herzog, *Defining Nations: Immigrants and Citizens in Early Modern Spain and Spanish America* (New Haven, CT: Yale University Press, 2003), chap. 8, for a discussion of Spain's exceptionalism vis-à-vis European citizenship.

100. The particular place of Afro-Latinos is an important component of this analysis. See George Reid Andrews, *Afro-Latin America* (New York: Oxford University Press, 2004); and

Herbert S. Klein and Ben Vinson, *African Slavery in Latin America and the Caribbean* (New York: Oxford University Press, 2007).

101. Race and sex are intimately connected through the idea of miscegenation, which involves mixing, sexuality, and different kinds of human types. See Joane Nagel, *Race, Ethnicity, and Sexuality* (New York: Oxford University Press, 2003). The link with imperial domination is explored in Ann Laura Stoler, *Carnal Knowledge and Imperial Power: Race and the Intimate in Colonial Rule* (Berkeley: University of California Press, 2002).

102. For a critique of liberal society's enabling of racism, see Falguni A. Sheth, *Toward a Political Philosophy of Race* (Albany: SUNY Press, 2009).

103. Following Cheryl Welch's understanding of the term as representing civil equality and certain freedoms, such as those in the areas of speech and press, trade, religion, and liberty from despotic power. Welch, *Liberty and Utility: The French Idéologues and the Transformation of Liberalism* (New York: Columbia University Press, 1984), chap. 4.

104. These include Will Kymlicka, *Multicultural Citizenship* (New York: Oxford University Press, 1996); Kwame Anthony Appiah, *The Ethics of Identity* (Princeton, NJ: Princeton University Press, 2005); and Sarah Song, *Justice, Gender, and the Politics of Multiculturalism* (New York: Cambridge University Press, 2007).

105. Thereby providing a critique of perspectives such as those of García Canclini, *Hybrid Cultures*; Walter D. Mignolo, "Globalization and the Borders of Latinity," in *Latin American Perspectives on Globalization,* ed. Mario Sáenz (Lanham, MD: Rowman and Littlefield, 2002); and Alcoff, *Visible Identities.*

106. This can often take the form of liberal accounts or republican perspectives on how a citizenry is to be defined. See D'Alembert's entry for *citoyen* in the *Encyclopedie* (1753). The liberal model originates in Roman law. See Michael Walzer, "Citizenship," in *Political Innovation and Conceptual Change*, eds. Terence Ball, James Farr, and Russell L. Hanson (New York: Cambridge University Press, 1989), 211.

107. Feminist critiques of canonical political theory have likewise shown that another key concept, gender, is used to regulate and restrict citizenship. See, e.g., Carole Pateman, *The Disorder of Women* (Palo Alto, CA: Stanford University Press, 1989); Susan Moller Okin, "Women, Equality and Citizenship," *Queen's Quarterly* 99 (1992): 56–71; Mary Dietz, "Context Is All: Feminism and Theories of Citizenship" *Daedalus* 116 (1987): 1–24.

CHAPTER 1

1. Bartolomé de Las Casas, *A Short Account of the Destruction of the Indies*, ed. Nigel Griffin (New York: Penguin, 1992), 74.

2. Another notable vivid description of death is the 1546 passage "Sobre la destrucción de los indios," in *Obras Completas*, Paulino Castañeda Delgado, ed. 14 vols. in 15 (henceforth OC) (Madrid: Alianza Editorial, 1994), vol. 13, chap. 28, p. 243, where he declares that "the name of Christ already releases a bad smell around these nations and races. It smells of an unprecedented and abominable odor" (my translation).

3. In the Walzerian understanding, one who seeks to reform from within and effect change out of love for his or her community.

4. See Bernasconi, *The Idea of Race*, viii.

5. See Daniel Castro, *Another Face of Empire: Bartolomé de Las Casas, Indigenous Rights, and Ecclesiastical Imperialism* (Durham, NC: Duke University Press, 2007), 150–158.

6. The French and British imperial justifications relied less on inquiries about definitions of humanity and the expansion of a Christian mission than on the concept of *res nullius*, the legitimate taking over of unoccupied territory (see Pagden, *Lords of All the World*, 76). The ideas of Juan Nuix are an exception.

7. As Pagden avers, the Spanish did not choose to enslave according to human phenotype. In other words, there was nothing particularly salient about Africans that made them more suitable for slavery; it was a matter of legal status. However, Pagden neglects to think critically about the term "race," even as he employs it. See *The Fall of Natural Man: The American Indian and the Origins of Comparative Ethnology* (New York: Cambridge University Press, 1982), 33. Before his own conversion, Las Casas advocated the use of African slaves, who, he argued, could do double the work of Indians. See Manuel Chaves González, ed., *V Centenario del Primer Viaje a América de Bartolomé de Las Casas* (Seville: Junta de Andalucía, 2003), 19.

8. I use the term "scientific" here in the broad sense of *Wissenschaft*: the pursuit of knowledge for its own sake. This is what is problematically implied in understandings of Las Casas as a proto-anthropologist or historian.

9. Castro does not point to the rhetorical method of Las Casas (see Castro, *Another Face of Empire*, 167).

10. See the letter of October 1543 written by Las Casas to Charles V, where he closes, "praying to God for the greater estate and domain of your Lordship" (OC, vol. 13, chap. 13, pp. 161–166).

11. Contra Howard J. Wiarda, *The Soul of Latin America* (New Haven, CT: Yale University Press, 2003), 84.

12. Contra Cary Nederman, *Worlds of Difference* (University Park: Pennsylvania State University Press, 2000), 110. The line from Ciceronian rationality does not lead directly to full equality and toleration because Las Casas urges the incorporation or integration of Amerindians into the Spanish fold through imperial means.

13. The Spanish Empire was "the true heir of Rome" in the sense of possessing a global, integrative mission (see Pagden, *Lords of All the World*, 127). Alfonso de Valdés and Juan Luis Vives both argued in favor of Spain's universal monarchy. Some did oppose it, such as Alonso de Castrillo.

14. Edmundo O'Gorman, *Cuatro historiadores de Indias, siglo XVI: Pedro Mártir de Anglería, Gonzalo Fernández de Oviedo y Valdés, Bartolomé de las Casas, Joseph de Acosta* (Mexico City: Secretaría de Educación Pública, 1963), 113–114.

15. Entitled *Brevísima Relación de la Destruición [sic] de las Indias*.

16. Joseph Hoffner, *La ética colonial Española del siglo de Oro* (Madrid: Cultural Hispánica, 1957), 260–261.

17. It is telling that J. A. Fernández-Santamaría pays scant attention to Las Casas and prefers to focus on Vives, Vitoria, and Sepúlveda in his otherwise instructive *The State, War, and Peace: Spanish Political Thought in the Renaissance, 1516–1559* (New York: Cambridge University Press, 1977). This is perhaps due to the polemical nature of Las Casas's oeuvre.

18. See OC, 1:30.

19. Chaves González, *V Centenario*, 7.

20. OC, 1:32, 396. Thus, even Las Casas's own identity is one of mixed, uncertain origins.

21. Ibid., 31.

22. Interestingly, Las Casas never mentions his mother in any of his writings. Thus, we do not have access to his possible Jewish origin from this perspective.

23. Anthony Grafton, Baldwin Lecture, Princeton University, March 30, 2009, http://www.princeton.edu/africanamericanstudies/news/baldwin/ (accessed January 26, 2010).

24. Huerga in OC, 1:31.

25. Ibid.

26. OC, 4:829.

27. The exact date is also uncertain (see OC, 1:39).

28. OC, 1:45.

29. Ibid., 53–54, 193.

30. Las Casas decried the *encomiendas* in the harshest terms (Pagden, *The Fall of Natural Man*, 36).

31. OC, 1:81.

32. Ibid., 157.

33. Ibid., 4:829.

34. Ibid., 10:296.

35. See Tzvetan Todorov, *The Conquest of America: The Question of the Other* (Norman: University of Oklahoma Press, 1999), chap. 1.

36. He is at the theoretical vanguard that engaged in "transgressing boundaries of difference" (Andrew B. Fisher and Matthew D. O'Hara, eds., *Imperial Subjects: Race and Identity in Colonial Latin America* [Durham, NC: Duke University Press, 2009], 3).

37. Las Casas, *Short Account*, 3.

38. Ibid.

39. If read as rhetoric rather than history, moral philosophy, or a chronicle, debates about the accuracy of its claims are made moot, such as those cited in *Brevísima relación de la destruición de las Indias* (Bayamón, Puerto Rico: Universidad Central de Bayamón, Centro de Estudios Dominicos del Caribe, Instituto de Estudios Históricos Juan Alejo de Arizmendi, 2000), 267–270 (henceforth *Brevísima*).

40. It was written the same year that the *Nuevas Leyes* were promulgated by King Charles V, regulating the treatment of the "Indians." These laws were largely a result of Las Casas's work on behalf of the natives (OC, 1:191). These laws caused widespread uproar in colonial cities (OC, 1:208), and many blamed Las Casas personally.

41. *Brevísima,* 72.

42. Ibid., 126.

43. Ibid., 55.

44. For the influence of Machiavelli on Spanish Renaissance thinkers, especially on Furió Ceriol, see Fernández-Santamaría, *State, War, and Peace,* 250, 277.

45. See Lewis Hanke's critique of Las Casas's *Historia de las Indias* in *Bartolomé de Las Casas: An Interpretation of his Life and Writings* (The Hague: Martinus Nijhoff, 1951). Las Casas never sought to publish it. In fact, he asked his colleagues at the Colegio de San Gregorio not to publish it for at least forty years (OC, 1:298–299). Contra Castro's belief that "the *Brevísima* is little more than a synoptic version of his Historia de Indias" (*Another Face of Empire*, 109).

46. *Brevísima,* 541.

47. Evangelization is a persuasive project in the realm of words and language (see Don Paul Abbott, *Rhetoric in the New World* [Columbia: University of South Carolina Press, 1996], 2).

48. Hanke recognizes that the *Short Account* "establishes Las Casas as a polemical writer, not a historian." *Bartolomé de Las Casas*, 59.

49. See Abbott, *Rhetoric*, 4.

50. The most evident passage of this is when Las Casas states, against the colloquial Machiavellism, that "one must never use evil means to reach a good end, even if those ends bring goodness." *Historia de Indias,* ed. Agustín Millares Carlo, introduction by Lewis Hanke, 3 vols. (Mexico City: Fondo de Cultura Económica, 1981), vol. 1, chap. 94, p. 382. Henceforth HDI.

51. Much as Vitoria's thought is an alternative to Machiavellianism (see Fernández-Santamaría, *State, War, and Peace*, 103).

52. Some, such as Giménez Fernández, argue that Las Casas sought the readership of the prince in subterfuge in order that his book would receive official imprimatur and be taken to the New World by Spanish soldiers (see OC, 1:284). Friar Motolinía believed that Las Casas hoped copies of the book would be shipped to the New World by Las Casas (see *Brevísima*, 126).

53. His Spanish surname was Borja.

54. See *Brevísima*, 315–316.

55. Docile like "lambs to the slaughter" (*Short Account*, 60).

56. Las Casas tells us that he wrote it so that "his Highness could read it with greater comfort" (OC, 1:284; see also *Brevísima*, 117).

57. Written texts have a certain power that unwritten stories do not. Witness the permanence of the Bible.

58. OC, 1:305.

59. Culturalist interpretations of the oeuvre of Las Casas, that is, those which seek to underscore the proto-anthropological contributions of the Dominican priest, do not fully articulate what "culture" and "cultural groups" or "race" are per se (see Pagden, *Fall of Natural Man*, introduction).

60. OC, 1:306.

61. Ibid., 386.

62. Moreover, it was written for a wide audience, not as a precise tract (see Pagden, *Fall of Natural Man*, 120).

63. Abbott, *Rhetoric*, 61.

64. See OC, 1:303. Menéndez Pelayo agrees with this assessment. Even its admirers call it a work of "ideology" (ibid., 304).

65. In 1537, Las Casas visited Guatemala. He was in Peru in 1581 (see OC, 1:177, 352).

66. It is telling that in a letter to the Council of the Indies, Las Casas uses the Caribbean Taíno term *bohío* (meaning "hut") in the very different linguistic and cultural context of Charcas and the city of La Paz, in present-day Bolivia (OC, vol. 13, chap. 52, p. 349).

67. As Roberto Levillier writes, Las Casas did not generally distinguish between the Tekestas and Tahinos of Cuba, the cannibalistic Caribs, the Otomí, Jívaros, Uros, Maya, Chibcha, Collas, Aztecs, Chiriguanes, Diaguitas, Araucanians, Juri, Iule, Comechingon, Aymara, Quechua, or Guaraní peoples. See Lewis Hanke, *The Spanish Struggle for Justice in the Conquest of America* (Dallas, TX: Southern Methodist University Press, 2002), 128.

68. Fernández-Santamaría provides extensive analyses of Sepúlveda's thought, but practically nothing on Las Casas (see Fernández-Santamaría, *State, War, and Peace*, 201, 206, 220).

69. One motivation for the publishing of the *Short Account* in 1552 was the fact that Sepúlveda published his *Apología* in Rome in 1550, which Las Casas wanted to counter (*Brevísima*, 113).

70. Antonio Mosquera Aguilar makes the insightful claim that Sepúlveda laid the intellectual bases of racism, thus locating him at the antipode of Las Casas's construction of the idea of race in a nonracist way. *El Pensamiento Lascasiano en el Pensamiento Latinoamericano y de Europa* (San Cristóbal de Las Casas: UNAM-CIHMECH, 1994), 69–81.

71. OC, 1:261.

72. "An exercise," as well, "in the persuasive art of eloquence" (Pagden, *Fall of Natural Man*, 112). See Fernández-Santamaría, *State, War, and Peace*, 220–230.

73. Which was anti-Erasmian and (importantly), anti-Machiavellian (Fernández-Santamaría, *State, War, and Peace*, 187).

74. OC, 1:263.

75. Ibid., 266.

76. Todorov, *The Conquest of America*, 160.

77. It is correct to state that "no one provided as much clarity on the theological problems of the New World as Vitoria" (OC, 1:268). Las Casas makes mention of Vitoria in one page of the *Apología*. See also OC, 1:273, on the fact that Las Casas never attended any university.

78. The *Short Account* is "quite inferior" as a work of "science" (Queraltó, OC, 1:288).

79. According to Hanke, even his more cogent historiographic work, the *Historia de las Indias*, is badly organized, and its narrative is haphazard, without order, and circuitous (see OC, 1:298).

80. Hence his principal obligation was "evangelization" (OC, 1:308. 316).

81. *Brevísima*, 379. The term *linaje* reappears (*Brevísima*, 384–385).

82. *Short Account*, 5.

83. See Pagden, *Fall of Natural Man*, 122.

84. "To call Bartolomé de Las Casas an anthropologist may seem to some not only inaccurate but presumptuous as well" (Hanke, *Bartolomé de Las Casas: An Interpretation of his Life and Writings*, 61). Recall that Las Casas did not speak Amerindian indigenous languages at all.

85. Pagden, *Fall of Natural Man*, 122.

86. Just as Leo Strauss argues that Machiavelli's principal teaching lies at the center of his brief and infamous text, I posit that the core of Las Casas's ideas is in his most well-known work.

87. Columbus himself makes note of the Indians' beauty in his diary of the first voyage to the Americas. "They all walk naked … even the women … with beautiful bodies and pretty faces … and have thick hair" (Archivos de la Biblioteca Nacional, Madrid, MS 10255), 15.

88. *Short Account*, 21, 103, 105. The Spanish original is "lindeza y hermosura" (*Brevísima*, 400–401), which means "prettiness and beauty." He also calls them "muy bien dispuestas" (*Brevísima*, 494–495, 498–499).

89. The Amerindians possess "physical beauty" (OC, 1:310).

90. "[El] color, hermosura de los indios" (OC, 3:551).

91. Columbus describes the harmony or "friendship" of the Cuban Indians (Archivos de la Biblioteca Nacional, Madrid, MS 10255), entry of November 1, 1492. He goes on to say that they possess no evil (entry of November 5, 1492).

92. *Apologética Historia Sumaria*, in Pagden, *Fall of Natural Man*, 46.

93. "Insensibles" (*Brevísima*, 375).

94. *Short Account*, 3.

95. Las Casas grants that the Amerindians are barbarians in this sense; they are non-Christians and hence barbarous. *Apologética Historia Sumaria* (in Las Casas, *Obras Completas*, volume 8, chap. 267 (hereafter AHS); and epilogue, OC, 8:1587–1592.

96. Las Casas's transvaluation of the values "civilized" and "barbarian" is similar to Machiavelli's transvaluation of the term *virtù*. They both reject the existing meaning assigned to those values and posit their own, going back to older definitions (pagan for Machiavelli and biblical for Las Casas).

97. The trope associating Amerindians with barbarism and Europeans with civilization, however, remained alive up to the nineteenth century in the works of Sarmiento and the Bolivian thinker Alcides Arguedas (see *The Sick People*, in Burke and Humphrey, *Nineteenth-Century Nation Building*, 354).

98. *Short Account*, 56; emphasis added.

99. Las Casas added this simile in his revision of the text in 1546 and modified it for the 1552 edition (*Brevísima*, 76, 80).

100. See *Brevísima*, 522–523.

101. *Short Account*, 108, 110, 114.

102. In this sense, Las Casas did not have a literal reading of Aristotle (contra Pagden, *Fall of Natural Man*, 123).

103. "In Las Casas's work, the reading of Aristotle and Thomas [is sometimes] wildly inaccurate" (ibid., 122).

104. This is different from merely showing that different cultural groups have similarities, which is what Pagden argues Las Casas was attempting (Pagden, *Fall of Natural Man*, 122).

105. Herder recognized Las Casas's ability to promote the equality of Amerindians without falling into relativism. "The best historians and anthropologists are driven by moral passion." Michael Frazer, *The Enlightenment of Sympathy* (New York: Oxford University Press, 2010), 161.

106. *Short Account*, 3 ("insensibles," *Brevísima*, 375).

107. *Short Account*, 47.

108. In the *Historia Apologética*, Las Casas denounces the "ill effects of Sadness and Fear" (see Hanke, *Bartolomé de Las Casas*, 71).

109. *Short Account*, 80, 92, 126. Las Casas writes of the "compasión del humano linaje" (*Brevísima*, 466–467).

110. As Pagden states, "barbarism" was defined by the Greeks in terms of behavior and practices, based on what people *did* (see Pagden, *Fall of Natural Man*, 18).

111. See OC, 1:306, on the fact that many of Las Casas's contemporaries viewed the Amerindians as "subhuman."

112. This is in spite of the possibility that he himself believed the natives did engage in cannibalism. Pagden, *Fall of Natural Man*, 83.

113. Ibid., 40.

114. See OC, 1:303.

115. Las Casas also argues that cannibalism was quite pervasive in the ancient world. The Greeks, Africans, Thracians, Scythians, the people of Rhodes, Athens, Egypt, Phoenicia, Libya, and Syria all committed human sacrifices according to Eusebius of Caesarea as quoted by Las Casas (AHS, chap. 162, p. 1128).

116. *Short Account*, 39. Las Casas's experience in Nicaragua and his fascination with its natural beauty are recounted in OC, 1:167.

117. *Short Account*, 63, 125.

118. In reference to Yucatán, Las Casas argues wishfully that the natives were free from "sin and vice" (ibid., 71). Las Casas also tries to minimize the Mexicas' acts of human sacrifice (Pagden, *Fall of Natural Man*, 90).

119. *Short Account*, 86.

120. It is interesting to note that, according to Quentin Skinner, Thomas Hobbes in his *De Cive* (1642) offers a late-Renaissance view that American Indians represent the anarchy, fear, and insecurity of "Liberty," as opposed to the peace and order of "Imperium." Las Casas argues that the Amerindians in fact represent good, peaceful subjects of empire (Skinner, Princeton University lecture, November 20, 2008).

121. *Short Account*, 13.

122. See ibid., 63.

123. Las Casas calls slavery "Hell" (ibid., 60, 72, 99) and "Infernal servidumbre" (*Brevísima*, 444–445). Las Casas believes *all* "Indians" in the Americas had been unjustly enslaved (see "Este es un tratado . . . sobre la materia de los indios que se han hecho esclavos," OC, 10:221).

124. See *Brevísima*, 82, 335.

125. Beltrán Nuño de Guzmán "bartered one mare against eight locals: against, that is, eight members of the human race" (*Short Account*, 65). Las Casas actually calls them "rational souls" (*Brevísima*, 448–449).

126. They all possess souls ("animas," *Brevísima*, 424–425).

127. That is, Amerindians are not merely culturally different, but they possess moral and aesthetic qualities fundamentally different from those belonging to Europeans. This distinction is reflected in their political organization.

128. *Short Account*, 54.

129. Las Casas did not question the basic issue of whether Spain could have political rule over the Americas. See Anthony Pagden, *Spanish Imperialism and the Political Imagination: Studies in European and Spanish-American Social and Political Theory, 1513–1830* (New Haven, CT: Yale University Press, 1998), 15.

130. *Short Account*, 69.

131. Ibid., 77.

132. Ibid., 101. "Alemanes o animales."

133. Ibid., 9.

134. Abbott, *Rhetoric*, 63; see also Lewis Hanke, *Estudios sobre Fray Bartolomé de Las Casas y sobre la lucha por la justicia en la conquista española de América* (Caracas: Universidad Central de Venezuela, Ediciones de la Biblioteca, 1968), 111.

135. Abbott, *Rhetoric*, does not remark on this.

136. *Short Account*, 10; emphases added.

137. See Hanke, introduction to the HDI, xv. Manuel José de Quintana shared this view.

138. Ibid., xvii.

139. See Pagden, *Fall of Natural Man*, chap. 6.

140. Even Hanke has to grant that the work is "disorganized" and seems to be written "willy nilly" (introduction to HDI, lxix, lxx).

141. Even Pagden, who argues for an ethnological reading of Las Casas, grants that the *Apologética Historia* was intended to be read out loud for the purpose of rhetorical persuasion (*Fall of Natural Man,* 122). See also Pagden, *European Encounters with the New World* (New Haven, CT: Yale University Press, 1993), 79.

142. See Hanke, *Spanish Struggle for Justice,* 11.

143. Ibid., lix.

144. See HDI, 1:28. See Santa Arias, *Retórica, historia y polémica: Bartolomé de las Casas y la tradición intelectual renacentista,* (Lanham, MD: University Press of America 2001), 40.

145. See HDI, 2:354.

146. Las Casas argues almost the exact same point in the *Historia Apologetica*: "Destos ejemplos antiguos y modernos claramente no parece haber naciones en el mundo, por rudas e incultas, silvestres y bárbaras, groseras, fieras o bravas y cuasi brutales que sean, que no puedan ser persuadidas, traidas y reducidas a toda buena orden y policía y hacerse domesticas [*sic*], mansas, y tratables, si se usare de industria y de arte y se llevare aquel camino que es propio y natural a los hombres, mayormente (conviene saber) por amor y mansedumbre, suavidad y alegría, y se pretende sólo aqueste fin." *Historia Apologetica* (Madrid: 1909), 127–128.

147. HDI, 2:515, 3:179.

148. Nederman, *Worlds of Difference,* 101–103.

149. See Santa Arias, 65–68.

150. This dimension of Las Casas's thought is perhaps the one that is farthest from his juridical legacy.

151. Not merely "cultural," as Pagden declares (*Fall of Natural Man,* 140).

152. See Diego von Vacano, *The Art of Power: Machiavelli, Nietzsche, and the Making of Aesthetic Political Theory* (Lanham, MD: Lexington Books, 2007).

153. Ibid., introduction.

154. AHS, 285.

155. Ibid., 382.

156. Contra Pagden, who believes that Las Casas and others "rejected [the idea of physical attributes of the Indians] not because they knew that the Indians were not strong.... They rejected it because they found it intellectually incoherent" (*Fall of Natural Man,* 3). In fact, as we have seen, Las Casas argued that the Amerindians were physically weak and defenseless.

157. *Summa Theologica,* Ia, q. 76, a. 5.

158. von Vacano, *Art of Power,* chaps. 1–2.

159. "*All* of the dwellers of these Indies are, on the whole . . . of good appearance, of beautiful faces and well-proportioned members and bodies . . . which show noble natural souls as well as good reason and understanding." *Apologetica Historia Sumaria* (selections), Ch. 34, in *Historia de las Indias* (Madrid: Imprenta de Miguel Ginesta, 1876), 5:395. Emphasis added.

160. The text on Africa is thought to have been written independently of the *Historia de Indias,* although it was incorporated into it later as chapters 17–27. Thus, it only came to light when the HDI was published in 1875. *Brevísima relación de la destrucción de África* [*A Short Account of the Destruction of Africa*], ed. Isacio Pérez Fernández (Santa Cruz de Tenerife: Gobierno de Canarias, 1989) (henceforth SADA), "Estudio Preliminar" (preliminary study), 13.

161. Pérez Fernández, "Estudio Preliminar," 35.

162. In the time of Las Casas, "Africa" referred to the area between Tangiers and Senegal, and "Ethiopia" was the area from the Senegal River to the South.

163. Even historians and "lascasistas" have largely missed this document (see Pérez Fernández, "Estudio Preliminar," 17). For example, P. André-Vincent wrote that "Las Casas, dans aucun de ses écrits ne s'interesse à l'Afrique si ce n'est dans quelques passages de l'Histoire des Indes." *Bartolomé de Las Casas: Prophète du Nouveau Monde* (Paris: Jules Tallandier, 1980), 224. In fact, these are not brief passages but extensive discourses in the first volume of the HDI.

164. For this reason, he cannot be presented as the founder of modern human rights, which are universalistic.

165. SADA, 249.

166. Ibid., 202.

167. "No tenían otra razón ni causa, ni justicia para invadirles con violencia." HDI, 1:108.

168. "Guerras crueles." Ibid., 136.

169. "Negros." Ibid., 143.

170. Ibid., 144.

171. Ibid., 3:177.

172. See also Silvia Soriano Hernández, "La no tan breve destrucción de las Indias," in *El Pensamiento Lascasiano en la conciencia de América y Europa*, ed. P. González Casanova H. (Mexico City: UNAM, 1994), 100.

173. SADA, 195, 219.

174. Ibid., 198. Las Casas used the aesthetic term "blindness" frequently to refer to the inability of Christians to see the moral status of nonwhite peoples. See Pérez Fernández, "Estudio Preliminar," 107–109.

175. SADA, 229, 231.

176. Ibid., 235.

177. Ibid., 244; emphasis added. He also calls Africans "prójimos," or "fellows" of the Europeans (257).

178. Las Casas uses the expression "poco seso" (lacking brains) often, employing an ad hominem weapon from his rhetorical arsenal (see, for instance, the letter to Prince Philip of November 9, 1544, in OC, vol. 13, chap. 19, p. 183).

179. SADA, 253; HDI, 1:134.

180. Ibid.

181. As Pagden tells us, "Las Casas was one of the few to endorse . . . both the validity of the Papal Bulls and the emperor's claim to universal sovereignty" (*Lords of All the World*, 52).

182. Contra Nederman's claim that Las Casas aimed to "refute justifications of Spanish imperialism." Nederman, *Worlds of Difference*, 100.

183. See Hanke, *Bartolomé de Las Casas*, 2, 38.

184. Las Casas valued the virtue of poverty profoundly. In 1542, the year he wrote the *Short Account*, he declined the bishopric of wealthy Cuzco. A year later, he accepted that of the much poorer Chiapas (OC, 1:212).

185. While Pagden interprets much of Las Casas's work as proto-ethnographical or anthropological, and he himself uses the term "racial" sometimes, it is peculiar that he does not provide either an analysis of the term "race" or of how Las Casas contributes to the construction of it (see, for instance, *Lords of All the World*, 149) in his otherwise invaluable work on the Dominican and on European ideologies of empire.

186. *Short Account*, 13.

187. Ibid., 109.

188. Castro does not point to these moments in Las Casas's thought. Instead he characterizes Las Casas as basically an apologist for others' material despoliation of the Indies, which is not what Las Casas does as a rhetorician (see Castro, *Another Face of Empire*, 170).

189. *Short Account*, 69.

190. Ibid., 101.

191. Even while Spain had *political* sovereignty over the Indies, it did not have a right to expropriate the property or patrimony of the Amerindians. See, for instance, his general conclusion in "De Thesauris" ("On the Treasures of Peru"), OC, vol. 11.1, chap. 4, p. 47.

192. "Tratado comprobatorio del imperio soberano," *Seventh Treatise*, OC, 10:400.

193. Such as "ethnology," as Pagden avers. *Fall of Natural Man*, 119.

194. Ibid., 121.

195. In *Democrates Alter*, where this means half-men or little men.

196. See Hanke, *Spanish Struggle for Justice*, 124.

197. Pagden, *Fall of Natural Man*, 135.

198. "The Indians are our brothers" (OC, 9:664).

CHAPTER 2

1. In *The Political Thought of Bolívar: Selected Writings*, ed. Gerald Fitzgerald (The Hague: Martinus Nijhoff, 1971), 63.

2. Contra Enrique de Gandía, *Simón Bolívar: Su pensamiento político* (Caracas: Academia Nacional de La Historia, 1984), 53. See also, contra, Ángel Francisco Brice, *Bolívar y Fray Bartolomé de Las Casas ante sus Críticos* (Caracas: Italgráfica, 1969), 8–11.

3. Manifesto of Carúpano, September 7, 1814, in *El Libertador: Writings of Simón Bolívar*, ed. David Bushnell (New York: Oxford University Press, 2003), 128.

4. Venezuela, Colombia, Ecuador, Peru, Bolivia, and Panama.

5. See Simón Collier, "Simón Bolívar as Political Thinker," in *Simón Bolívar: Essays on the Life and Legacy of the Liberator*, eds. David Bushnell and Lester Langley (Lanham, MD: Rowman and Littlefield, 2008), 22.

6. Bolívar, Angostura Discourse, in *Political Thought of Bolívar*, 28.

7. As he tells José Joaquín de Olmedo in a letter of June 27, 1825 (in *Writings of Simón Bolívar*, 209). Bolívar accepted the "black legend" depicting the Spanish conquistadores as brutal and inhumane (see Collier, "Bolívar as Political Thinker," 22).

8. See, for instance, Paul Rahe's monumental *Republics Ancient and Modern* (Chapel Hill: University of North Carolina Press, 1994); Daniel Weinstock and Christian Nadeau, *Republicanism* (Portland, OR: Frank Cass, 2004).

9. For Bolívar the term "America" refers to Latin America, not the United States.

10. For the extent of Bolívar's ultimately tragic final days, see de Gandía, *Simón Bolívar*, 207–210; for a vivid fictionalized account, see Gabriel García Márquez, *El General en su Laberinto* (Mexico City: Editorial Diana, 1989).

11. The place of race in republican thought is usually not examined in historico-theoretical accounts. See, for instance, Philip Pettit, *Republicanism: A Theory of Freedom and Government* (New York: Oxford University Press, 1999); Patrice Higonnet, *Sister Republics: The Origins of French and American Republicanism* (Cambridge, MA: Harvard University Press, 1998); and

Quentin Skinner and Martin van Gelderen, eds., *Republicanism and Constitutionalism in Early Modern Europe* (New York: Cambridge University Press, 2005).

12. Letter to General Nariño, in *Political Thought of Bolívar*, 72; emphasis added.

13. See Hermes Tovar Pinzón, "Bolívar and the Future of Democracy," in Bushnell and Langley, *Simón Bolívar*, 154.

14. It is not correct that "Liberal independence thinker Bolívar saw racial 'diversity' as a central impediment to 'perfect' democracy" (Appelbaum, Macpherson, and Rosemblatt, *Race and Nation*, 4). Bolívar was not squarely liberal, nor was he a believer in perfect democracy. Moreover, he did not see Latin America's diversity as an impediment, but simply as a unique reality to be dealt with politically by a martial republicanism with a strong executive.

15. He contributes to and explains the process by which colonial identities were shaped into republican ones. See Anthony McFarlane and Eduardo Posada-Carbó, eds., *Independence and Revolution in Spanish America* (London: University of London, ILAS, 1999), 38.

16. Bolívar was "a liberator who scorned liberalism." John Lynch, *Caudillos in Spanish America, 1800–1850* (New York: Oxford University Press, 1992), 1.

17. See Augusto Mijares, *El Libertador* (Caracas: Grolier Panamericana, 1987), 101–102; Victor Andres Belaúnde, *Bolívar and the Political Thought of the Spanish American Revolution* (Lenox, MA: Hard Press Editions, 2008), 34; Wiarda, *Soul of Latin America*, 114.

18. Most accounts of Bolívar's intellectual origins principally point to Montesquieu, largely because of Bolívar's explicit declarations of theoretical debt, but this association neglects implicit affinities with other thinkers. See for instance Jaime Urueña Cervera, *Bolívar Republicano: Fundamentos ideológicos e históricos de su pensamiento político* (Bogotá: Ediciones Aurora, 2004), 36–45. See also David Bushnell, *Simón Bolívar: Hombre de Caracas, proyecto de América* (Buenos Aires: Biblos, 2002), 18. Also contra Wiarda, *Soul of Latin America*, 129.

19. See Urueña, *Bolívar Republicano*, 18. For a brief treatment of the parallels between Bolívar and Machiavelli that does not refer to the issue of race, see Carlos Lozano y Lozano, "Bolívar maquiavélico," in *Bolívar: Antología de autores colombianos* (Caracas: Ediciones Presidencia de la República, 1983), 1:183–217.

20. For the Florentine, "the problem of war" is "inseparable from his view of the state." Fernández-Santamaría, *State, War, and Peace*, 115. Or vice versa: the problem of politics is the problem of war writ large.

21. While the literature on Bolívar seems exhaustive, the ties to Machiavellian thought are central to "what is left to say about Bolívar." See Simón Collier, "Nationality, Nationalism, and Supranationalism in the Writings of Simón Bolívar," *Hispanic American Historical Review* 63 (1983): 37.

22. His Irish aide Daniel O'Leary wrote that "his skin was dark and rough" (in Lynch, *Simón Bolívar: A Life* [New Haven, CT: Yale University Press, 2006], 22).

23. Ibid., 2. It is doubtful that after such a long time, any Latin American would be "pure" white.

24. See Iván Jaksic, *Andrés Bello: Scholarship and Nation-Building in Nineteenth-Century Latin America* (New York: Cambridge University Press, 2001), 8.

25. Lynch, *Simón Bolívar*, 17.

26. Ibid., 9. See also Lynch, *Caudillos in Spanish America*, 56.

27. Pardos were not "late-colonial blacks," but rather mixed-race (of white, black, or African *canario* descent) persons. They may have been "blacks" in a U.S.-centered purview, but not in the context of late-colonial South America (contra Fisher and O'Hara, *Imperial Subjects*, 26).

28. These figures are taken from John Lynch, *Simón Bolívar: A Life* (New Haven, CT: Yale University Press, 2007), 10.

29. Through a law of February 10, 1795, *pardos* could purchase certificates of whiteness (*cédulas de gracias al sacar*). See Ann Twinam, "Purchasing Whiteness: Conversations on the Essence of Pardo-ness and Mulatto-ness at the End of Empire," in Fisher and O'Hara, *Imperial Subjects*, chap. 6.

30. Lynch, *Simón Bolívar: A Life*, 21.

31. Ibid., 15. One member of the lower classes was Bolívar's nanny, a black slave nurse called Hipólita. In effect, she raised Bolívar in the absence of his parents. See José Ignacio García Hamilton, *Simón: Vida de Bolívar* (Buenos Aires: Editorial Sudamericana, 2004), 259.

32. See Carlos Fuentes, *The Buried Mirror* (New York: Houghton Mifflin, 1992), 249.

33. In Lynch, *Simón Bolívar: A Life*, 21.

34. Among his favorite authors were Montesquieu, Rousseau, Hobbes, Locke, Spinoza, Helvetius, Holbach, Hume, and Bentham (Lynch, *Simón Bolívar: A Life*, 28, 32).

35. Ibid., 23.

36. D. A. Brading, *The First America* (New York: Cambridge University Press, 1991), 609.

37. Lynch, John, *Simón Bolívar: A Life*, 26.

38. Oath of Rome, in *Writings of Simón Bolívar*, 113. See also Juramento de Roma, in *Doctrina del libertador*, ed. Pérez Vila (Caracas: Biblioteca Ayacucho, 1979), 3.

39. Oath of Rome, in *Writings of Simón Bolívar*, 113.

40. See Marixa Lasso, *Myths of Harmony: Race and Republicanism during the Age of Revolution, Colombia 1795–1831* (Pittsburgh, PA: University of Pittsburgh Press, 2007), 4. See also Eduardo Rozo Acuña, *Bolívar y la organización de los poderes políticos* (Bogotá: TEMIS, 1988).

41. Social bases created pressures from below to shape political order in Latin America and Spain (see Herzog, *Defining Nations*, 205).

42. Jamaica Letter, in *Political Thought of Bolívar*, 33.

43. Bolívar, Angostura Discourse, 48. See Urueña, *Bolívar Republicano*, 66–67.

44. See Lasso, *Myths of Harmony*, 62. See also Gerhard Masur, *Simón Bolívar* (Whitefish, MT: Kessinger, 2007), 52

45. See Frank Safford, "Bolívar as Triumphal State Maker and Despairing 'Democrat,'" in Bushnell and Langley, *Simón Bolívar*, 100.

46. See de Gandía, *Simón Bolívar*, 65–70.

47. The United States could be said to be multiethnic at the time as well, but race admixture was not as pervasive. Most *mestizaje* could be said to occur among whites (e.g. Germans marrying Irish or Norwegians, etc.). *Mulattos* were seen as inferior, and the one-drop rule classified people into white/nonwhite groups. There was no widespread European-Indian mixing as there was in Spanish America.

48. H. Micheal Tarver and Julia C. Frederick, *The History of Venezuela* (Westport, CT: Greenwood Press, 2005), 43.

49. Ibid., 44.

50. The *Nuevas Leyes de Indias* of 1542 limited Indian slavery.

51. Tarver and Frederick, *The History of Venezuela*, 45.

52. Bolívar, Angostura Discourse, 53; emphases added.

53. This would be Jorge Gracia's understanding of being "Latin American." *Hispanic/Latino Identity: A Philosophical Perspective* (Malden, MA: Blackwell, 2000), 48.

54. Gracia's understanding of Latin American identity is not political but purely philosophical.

55. An exception is when he refers to the social dimension of mixing when he urges migration to Venezuela. He states, "Caracas not only welcomes you but eagerly awaits the arrival in its ports of all able men who come seeking refuge among us and who can help us with their skill and knowledge, *without concern for their place of origin*" (Manifesto to the Nations of the World, September 20, 1813, in *Writings of Simón Bolívar*, 125; emphasis added).

56. Bolívar sometimes defends a "democratic republic" as a model, but his thought involves a significant elite element as well as a strong executive (see Bolívar, Angostura Discourse, 50). In reality he opposed full freedom, for it lapses "into absolute power" (Angostura Discourse, 62).

57. Lynch, *Simón Bolívar: A Life*, 28.

58. See ibid., 26; Mijares, *El Libertador*, 112; John Brande Trend, *Bolívar and the Independence of Spanish America* (New York: Harper & Row), 50; Salvador de Madariaga, *Bolívar* (Buenos Aires: Editorial Sudamericana, 1975), 160; Elías Pino Iturrieta, *El divino Bolívar: Ensayo sobre una religión republicana* (Madrid: Los Libros de la Catarata, 2003), 127. Bolívar recognized that he only acquired a "vulgar concept" of Machiavelli's works. See Alfonso Rumazo Gonzáles, *Simón Bolívar* (Caracas: Reproducciones Gráficas S.A., 1971), 44.

59. There was a clear anti-Machiavellism in the Hispanic world. See José Antonio Aguilar Rivera, "Dos conceptos de la república," in *El Republicanismo en Hispanoamérica*, eds. José Antonio Aguilar Rivera and Rafael Rojas (Mexico City: Fondo de Cultura Económica, 2002), 74. Manuel Lorenzo de Vidaurre (1773–1841) was an exception in recognizing the republican qualities of the Florentine.

60. Urueña points out that Machiavelli might be considered a key influence on Bolívar, but does not analyze this link (see Urueña, *Bolívar Republicano*, 19, 42, 78).

61. Pagden, *Spanish Imperialism*, 139.

62. See Belaúnde, *Bolívar and Political Thought*, 26.

63. See Iván Jaksic, "Simón Bolívar and Andrés Bello: The Republican Ideal," in Bushnell and Langley, *Simón Bolívar*, 84.

64. Montesquieu decries racism satirically but nonetheless believes it will likely persist. *The Spirit of Laws: A Compendium of the First English Edition*, ed. David Wallace Carrithers, trans. Thomas Nugent (Berkeley: University of California Press, 1977), book 15, chap. 5, p. 257.

65. Freedom from interference is not a preoccupation for Bolívar. For a distinction between liberal and republican concerns, see Maurizio Viroli, *Republicanism* (New York: Hill and Wang, 2001), 10.

66. See Bernard Manin, "Montesquieu, la república y el comercio," in Aguilar Rivera and Rojas, *El Republicanismo en Hispanoamérica*, 13–56.

67. See Viroli, *Republicanism*, 76.

68. Ibid., 70.

69. This may be due to the fact that Rousseau was the most widely read European author, along with Reynal, in Latin America. Belaúnde, *Bolívar and Political Thought*, 24. Emphasis on Rousseau's influence on Bolívar is also probably due to the fact that the citizen of Geneva was the favorite author of Simón Rodríguez, Bolívar's tutor.

70. For a clear statement of this, see ibid., 187.

71. One of the few commentators to see the wide gulf between Bolívar and Rousseau was Laureano Vallenilla Lanz. Bolívar, he tells us, "was not in favor of pure democracy, because—having

lived in the midst of our [racially] heterogeneous peoples—[he] did not need, like Napoleon, to look at those of so-called inferior races to realize the sophistry of the ideas of Jean-Jacques." Vallenilla Lanz, *El Libertador juzgado por los miopes* (Caracas: Comercio, 1914), 10. Vallenilla goes on to say that in this case, he uses the term "race" in sociocultural, not biological, terms.

72. Collier, "Bolívar as Political Thinker," 29.

73. Moreover, Rousseau's preference for small republics goes against Bolívar's belief that Spanish America could be, and should be, one large republic.

74. The erasure of this distinction is one interpretation of Las Casas's oeuvre. In the *Social Contract*, Rousseau tells us that Amerindians somehow stand outside the realm of human necessity, for "the Caribs of Venezuela among others live in this respect in absolute security and without the smallest inconvenience." *The Social Contract, and Discourses*, trans. G. D. H. Cole (New York: E. P. Dutton, 1950), 203.

75. *Jean-Jacques Rousseau: The Basic Political Writings*, ed. Donald A. Cress (Cambridge, MA: Hackett, 1987), 56.

76. Rousseau, *Emile* (Fairford, Gloucestershire, England: Echo Library, 2007), 11.

77. Bolívar, Angostura Discourse, 53.

78. Mazzini is instructive for a related view of race in relation to republicanism (in Viroli, *Republicanism*, 33).

79. Contra D. A. Brading, *Classical Republicanism and Creole Patriotism: Simón Bolívar (1783–1830) and the Spanish American Revolution* (Cambridge: Centre of Latin American Studies, University of Cambridge, 1983).

80. For his reference to African hordes, which is tinged by racism, see Letter to Santander of August 8, 1826, in *Cartas del Libertador* (Caracas: Banco de Venezuela, 1968), 5:234. He also refers to black revolts as the product of an "inhuman and savage mob" (in Manifesto to the Nations of the World, September 20, 1813, in *Writings of Simón Bolívar*, 118). For Bolívar's fear of *pardocracia* see also Lynch, *Simón Bolívar: A Life*. New Haven, CT: Yale University Press, 2007, p. 149; see also Lynch, *Caudillos in Spanish America*, 112; and Lasso, *Myths of Harmony*, 61.

81. Bolívar, Angostura Discourse, 53.

82. Ibid.

83. See Eduardo Rozo Acuña, *Obra política y constitucional de Simón Bolívar*, lvi.

84. Letter to Guillermo White, in *Political Thought of Bolívar*, 69.

85. Contra Clare Mar-Molinero, *The Politics of Language in the Spanish-Speaking World* (New York: Routledge, 2005), 32.

86. See Aline Helg, *Liberty and Equality in Caribbean Colombia, 1770–1835* (Chapel Hill: University of North Carolina Press, 2004), 196.

87. See Message to the Congress of Bolivia, in *Political Thought of Bolívar*, 95.

88. Letter to Sucre, in *Political Thought of Bolívar*, 90.

89. *Writings of Simón Bolívar*, 220 n. 5.

90. Ibid., 54.

91. Ibid., 135.

92. On his leadership, see Safford, "Triumphal State Maker," 101. On his heroism, see José Enrique Rodó, "Bolívar," in *Bolívar* (Caracas: Biblioteca Ayacucho, 1983), 243–264.

93. Bolívar admired Draco as a good example of the value of firm laws. See Letter to Guillermo White, in *Political Thought of Bolívar*, 70. See also Lynch, *Caudillos in Spanish America*, 108.

94. See Bolívar, Angostura Discourse, 46. See also de Gandía, *Simón Bolívar*, 19.

95. See Tarver and Frederick, *The History of Venezuela*, 59. Still, he believed that unconstitutional permanence of one person in power would lead to tyranny (Bolívar, Angostura Discourse, 47).

96. Being subject to another man in a hierarchical structure is not, for Bolívar, necessarily a loss of freedom. This is another mark of distinction with Rousseau, who believed that one is not free "when one must obey another man; because [in that] case I must obey the will of another" (in Viroli, *Republicanism*, 38).

97. *Portable Machiavelli*, eds. Peter Bondanella and Mark Musa (New York: Penguin, 1979), 124–126.

98. "Bolívar was a master of the art of war." John Johnson and Doris Ladd, *Simón Bolívar and Spanish American Independence, 1783–1830* (Malabar, FL: Krieger, 1992), 115. Some accounts of Machiavelli seek to portray him as a whitewashed, domesticated proto-liberal or proto-democrat, but they miss a substantial part of the Florentine's ideas when they do not address his perennial concern with war, expansionism, and the martial life. One example is Viroli's attempt to situate Machiavelli at the origins of the history of liberalism in his *Republicanism*.

99. See Rozo Acuña's brief but penetrating parallel between Bolívar and Machiavelli in *Obra política y constitucional de Simón Bolívar*, xxxvi–xxxix.

100. See Michael Mallet, "The Theory and Practice of Warfare in Machiavelli's Republic," in *Machiavelli and Republicanism*, eds. Gisela Bock, Quentin Skinner, and Maurizio Viroli (New York: Cambridge University Press, 1990), 173.

101. This perspective distinguishes Bolívar's concept from Rousseau's theory of the social contract. Bolívar believed that social order can emerge out of the imposition of the authority of one man over a situation of social conflict, not through a bargaining process or one of deliberation.

102. Brading, *The First America*, 610.

103. Cartagena Manifesto, in *Political Thought of Bolívar*, 12.

104. This concern with nondomination vis-à-vis an external, *foreign* threat is, I believe, an extension of the republican idea of freedom that Pettit describes, as opposed to noninterference. See Pettit, *Republicanism*, 51.

105. Sarah Chambers shows the centrality of masculinity to Bolívar's republican approach to race (see "Masculine Virtues and Feminine Passions: Gender and Race in the Republicanism of Simón Bolívar," *Hispanic Research Journal* 7.1 [March 2006]: 20).

106. See Brading, *The First America*, 45.

107. See Rozo Acuña, *Bolívar y la organización de los poderes públicos*, 8.

108. See Lynch, *Simón Bolívar: A Life*, 34–35.

109. See Rozo Acuña, *Obra política y constitucional de Simón Bolívar*, xxxvii.

110. See Winthrop Wright, *Café Con Leche: Race, Class, and National Image in Venezuela* (Austin: University of Texas Press, 1993), 27.

111. "What is surprising is not that slaves sought to avoid military service, but that so many agreed to serve." Andrews, *Afro-Latin America*, 62.

112. Contra Pettit, *Republicanism*, 51–52.

113. According to Pettit's citation of Weber's *Economy and Society* (1978) and Connolly's *Terms of Political Discourse* (1983).

114. For Pettit, it is not law that restrains arbitrariness, but the extent to which the dominant person "tracks" the "interests and ideas" of a person being interfered with. This makes us ask,

how we can track the person doing the tracking of something as intangible as ideas? See Pettit, *Republicanism*, 55. Rhetoric here would trump deliberation, since there is no easy way for the dominator to see the ideas of the dominated.

115. Citizenship went hand in hand with military participation. "La acción política y la acción militar estaban por supuesto entrelazadas" (Veronique Hebrard in McFarlane and Posada-Carbó, *Independence and Revolution*, 137).

116. See Pettit, *Republicanism*, chap. 6 for a discussion of *imperium*.

117. A republic must "molest others," otherwise "others will molest her." *Discourses on Livy*, eds. Harvey Mansfield and Nathan Tarcov (Chicago: University of Chicago Press, 1996), 2:19, 173.

118. See Lozano y Lozano, "Bolívar maquiavélico," 201.

119. Bolívar, Jamaica Letter, 39.

120. Ibid.

121. In this manner, Bolívar contributes to a fuller understanding of republicanism as a theory of freedom from domination, as Pettit, *Republicanism*, has argued. Rather than merely focusing on freedom from interference, as liberalism does, or from internal despotism, as some forms of republicanism do, Bolívar's theory is more complete because it considers foreign domination just as pernicious (see Viroli, *Republicanism*, 36–37). Thus, it provides a critique of colonialism.

122. See his reference to *pardocracia* in his letter to Santander of April 7, 1825, and to Sucre of May 12, 1826, in *Selected Writings of Bolívar*, ed. Vicente Lecuna and Harold Bierck, Jr., trans. Lewis Bertrand (New York: Colonial Press, 1951).

123. Letter to Sucre, in *Political Thought of Bolívar*, 89. Bolívar feared a kind of Jacobinism if the *pardos* were to take over. See Belaúnde, *Bolívar and Political Thought*, 136.

124. Introduction, Appelbaum, Macpherson, and Rosemblatt, *Race and Nation*, 4–5.

125. Thus, he cannot be blamed for perpetuating the "myth of racial democracy" in Venezuela, since he never believed it would be possible (see Wright, *Café Con Leche*, chap. 1).

126. See Aline Helg, "Bolívar and the Spectre of *Pardocracia*: José Padilla in Post-independence Cartagena," *Journal of Latin American Studies* 35 (2003): 447–471.

127. Contra Wright, *Café Con Leche*, 28, 36.

128. Bolívar, Cartagena Manifesto, 11.

129. As Helg shows, Bolívar was aware of his own immorality in his implication in the deaths of Piar and Padilla and the light treatment received by Santander (Helg, *Liberty and Equality*, 209).

130. He did not endorse this religion in his model constitution for Bolivia (see Message to the Congress of Bolivia, 103) because religion "governs man in his home, within his own walls, within himself." Ibid.

131. In Lynch, *Simón Bolívar: A Life*, 37.

132. Bolívar was critical of ecclesiastical influence after the earthquake in Venezuela that led to the collapse of the first republic (see Bolívar, Cartagena Manifesto, 15). Priests, in his eyes, became traitors to the republican cause. See also Lynch, *Simón Bolívar: A Life*, 32.

133. See Lozano y Lozano, "Bolívar maquiavélico," 189.

134. Bolívar, Cartagena Manifesto, 16.

135. Ibid.

136. See Manifesto to the Nations of the World, September 20, 1813, in *Writings of Simón Bolívar*, 118.

137. Decree of March 12, 1828, in *Writings of Simón Bolívar*, 214. See Bolívar, Angostura Discourse, 54. See also Lynch, *Simón Bolívar: A Life*, 38, for Bolívar's valuation of utilitarianism.

138. In his "Method to be Employed in the Education of My Nephew Fernando Bolívar," in *Writings of Simón Bolívar*, 206.

139. Lynch, *Simón Bolívar: A Life*, 287.

140. Bolívar, Cartagena Manifesto, 17.

141. See Lozano y Lozano, "Bolívar maquiavélico," 186. Bolívar was a "violent" soldier, according to Germán Arciniegas (Urueña, *Bolívar Republicano*, 18).

142. Belaúnde, *Bolívar and Political Thought*, 184.

143. See Karen Racine, "Simón Bolívar, Englishman: Elite Responsibility and Social Reform in Spanish American Independence," in Bushnell and Langley, *Simón Bolívar*, 67.

144. For the importance of this document, see Lynch, *Simón Bolívar: A Life*, 201.

145. Bolívar believed it was his political *chef d'oeuvre* (see Collier, "Bolívar as Political Thinker," 21).

146. Bolívar, Jamaica Letter, 40.

147. Ibid., 29–32.

148. Ibid., 32.

149. Ibid., 33.

150. Ibid., 42–43.

151. Its strong centralism is similar to the Napoleonic plan. See Belaúnde, *Bolívar and Political Thought*, 239.

152. See Jeremy Adelman, *Sovereignty and Revolution in the Iberian Atlantic* (Princeton, NJ: Princeton University Press, 2009), 345. Contra *Writings of Simón Bolívar*, 85.

153. See Rozo Acuña, *Obra política y constitucional de Simón Bolívar*, clxiv–clxxi. See also de Gandía, *Simón Bolívar*, 17.

154. Bolívar, Cartagena Manifesto, 13.

155. See Bolívar, Message to the Congress of Bolivia, 96.

156. Bolívar, Jamaica Letter, 33.

157. For example, he favored the use of the term *curaca* for the elected provincial executives. Belaúnde, *Bolívar and Political Thought*, 82. Also Rozo Acuña, *Obra política y constitucional de Simón Bolívar*, xliv. Miranda was accused by some of being mulatto and of coming from the lower ranks of society (see Lynch, *Simón Bolívar: A Life*, 9) although he favored a Spanish American monarchy for the continent.

158. See Rozo Acuña, *Obra política y constitucional de Simón Bolívar*, ccvii. Both Bolívar and San Martín had initially seen no tension between republicanism and slavery but did change their minds (see Andrews, *Afro-Latin America*, 56).

159. Bolívar, Message to the Congress of Bolivia, 102.

160. See Lynch, *Simón Bolívar: A Life*, 152.

161. Jefferson did not believe a multiracial republic was possible. See Rahe, *Republics Ancient and Modern*, 619.

162. His earliest such action was the Decree of Carúpano of 1816 granting freedom to slaves if they fought for independence.

163. "[A]ccidente de su cutis." See Proclamation of August 5, 1817 in Pérez Vila, *Doctrina del Libertador*, 84.

164. Letter to Santander of April 18, 1820, in *Writings of Simón Bolívar*, 182.

165. Decree of War to the Death, June 15, 1813, in *Writings of Simón Bolívar*, 116. See also Pérez Vila, *Doctrina del libertador*, 20.

166. Decree of War to the Death, 116.

167. Decree for the Emancipation of the Slaves, June 2, 1816, in *Writings of Simón Bolívar*, 177.

168. He was a "calculating manipulator" (Safford, "Triumphal State Maker," 102).

169. Letter to Santander of April 18, 1820, in *Writings of Simón Bolívar*, 182.

170. See Sarah Chambers, "Little Middle Ground: The Instability of a Mestizo Identity in the Andes, Eighteenth and Nineteenth Centuries," in Applebaum, Macpherson and Rosenblatt, *Race and Nation*, 39. Bolívar abolished *mita* forced Indian labor (García Hamilton, *Simón*, 258).

171. Decree on Indian Lands, May 20, 1820, in *Writings of Simón Bolívar*, 184. See also Pérez Vila, *Doctrina del libertador*, 140.

172. Decree on Indian Lands, 184.

173. Proclamation of the Civil Rights of Indians, Cuzco, July 4, 1825, in *Writings of Simón Bolívar*, 187.

174. Manifesto of Carúpano, in *Writings of Simón Bolívar*, 128.

175. Letter to Sucre, in *Political Thought of Bolívar*, 88.

176. Ideas on Union of All America, in *Political Thought of Bolívar*, 20.

177. Bolívar was always wary of the United States (see de Gandía, *Simón Bolívar*, 24).

178. See Rozo Acuña, *Obra política y constitucional de Simón Bolívar*, cxcv.

179. Letter to Sir Richard Wellesley, in *Writings of Simón Bolívar*, 153.

180. Ibid., 154.

181. Thoughts on the Congress of Panama, *Writings of Simón Bolívar*, 170.

182. Bolívar, Jamaica Letter, 38.

183. Caracciolo Parra Pérez, *Bolívar: Contribución al estudio de sus ideas políticas* (Paris: Excelsior, 1928), 114; my translation.

184. Ibid.

185. Letter to Santander, May 30, 1825, in *Cartas del Libertador*, 4:343.

186. Ibid.

187. Bolívar would go on to comment that the United States "seems destined by Providence to plague [Latin] America with miseries in the name of freedom." Letter to Colonel Patrick Campbell, August 5, 1829, in *Writings of Simón Bolívar*, 172.

188. In his Thoughts on the Congress of Panama, Bolívar defends the idea of the unity of the Americas partly on the grounds that most of the continent would be able to thus avoid the race war of Santo Domingo and the preponderance of indigenous populations (170).

189. Thoughts on the Congress of Panama, 78.

190. See Collier, "Bolívar as Political Thinker," 26.

191. What Lynch calls *"mestization"* (Lynch, *Simón Bolívar: A Life*, 65).

192. Bolívar, Thoughts on the Congress of Panama, 78.

193. Belaúnde, *Bolívar and Political Thought*, 373.

194. Bolívar, Jamaica Letter, 41; emphasis added.

195. Ibid.

196. Viroli, *Republicanism*, 89.

197. Bolívar, Jamaica Letter, 44.

198. Manifesto on the Execution of General Manuel Piar, October 17, 1817, in *Writings of Simón Bolívar*, 130.

199. See Lasso, *Myths of Harmony*, 124; Lynch, *Caudillos in Spanish America*, 106.

200. Letter to José Antonio Páez, March 6, 1826, in *Writings of Simón Bolívar*, 138. Bolívar uses the term "los colores" in Pérez Vila, *Doctrina del libertador*, 222.

201. Lynch, *Simón Bolívar: A Life*, 120.

202. Bolívar was "prone to disenchantment with his own cause" (Adelman, *Sovereignty and Revolution*, 307).

203. Letter to General Flores, November 9, 1830, in *Writings of Simón Bolívar*, 146.

204. Letter to Santander of July 8, 1826, in *Cartas del Libertador*, 5:193; my translation. Lynch's translation loses all of the rhetorical potency of the original, where Bolívar's use of animal imagery reminds of us Las Casas's critique of the conquistadores (see Lynch, *Simón Bolívar: A Life*, 218).

205. We cannot say that Bolívar espoused an "ideal Spanish American democracy" (contra Fuentes, *The Buried Mirror*, 262).

CHAPTER 3

1. "The rebellion of Venezuela against the centralist régime of Bogotá was not due solely, as many believed, to the personal ambitions of Páez. It was rather a manifestation of the *nationalist* spirit which existed in Venezuela. This was the fundamental cause of the movement" (Belaúnde, *Bolívar and Political Thought*, 322; emphasis added).

2. In an ornate, nineteenth-century building in Saint-Germain-en-Laye, a few miles northwest of Paris, the archives of Laureano Vallenilla Lanz are ensconced. His grandson, a professor of history who left Venezuela in the 1960s, maintains a well-ordered record of the eminent sociologist and historian's files. It is a fitting setting for a thinker who was deeply influenced by French thought. Hereafter this material is cited as "Vallenilla Archives." Vallenilla also had influence on the French intellectual milieu. See, for instance, Ernest Martinenche, *Revue de l'Amérique latine* (Paris, 1923), 4:272; also Margaret E. Beeson, *Hispanic Writers in French Journals: An Annotated Bibliography* (Berkeley: University of California Press, 1978).

3. Bolívar thought in continental terms. For him, "Nationalism was never enough." Collier, "Nationality, Nationalism, and Supranationalism," 48.

4. In "Por qué escribí mi 'césarismo demócratico,'" in *Sentido americano de la democracia* (Caracas: Universal, 1926), 47.

5. Vallenilla, *Sentido americano*, 45.

6. Vallenilla, "Por qué escribí mi 'césarismo demócratico,'" 48.

7. See Nikita Harwich Vallenilla, "Arma y coraza," in Laureano Vallenilla Lanz, *Obras Completas* (Caracas: Universidad Santa María, 1983), 1:xxix. Some commentators have recognized the "innovative sociological interpretation" of Vallenilla Lanz. See Fernando Coronil, *The Magical State: Nature, Money and Modernity in Venezuela* (Chicago: University of Chicago Press, 1997), 175, n. 7.

8. The inadequacy of the terms "liberal" and "conservative" can be seen in the tension between Vallenilla's defense of dictatorship and his long-held animosity toward Venezuelan oligarchies, *godos*, clericalism, and racism. See Ángel Cappelletti, *Positivismo y evolucionismo en Venezuela* (Caracas: Monte Ávila, 1992), 263.

9. "A republic is not a purely or essentially political institution, distinct from a nation understood as a cultural reality" (Viroli, *Republicanism*, 87).

10. See Ernest Sosa, *La filosofía política del gomecismo* (Barquisimeto, Venezuela: Centro Gumilla, 1974), 42.

11. Vallenilla, *El Libertador juzgado*, 6–7. Bolívar called the idea of a Latin American monarchy a "chimera." Vallenilla, *El Libertador juzgado*, 12.

12. Ibid., 10.

13. Ibid.

14. Hugo Chávez's rule can be elucidated with the use of Vallenilla's idea of democratic Caesarism.

15. See Elena Plaza, *La tragedia de una amarga convicción: Historia y política en el pensamiento de Laureano Vallenilla Lanz, 1870–1936* (Caracas: Facultad de Ciencias Jurídicas y Políticas, Universidad Central de Venezuela, 1996), 38.

16. Harwich, "Arma y coraza," 1:xii.

17. See Luis Salamanca, *Los pensadores positivistas y el gomecismo* (Caracas: Congreso de la República, 1983), 7, 15. See Cappelletti, *Positivismo y evolucionismo.*

18. With whom he maintained a long friendship and correspondence of about forty years until they had a falling out over control of the newspaper *El Nuevo Diario* (see Plaza, *La tragedia*, 81).

19. See Wright, *Café Con Leche*, 81.

20. Sosa, *La filosofía política del gomecismo*, 40.

21. See *Disgregación e Integración*, in Vallenilla Lanz, *Cesarismo democrático y otros textos*, ed. Nikita Harwich Vallenilla (Caracas: Biblioteca Ayacucho, 1991), 229.

22. *Disgregación e Integración*, 333.

23. Ibid., 242.

24. From December 19, 1908, to December 17, 1935. Vallenilla was not "pessimistic" about Venezuelan politics because it could not reach liberal aims. He was deeply inimical to liberalism's individualist orientation as such. Contra Leslie Bethell, *Ideas and Ideologies in Twentieth Century Latin America* (Cambridge: Cambridge University Press, 1996), 178.

25. Harwich, "Arma y coraza," 1:xxii.

26. Contra Wright, *Café Con Leche*, 81.

27. Plaza, *La tragedia*, 85. Vallenilla was attacked for being "our Machiavelli" in Venezuela (Plaza, *La tragedia*, 457).

28. In *Cesarismo Democrático* (Caracas: Biblioteca Ayacucho, 1991), 208.

29. Vallenilla provides a relatively short list of the main elite families in Venezuela. See Federico Brito Figueroa, "La contribución de Laureano Vallenilla Lanz," in *Vallenilla: Obras Completas* (Caracas: Centro de Investigaciones Históricas, 1983), 1:viii.

30. Vallenilla, *Sentido americano*, 32.

31. Ibid.

32. Brito Figueroa, "Apuntes para una crítica de 'Sinceridad y Exactitud,'" in *Vallenilla: Obras Completas*, Caracas: Centro de Investigaciones Históricas, 1983, 3:17.

33. This assessment comes from Venezuelan Marxist historians such as Brito Figueroa.

34. Brito Figueroa, "Apuntes para una crítica," 22.

35. Gómez's motto was "Paz, Unión y Trabajo"(Peace, Unity, and Work), reflecting a positivist orientation that Vallenilla would find theoretically appealing.

36. The idea of the "necessary gendarme" state has some origins in the Peruvian Francisco García Caderón.

37. See James Henderson, *Conservative Thought in Twentieth Century Latin America* (Athens: Ohio University Center for International Studies, Center for Latin American Studies, 1988), 15.

38. Brito Figueroa, "Apuntes para una crítica," 26.

39. Ibid., 28.

40. Contra Fernando Coronil and Julie Skurski, *States of Violence* (Ann Arbor: University of Michigan Press, 2006), 65. Neither Vallenilla nor Sarmiento was, in fact, a proponent of tyranny. Both opposed autocratic, personalist rule. Vallenilla sought to justify a strong executive within institutional mechanisms to delimit dictatorial powers, just as Bolívar did. Moreover, Vallenilla valued miscegenation, not racial extermination as Sarmiento did.

41. Bolívar, Letter to Santander, Lima, April 7, 1925, in *Obras Completas* (Havana: Les, 1950), 2:114.

42. Laureano Vallenilla Lanz, Jr., *Razones de Proscrito* (Choisy-le-Roi: Les Gondoles, 1965), 145; emphasis added.

43. See Carmen Bohórquez, "Caudillismo y modernidad en Laureano Vallenilla," in *Los intelectuales latinoamericanos entre la modernidad y tradición siglos XIX y XX*, ed. Reseña de Hugo Cancino (Madrid: Iberoamericana, 2004).

44. Ibid., 36.

45. Cappelletti, *Positivismo y evolucionismo*, 264. For an elaboration of the eclecticism, see Plaza, *La tragedia*, 131–133.

46. Harwich, "Arma y coraza," 1:xxxv.

47. Plaza, *La tragedia*, 3.

48. Vallenilla was in favor of open debate and secularism, but he was not pointedly anticlerical (Plaza, *La tragedia*, 142).

49. "Le milieu, le moment, et la race" (Plaza, *La tragedia*, 139). See also Cappelletti, *Positivismo y evolucionismo*, 271.

50. See Marisa Kohn, *Tendencias positivistas en Venezuela* (Caracas: Universidad Central, 1970), 7.

51. Plaza, *La tragedia*, 144.

52. In Nikita Harwich Vallenilla, "Crítica y métodos de la historia en Laureano Vallenilla Lanz," Suplemento Cultural, *Ultimas Noticias*, January 4, 1987, 65.

53. Ibid., 68.

54. See Wright, *Café Con Leche*, 82.

55. In Harwich. "Crítica y métodos," 68.

56. Vallenilla does not rely on Spencer for his conceptions of evolution and the social organism, but is closer to René Worms's eclectic positivism evident in *Philosophie des Sciences Sociales*, 3 vols. (Paris: V. Giard and E. Brière, 1903–1907). Vallenilla found Spencer to be too ahistorical.

57. Plaza, *La tragedia*, 192–193.

58. Cappelletti, *Positivismo y evolucionismo*, 265.

59. "Fiesta de la Raza," *El Nuevo Diario* (Caracas), October 12, 1916, in Vallenilla Archives, 2:315.

60. One reason is that Spain itself was a cauldron of racial admixture, similar to Latin America. See Wright, *Café Con Leche*, 83.

61. See Torcuato Di Tella, *Latin American Politics: A Theoretical Framework* (Austin: University of Texas Press, 1990), 49.

62. See Vallenilla, *Disgregación e Integración*, 225.

63. Vallenilla, *Cesarismo Democrático*, 21.

64. *Confraternidad Hispano-Americana* (Vallenilla Archives, 1915), 3:323.

65. Ibid., 353.

66. See *Selected Writings of Andrés Bello*, ed. Iván Jaksic (New York: Oxford University Press, 1997), 162.

67. *Los Hijos del Invasor*, 372, in Vallenilla Archives, vol. 3.

68. Martí, in Vallenilla, "Notas al margen de la proclama," 112, in *Cesarismo Democrático*, Ayacucho ed.

69. Vallenilla is thus closer to Martí's emphasis on the mixing of races in Spanish America than to the dualistic theme of civilization and barbarism espoused by Sarmiento's Manichaean view of race (contra John Lombardi, *Venezuela: The Search for Order, the Dream of Progress* [New York: Oxford University Press, 1982], 260).

70. Harwich, introduction to *Cesarismo Democrático y otros textos*, xxx.

71. Many of the ideas from this speech found their way into *Cesarismo Democrático*.

72. Vallenilla, *Concepto de Raza en la evolución venezolana*, in Vallenilla Archives, 3:287.

73. Spain, much more so than Britain, shows miscegenation, according to Vallenilla. This is the reason for the different modes of conquest by the Spanish and the British in their colonial ventures. The Spanish did intermix, but the British did not (see "Fiesta de la Raza," 313).

74. Vallenilla, *Concepto de Raza*, 289. See also his "Comentario Sobre el Concepto de Raza en la Evolución Venezolana," *El Nuevo Diario* (Caracas), August 6, 1914, 303; also his "Fiesta de la Raza," *El Nuevo Diario* (Caracas), October 12, 1916, 312. All in Vallenilla Archives, vol. 2.

75. See *Disgregación e Integración*, 326, where Vallenilla calls Gobineau's ideas a "pseudoscience."

76. Vallenilla, *Concepto de Raza*, 290.

77. Writing about the United States, Vallenilla states that railway conductors, in 1916, were sometimes baffled as they tried to classify Spanish or Italian people into their rigid racial categories (in "Fiesta de La Raza," 312).

78. In Vallenilla, *Disgregación e Integración*, 326.

79. Vallenilla, *Concepto de Raza*, 293.

80. Ibid.

81. See "Monsieur Le Bon y la América Latina," *El Universal* (Caracas), July 15, 1911 (Vallenilla Archives, vol. 4). See also *Disgregación e Integración*, 328.

82. Vallenilla, *Concepto de Raza*, 294.

83. Ibid.

84. Ibid. See also *Disgregación e Integración*, 326. See his "Fiesta de la Raza," *El Nuevo Diario* (Caracas), October 12, 1916. Vallenilla tells us also that the Spanish did not annihilate the native American peoples; they did destroy most of the men, but they kept the women, which led to intermixing (311–313). See also "Los hijos del Invasor," Caracas, May 30, 1915, 372.

85. In "Fiesta de la Raza," *El Nuevo Diario* (Caracas), October 12, 1916, Vallenilla writes against the idea that there is such a thing as "sangre azul" (blue blood).

86. In Vallenilla, *Concepto de Raza*, 295.

87. In Vallenilla, *Disgregación e Integración*, 327.

88. In Vallenilla, *Concepto de Raza*, 295.

89. See also his "Fiesta de la Raza," *El Nuevo Diario* (Caracas), October 12, 1916.

90. Le Bon classed races into primitive, inferior, middle, and superior. Alcides Arguedas writes approvingly of Le Bon (Arguedas, *The Sick People*, 354).

91. See also "Monsieur Le Bon y la América Latina," *El Universal* (Caracas), July 15, 1911.

92. Vallenilla was inconsistent with regards to immigration. He did argue at certain points that increased European immigration would benefit the cultural level of some Latin American nations. See "Notas al Margen de la proclama del 5 de Julio de 1902," *Cesarismo Democrático*, Biblioteca Ayacucho, 5.

93. Vallenilla, *Disgregación e Integración*, 327.

94. Ibid., 329.

95. Vallenilla, *Concepto de Raza*, 299. See also his "Fiesta de la Raza," *El Nuevo Diario* (Caracas), October 12, 1916, 311.

96. Vallenilla, *Concepto de Raza*, 302.

97. Vallenilla, "Fiesta de la Raza," 314.

98. Palante, "Précis de Sociologie," quoted in *Disgregación e Integración*, 328.

99. Vallenilla, *Disgregación e Integración*, 309.

100. Ibid.

101. "La raza es la expresión del medio" (in *Cesarismo Democrático*, Biblioteca Ayacucho, 339).

102. Vallenilla is diametrically opposed to Sarmiento when it comes to race. For the Venezuelan thinker, there is no such thing as a pure race; and indeed, racial mixing is both a fact and normatively valuable. For Sarmiento, nonwhite races are inferior to European extraction. Montaner is completely incorrect on this account. See Carlos Alberto Montaner, *Twisted Roots: Latin America's Living Past* (New York: Algora, 2003), 60. To say that liberal democracy has no effect in Latin America does not mean that Latin America "has no future." For Vallenilla, this future is that of *Cesarismo democrático*.

103. The Argentine decried the presence of Indians and blacks in his country. See Domingo Faustino Sarmiento, *Life in the Argentine Republic in the Days of the Tyrants* (New York: Hafner, 1974), 10–11.

104. Vallenilla, *Cesarismo Democrático*, Biblioteca Ayacucho, 345.

105. Hence the term "social race" that was used by Vallenilla and Gil Fortoul. See Wright, *Café Con Leche*, 81.

106. This argument is not entirely convincing, since the United States also shows a history of cowboy life; but this did not lead to tyrannical, despotic, or "democratic-Caesarist" politics. See Richard Slatta, *Cowboys of the Americas* (New Haven, CT: Yale University Press, 1990).

107. See Brito Figueroa, "La contribución de Laureano Vallenilla Lanz," 1:xx.

108. See Juan Pablo Dabove, *Nightmares of the Lettered City* (Pittsburgh, PA: University of Pittsburgh Press, 2007), 146, 165.

109. Vallenilla did not share with Alcides Arguedas the negative view of native Americans (contra Bethell, *Ideas and Ideologies*, 177). Arguedas saw a *pueblo enfermo* where Vallenilla saw indigenous blood as the principal component of national identity.

110. Figures such as Rosas, Quiroga, and Boves are not too distant from Machiavelli's Cesare Borgia, who pacified the Romagna by means of brutal violence.

111. Vallenilla, *Disgregación e Integración*, 311.

112. Ibid., 313.

113. Ibid., 317.

114. Vallenilla did try to comprehend the role of blacks in the formation of Venezuelan national identity. See Wright, *Café Con Leche*, 83.

115. See Ángel Rosenblat, *La Población indígena y el Mestizaje en América* (Buenos Aires: Nova, 1954), 79.

116. Vallenilla, *Disgregación e Integración*, 320.

117. On the term "heterogeneity" and positivism, see Bernard Lavallé, *Transgressions et Strategies du Métissage en Amérique Coloniale* (Paris: Sorbonne nouvelle, 1999), 248.

118. Vallenilla, *Disgregación e Integración*, 323.

119. Vallenilla, *Cesarismo democrático*, Biblioteca Ayacucho, 114.

120. See Wright, *Café Con Leche*, 84.

121. See Georges Gurvitch, ed., *La Sociologie au XXe Siècle* (Paris: PUF, 1947), 634.

122. Plaza, *La tragedia*, 358.

123. As did Donato Gianotti.

124. Machiavelli, *Discourses on Livy*, 74.

125. We must recall that the Venetian republic's doge or gonfalonier was a position for life.

126. Viroli, *Republicanism*, 4; emphasis added.

127. Vallenilla, *Sentido Americano*, 6.

128. Ibid., 18.

129. Ibid.

130. Ibid., 22.

131. Ibid., 19.

132. Vallenilla feared and detested Communism for its "barbaric" qualities (*Sentido Americano*, 7).

133. The publication of the text had a substantial impact across Latin America as well as in Spain. The critiques were mostly negative owing to the erroneous belief that Vallenilla had written it in defense of Gómez (see Plaza, *La tragedia*, 98).

134. Ibid., 487, 496.

135. Vallenilla, *Disgregación e Integración*, 309.

136. As Viroli points out, republican ideas are not abstract; rather, they should be implemented in and for particular cultural locales and contexts (*Republicanism*, 13, 87). This means a *patria* is a land where the law rules, but it also means that the word refers to a particular way of life. For Machiavelli, it meant the streets of Florence and the countryside of Tuscany, and for Vallenilla it is the cities and towns of Venezuela with their particular cultural texture, which in this case includes racial heterogeneity.

137. See Caracciolo Parra Pérez, *Bolívar: Contribución al estudio de sus ideas políticas* (Paris: Excelsior, 1928), 157.

138. Bolívar, Angostura Discourse, 48.

139. Plaza, *La tragedia*, 330.

140. Vallenilla, *Cesarismo Democrático* (Caracas: El Cojo, 1919), 93.

141. Ibid., 98.

142. Ibid., n. 2.

143. Ibid., 104.

144. Ibid., 106.

145. Ibid., 108.

146. Arlene J. Díaz, *Female Citizens, Patriarchs, and the Law in Venezuela, 1786–1904* (Lincoln: University of Nebraska Press, 2004), 237.

147. Vallenilla, *Cesarismo Democrático*, El Cojo ed., 116.

148. Ibid.

149. "Essai sur l'inégalité des races humaines," in *Cesarismo Democrático*, El Cojo ed., 116 n. 1.

150. *Cesarismo Democrático*, El Cojo ed., 116.

151. This idea fits squarely within the republican tradition as defined against the idea of *natio*, or common birth. Nationalism emphasizes ethnic and racial unity, whereas republicanism does not (see Viroli, *Republicanism*, 86).

152. "El Gendarme necesario," in *Cesarismo Democrático*, El Cojo ed., 189.

153. For Vallenilla, "Leaders impose themselves." Hugh Hamill, ed., *Caudillos: Dictators in Spanish America* (Norman: University of Oklahoma Press, 1992), 93.

154. "Verdugo," in *Cesarismo Democrático*, El Cojo ed., 195.

155. Ibid., 196.

156. Ibid., 200.

157. "Gendarme Necesario," ibid., 203.

158. Ibid.

159. Ibid., 206.

160. See, for example, Winfield J. Burggraaff, *The Venezuelan Armed Forces in Politics, 1935–1959* (Columbia: University of Missouri Press, 1972), 130; Arturo Sosa Abascal, *La filosofía política del gomecismo: Estudio del pensamiento de Laureano Vallenilla Lanz* (Barquisimeto: Centro Gumilla, 1974); and Slatta, *Cowboys of the Americas*, 5.

161. Good rulers, not widespread citizen participation, are more central to republicanism. See Viroli, *Republicanism*, 66.

162. Ibid., 87.

163. Vallenilla was a contemporary of Weber and twenty-four years younger than Schmitt.

164. McCormick explains that Schmitt's effort to distinguish dictatorship from Bonapartism and Caesarism in fact culminated in a harmonization of the first and third terms. John McCormick, "From Constitutional Technique to Caesarist Ploy: Carl Schmitt on Dictatorship," in *Dictatorship in History and Theory*, eds. Peter Baehr and Melvin Richter (New York: Cambridge University Press, 2004), 197.

165. John McCormick, *Carl Schmitt's Critique of Liberalism* (New York: Cambridge University Press, 1997), 129.

166. McCormick also sees a fundamentally Machiavellian basis in the thought of Schmitt (ibid., 8).

167. Schmitt, *Die Diktatur: Von den Anfängen des modernen Souveränitätsgedankens bis zum proletarischen Klassenkampf* (Berlin: Duncker & Humblot, 1989), 1–2, cited in McCormick, *Schmitt's Critique of Liberalism*, 129.

168. Ibid.

169. Schmitt, *Diktatur*, 6.

170. Schmitt shows the movement away from "commissarial" to "sovereign" dictatorship, or from temporary to permanent Caesarism. See McCormick, "Constitutional Technique," 198.

171. Vallenilla, "Cesarismo teocrático," in *Cesarismo democrático y otros textos*, 151–178.

172. See McCormick, "Constitutional Technique," 203.

173. McCormick, *Schmitt's Critique of Liberalism*, 135.

174. "We in Central Europe live under the eyes of the Russians" (McCormick, *Schmitt's Critique of Liberalism*, 140).

175. Peter Baehr, "Max Weber and the Avatars of Caesarism," in Baehr and Richter, *Dictatorship*, 165.

176. Ibid., 173.

177. Ibid., 160.

178. Ibid., 163.

179. Plaza, *La tragedia*, 257.

180. In contrast, Gil Fortoul remained committed to liberal principles throughout his life.

181. Plaza, *La tragedia*, 269.

182. Weber declared, somewhat ambiguously, that *"only a politically mature people* is a 'nation of masters' [*Herrenvolk*]" (Baehr, "Max Weber," 160).

183. See Bohórquez, "Caudillismo y modernidad," 35.

184. *Disgregación e Integración*, 334. Alcides Arguedas also refers to Novicow (also spelled Novikow) in his endorsement of the idea that there are no basic races (see Arguedas, *The Sick People*, 344).

185. *Disgregación e Integración*, 334

186. Arguedas agrees with the specifically "social" construction of race (*The Sick People*, 344) but nonetheless believed the predominance of indigenous "blood" in Bolivia was negative (*The Sick People*, 345).

CHAPTER 4

1. "Whoever synthesizes, also augments." José Vasconcelos, *Indología* (Paris: Mundial, 1926), 5. All translations are my own.

2. Friedrich Katz, *La guerra secreta en México* (Mexico City: Ediciones Era, 1982), 21.

3. See William Rex Crawford, *A Century of Latin American Thought* (Cambridge, MA: Harvard University Press, 1945), 260.

4. Indeed, his thought can be seen as germinating in the "labor-based populism" associated with the Mexican Revolution. See Andrews, *Afro-Latin America*, 165.

5. See Christopher Domínguez Michael in Vasconcelos, *Obra Selecta*, ed. Michael (Caracas: Biblioteca Ayacucho, 1992), ix. While he was a committed Mexican educator, his thought also fomented the demise of nationalism.

6. "Bolívar was to see in the fusion of races the formation of a new stock—forecast of the cosmic race of Vasconcelos" (Belaúnde, *Bolívar and Political Thought*, 166).

7. Vasconcelos, *La Raza Cósmica* (Baltimore, MD: Johns Hopkins University Press, 1997), 13.

8. "The task of a philosopher [such as Vasconcelos] in a country where Indians form a major part of the population is a task of synthesis" (Crawford, *Latin American Thought*, 264).

9. Crawford posits that his corpus is held together by his philosophical approach (ibid., 260).

10. Lima is where he showed his first public interest in the "cosmic race." Martha Robles, *Entre el Poder y las Letras: Vasconcelos en sus Memorias* (Mexico City: Fondo de Cultura Económica, 1989), 57.

11. Vasconcelos, *En el ocaso de mi vida* (Mexico City: Populibros La Prensa, 1957), 165.

12. Vasconcelos, *Ideario de Acción* (Lima: Actual, 1924), 33. Vasconcelos was very critical of the Church in 1921.

13. Vasconcelos, *Ocaso*, 94.

14. See José Enrique Rodó, *Ariel* (Austin: University of Texas Press, 1988), 49–51.

15. Rodó merely states that "Latin Americans have a great heritage of race, a great ethnic tradition" (ibid., 73).

16. "Pero aparte de las relaciones literarias [a Eça de Queiros], el arte intenso y espontánea de la bailarina nos producía goces como de quien vuelve a algo suyo ignorado o muy distante, o como si del fondo nuestra conciencia étnica naciesen emociones de dicha profunda jamás gustada. Aquello era extraño pero no discorde" (Vasconcelos, *Ideario de Acción*, 62).

17. Vasconcelos, "El Problema del Brasil," in *Ideario de Acción,* 61.

18. No extensive treatment of the Nietzschean themes in Vasconcelos has been carried out heretofore. In fact, many scholars, especially in comparative literature, treat Vasconcelos's writing as "ideological" rather than philosophical. See Miller, *Cosmic Race*, 35. However, the two thinkers shared some key themes and concerns beyond aesthetic metaphysics.

19. In the history of European political thought, we see a serious engagement with the problem of race only with the advent of Hannah Arendt.

20. Even Vasconcelos himself appreciated (perhaps to an exaggerated degree) his own significance. He wrote three autobiographical works, one of which was entitled *Creole Ulysses*, which documented every exiguous detail of his life and travels.

21. Nietzsche has no "unambiguous theory of race," as James Winchester tells us, but we can attempt to see what can be of use to understand Vasconcelos better. "Nietzsche's Racial Profiling," in *Race and Racism in Modern Philosophy*, ed. Andrew Valls (Ithaca, NY: Cornell University Press, 2005), 255.

22. Much of the secondary literature on Vasconcelos's treatment of race is carried out in nonphilosophical disciplines, such as comparative literature, history, and cultural studies.

23. Kathleen Higgins, "Comparative Aesthetics," in *Oxford Handbook of Aesthetics* (New York: Oxford University Press: 2005), 688.

24. This is not the place for an extensive discussion of Nietzsche's location vis-à-vis modernity, but we can provide a framework that is useful in our effort to see the links to Vasconcelos.

25. Matthew Rampley, *Nietzsche, Aesthetics, and Modernity* (New York: Cambridge University Press, 2000), 45.

26. Ibid., 6.

27. See Julian Young, *Nietzsche's Philosophy of Art* (New York: Cambridge University Press, 1992), 1–2. Nietzsche has an integral conception of art, since it is connected with "everything else."

28. Ibid., 134.

29. Ibid., 35; emphasis added.

30. Nietzsche tells us that "art raises its head when religions relax their hold . . . the feelings expelled from the sphere of religion by the Enlightenment throw themselves into art." *Human, All Too Human*, trans. R. J. Hollingdale (New York: Cambridge University Press, 1996), 150.

31. See Nietzsche, *Gay Science*, 370, ed. by Bernard Williams (New York: Cambridge University Press, 2001).

32. However, Nietzsche praises Wagner's *Ring of Nibelungen* as a "tremendous system of thought" (*Untimely Meditations,* ed. Daniel Brazeale [New York: Cambridge University Press, 1997], IV.9, 236).

33. *Genealogy of Morals*, in Rampley, *Nietzsche, Aesthetics, and Modernity*, 47.

34. See Alexander Nehamas, *Life as Literature* (Cambridge, MA: Harvard University Press, 1985).

35. There is no monograph specifically on the subject in the English language. Only one book deals with race and Nietzsche, but that is with a focus on British eugenics. See Dan Stone, *Breeding Superman* (Liverpool: Liverpool University Press, 2002). The one monograph on the

topic is Gerd Schank, *"Rasse" und "Züchtung" bei Nietzsche* (Berlin: de Gruyter, 2000). There are some edited volumes with relevant essays. See Salim Kemal, Ivan Gaskel, and Daniel Conway, eds., *Nietzsche, Philosophy and the Arts* (New York: Cambridge University Press, 2002); Jacob Golomb, *Nietzsche and Jewish Culture* (New York: Routledge, 1997); Gooding-Williams, *Look, a Negro!*; Jacqueline Scott and A. Todd Franklin, eds., *Critical Affinities: Nietzsche and African American Thought* (Albany: SUNY Press, 2006); Robert Bernasconi, ed., *Race and Racism in Continental Philosophy* (Bloomington: Indiana University Press, 2003); Ward and Lott, *Philosophers on Race*.

36. Thus, this chapter focuses on how Vasconcelos may be read in light of Nietzschean aesthetic ideas, rather than under the scope what the German thinker said about Jews, Aryans, or other "races." The attempt to "de-Nazify" Nietzsche is not philosophically fruitful (contra Jacob Golomb, "How to De-Nazify Nietzsche's Philosophical Anthropology?" in Golomb and Wistrich, *Nietzsche, Godfather of Fascism?* 19–20).

37. Conway, "Great Play and Fight," 167–190.

38. Gooding-Williams, *Look, A Negro!* 132.

39. See Eric Blondel's comprehensive *Nietzsche, the Body and Culture: Philosophy as a Philological Genealogy* (Palo Alto, CA: Stanford University Press, 1991).

40. See Rampley, *Nietzsche, Aesthetics, and Modernity*, 168–172.

41. *The Genealogy of Morals*, First Essay, §5 in *Basic Writings of Nietzsche*, ed. Kaufmann, (New York: Modern Library, 1968), 466.

42. See Winchester, "Nietzsche's Racial Profiling," 262–263.

43. Understood here as cognition through the senses, not in art or beauty.

44. This context immediately questions his purported association with proto-Nazi ideological projects, and thus can be misleading in an effort to find solely philosophical groundings for the place of race in society and culture.

45. The aesthetic is not, as Miller asserts, merely "a helpful metaphor" (*Cosmic Race*, 32). Robles provides ample textual evidence of Nietzsche's influence on Vasconcelos (*Entre el Poder y las Letras*, 17, 20, 23, 67).

46. See Vasconcelos, *Indología*, 93.

47. Vasconcelos also values Nietzsche's poetic philosophy. See "Nietzsche," in *Manual de Filosofía*, in *Obras Completas* (Mexico City: Libreros Mexicanos Unidos, 1957–1961).

48. Robles, *Entre el Poder y las Letras*, 101.

49. In Vasconcelos, *Obras Completas*, 4:12.

50. Vasconcelos also praises Nietzsche's *Thus Spoke Zarathustra*, as a book that "has a thousand different themes, which has an ethical rhythm," for it "awakens slumbering notions; pulls out unsuspected convictions; gives growth to all latent faculties" (*Monismo Estético*, in *Obras Completas*, 4:38).

51. See Omi and Winant, *Racial Formation*, 61–62.

52. See Isaac, *The Invention of Racism*.

53. "Mas que sus coetáneos mexicanos . . . se levanta por encima de sus paginas la figura Nietzscheana, que apela por la cultura de la grandeza" (Robles, *Entre el Poder y las Letras*, 66).

54. Nietzsche was, similarly, concerned with his own (German) nation, but principally as a vehicle for continental cultural transformation. To be a nationalist is not the same as being a colonialist or imperialist (contra Gooding-Williams's endorsement of Holub's claim that Nietzsche was a colonialist thinker, *Look, a Negro!* 132). Furthermore, for Vasconcelos

nationalism need not be "aggressive." See Vasconcelos, *Hispanoamérica frente a los nacionalismos agresivos de Europa y Norteamérica* (La Plata: Universidad de Buenos Aires, 1934).

55. Vasconcelos points to the power of Jewish identity, transnational in character, to show that nationalism is not the supreme form of social cohesion ("Bolivarismo y Monroismo," in *Obras Completas*, 2:1366; see also 1378).

56. Vasconcelos, "Discurso Hecho en Chile," in *Ideario de Acción*, 37; emphasis added.

57. Vasconcelos, "Día de la Raza," in *Ideario de Acción*, 40.

58. There is indeed a biological basis for Vasconcelos, as Vargas points out, referring to his use of Mendel. Manuel Vargas, "La biología y la filosofía de la 'raza' en México: Francisco Bulnes y José Vasconcelos," in *Construcción de las identidades latinoamericanas*, eds. Aimer Granados García and Carlos Marichal (Mexico City: El Colegio de México, 2004).

59. "La tiranía es la causa principal del atraso de los pueblos españoles de América." Vasconcelos, *Ideario de Acción*, 40.

60. See *La Raza Cósmica*, 26, where Vasconcelos speaks of "free choice of personal taste" as the guiding criterion of a new society.

61. Vasconcelos, *Ideario de Acción*, 40.

62. At the very least, Vasconcelos's work can be seen as a "riposte to Spencer" (Alan Knight, "Racism, Revolution, and *Indigenismo*," in Graham, *Idea of Race*, 92).

63. See *La Raza Cósmica*, 38: "the mestizo people of the Ibero-American continent, people for whom beauty is the reason for everything [because of a] fine aesthetic sensitivity and a profound love of beauty."

64. "el conjuro creador de una raza nueva, fuerte, y gloriosa" (*Ideario de Acción*, 44). Vasconcelos also praises the indigenous American peoples in *Indología*, 86.

65. Vasconcelos, *Indología*, 191.

66. Ibid., 73.

67. "El Bronce del Indio Mexicano se apoya en el Granito Bruñido del Brasil" (*Ideario de Acción*, 45).

68. Vasconcelos is not unaware of the viciousness of the Spanish in the Americas. He knows of the "atrocious cruelties" perpetrated by the conquistadores (*Obras Completas*, 2:994).

69. *La Raza Cósmica*, 21.

70. Later in his life Vasconcelos denigrated the significance of pre-Columbian civilizations (see Robles, *Entre el Poder y las Letras*, 47).

71. In contrast, Arguedas finds that the aesthetic qualities of the Aymara in Bolivia are inchoate and primitive (Arguedas, *The Sick People*, 346–347; Crawford, *Latin American Thought*, 107).

72. *Ideario de Acción*, 48; emphases added.

73. Vasconcelos is well aware of the prevalence of racism in modern societies (see "Bolivarismo y Monroismo," 2:1361, 1370). Equality is part of Vasconcelos's philosophical system, as he proposes that Pythagorean gnosis represents "the ideal of the equality of all men" (*La Raza Cósmica*, 39).

74. Vasconcelos speaks in self-contradictory terms when he also wants to posit that the future will actually have no specific guidelines: "Life will be without norms" (*La Raza Cósmica*, 29).

75. Vasconcelos, *Ideario de Acción*, 54.

76. Vasconcelos is critical of mimetic action; he wants original, creative practices (see *Obras Completas*, 2:1379).

77. Vasconcelos, *Ideario de Acción*, 56.

78. His work *Indología*, in his eyes, is merely an "expansion" of the ideas of *La Raza Cósmica* (see *Indología*, lv).

79. Nietzsche was equally critical of the marginalization of art and beauty in modern culture (see *Human, All Too Human*, trans. R.J. Hollingdale [New York: Cambridge University Press, 1996], II.2, §170, 350).

80. *La Raza Cósmica*, 3.

81. Introduction, *La Raza Cósmica*, xix.

82. Walter Kaufmann, *Nietzsche: Philosopher, Psychologist, Antichrist* (Princeton, NJ: Princeton University Press, 1974), 286.

83. Ibid.

84. "Contra Aryan and Semitic. Where races are mixed, there is the source of great cultures" (quoted in Kaufmann, *Nietzsche*, 303).

85. Ibid., 295.

86. His work *Pitágoras*, also concerned with the ideas of harmony and rhythm as integral to the human nexus with the world, appeared in 1919.

87. His fascination with the aesthetic is visible even in his earliest writings, such as "La estética de Sevilla." *Pesimismo Alegre* (Madrid: Aguilar Editores, 1931), 49.

88. In his *Indología*, Vasconcelos shows he is tired of the topic of race, and wants to move to what he considers more important topics such as aesthetics, metaphysics, and religion. ("Ya no escribiré más sobre estas trilladas cuestiones de la raza y el iberoamericanismo." *Indología*, lvii).

89. *La Raza Cósmica*, 24. For Vasconcelos, the aesthetic is the central notion of his metaphysics, as he explains in his work *Monismo Estético*, published in 1918.

90. "Perhaps there is nothing useless in historical developments" (*La Raza Cósmica*, 21).

91. Ibid., 28.

92. See Winchester, "Nietzsche's Racial Profiling," 260.

93. Vasconcelos would say, "no one in submission, and every one in his mission" ("La cultura en hispano-América," in Crawford, *Latin American Thought*, 261), thereby positing an egalitarian Hegelianism in his philosophy of culture and history.

94. See *La Raza Cósmica*, 20.

95. Nietzsche believes "the demand for art and beauty is an indirect demand for the ecstasies of sexuality" (*Will to Power*, 805). Elsewhere, Nietzsche tells us that sexual drives exist deep in the original artist (801). *The Will to Power*, ed. and trans. Walter Kaufmann (New York: Vintage, 1968).

96. See my *Art of Power*, chap. 6.

97. See ibid., 73–77.

98. He calls it the "new universal era of Humanity" (*La Raza Cósmica*, 39).

99. It may be the case that Nietzsche's usage of the term "breeding" refers to improvement through more miscegenation (see Winchester, "Nietzsche's Racial Profiling," 264–265).

100. In *Indología*, Vasconcelos speaks for universalism, and he believes the Hispanic roots of the conquest allow for a universal conception of the eventual unification of humanity (*Indología*, 9).

101. *Beyond Good and Evil*, in *Basic Writings of Nietzsche*, ed. and trans. Walter Kaufmann (New York: Modern Library, 1968), II § 44, 244. Nietzsche also writes even the wisest among men is only a disharmony (or discord) of plant and ghost (*Thus Spoke Zarathustra*, Prologue, § 3, 256 in *The Nietzsche Reader*, eds. Keith Ansell Pearson and Duncan Large, Blackwell, 2006).

102. Rodó, *Ariel*, 69. Still, Rodó admires the "formidable Nietzsche" (ibid., 64). Antonio Caso also critiqued Nietzsche's negative view of Christianity. See Crawford, *Latin American Thought*, 290.

103. See José Carlos Mariátegui, "El factor religioso," in *Siete ensayos de interpretación de la realidad peruana* (Caracas: Biblioteca Ayacucho, 1979), 105–125. See also Jorge Coronado, *The Andes Imagined* (Pittsburgh, PA: University of Pittsburgh Press, 2009), 26.

104. See *La Raza Cósmica*, 35.

105. Ibid., 21.

106. *Beyond Good and Evil*, Part II §28, 230-231 in *Basic Writings of Nietzsche*, ed. and trans. by Walter Kaufmann (New York: Modern Library, 1968).

107. Genaro Fernández Mac Gregor, ed., *Vasconcelos* (Mexico City: Ediciones de la Secretaría de Educación Pública, 1942), 195.

108. "La célula biológica también está agitada por el ritmo confuso de sus apetencias y anhelos varios" (ibid., 213).

109. Ibid., 206.

110. Ibid.,196.

111. Ibid., 206.

112. Ibid., 212; emphasis added.

113. Ibid., 229.

114. *La Raza Cósmica*, 19. On their similar use of *pathos*, see Robles, *Entre el Poder y las Letras*, 43.

115. *La Raza Cósmica*, 30.

116. As Menahem Brinker states, "For Nietzsche 'race' connotes a combination of spiritual internalizations of historical experience, with the biological mechanism securing their transmission" ("Nietzsche and the Jews," in Golomb and Wistrich, *Nietzsche, Godfather of Fascism?* 124 f. 2).

117. Kaufmann argues that Nietzsche advances racial mixing (*Nietzsche*, 288–289, 293).

118. Barbara Stiegler, *Nietzsche et la biologie* (Paris: PUF, 2001), 95.

119. He believed in the importance of "weakness" in a system (*Human, All Too Human*, §224).

120. *La Raza Cósmica*, 31. This statement recalls Nietzsche's parallel between art and love (*Gay Science*, 59).

121. Robles tell us that "a temperamental sympathy, visible in Vasconcelos's memories, show an inescapable lineage relating him to Nietzsche" (*Entre el Poder y las Letras*, 72). Vasconcelos was to publish an essay on dance that was inflected by Nietzschean influences, specifically *The Birth of Tragedy* (see *Monismo Estético*, 4:13).

122. See my argument in *The Art of Power*.

123. This, in spite of the fact that he had positive things to say about Lenin earlier in his life (see Robles, *Entre el Poder y las Letras*, 44).

124. Vasconcelos, *Ocaso*, 185.

125. Ibid., 187.

126. Ibid., 94.

127. He is very critical of the unworldliness of Hegel. See Nicotra Di Leopoldo, *Pensamientos Inéditos de Vasconcelos* (Mexico City: Botas, 1970), 81.

128. Vasconcelos, *Ocaso*, 189.

129. "The motives of the shield," in ibid., xxv.

130. Vasconcelos, ibid., 266.

131. "Raza y arte," in ibid., 280.

132. This is, in part, because "human differences are not intrinsic" (*Ideario de Acción*, 86).

133. Vasconcelos, *Ocaso*, 281.

CONCLUSION

1. Friedrich Nietzsche, *On the Advantage and Disadvantage of History for Life*, trans. Peter Preuss (Indianapolis, IN: Hackett, 1980), preface, 7.

2. See Andrew Wilson Nightingale, *Spectacles of Truth in Classical Greek Philosophy: "Theoria" in its Cultural Context* (New York: Cambridge University Press, 2004), 40.

3. See Sheldon Wolin, *Politics and Vision: Continuity and Innovation in Western Political Thought* (Princeton, NJ: Princeton University Press, 2004), 17–18.

4. This was part of the germination of racial thinking during the Spanish Inquisition. See Henry Kamen, *The Spanish Inquisition* (New Haven, CT: Yale University Press, 1997), 231.

5. See Walzer, "Citizenship," 214, for the relationship between heterogeneity and trust in republican thought.

6. See Viroli, *Republicanism*.

7. See Pettit, *Republicanism*.

8. See Kymlicka, *Multicultural Citizenship: Politics in the Vernacular* (New York: Oxford University Press, 2001); and *Multicultural Odysseys* (New York: Oxford University Press, 2007).

9. The valuable work by Sarah Song is also principally concerned with cultural diversity, not the role of race in politics. Hence, it has a focus different from that of my enterprise here. Song takes cultural groups as relatively clearly bounded, even though she recognizes that they are constantly reshaped by cultural interactions. See Song, *Justice*, 26, 29, 40.

10. The chief focus for Kymlicka is cultural diversity in a liberal democratic state. The issue of race as somatic difference in political life is an ancillary issue. See, for example, *Politics in the Vernacular*, chap. 9.

11. Wiarda is correct on this point. See Wiarda, *Soul of Latin America*, 228.

12. In Mariátegui, *Siete ensayos*.

13. García Linera, *La potencia plebeya: Acción colectiva e identidades indígenas, obreras y populares en Bolivia* (Buenos Aires: Prometeo, 2008).

14. Thus, while critiques of the Western canon are useful, we ought to look for positive arguments on race that come from non-Western sources such as East Asia or Africa.

15. In spite of the immigration of nonblack and nonwhite groups into the United States, the dualistic paradigm remains in force, given that elites from these new immigrant groups can become "honorary whites" under the current racial schemas in the United States. See Eduardo Bonilla-Silva and David Embrick, "Black, Honorary White, White: The Future of Race in the United States?" in *Negotiating the Color Line: Doing Race in the Color-Blind Era and Implications for Racial Justice*, ed. David Brunsma (Boulder, CO: Lynne Rienner, 2005). Hence, a new paradigm is needed, one that undermines such stratifications.

16. Kwame Anthony Appiah, "The Uncompleted Argument: Du Bois and the Illusion of Race," in Bernasconi and Lott, *The Idea of Race*, 134–135.

17. Mark Bevir, *Logic of the History of Ideas* (New York: Cambridge University Press, 2002), 222.

18. The work of Leopoldo Zea is cardinal to the understanding of Latin American identity as being in part defined by its intellectual history. See for instance *El pensamiento latinoamericano*

(Mexico City: Pórmaca, 1965); *Precursores del pensamiento latinoamericano contemporáneo* (Mexico City: Secretaría de Educación Pública, 1971).

19. The case of Portugal's relationship to Brazil is a particular one that differs in many ways from that of Spain to Spanish America, principally owing to the extent of African slavery.

20. See Gracia, *Hispanic/Latino Identity*, 87, 129. See also Crawford, *Latin American Thought*, 6.

21. I thank Mark Bevir for discussions of these issues.

22. See Rosemary Joyce, "Performing the Body in Pre-Hispanic Central America," *RES: Anthropology and Aesthetics* 33 (1998): 147–165. In effect, cranial modification was not uncommon as a way to define ethnic identity.

23. Bevir explains that webs of beliefs compose particular intellectual traditions (*Logic*, 258). For the idea of a chain of intellectual links. See Crawford, *Latin American Thought*, 136.

24. Martí critiqued the very notion of race, while Sarmiento proposed that whitening and increased European migration to the Americas was the best policy. Although at polar opposites on the issue of race, they both believed the nation-state—Cuba and Argentina, respectively—would be the most adequate vehicle for progress. José María Samper of Colombia shared in Sarmiento's and Alberdi's dichotomy of European civilization and Amerindian barbarism. See Alfredo Gómez-Muller, *Alteridad y ética desde el descubrimiento de América* (Madrid: Akal, 1997), 13, 23.

25. Bevir, *Logic*, 309.

26. Ibid., 310.

27. Gracia, *Hispanic/Latino Identity*, 48.

28. I thank Kanchan Chandra for discussions that led to these concepts.

29. I thank Konstantin Pollok for discussions of these issues.

30. A similar enterprise is that of critical race theory in that it also seeks to deconstruct the notion of race. Critical race theory emerged in the mid-1990s as a field in American law schools. Hence, its chief focus has been to confront critically the "complicity of law in upholding white supremacy." See Cornel West, foreword to *Critical Race Theory: The Key Writings That Formed the Movement*, eds. Kimberly, Crenshaw, Neil Gotanda, Gary Peller, and Kendall Thomas (New York: New Press, 1996), xi. As such, it is chiefly located in a U.S. context, and maintains a relatively dualistic approach, given that it is largely an African American critique of "white" supremacy. Its value is thus distinct from my synthetic paradigm of race that emerges from Latin American political thought.

31. One important connection here is that I locate the emergence of race within the value system associated with Christianity. Nietzsche's critique of Christianity as a set of values is useful to unearth the power dynamics that underlie the early Christian encounter with Amerindians.

32. See Raymond Geuss, "Genealogy as Critique," *European Journal of Philosophy* 10 (2010): 209–215; and Tyler Krupp, "Genealogy as Critique," *Journal of the Philosophy of History* 2 (2008): 315–337.

33. See Gooding-Williams, *Look, a Negro!* chap. 9.

34. "Synthesis means adding the heterogenous to the homogenous." Crawford, *Latin American Thought*, 264.

35. I thank Kazuko Suzuki for this insight.

36. See Andrews, *Afro-Latin America*, chap. 4.

37. Alcides Arguedas must also be classified as a racialist thinker owing to his attempt to find essential traits (albeit psychological) of "races." See *The Sick People*, 348.

38. See Darío Euraque, Jeffrey Gould, and Charles Hale, eds., *Memorias del Mestizaje: Cultura política en Centroamérica de 1920 al presente* (Guatemala: Librería Nawal Wuj, 2005).

39. See Robert Pippin, *Modernism as a Philosophical Problem: On the Dissatisfactions of European* (Malden, MA: Blackwell, 1999), 7.

40. Pippin defines it as "recently" or "of this time." Ibid., 17.

41. Contra Pippin's location of the emergence of modernity in European culture. Ibid., 16.

42. For Pippin, Descartes's treatment as false of whatever was possibly untrue "created the first horn of the dilemma." Ibid., 23.

43. Pippin does not mention Machiavelli in *Modernism as a Philosophical Problem*.

44. Contra Pippin, *Modernism as a Philosophical Problem*, 10. In fact, Nietzsche's "death of God" thesis owes much to the philosophical and theoretical groundwork laid by Machiavelli.

45. von Vacano, *Art of Power*, 4–5.

46. Las Casas made analogies of Amerindian culture to the premodern European world, but he still saw the Amerindians as categorically distinct from Europeans.

47. Dussel, *El Encubrimiento del Otro*.

48. The multiple dimensions of this intersectionality are beyond the scope of this book.

49. The concept "hybrid" ultimately originates in biology and genetics. It carries with it an implicit naturalistic essence (the word *hibrida* meant a crossbred animal in the 1600s) and thus should not be used for understanding the idea of race. The concept of the synthetic does not, as it denotes that which is artificial and constructed.

50. As Charles Hale believes, Mexican liberalism and conservatism were not that far apart. See *Mexican Liberalism in the Age of Mora, 1821–1853* (New Haven, CT: Yale University Press, 1968), introduction.

51. It is closer, I would argue, to the phenomenon of a *Kulturkampf.* Thus, citizenship in the Latin American tradition is about the shifting line of demarcation between those inside and those outside the polity over time. This is closer to Rogers Brubaker's conception of exclusionary citizenship (Brubaker, *Citizenship and Nationhood*) than to the idea of citizenship as defined by the incremental right to have rights, as in the work of T. H. Marshall or Hannah Arendt. See Margaret Somers, *Genealogies of Citizenship: Markets, Statelessness, and the Right to Have Rights* (New York: Cambridge University Press, 2008).

52. Hale, *Mexican Liberalism*, chap. 2.

53. Ibid., 155.

54. See Kymlicka, *Politics in the Vernacular*.

55. See Stephen Cornell and Douglas Hartmann, *Ethnicity and Race: Making Identities in a Changing World* (Newbury Park, CA: Pine Forge Press, 1998), 27–29.

56. The United States is probably the only country where the distinction between "race" and "ethnicity" is an important issue. This is mostly due to its history of immigration. In Spanish, the term *etnia* is mostly academic.

57. For example, a "white" Anglo-Saxon American, a Hispanic American, and an African American (of putatively different races) may be seen as ethnically the same ("American") if they happen to have similar cultural practices (such as speaking English fluently, watching U.S. sports, and having similar educational experiences).

58. Education policy is one central instance where moral pedagogy can help contribute to "prepare each new generation for their responsibilities as citizens." Kymlicka, *Politics in the Vernacular*, 293. A critical approach to race and the promotion of a synthetic paradigm can be carried out in schools as part of moral education.

59. Alcides Arguedas is not a useful point of reference here, for he essentializes the nature of the "Indian," describing it as "embittered, egotistical, cruel, vengeful, and distrustful." *The Sick People*, 348. See, for instance, his novel *Raza de Bronce* (Buenos Aires: Losada, 1957), 88.

60. Latino immigrants tend to feel pride in having "mixed racial roots." Douglas Massey, *Brokered Boundaries* (New York: Russell Sage, 2010), 22.

61. The intellectual legacy of Bolívar and his dream of a united Latin America is one example. Michael Jones-Correa, *Between Two Nations: The Political Predicament of Latinos in New York City* (Ithaca, NY: Cornell University Press, 1998), 118, 122.

62. For a historical deconstruction of the U.S. majority group, see the excellent work by Nell Irvin Painter, *The History of White People* (New York: Norton, 2010).

63. One reason for this is that Latin American polities are moving toward greater political, social, and economic integration in the early twenty-first century. A common conceptualization of race as fluid and nondiscrete would fit with this process of finding a more unified continental identity.

Bibliography

Abbott, Don Paul. *Rhetoric in the New World*. Columbia: University of South Carolina Press, 1996.

Aguilar Rivera, José Antonio. "Dos conceptos de la república." In *El Republicanismo en Hispanoamérica*, ed. José Antonio Aguilar Rivera and Rafael Rojas. Mexico City: Fondo de Cultura Económica, 2002.

Alberdi, Juan Bautista. "Foundations and Points of Departure for the Political Organization of the Republic of Argentina." In *Nineteenth-Century Nation Building and the Latin American Intellectual Tradition*, ed. and trans. Janet Burke and Ted Humphrey. Indianapolis, IN: Hackett, 2007.

Alcoff, Linda Martín. *Visible Identities*. New York: Oxford University Press, 2005.

Allen, Danielle S. *Talking to Strangers*. Chicago: University of Chicago Press, 2006.

André-Vincent, P. *Bartolomé de Las Casas: Prophète du Nouveau Monde*. Paris: Jules Tallandier, 1980.

Andrews, George Reid. *Afro-Latin America*. New York: Oxford University Press, 2004.

Appelbaum, Nancy, Anne Macpherson, and Karin Alejandra Rosemblatt, eds. *Race and Nation in Modern Latin America*. Chapel Hill: University of North Carolina Press, 2003.

Appiah, Kwame Anthony. "The Uncompleted Argument: Du Bois and the Illusion of Race." In *The Idea of Race*, ed. Robert Bernasconi and Tommy Lee Lott. Indianapolis, IN: Hackett, 2000.

———. *The Ethics of Identity*. Princeton, NJ: Princeton University Press, 2005.

Appiah, Kwame Anthony, and Amy Gutmann. *Color Conscious: The Political Morality of Race*. Princeton, NJ: Princeton University Press, 1996.

Arendt, Hannah. *The Origins of Totalitarianism*. New York: Schocken, 2004.

Arguedas, Alcides. *Raza de Bronce*. Buenos Aires: Losada, 1957.

———. *The Sick People*. In *Nineteenth-Century Nation Building and the Latin American Intellectual Tradition*, ed. Janet Burke and Ted Humphrey. Indianapolis, ID: Hackett, 2007.

Arias, Santa, *Retórica, historia y polémica: Bartolomé de las Casas y la tradición intelectual renacentista*. Lanham, MD: University Press of America, 2001.

Armitage, David. "John Locke, Carolina, and the Two Treatises of Government." *Political Theory* 32 (2004): 602–627.

Avineri, Shlomo. *Karl Marx on Colonialism and Modernization*. Garden City, NY: Doubleday Anchor, 1969.

Baehr, Peter. "Max Weber and the Avatars of Caesarism." In *Dictatorship in History and Theory*, ed. Peter Baehr and Melvin Richter. New York: Cambridge University Press, 2004.

Balfour, Lawrie. *Democracy's Reconstruction: Du Bois in the 21st Century*. New York: Oxford University Press, 2009.

Balibar, Étienne, and Immanuel Maurice Wallerstein. *Race, Nation, Class*. New York: Verso, 1991.

Beeson, Margaret. *Hispanic Writers in French Journals: An Annotated Bibliography*. Berkeley: University of California Press, 1978.

Belaúnde, Victor Andrés. *Bolívar and the Political Thought of the Spanish American Revolution*. Baltimore, MD: Johns Hopkins Press, 1938.

Bernasconi, Robert, ed. *Race and Racism in Continental Philosophy*. Bloomington: Indiana University Press, 2003.

Bernasconi, Robert, and Tommy Lee Lott, eds. *The Idea of Race*. Indianapolis, IN: Hackett, 2000.

Bindman, David. *Ape to Apollo: Aesthetics and the Idea of Race in the 18th Century*. London: Reaktion, 2002.

Blondel, Eric. *Nietzsche, the Body and Culture: Philosophy as a Philological Genealogy*. Palo Alto, CA: Stanford University Press, 1991.

Bohórquez, Carmen. "Caudillismo y modernidad en Laureano Vallenilla." In *Los intelectuales latinoamericanos entre la modernidad y tradición siglos XIX y XX*, ed. Hugo Cancino. Madrid: Iberoamericana, 2004.

Bolívar, Simón. *Selected Writings of Bolívar*, ed. Vicente Lecuna and Harold Bierck, Jr. Trans. Lewis Bertrand. New York: Colonial Press, 1951.

———. *Cartas del Libertador*. Caracas: Banco de Venezuela, 1968.

———. *Doctrina del Libertador*, ed. Pérez Vila. Caracas: Biblioteca Ayacucho, 1979.

———. *El Libertador: Writings of Simón Bolívar*, ed. David Bushnell. New York: Oxford University Press, 2003.

Bonilla-Silva, Eduardo. "New Racism." In *White Out: The Continuing Significance of Racism*, ed. Bonilla-Silva and Ashley Doane. London: Routledge, 2003.

Bonilla-Silva, Eduardo, and David Embrick. "Black, Honorary White, White: The Future of Race in the United States?" In *Negotiating the Color Line: Doing Race in the Color-Blind Era and Implications for Racial Justice*, ed. David Brunsma. Boulder, CO: Lynne Rienner, 2005.

Brading, D. A. *Classical Republicanism and Creole Patriotism: Simón Bolívar (1783–1830) and the Spanish American Revolution*. Cambridge: Centre of Latin American Studies, University of Cambridge, 1983.

———. *The First America: The Spanish Monarchy, Creole Patriots, and the Liberal State*. New York: Cambridge University Press, 1991.

Brande Trend, John. *Bolívar and the Independence of Spanish America*. New York: Harper & Row, 1968.

Brice, Ángel Francisco. *Bolívar y Fray Bartolomé de Las Casas ante sus críticos*. Caracas: Italgráfica, 1969.

Brito Figueroa, Federico. "Apuntes para una crítica de 'Sinceridad y Exactitud.'" In *Vallenilla: Obras Completas*. Caracas: Centro de Investigaciones Históricas, 1983.

———. "La contribución de Laureano Vallenilla Lanz." In *Vallenilla: Obras Completas*. Caracas: Centro de Investigaciones Históricas, 1983.

Brubaker, Rogers. *Citizenship and Nationhood in France and Germany*. Cambridge, MA: Harvard University Press, 1998.

Burggraaff, Winfield J. *The Venezuelan Armed Forces in Politics, 1935–1959*. Columbia: University of Missouri Press, 1972.

Bushnell, David. *Simón Bolívar: Hombre de Caracas, proyecto de América*. Buenos Aires: Biblos, 2002.

Canclini, Néstor García. *Hybrid Cultures*. Minneapolis: University of Minnesota Press, 1997.

Cappelletti, Ángel. *Positivismo y evolucionismo en Venezuela*. Caracas: Monte Ávila, 1992.

Castro, Daniel. *Another Face of Empire: Bartolomé de Las Casas, Indigenous Rights, and Ecclesiastical Imperialism*. Durham, NC: Duke University Press, 2007.

Chaves González, Manuel, ed. *V Centenario del Primer Viaje a America de Bartolomé de Las Casas*. Seville: Junta de Andalucía, 2003.

Chorba, Carrie C. *Mexico, from Mestizo to Multicultural*. Nashville: Vanderbilt University Press, 2007.

Collier, Simon. "Nationality, Nationalism, and Supranationalism in the Writings of Simón Bolívar." *Hispanic American Historical Review* 63 (1983): 37–64.

———. "Simón Bolívar as Political Thinker." In *Simón Bolívar: Essays on the Life and Legacy of the Liberator*, ed. David Bushnell and Lester Langley. Lanham, MD: Rowman and Littlefield, 2008.

Conway, Daniel. "'The Great Play and Fight of Forces': Nietzsche on Race." In *Philosophers on Race*, ed. Julie K. Ward and Tommy Lee Lott. Malden, MA: Blackwell, 2000.

Cornell, Stephen and Douglas Hartmann. *Ethnicity and Race: Making Identities in a Changing World*. Newbury Park, CA: Pine Forge Press, 1998.

Coronado, Jorge. *The Andes Imagined*. Pittsburgh, PA: University of Pittsburgh Press, 2009.

Coronil, Fernando. *The Magical State: Nature, Money, and Modernity in Venezuela*. Chicago: University of Chicago Press, 1997.

Coronil, Fernando, and Julie Skurski. *States of Violence*. Ann Arbor: University of Michigan Press, 2006.

Craig, Maxine Leeds. *Ain't I a Beauty Queen?* New York: Oxford University Press, 2002.

Crawford, William Rex. *A Century of Latin American Thought*. Cambridge, MA: Harvard University Press, 1945.

Crenshaw, Kimberly, Neil Gotanda, Gary Peller, and Kendall Thomas, eds. *Critical Race Theory: The Key Writings That Formed the Movement*. New York: New Press, 1996.

Dawson, Michael C. *Black Visions: The Roots of Contemporary African-American Political Ideologies*. Chicago: University of Chicago Press, 2001.

De Castro, Juan. *Mestizo Nations*. Tucson: University of Arizona Press, 2002.

De Gandía, Enrique. *Simón Bolívar: Su pensamiento político*. Caracas: Academia Nacional de La Historia, 1984.

Di Leopoldo, Nicotra. *Pensamientos inéditos de Vasconcelos*. Mexico City: Botas, 1970.

Di Tella, Torcuato. *Latin American Politics: A Theoretical Framework*. Austin: University of Texas Press, 1990.

Díaz, Arlene J. *Female Citizens, Patriarchs, and the Law in Venezuela, 1786–1904*. Lincoln: University of Nebraska Press, 2004.

Dietz, Mary. "Context Is All: Feminism and Theories of Citizenship." *Daedalus* 116 (1987): 1–24.

Dussel, Enrique. *El Encubrimiento del Otro*. Barcelona: Antropos Editorial, 1992.

Euraque, Darío, Jeffrey Gould, and Charles Hale, eds. *Memorias del Mestizaje: Cultura política en Centroamérica de 1920 al presente*. Guatemala: Librería Nawal Wuj, 2005.

Fanon, Frantz. *Black Skin, White Masks*. Trans. Charles Lam Markmann. New York: Grove Press, 2008.

Farr, James. "Locke, Natural Law, and New World Slavery." *Political Theory* 36 (2008): 495–522.

Feagin, Joe R. *Systemic Racism*. New York: Routledge, 2006.

Fernández-Santamaría, J. A. *The State, War and Peace: Spanish Political Thought in the Renaissance*. New York: Cambridge University Press, 1977.

Fisher, Andrew B., and Matthew D. O'Hara, eds. *Imperial Subjects: Race and Identity in Colonial Latin America*. Durham, NC: Duke University Press, 2009.

Fitzgerald, Gerald. *The Political Thought of Simón Bolívar*. The Hague: Martinus Nijhoff, 1971.

Forcada, Helena Puigdomenech. *Maquiavelo en España*. Madrid: Fundación Universitaria Española, 1988.

Frazer, Michael. *The Enlightenment of Sympathy*. New York: Oxford University Press, 2010.

Fredrickson, George M. *Black Image in the White Mind: The Debate on Afro-American Character and Destiny, 1817–1914*. New York: Harper and Row, 1971.

———. *Racism: A Short History*. Princeton, NJ: Princeton University Press, 2002.

———. *Big Enough to Be Inconsistent: Abraham Lincoln Confronts Race and Slavery*. Cambridge, MA: Harvard University Press, 2008.

Fuentes, Carlos. *The Buried Mirror*. New York: Houghton Mifflin, 1992.

García Hamilton, José Ignacio. *Simón: Vida de Bolívar*. Buenos Aires: Editorial Sudamericana, 2004.

García Linera, Álvaro. *La potencia plebeya: Acción colectiva e identidades indígenas, obreras y populares en Bolivia*. Buenos Aires: Prometeo, 2008.

García Márquez, Gabriel. *El General en Su Laberinto*. Mexico City: Editorial Diana, 1989.

Gargarella, Roberto. "Towards a Typology of Latin American Constitutionalism, 1810–1860." *Latin American Research Review*, vol. 39, no. 2, p. 141–153, 2004.

Gates, Henry Louis, Jr., ed. *Lincoln on Slavery and Race*. Princeton, NJ: Princeton University Press, 2009.

———. *Tradition in the Black Atlantic*. New York: Basic Civitas, 2010.

Geuss, Raymond. *Morality, Culture, and History*. New York: Cambridge University Press, 1999.

———. "Genealogy as Critique." *European Journal of Philosophy* 10 (2010): 209–215.

Goldberg, David Theo. *The Racial State*. Malden, MA: Blackwell, 2002.

Golomb, Jacob. *Nietzsche and Jewish Culture*. New York: Routledge, 1997.

Golomb, Jacob, and Robert S. Wistrich, eds. *Nietzsche, Godfather of Fascism?* Princeton, NJ: Princeton University Press, 2002.

Gómez-Muller, Alfredo. *Alteridad y ética desde el descubrimiento de América*. Madrid: Akal, 1997.

Gooding-Williams, Robert. *Look, A Negro!* New York: Routledge, 2005.

———. *In the Shadow of Du Bois*. Cambridge, MA: Harvard University Press, 2009.

Gordon-Reed, Annette. *The Hemingses of Monticello*. New York: Norton, 2008.

Gossett, Thomas F. *Race: A History of an Idea in America*. New York: Oxford University Press, 1963.

Gracia, Jorge J. E. *Hispanic/Latino Identity: A Philosophical Perspective*. Hoboken, NJ: Wiley-Blackwell, 1999.

———, ed. *Race or Ethnicity? On Black and Latino Identity*. Ithaca, NY: Cornell University Press, 2007.

Grafton, Anthony. Baldwin Lecture, Princeton University, March 30, 2009, http://www.princeton.edu/africanamericanstudies/news/baldwin/ (accessed January 26, 2010).

Graham, Richard. *The Idea of Race in Latin America*. Austin: University of Texas Press, 1990.

Graves, Joseph. *The Emperor's New Clothes: Biological Theories of Race at the Millennium*. Piscataway, NJ: Rutgers University Press, 2002.

Gurvitch, Georges, ed. *La Sociologie au XXe Siècle*. Paris: PUF, 1947.

Hacking, Ian. "Why Race Still Matters." *Daedalus* 134 (2005): 102–116.

Hale, Charles. *Mexican Liberalism in the Age of Mora, 1821–1853*. New Haven, CT: Yale University Press, 1968.

Hanchard, Michael. *Party/Politics*. New York: Oxford University Press, 2006.

Haney López, Ian F. *White by Law*. New York: New York University Press, 1996.

Hanke, Lewis. *Bartolomé de Las Casas: An Interpretation of His Life and Writings*. The Hague: Martinus Nijhoff, 1951.

———. *Estudios sobre Fray Bartolomé de Las Casas y sobre la lucha por la justicia en la conquista española de América*. Caracas: Universidad Central de Venezuela, Ediciones de la Biblioteca, 1968.

———. *The Spanish Struggle for Justice in the Conquest of America*. Dallas, TX: Southern Methodist University Press, 2002.

Hannaford, Ivan. *Race: The History of an Idea in the West*. Baltimore, MD: Johns Hopkins University Press, 1996.

Harwich Vallenilla, Nikita. "Crítica y metódos de la historia en Laureano Vallenilla Lanz." Suplemento Cultural, *Ultimas Noticias*, January 4, 1987.

———, ed. *Laureano Vallenilla Lanz: Obras Completas*. Caracas: Universidad Santa María, 1983.

Helg, Aline. "Bolívar and the Spectre of Pardocracia: José Padilla in Post-independence Cartagena." *Journal of Latin American Studies* 35 (2003): 447–471.

———. *Liberty and Equality in Caribbean Colombia, 1770–1835*. Chapel Hill: University of North Carolina Press, 2004.

Henderson, James. *Conservative Thought in Twentieth Century Latin America*. Athens: Ohio University Center for International Studies, Center for Latin American Studies, 1988.

Herzog, Tamar. *Defining Nations: Immigrants and Citizens in Early Modern Spain and Spanish America*. New Haven, CT: Yale University Press, 2003.

Higgins, Kathleen. "Comparative Aesthetics." In *Oxford Handbook of Aesthetics*. New York: Oxford University Press: 2005.

Higonnet, Patrice. *Sister Republics: The Origins of French and American Republicanism*. Cambridge, MA: Harvard University Press, 1998.

Hirschman, Albert O. *The Passions and the Interests: Political Arguments for Capitalism before Its Triumph*. Princeton, NJ: Princeton University Press, 1977.

Isaac, Benjamin. *The Invention of Racism in Classical Antiquity*. Princeton, NJ: Princeton University Press, 2004.

Isaacson, Walter. *Benjamin Franklin: An American Life*. New York: Simon and Schuster, 2004.

Israel, Jonathan. *Enlightenment Contested*. New York: Oxford University Press, 2006.

Jacobson, Matthew Frye. *Whiteness of a Different Color*. Cambridge, MA: Harvard University Press, 1998.

Jaksic, Iván, ed. *Selected Writings of Andrés Bello*. New York: Oxford University Press, 1997.

———. *Andrés Bello: Scholarship and Nation-Building in Nineteenth-Century Latin America*. New York: Cambridge University Press, 2001.

———. "Simón Bolívar and Andrés Bello: The Republican Ideal." In *Simón Bolívar: Essays on the Life and Legacy of the Liberator*, ed. David Bushnell and Lester Langley. Lanham, MD: Rowman and Littlefield, 2008.

Jefferson, Thomas. *Notes on the State of Virginia*, ed. David Waldstreicher. New York: Palgrave Macmillan, 2002.

Johnson, John, and Doris Ladd. *Simón Bolívar and Spanish American Independence, 1783–1830*. Malabar, FL: Krieger, 1992.

Jones-Correa, Michael. *Between Two Nations: The Political Predicament of Latinos in New York City*. Ithaca, NY: Cornell University Press, 1998.

Jordan, Winthrop D. *White over Black: American Attitudes towards the Negro, 1520–1812*. Chapel Hill: University of North Carolina Press, 1968.

Joyce, Rosemary. "Performing the Body in Pre-Hispanic Central America." *RES: Anthropology and Aesthetics* 33 (1998): 147–165.

Kamen, Henry. *The Spanish Inquisition*. New Haven, CT: Yale University Press, 1997.

Kaufmann, Walter. *Nietzsche: Philosopher, Psychologist, Antichrist*. Princeton, NJ: Princeton University Press, 1974.

Kemal, Salim, Ivan Gaskel and Daniel Conway, eds. *Nietzsche, Philosophy and the Arts*. New York: Cambridge University Press, 2002.

King, Desmond. *Making Americans: Immigration, Race, and the Origins of the Diverse Democracy*. Cambridge, MA: Harvard University Press, 2002.

Kitcher, Philip. "Does 'Race' Have a Future?" *Philosophy & Public Affairs* 35 (2007): 293–317.

Klein, Herbert S., and Ben Vinson. *African Slavery in Latin America and the Caribbean*. New York: Oxford University Press, 2007.

Kohn, Marisa. *Tendencias positivistas en Venezuela*. Caracas: Universidad Central, 1970.

Kojève, Alexandre. *Introduction to the Reading of Hegel: Lectures on the "Phenomenology of Spirit"*. Assembled by Raymond Queneau, ed. Allan Bloom, trans. James H. Nichols, Jr. New York: Basic Books, 1969.

Krupp, Tyler. "Genealogy as Critique." *Journal of the Philosophy of History* 2 (2008): 315–337.

Kymlicka, Will. *Multicultural Citizenship: A Liberal Theory of Minority Rights*. New York: Oxford University Press, 1996.

——. *Politics in the Vernacular*. New York: Oxford University Press, 2001.

——. *Multicultural Odysseys*. New York: Oxford University Press, 2007.

Las Casas, Bartolomé de. *Apologética Historia Sumaria*. In *Historia de las Indias*. Madrid: Imprenta de Miguel Ginesta, 1876.

——. *Historia Apologética*. Madrid, 1909.

——. *Historia de Indias*. Ed. Agustín Millares Carlo. Introduction by Lewis Hanke. Mexico City: Fondo de Cultura Económica, 1981.

——. *Brevísima relación de la destrucción de África*, ed. Isacio Pérez Fernández. Santa Cruz de Tenerife: Gobierno de Canarias, 1989.

——. *A Short Account of the Destruction of the Indies*, ed. Nigel Griffin. New York: Penguin, 1992.

——. *Obras Completas*, ed. Paulino Castañeda Delgado. 14 vols. in 15. Madrid: Alianza Editorial, 1994.

——. *Brevísima relación de la destruición de las Indias*. Bayamón, Puerto Rico: Universidad Central de Bayamón, Centro de Estudios Dominicos del Caribe, Instituto de Estudios Históricos Juan Alejo de Arizmendi, 2000.

Lasso, Marixa. *Myths of Harmony: Race and Republicanism during the Age of Revolution, Colombia 1795–1831*. Pittsburgh, PA: University of Pittsburgh Press, 2007.

Lavallé, Bernard. *Transgressions et Strategies du Métissage en Amérique Coloniale*. Paris: Sorbonne nouvelle, 1999.

Linke, Uli. *Blood and Nation: The European Aesthetics of Race*. Philadelphia: University of Pennsylvania Press, 1999.

Lombardi, John. *Venezuela: The Search for Order, the Dream of Progress*. New York: Oxford University Press, 1982.

Lozano y Lozano, Carlos. *Bolívar: Antología de autores colombianos*. Caracas: Ediciones Presidencia de la República, 1983.

Lynch, John. *Caudillos in Spanish America, 1800–1850*. New York: Oxford University Press, 1992.

——. *Simón Bolívar: A Life*. New Haven: Yale University Press, 2006.

Mac Gregor, Genaro Fernández, ed. *Vasconcelos*. Mexico City: Ediciones de la Secretaría de Educación Pública, 1942.

Machiavelli, Niccolò. *Portable Machiavelli*, ed. Peter Bondanella and Mark Musa. New York: Penguin, 1979.

——. *Discourses on Livy*, ed. Harvey Mansfield and Nathan Tarcov. Chicago: University of Chicago Press, 1996.

——. *The Prince*, ed. Harvey Mansfield. Chicago: University of Chicago Press, 1998.

Madariaga, Salvador de. *Bolívar*. Buenos Aires: Editorial Sudamericana, 1975.

Mallet, Michael. "The Theory and Practice of Warfare in Machiavelli's Republic." In *Machiavelli and Republicanism*, ed. Gisela Bock, Quentin Skinner, and Maurizio Viroli. New York: Cambridge University Press, 1990.

Manin, Bernard. "Montesquieu, la república y el comercio." In *El Republicanismo en Hispanoamérica*, ed. José Antonio Aguilar Rivera and Rafael Rojas. Mexico City: Fondo de Cultura Económica, 2002.

Mariátegui, José Carlos. *Siete ensayos de interpretación de la realidad peruana*. Mexico City: Biblioteca Era, 1979.

Mar-Molinero, Clare. *The Politics of Language in the Spanish-Speaking World*. New York: Routledge, 2005.

Martí, José. *José Martí Reader: Writings on the Americas*, ed. Deborah Shnookal and Mirta Muñiz. New York: Ocean Press, 1999.

Martinenche, Ernest. *Revue de l'Amérique latine*. Paris: 1923.

Marx, Anthony. *Making Race and Nation: A Comparison of the United States, South Africa, and Brazil*. New York: Cambridge University Press, 1998.

Massey, Douglas. *Brokered Boundaries*. New York: Russell Sage, 2010.

Masur, Gerhard. *Simón Bolívar*. Whitefish, MT: Kessinger, 2007.

McCarthy, Thomas. *Race, Empire, and the Idea of Human Development*. Cambridge: Cambridge University Press, 2009.

McCormick, John. *Carl Schmitt's Critique of Liberalism*. New York: Cambridge University Press, 1997.

———. "From Constitutional Technique to Caesarist Ploy: Carl Schmitt on Dictatorship." In *Dictatorship in History and Theory*, ed. Peter Baehr and Melvin Richter. New York: Cambridge University Press, 2004.

McFarlane, Anthony, and Eduardo Posada-Carbó, eds. *Independence and Revolution in Spanish America*. London: University of London, ILAS, 1999.

McWilliams, Wilson Carey. *The Idea of Fraternity in America*. Berkeley: University of California Press, 1973.

Mignolo, Walter D. *The Darker Side of the Renaissance*. Ann Arbor: University of Michigan Press, 2002.

———. "Globalization and the Borders of Latinity." In *Latin American Perspectives on Globalization*, ed. Mario Sáenz. Lanham, MD: Rowman and Littlefield, 2002.

———. *The Idea of Latin America*. Malden, MA: Blackwell, 2005.

Mijares, Augusto. *El Libertador*. Caracas: Grolier Panamericana, 1987.

Miller, Marilyn Grace. *The Rise and Fall of the Cosmic Race: The Cult of Mestizaje in Latin America*. Austin: University of Texas Press, 2004.

Mills, Charles. *The Racial Contract*. Ithaca, NY: Cornell University Press, 1997.

Montaner, Carlos Alberto. *Twisted Roots: Latin America's Living Past*. New York: Algora, 2003.

Montesquieu, Charles-Louis de Secondat, Baron de. *The Spirit of Laws: A Compendium of the First English Edition*. Ed. David Wallace Carrithers, trans. Thomas Nugent. Berkeley: University of California Press, 1977.

Mosquera Aguilar, Antonio. *El Pensamiento Lascasiano en el Pensamiento Latinoamericano y de Europa*. San Cristóbal de Las Casas: UNAM-CIHMECH, 1994.

Muthu, Sankar. *Enlightenment against Empire*. Princeton, NJ: Princeton University Press, 2003.

Nederman, Cary. *Worlds of Difference*. University Park: Pennsylvania State University Press, 2000.

Nietzsche, Friedrich. *Beyond Good and Evil*. In *Basic Writings of Nietzsche*, Ed. and trans. Walter Kaufmann. New York: Modern Library, 1968.

———. *Human, All Too Human*. Trans. R. J. Hollingdale. New York: Cambridge University Press, 1996.

———. *Untimely Meditations*. Ed. Daniel Brazeale. Cambridge: Cambridge University Press, 1997.

———. *Gay Science*. ed. Bernard Williams. Cambridge: Cambridge University Press, 2001.

———. *The Birth of Tragedy.* Ed. Raymond Geuss and Ronald Speirs. Cambridge: Cambridge University Press, 1999.

———. *The Will to Power.* Ed. and trans. Walter Kaufmann. New York: Vintage, 1968.

———. *On the Advantage and Disadvantage of History for Life.* Trans. Peter Preuss. Indianapolis, IN: Hackett, 1980.

———. *Thus Spoke Zarathustra*, in *The Nietzsche Reader*, eds. Ansell Pearson and Duncan Large, Oxford: Blackwell, 2006.

Nightingale, Andrew Wilson. *Spectacles of Truth in Classical Greek Philosophy: Theoria in Its Cultural Context.* New York: Cambridge University Press, 2004.

Norrell, Robert Jefferson. *Up from History: The Life of Booker T. Washington.* Cambridge, MA: Belknap Press, 2009.

O'Gorman, Edmundo. *Cuatro historiadores de Indias, siglo XVI: Pedro Mártir de Anglería, Gonzalo Fernández de Oviedo y Valdés, Bartolomé de las Casas, Joseph de Acosta.* Mexico City: Secretaría de Educación Pública, 1963.

Obama, Barack. *Dreams from My Father.* New York: Three Rivers Press, 2004.

Olson, Joel. *The Abolition of White Democracy.* Minneapolis: University of Minnesota Press, 2004.

Omi, Michael, and Howard Winant. *Racial Formation in the United States.* New York: Routledge, 1994.

Pagden, Anthony. *The Fall of Natural Man: The American Indian and the Origins of Comparative Ethnology.* New York: Cambridge University Press, 1982.

———. *European Encounters with the New World.* New Haven, CT: Yale University Press, 1993.

———. *Lords of All the World: Ideologies of Empire in Spain, Britain and France c. 1500–c. 1800.* New Haven, CT: Yale University Press, 1995.

———. *Spanish Imperialism and the Political Imagination: Studies in European and Spanish-American Social and Political Theory, 1513–1830.* New Haven, CT: Yale University Press, 1998.

Painter, Nell Irvin. *The History of White People.* New York: Norton, 2010.

Palti, Elías. *Mito y realidad de la cultura política latinoamericana.* Buenos Aires: Prometeo, 2010.

Parra Pérez, Caracciolo, *Bolívar: Contribución al estudio de sus ideas políticas.* Paris: Excelsior, 1928.

Pascoe, Peggy. *What Comes Naturally: Miscegenation Law and the Making of Race in America.* New York: Oxford University Press, 2009.

Pateman, Carole. *The Disorder of Women.* Palo Alto, CA: Stanford University Press, 1989.

Persram, Nalini, ed. *Postcolonialism and Political Theory.* Lanham, MD: Lexington Books, 2007.

Pettit, Philip. *Republicanism: A Theory of Freedom and Government.* New York: Oxford University Press, 1999.

Pino Iturrieta, Elías. *El divino Bolívar: Ensayo sobre una religión republicana.* Madrid: Los Libros de la Catarata, 2003.

Pinzón, Hermes Tovar. "Bolívar and the Future of Democracy." In *Simón Bolívar: Essays on the Life and Legacy of the Liberator*, ed. David Bushnell and Lester Langley. Lanham, MD: Rowman and Littlefield, 2008.

Pippin, Robert. *Modernism as a Philosophical Problem: On the Dissatisfactions of European High Culture.* Malden, MA: Blackwell, 1999.

Pitts, Jennifer. *A Turn to Empire: The Rise of Imperial Liberalism in Britain and France.* Princeton, NJ: Princeton University Press, 2005.

Plaza, Elena. *La tragedia de una amarga convicción: Historia y política en el pensamiento de Laureano Vallenilla Lanz, 1870–1936*. Caracas: Facultad de Ciencias Jurídicas y Políticas, Universidad Central de Venezuela, 1996.

Rahe, Paul. *Republics Ancient and Modern*. Chapel Hill: University of North Carolina Press, 1994.

Rampley, Matthew. *Nietzsche, Aesthetics, and Modernity*. New York: Cambridge University Press, 2000.

Rich Greer, Margaret, Walter Mignolo, and Maureen Quilligan. *Rereading the Black Legend: The Discourses of Religious and Racial Difference in the Renaissance Empires*. Chicago: University of Chicago Press, 2007.

Robles, Martha. *Entre el Poder y las Letras: Vasconcelos en sus memorias*. Mexico City: Fondo de Cultura Económica, 1989.

Rodó, José Enrique. "Bolívar." In *Bolívar*. Caracas: Biblioteca Ayacucho, 1983.

———. *Ariel*. Austin: University of Texas Press, 1988.

Romo Cedano, Pablo. "Las bases filosóficas del pensamiento de fray Bartolomé de Las Casas." In *El Pensamiento Lascasiano en la Conciencia de América y Europa*, ed. P. González Casanova H. Mexico City: UNAM, 1994.

Rosenblat, Ángel. *La población indígena y el mestizaje en América*. Buenos Aires: Nova, 1954.

Rousseau, Jean-Jacques. *The Social Contract, and Discourses*. Trans. G. D. H. Cole. New York: E. P. Dutton, 1950.

———. *The Basic Political Writings*. Ed. Donald A. Cress. Indianapolis, IN: Hackett, 1987.

———. *Emile*. Fairford, Gloucestershire, England: Echo Library, 2007.

Rozo Acuña, Eduardo. *Bolívar: Pensamiento Constitucional*. Bogotá: Universidad Externado de Colombia, 1983.

———. *Bolívar y la organización de los poderes políticos*. Bogotá: TEMIS, 1988.

———. *Obra política y constitucional de Simón Bolívar*. Madrid: Tecnos, 2007.

Rumazo Gonzáles, Alfonso. *Simón Bolívar*. Caracas: Reproducciones Gráficas, 1971.

Safford, Frank. "Bolívar as Triumphal State Maker and Despairing 'Democrat.'" In *Simón Bolívar: Essays on the Life and Legacy of the Liberator*, ed. David Bushnell and Lester Langley. Lanham, MD: Rowman and Littlefield, 2008.

Salamanca, Luis. *Los pensadores positivistas y el gomecismo*. Caracas: Congreso de la República, 1983.

Sanjinés, Javier. *Mestizaje Upside Down*. Pittsburgh, PA: University of Pittsburgh Press, 2004.

———. *El espejismo del mestizaje*. La Paz: IFEA, 2005.

Sarmiento, Domingo Faustino. *Life in the Argentine Republic in the Days of the Tyrants*. New York: Hafner, 1974.

Schank, Gerd. *"Rasse" und "Züchtung" bei Nietzsche*. Berlin: de Gruyter, 2000.

Schmitt, Carl. *Die Diktatur: Von den Anfängen des modernen Souveränitätsgedankens bis zum proletarischen Klassenkampf*. Berlin: Duncker & Humblot, 1989.

Scott, Jacqueline, and A. Todd Franklin, eds. *Critical Affinities: Nietzsche and African American Thought*. Albany: SUNY Press, 2006.

Shelby, Tommie. *We Who Are Dark: The Philosophical Foundations of Black Solidarity*. Cambridge, MA: Belknap Press, 2007.

Sheth, Falguni A. *Toward a Political Philosophy of Race*. Albany: SUNY Press, 2009.

Shulman, George. *American Prophecy: Race and Redemption in American Political Culture*. Minneapolis: University of Minnesota Press, 2008.

Silver, Peter. *Our Savage Neighbors: How Indian War Transformed Early America*. New York: Norton, 2007.

Skinner, Quentin. *Hobbes and Republican Liberty*. Cambridge: Cambridge University Press, 2008.

Skinner, Quentin, and Martin van Gelderen, eds. *Republicanism and Constitutionalism in Early Modern Europe*. New York: Cambridge University Press, 2005.

Slatta, Richard. *Cowboys of the Americas*. New Haven, CT: Yale University Press, 1990.

Smedley, Audrey. *Race in North America*. Boulder, CO: Westview Press, 1999.

Smith, Rogers. *Civic Ideals: Conflicting Visions of Citizenship in U.S. History*. New Haven, CT: Yale University Press, 1997.

Somers, Margaret. *Genealogies of Citizenship: Markets, Statelessness, and the Right to Have Rights*. New York: Cambridge University Press, 2008.

Song, Sarah. *Justice, Gender, and the Politics of Multiculturalism*. New York: Cambridge University Press, 2007.

Soriano Hernández, Silvia. "La no tan breve destrucción de las Indias." In *El Pensamiento Lascasiano en la conciencia de América y Europa*, ed. P. González Casanova H. Mexico City: UNAM, 1994.

Sosa, Ernest. *La filosofía política del gomecismo*. Barquisimeto, Venezuela: Centro Gumilla, 1974.

Stepan, Nancy. *The Hour of Eugenics: Race, Gender, and Nation in Latin America*. Ithaca, NY: Cornell University Press, 1991.

Stiegler, Barbara. *Nietzsche et la biologie*. Paris: PUF, 2001.

Stoler, Ann Laura. *Carnal Knowledge and Imperial Power: Race and the Intimate in Colonial Rule*. Berkeley: University of California Press, 2002.

Stone, Dan. *Breeding Superman*. Liverpool: Liverpool University Press, 2002.

Tarica, Estelle. *The Inner Life of Mestizo Nationalism*. Minneapolis: University of Minnesota Press, 2008.

Tarver, H. Micheal, and Julia C. Frederick. *The History of Venezuela*. Westport, CT: Greenwood Press, 2005.

Tocqueville, Alexis de. *Oeuvres Complètes*. Paris: Éditions Gallimard, 1952.

———. *Democracy in America*. New York: Library of America, 2004.

Todorov, Tzvetan. *The Conquest of America: The Question of the Other*. Norman: University of Oklahoma Press, 1999.

Twinam, Ann. "Purchasing Whiteness: Conversations on the Essence of Pardo-ness and Mulatto-ness at the End of Empire." In *Imperial Subjects: Race and Identity in Colonial Latin America*, ed. Andrew Fisher and Matthew O'Hara. Durham, NC: Duke University Press, 2009.

Urueña Cervera, Jaime. *Bolívar Republicano: Fundamentos ideológicos e históricos de su pensamiento político*. Bogotá: Ediciones Aurora, 2004.

Vallenilla Lanz, Laureano. *Cesarismo Democrático*. Caracas: Biblioteca Ayacucho, 1991.

———. *El Libertador juzgado por los miopes*. Caracas: Comercio, 1914.

———. "Fiesta de la Raza." *El Nuevo Diario* (Caracas), October 12, 1916. Vallenilla Archives, Saint-Germain-en-Laye, France, vol. 2.

———. *Cesarismo Democrático*. Caracas: El Cojo, 1919.

———. *Sentido americano de la democracia*. Caracas: Universal, 1926.

———. *Disgregación e Integración*. In *Cesarismo democrático y otros textos*, ed. Nikita Harwich Vallenilla. Caracas: Biblioteca Ayacucho, 1991.

———. *Obras Completas*. Caracas: Centro de Investigaciones Históricas, 1983.

———. *Obras Completas*. Havana: Les, 1950.

Vallenilla Lanz, Laureano, Jr. *Razones de Proscrito*. Choisy-le-Roi: Les Gondoles, 1965.

Vargas, Manuel. "La biología y la filosofía de la 'raza' en México: Francisco Bulnes y José Vasconcelos." In *Construcción de las identidades latinoamericanas*, ed. Aimer Granados García and Carlos Marichal. Mexico City: El Colegio de México, 2004.

Vasconcelos, José. *Ideario de Acción*. Lima: Actual, 1924.

———. *Indología*. Paris: Mundial, 1926.

———. *Pesimismo Alegre*. Madrid: Aguilar Editores, 1931.

———. *Hispanoamérica frente a los nacionalismos agresivos de Europa y Norteamérica*. La Plata: Universidad de Buenos Aires, 1934.

———. *En el ocaso de mi vida*. Mexico City: Populibros La Prensa, 1957.

———. *Obras Completas*. Mexico City: Libreros Mexicanos Unidos, 1957–1961.

———. *Obra Selecta*. Ed. Christopher Domínguez Michael. Caracas: Biblioteca Ayacucho, 1992.

———. *La Raza Cósmica*. Baltimore, MD: Johns Hopkins University Press, 1997.

Viroli, Maurizio. *Republicanism*. New York: Hill and Wang, 2001.

Vitoria, Francisco de. *Political Writings*. Ed. Anthony Pagden and Jeremy Lawrance. New York: Cambridge University Press, 1991.

Voegelin, Eric. *The History of the Race Idea*. Columbia: University of Missouri Press, 1998.

von Vacano, Diego. *The Art of Power: Machiavelli, Nietzsche, and the Making of Aesthetic Political Theory*. Lanham, MD: Lexington Books, 2007.

Waldstreicher, David. *Runaway America: Benjamin Franklin, Slavery, and the American Revolution*. New York: Hill and Wang, 2005.

Walzer, Michael. "Citizenship." In *Political Innovation and Conceptual Change*, ed. Terence Ball, James Farr, and Russell L. Hanson. New York: Cambridge University Press, 1989.

Ward, Julie, and Tommy Lee Lott, eds. *Philosophers on Race*. Malden, MA: Blackwell, 2002.

Weinstock, Daniel, and Christian Nadeau, eds. *Republicanism*. Portland, OR: Frank Cass, 2004.

Welch, Cheryl. *Liberty and Utility: The French Idéologues and the Transformation of Liberalism*. New York: Columbia University Press, 1984.

West, Cornel. *Prophesy Deliverance! An Afro-American Revolutionary Christianity*. Philadelphia: Westminster Press, 1982.

Wiarda, Howard J. *The Soul of Latin America*. New Haven, CT: Yale University Press, 2003.

Winchester, James. "Nietzsche's Racial Profiling." In *Race and Racism in Modern Philosophy*, ed. Andrew Valls. Ithaca, NY: Cornell University Press, 2005.

Wolin, Sheldon. *Politics and Vision: Continuity and Innovation in Western Political Thought*. Princeton, NJ: Princeton University Press, 2004.

Worms, René. *Philosophie des Sciences Sociales*. 3 vols. Paris: V. Giard and E. Brière, 1903–1907.

Wright, Winthrop. *Café Con Leche: Race, Class, and National Image in Venezuela*. Austin: University of Texas Press, 1993.

Young, Iris Marion. "Polity and Group Difference." *Ethics* 99 (1989): 250–274.

———. *Inclusion and Democracy*. Oxford: Oxford University Press, 2000.

Young, Julian. *Nietzsche's Philosophy of Art*. New York: Cambridge University Press, 1992.

Zack, Naomi. *Race/Sex: Their Sameness, Difference and Interplay*. New York: Routledge, 1997.

Zea, Leopoldo. *El pensamiento latinoamericano*. Mexico City: Pórmaca, 1965.

———. *Precursores del pensamiento latinoamericano contemporáneo*. Mexico City: Secretaría de Educación Pública, 1971.

Index

Africa, 10, 13, 50–52, 82, 94, 178nn160, 162, 202n14

African, x, 8–9, 12–15, 20–21, 27, 29, 49–52, 58–61, 66, 79, 88, 95, 98, 100, 104, 115, 154–155, 159–164, 172n7, 179n177, 176n115, 181n27, 184n80, 203n19

African American, 11, 14–15, 160, 164, 203n30, 204n57

Afro-Latino, 18, 23, 170n100

Agon/agonism, 109, 118, 120, 127–128, 152

Alberdi, Juan Bautista, 16, 170n84, 203n24

Allen, Danielle, xi, xiii, 165n9

Amoral, 33, 147, 152

Anderson, Marian, 140

Angostura Discourse, 56, 60 at n43, 61 at n52, 65 at n77, 68 at n94, 75, 88, 103, 183n56

Animal, 8, 38, 42, 55, 98, 135, 189n204, 204n49

Anthropology, 6, 27, 29, 43, 65, 90, 142

Aquinas, 38, 47–48, 118, 125

Arendt, Hannah, 6, 8, 10, 166n15, 197n19, 204n51

Argentina, 16, 91, 96, 98, 101, 126, 132, 140, 203n24

Aristotle, 6, 8, 38, 48, 125, 157, 176nn102–103

Art, 22, 113–126, 130–135, 140, 145, 154, 156, 175n72, 178n146, 185n98, 197n16, 198n43, 200n79

Asia, 10, 80, 94, 146, 155, 158, 163–164, 169n80, 202n14

Asian, ix, 10, 15, 22, 154, 169n81

Athens, 82, 176

Autonomy, 33, 49, 156, 160

Aymara, 73, 162–163, 174n67, 199n71

Aztec, 10, 127, 174n67

Bacon, Francis, 7

Barbarian, 6, 8, 10, 27, 32–34, 37–40, 45, 49, 55, 130, 139, 157, 176nn95–96

Beautiful, 9, 49, 51, 82, 120–121, 133, 135, 175n87, 178n159

Beauty, 22, 37, 46–50, 113, 116, 117, 120–122, 126, 128–137, 149, 158, 159, 175nn87–89, 177n116, 198n43, 199n63, 200n79

Bello, Andrés, 58, 92

Beltrán, Aguirre, 16

Bentham, Jeremy, 72, 168n48, 182n34

Bevir, Mark, xi, 202n17, 203nn21, 23

Bible, 8, 174n57

Biological, 18, 28, 42–45, 47, 49, 50, 55, 61–63, 80, 84, 93–98, 105, 111, 117, 127, 129–136, 148, 150–151, 155, 165n2, 170n96, 184n71, 199n58, 201n116

Biology, 28, 55, 90, 135, 136, 204n49

Blumenbach, Johann, 9, 117
Body, 12, 14, 39, 46–50, 65, 67, 79, 118, 122, 123, 131, 135, 161
Bolívar, Simón:
  civic, 63, 71–72
  constitution, 66, 73–77
  dictatorship, 64, 68, 79
  diversity, 62, 64–65, 73
  imperialism, 68–70, 81
  Machiavellian, 70–76
  martial, 68, 81
  Montesquieu 68–69, 76
  pardos, 58–59
  race, 56–59, 62, 75
  republicanism, 63–66, 82
  Rome, 59, 70
  Rousseau, 64–68, 71
Bolivia, ix, xii, 24, 62, 66–67, 73–75, 79, 83, 91, 98, 101, 148, 162, 163, 174n66, 180n4, 186n130, 196n186, 199n71
Borgia, Cesare, 32, 39, 105, 193n110
Bouglé, Celestin, 90
Brazil, 96, 117–118, 126–128, 134, 139, 159, 203n19
Britain, 59, 78, 192n73
Bruno, Giordano, 8, 157
Buffon, Georges de, 9, 62
Burke, Edmund, 9, 168n46

Cambas, 163
Canarians, 58, 59, 76
Canary Islands, 46, 51, 58
Cannibalism, 9, 40, 174, 176
Capitalism, 88, 156, 159
Caribs, 9, 61, 65, 99, 174n67
Caso, Antonio, 16, 201n102
Casta paintings, x
Castro, Cipriano, 86, 110
Catholic Church, 36, 40, 72, 146, 149, 160
Catholicism, 17–19, 22–23, 28, 40–45, 50–54, 112–115, 118, 133–134, 138–140, 146, 149
Caudillismo, 85, 98, 102, 105
Caudillo, 58, 86, 98, 105, 110
Censorship, 65
Charles V, 27, 172n10, 173n40
Chávez, Hugo, 190n14
Chile, 73, 79, 126, 155, 162
Chinese, 139
Cholos, ix, 74

Christian, 27, 29, 31–32, 34, 37, 40–42, 45–48, 52–55, 72, 75, 77, 104, 121, 133–134, 139–140, 158, 167n29, 172n6, 176n95, 179n174, 203n31
Christianity, 27, 29, 39, 42, 45, 52, 53, 55, 72, 77, 118, 134, 151, 201n102, 203n31
Christendom, 46
Cicero, 8, 45, 172n12
Citizenship, ix, 5, 13–14, 17–18, 25, 66, 69, 75, 89, 132, 135, 142–144, 149–153, 158, 164, 166n13, 170n99, 171n107, 186n115, 204n51
Civilized, 8–9, 27, 37, 41–42, 49, 55, 65, 95, 153, 176n96
Class, ix, 6, 10, 14, 23, 45, 50, 57–60, 69–72, 81, 84, 87–88, 94, 103, 106, 109–110, 138, 143, 159, 163, 182n31
Coll, Emilio, 86
Collas, 163
Colombia, 57, 60, 64, 67, 77–81, 86, 87, 101, 108–110, 125, 148, 155, 180n4
Colonial/colonialism, 9–11, 16–17, 21, 58, 69, 71, 82, 87, 91, 104–105, 109, 112–115, 141–142, 146–152, 155, 157, 159, 163, 164, 167n37, 168n43, 173n40, 181n15, 186n121, 192n73, 198n54
Color, ix, 6, 9, 15, 17, 46, 59, 61–63, 69, 79, 81–82, 88–89, 96, 100, 104, 123, 128, 135, 137, 140, 145, 157, 161, 175n90, 189n200
Color-blind/color-blindness, 142, 145
Columbus, 16, 20, 30, 43–44, 46, 175nn87, 91
Comte, Auguste, 86–90, 96, 114–115
Constitution, 13, 43, 66–68, 71, 74, 77, 80, 83, 103, 106, 108, 110, 186
Constitutionalism, 19, 58, 60, 65, 72–75, 84–85, 93, 101, 108–109, 160
Corruption, 71–73, 103, 106, 162, 166n18
Cosmopolitanism, 17, 22–23, 45, 85, 117, 132, 147–149
Cosmos, 134
Creativity, 6, 126, 132–133
Creoles, 58–59, 92, 105
Criollos, 60–61, 73–74, 148, 159, 163
Croly, David Goodman, 4
Cruelty, 39, 51, 53
Cuba, 4, 112, 132, 174n67, 175n91, 203n24

Dance, 22, 50, 118, 121, 125, 127, 159, 201n121
Darwin, Charles, 86, 91, 96, 117
De Soto, Domingo, 35

Deleuze, Gilles, 119–120
Delfino, Victor, 16
Deliberation, 66, 102, 142, 185n101, 186n114
Democracy, 11, 63, 66, 71, 82, 87, 88, 90, 92, 95,
    101, 102, 103, 109, 114, 160, 181n14, 183n71,
    186n125, 189n205, 193n102
Demos, 66, 84–87, 102, 106
Descartes, René, 7, 157, 204n42
Despotism, 10, 42, 70, 77, 82, 87, 89, 186n121
Development, 7, 15–19, 23–24, 44, 53, 55, 85,
    88–93, 96–100, 104, 110–111, 119–120, 134,
    142, 149, 151–152, 162, 167n34, 200n90
Díaz, Porfirio, 114, 148
Dictator, 21, 69, 79, 87–89, 102, 104,
    107–108, 127
Dictatorship, 64, 68, 79, 84, 87, 89, 91, 101,
    108–109, 127, 148, 189n8, 191n40,
    195n164
Diversity, 16, 21–22, 25, 28, 52–53, 62, 64–65, 71,
    73, 84–85, 91, 92, 101, 104–106, 110, 140,
    181, 202
Docility, 13, 27, 46–47
Domination, 10, 24, 64, 69, 71, 95, 108, 139,
    142–143, 151, 171, 185–186
Domination paradigm, 7, 9, 11, 15, 20, 111, 122,
    144, 162
Dominium, 54
Douglass, Frederick, 13–14, 169n74
Du Bois, W.E.B., 14–15, 169n82
Dualistic paradigm, 11, 14–15, 145, 151, 161,
    202n15, 203n30
Durkheim, Émile, 90–91
Dussel, Enrique, 158

Education, 12, 14, 44, 62, 66, 72–75, 86, 114,
    162–163, 187n138, 204n57, 205n58
Emotion, 32, 36–39, 45, 47–48, 67, 69, 116, 118,
    126, 131–132, 137, 140, 158
England, 10, 49, 114
Enlightenment, x, 9, 11, 15, 62–64, 82, 88, 116, 131,
    139, 167n37, 197n30
Equality, 9, 11, 13–15, 23, 64–66, 69, 71, 75–77, 81,
    84, 87, 89, 102, 109–110, 129, 140–143, 151,
    156, 158, 162, 168n51, 171n103, 172n12,
    176n105, 199n73
Erotic, 104, 159
Ethnicity, 16–17, 19, 34, 55, 58, 64, 80, 116, 136,
    142–143, 153, 161, 163, 166n10, 204n56
Ethnography, 50, 54

Eugenics, 7, 16, 96, 136, 197n35
Europe, 4–5, 7–15, 20–22, 26–27, 30, 34–43,
    47–77, 76, 78, 80–86, 91–105, 109–114,
    117–122, 127–132, 139–148, 151–159, 162,
    166n16, 170n84, 176n97, 177n127, 179n177,
    182n47, 183n69, 193nn92, 102, 195n174,
    197n19, 203n24, 204nn41, 46
Evil, 7, 33, 88–89, 123, 135, 152, 174n50, 175n91
Evolution, 91, 93, 136, 191n56
Executive, 21–23, 64–70, 81, 84–88, 93, 101–103,
    107–110, 146, 148, 181n14, 183n56, 187n157,
    191n40
Exploitation, 77, 99, 159

Fanon, Frantz, 6, 166n15
Fascism, 85, 106, 108, 127, 130
Fear, 4, 8, 13, 29, 39, 48, 59, 68, 70–71, 74, 89,
    105–106, 137, 142, 148, 153, 164, 177n120,
    184n80, 186n123, 194n132
Febvre, Lucien, 90
Federalism, 74, 79, 81, 110
Form, 17, 29, 37, 46, 48–49, 113, 120, 123, 128, 134,
    137, 149, 158
France, 59, 86, 91–92, 104, 114, 142, 168n59
Franklin, Benjamin, 12–13
Freedom, 8, 14, 23, 64–65, 69–70, 73–78, 106,
    131, 142, 156, 158, 171n103, 183nn56, 65,
    185nn96, 104, 186n121, 187n162, 188n187
Freyre, Gilberto, 95, 104, 149

Gamio, Manuel, 16
García Canclini, Néstor, 170n86, 171n105
García Linera, Álvaro, 143, 202n13
Garcilaso, Inca, 56, 149
Gates, Jr., Henry Louis, xi, 169nn72, 78
Gendarme, 21, 87–88, 105, 108, 190n36, 195nn152,
    157
Gender, 6, 23, 98, 159
Genealogical, 19, 45, 122, 152
Genealogy, 26, 34, 57, 84, 119–125, 152, 170n96
General Will, the, 64, 71, 81, 102
Germany, 34, 91, 109, 136
Gil Fortoul, José, 86, 105, 193n105, 196n180
Ginés de Sepúlveda, Juan, 20, 27, 34, 35
Gobineau, Arthur de, 4, 94–95, 105, 117, 148, 155,
    192n75
God, 8, 26, 33, 37, 42, 44, 67, 139, 157, 172n10,
    204n44
Godos, 57, 92, 110, 189n8

Gómez, Juan Vicente, 21, 84, 87–89, 107, 110, 127, 148, 190n35, 194n133

Good, 21, 27, 43, 46–47, 53, 55, 57, 69–71, 83–84, 88, 101–102, 107, 123, 142, 149, 152, 155, 174n51

Good and Evil, 135

Gracia, Jorge, xi, 150, 165n9, 183n54, 203nn20, 27

Grafton, Anthony, xi, 29, 167n29, 173n23

Gramsci, Antonio, 143

Greece, 7–8, 33–34, 46, 94, 104, 130, 137, 141, 145, 156, 158, 176nn110, 115

Guanches, 51

Guaraní, 73, 162, 174n67

Guarionex, 41

Guatemala, 34, 35, 62, 174n65

Guicciardini, Francesco, 101

Gumplowicz, Ludwig, 86

Habermas, Jürgen, 4

Haiti, 71, 79

Hanke, Lewis, 43, 173n45, 174nn48, 50, 175nn79, 84, 176n108, 177nn134, 137, 140, 178n142, 179n183, 180n196

Hegel, Georg W.F., 10–11, 17, 80, 117–118, 120–121, 124, 131–132, 139, 147, 149, 152, 156–157, 166n19, 200n93, 201n117

Heidegger, Martin, 119, 131

Herder, Johann, G. 9, 176n105

Hernández, Fortuno, 16

Heterogeneity, 84–85, 97, 100–105, 108, 110, 194nn117, 136, 202n5

Hirschman, Albert O., 3, 7, 24, 145, 165n1

Hispaniola, 16, 20, 33, 34, 37, 41, 46

Hobbes, Thomas, 8, 31, 142, 160, 167n34, 177n120, 182n34

Homogeneity, 64–65, 79–80, 104, 129

Homunculi, 27, 55

Humanism, 32–33, 157

Humanity, 9, 13, 23, 27, 29, 32–33, 36–38, 41, 44–45, 48–59, 75, 80, 95–96, 111, 124, 130, 146–148, 152, 155, 163, 170n93, 172n6, 200nn98–99

Hume, David, 9, 182n34

Huntington, Samuel, 163–164

Hybridity, 16, 24, 159

Identity, 5, 17–23, 57–63, 74–78, 83–85, 88–91, 94–105, 109, 113, 117–118, 122, 124, 132, 135, 138, 140–146, 149–154, 158–164, 172n20, 183n54, 193nn109, 114, 199n55, 202n18, 203n22, 205n63

Immigrants, ix, 24, 164, 169n80, 205n60

Immigration, 24, 91, 96, 100, 111, 164, 193n92, 202n15, 204n56

Immorality, 32, 75, 166n18, 186n129

Inca, 10, 41, 56, 73, 75, 99, 137, 149

Independence, 61, 69, 76, 85, 87–93, 106, 162, 181nn14–15

Indígena, 163

Indigenista, 16

Inequality, 4, 63, 66, 95, 103, 106, 142–143, 148

Ingenieros, José, 96

Inhuman, 32, 37, 39, 40, 180n7, 184n80

Islam, 134

Jackson, Andrew, 102

Japanese, 95, 132, 133

Jefferson, Thomas, 12–15, 75, 169nn67, 69, 187n161

Jesus Christ, 45, 171n2

Jews/Jewish, 8, 10, 29, 44, 46, 104, 122, 130, 141, 148, 163, 167n29, 173n22, 198nn35–36, 199n55, 201n116

Judaism, 29

Justice, 6, 9, 13, 25, 44, 51, 76, 78, 142–143, 162–163, 166n18

Kant, Immanuel, 9–11, 118, 120, 133, 142, 157, 160, 168nn43, 44, 49

Katz, Friedrich, 112, 196n2

Kehl, Renato, 16

Kymlicka, Will, xi, 143, 171n104, 202nn8, 10, 204n54, 205n58

La Paz, ix, 162, 174n66

Laboulaye, Édouard, 86–87, 90

Langlois, Charles, 86, 90

Las Casas, Bartolomé de:
    Aesthetic, 29, 32, 37, 46–49
    Barbarian, 27, 32, 37
    Catholicism, 28, 36, 40–45
    civilized, 27, 41, 55
    empire, 52–57
    linaje, 27, 44, 49
    modernity, 27, 31
    race, 27–29, 34, 44, 46–49
    rhetoric, 27–28, 32, 36–37
    sentience, 38–40
    universalism, 42

Latin America, ix-x, 3, 16–24, 57–58, 62, 67, 73, 77–86, 91–114, 125–126, 129–130, 137–143, 146–149, 158–159, 162, 169n80, 180n9, 181nn14, 23, 182n41, 183n54, 193nn92, 102, 194n133

Law, 18, 21, 24, 28, 32, 34, 42, 52, 59, 60, 64, 67–76, 82–84, 87–88, 102, 107, 108–109, 114, 129, 142, 165n7, 169n78, 171n106, 173n40, 182n29, 184n93, 185n114, 194n136, 203n30

Liberalism, 9, 12, 16–19, 23, 28, 57, 65, 67, 72–74, 80, 84, 87–88, 95, 103, 106–110, 115, 139–143, 148, 160–162, 171nn102, 106, 181nn14, 16, 183n65, 185n98, 186n121, 189n8, 190n24, 194n102, 196n180, 202n10, 202n50

Linaje, 20, 27, 36, 38, 41, 44–45, 49–50, 150, 152, 175n181, 176n109

Lincoln, Abraham, 13

Lineage, 15, 27–30, 44–45, 49–50, 58, 63, 111, 141, 167n37, 201n121

Linnaeus, Carolus, 9, 62, 117

Locke, John, 8–9, 136, 160, 167n35, 182n34

Logos, 32, 140

Lora, Guillermo, 143

Love, 42, 45, 50, 59, 65, 72, 83, 95, 115–116, 122, 132, 134, 140, 171n3, 199n63, 201n120

Mariátegui, José Carlos, 125, 134, 143, 149, 170n94, 201n103, 202n12

Markets, 110, 156–157, 162

Martí, José, 4, 93, 132, 149, 165n8, 170n94, 192nn68–69, 203n24

Martial, 21, 58, 63, 68–70, 75–76, 81, 85, 88, 105, 108, 148, 155, 159, 164, 181n14, 185n98

Marx, Karl, 6, 10, 106, 143

Marxism, 6, 88, 103, 131, 138–139, 142, 190n33

Maya, 10, 41, 99, 137, 174n67

Mestizaje, 16, 18, 91, 124, 139, 149, 153, 155, 163, 182n47

Mestizo, 22, 24, 59–60, 73–74, 89, 95, 99, 104–105, 113, 155, 199n63

Métissage, 96, 148

Mexico, 18, 22, 79, 91, 101, 111–114, 125, 126, 138–139, 148–149, 155

Mignolo, Walter, 16, 166n19, 170n86, 171n105

Military, 41, 59–60, 63, 68–69, 75–76, 79, 81, 88, 105, 148, 185n111, 186n115

Mill, John Stuart, 6, 9–10, 86, 97, 142, 160, 168nn48, 49, 51

Miranda, Francisco de, 75, 187n157

Miscegenation, x, 4, 11, 18, 21–24, 58, 60, 65, 78–80, 93, 95, 100–105, 111, 117, 129–130, 133–136, 139, 146, 149, 155, 162, 165n7, 170n92, 171n101, 191n40, 192n73, 200n9

Misery, 87–89, 103–106

Modern, 3, 5–12, 15–19, 21–34, 39, 41, 43, 45–46, 48–50, 54, 57–58, 60, 63–65, 73–74, 81–86, 89, 92–93, 101, 106–131, 136–147, 151, 154–159, 161, 164, 166, 178n146, 179n164, 199n73, 200n79

Modernity, 4, 7, 10, 16, 18, 20, 23–24, 27, 31, 33, 107, 111, 113, 117–120, 125, 128, 130, 137, 140, 143, 148, 156–159, 204n41

Monarchy, 27, 63, 66–67, 69, 81, 85, 172n13, 187n157

Monogenesis, 8–9, 136

Montaigne, Michel de, 9

Montesinos, Antonio de, 30

Montesquieu, Charles-Louis de, 9, 21, 57, 63–64, 68–70, 74, 76, 81, 147, 181n18, 182n34, 183n64

Moors, 51–52, 104, 148

Morales, Evo, 24, 162–163

Morality, 29, 32–33, 38, 40, 49, 53, 71–75, 82, 119–122, 125, 147, 157, 166n18

Motolinía, 31, 174n52

Multiculturalism, 23, 160

Muslim, 29, 44, 52, 104

Mussolini, Benito, 106–107

Napoleon, 59, 69, 81, 184n71, 187n151

Nationalism, 10, 22, 24, 79, 85, 107–113, 118, 126–127, 132, 138–140, 148, 153, 189n3, 195n151, 196n5, 199nn54–55

Native Americans, 9, 14, 22, 164, 192n84

Nature, 8, 21, 27, 38, 41, 45, 47, 49, 65, 76–77, 90, 96, 98, 132–136, 164

Nazi, 10, 108, 198nn36, 44

Nederman, Cary, x, 45, 172n12, 178n148, 179n182

Nehamas, Alexander, 197n34

Nero, 39, 59

Nicaragua, 40, 86, 177n116

Nietzsche, Friedrich, 6, 10, 22–23, 113, 118–137, 140–141, 149, 152, 156, 170n96, 178n152, 197nn18, 21, 24, 27, 30, 31, 198nn35, 36, 39–42, 45, 47, 50, 200nn79, 92, 95, 201nn102, 116–119, 203n31, 204n44

Nihilism, 120, 132–133

Nomos, 45, 109
Novicow, Jacques, 111, 196n184

Obama, Barack, x, 154, 166n9
Omi, Michael, 168n63
One-drop rule, 18, 24, 170n90, 182n47
Order, 19, 21, 28–29, 49–50, 52, 53, 66, 69, 72, 80,
    83, 85, 88–90, 100, 103–111, 116, 118,
    127–129, 132, 135, 149, 160, 175n79, 177n120,
    182n41, 185n101

Pagden, Anthony, 36, 53, 55, 167nn22, 25, 168n45,
    172nn6, 7, 13, 173n30, 174nn59, 62, 175nn72,
    83, 85, 176nn102, 104, 110, 112, 177nn129,
    139, 178nn141, 151, 156, 179nn181, 185,
    180nn193, 197, 183n61
Pain, 38–39, 48, 50, 128
Palante, Georges, 97, 193n98
Pardo, 51, 57–60, 66, 69–71, 82, 89, 99, 105–106,
    148, 159, 181n27, 182n29, 186n123
Pardocracia, 66, 71, 89, 106, 184n80, 186n122
Particularism, 17–18, 21–22, 113, 147, 149
Pathos, 32, 67, 116, 120, 135, 201n114
Patriotism, 19, 80, 164
Peace, 13, 33, 41–42, 45–46, 51–52, 65, 68, 71, 78,
    116, 177n120
People, the, 64, 66, 87–88, 102–103, 107
Performance, 118
Peru, 33–34, 56, 73, 79, 83, 91, 98, 114, 125–126,
    139, 162, 174n65, 180n4, 190n36
Petrarch, 52
Pettit, Philip, 180n11, 185nn103, 112–114,
    186nn114, 116, 121, 202n7
Phenotype, 63, 167nn32, 37, 172n7
Philip II, 27, 36, 179n178
Physis, 45
Pippin, Robert, 204nn39–44
Plato, 6–8, 120
Pluralism, 28, 71
Polis, 8, 54–55
Political science, x-xi
Politics, 3, 5–7, 22, 24–25, 31–34, 39, 46, 48, 58–59,
    65, 71, 77, 82, 85–87, 90–91, 101–103, 107–109,
    118, 132–133, 137, 142–145, 153, 156–160,
    166n18, 181n20, 190n24, 193n106, 202n9
Polygenesis, 8, 86, 136
Portugal, 50–51, 203n19
Positivism, 85–86, 89–01, 109, 114, 148–149,
    191n56, 194n117

Postcolonial, 58, 71, 82, 91, 109, 142
Postmodern, 23, 24, 130, 159
Poverty, 29, 53, 88–89, 103–106, 148, 159, 179n184
Power, x, 5, 17, 19, 28, 34–35, 39, 41, 61, 64, 69–81,
    102, 107, 109, 110, 120–125, 135, 140–141,
    143, 147, 151–156, 159–162, 171n103, 183n56,
    203n31
Premodern, 3, 7, 28, 46, 49, 54, 65, 123, 125, 142,
    156, 204n46
President, 13, 24, 66–68, 74, 78, 101–102, 107,
    114, 126, 154, 162
Prince, The, 8, 31–32, 36, 64, 68, 84, 101, 103, 105
Proletarian/proletariat, 10, 109, 138, 143
Protestantism, 20, 134, 163
Puerto Rico, 41
Punishment, 71, 106

Quechua, 73, 162–163, 174n67
Quetzalcoatl, 74
Quintilian, 32, 48

Racism, 9–11, 16, 84, 93, 125, 127, 145, 149, 153,
    163, 165n5, 168n44, 171n102, 175n70,
    183n64, 184n80, 189n8, 199n73
Rational/irrational, 10, 37, 39, 42, 45, 48–52, 92,
    125, 131–134, 140, 156, 177n125
Rationality, 7, 32, 43, 47, 55, 108, 115, 116, 120, 148,
    172n12
Rawls, John, 6, 142, 160
Razetti, Luis, 86
Reason, 4, 8, 12, 16, 29, 32, 37–39, 44–54, 82, 111,
    116, 118, 128–129, 133–136, 139–140, 149, 151,
    156–157, 178n159, 191n60, 199n63, 205n63
Regionalism, 19
Religion, 7, 42, 44–45, 52–54, 72, 74, 77, 80, 90,
    104, 116, 118, 121, 138–139, 151, 153, 157,
    171n103, 186n130, 197n30, 200n88
Renan, Ernest, 86, 90, 96, 111
Representation, 37, 48, 94, 107, 121
Republicanism, 19–23, 57–58, 63–70, 73, 75,
    81–85, 88–89, 92, 101–102, 106–108, 132,
    142, 147–149, 152, 160, 164, 181n14,
    184n78, 185n105, 186n121, 187n158,
    195nn151, 161
Revolution, 22, 59, 69, 72, 75, 82, 84, 88–90, 112,
    114, 121, 126–127, 139, 143, 162, 196n4
Rhetoric, 20, 27–46, 50, 55, 66–67, 78, 118, 132,
    142, 147, 150, 154, 172n9, 173n39, 178n141,
    179n178, 180n188, 186n114, 189n204

Rodó, José Enrique, 115, 117, 125, 133, 149, 184n92, 196nn14–15, 201n102

Rome, 30, 35, 39, 60, 63, 67, 70, 72, 82, 92, 102, 172n13, 175n69, 182nn38–39

Rousseau, Jean-Jacques, 6, 9, 57, 63–71, 71, 142, 147, 182n34, 183nn69, 71, 184nn73–76, 185nn96, 101

Sarmiento, Domingo Faustino, 16, 98, 106, 132, 149, 155, 176n97, 191n40, 192n69, 193nn102–103, 203n24

Savages, 32, 40–41, 44, 50, 99, 153

Schmitt, Carl, 22, 107–110, 195nn163–174

Scholastic, 20, 34, 37–38, 147

Schopenhauer, Arthur, 124, 130

Science, 7, 9, 28, 30, 54, 80, 95, 105, 114, 120, 130, 136, 138, 151, 153, 157, 175n78, 192n75

Seignobos, Charles, 86, 90

Self, 14, 68, 104, 121–122, 156

Senses, 48–50, 123, 131, 135, 141, 151, 198n43

Sentience, 29, 38–40, 47

Sex/sexual, 6, 41, 59, 61, 95, 132, 159, 171n101, 200n95

Skin, 6, 61–63, 75, 96, 104, 128, 137, 140, 145, 161

Skinner, Quentin, 8, 167n33, 177n120, 181n11, 185n100

Slave, 12, 14, 59, 120, 152, 182n31

Slavery, 4, 8, 12–14, 20, 38, 75, 105, 154, 157, 172n7, 177n123, 182n50, 187n158, 203n19

Smith, Adam, 9

Socialism, 108, 162

Sociology, 6, 90, 96, 111

Socratic, 120

Soldiers, 27, 33, 39, 81, 164, 174n52

Solórzano, Juan de, 92, 149

Somatic, 16, 29, 43, 45, 47, 49–50, 98–99, 122–124, 140–141, 145–149, 151, 153, 156, 161, 202n10

Soul, 29, 44, 47–50, 67, 78, 91, 128, 131, 139, 167n29, 177nn125–126, 178n159

Spain, 12, 18, 21, 27–36, 39–45, 50, 54–55, 59–62, 73, 75, 86, 90–94, 104, 106, 110, 114, 125, 162, 167n31, 170n99, 172n13, 177n129, 180n91, 181n41, 191n60, 192n73, 194n133, 203n19

Spectacle, 46, 141, 159

Spencer, Herbert, 86, 91, 115, 117, 136, 191n56, 199n62

Spirituality, 126, 132–134

State, the, 7, 18, 62, 65, 71–76, 81, 86, 106–111, 152, 159, 172, 181n20

Strauss, Leo, 175n86

Suffering, 37–43

Synthesis, 16–22, 28, 52–55, 60, 79–81, 112–113, 120–122, 134, 139, 147, 149, 154, 196n8, 203n34

Synthetic, 4–5, 15–24, 34, 55–60, 84, 89, 103, 108, 11, 113, 121–124, 134, 140, 144, 151–155, 160–164, 170n88, 203n30, 204n49, 205n58

Taine, Hyppolyte, 86, 87, 90, 105

Tarde, Gabriel, 91, 96

Taste, 48, 75, 116, 128, 129, 135, 199n60

Terror, 26, 39

Theology, 21, 27, 108–109, 113, 147

Theoria, 141, 145

Thomistic, 27–28

Tocqueville, Alexis de, 4, 11, 14, 104, 105, 165nn3–6, 168n60

Toleration, 9, 28, 172n12

Torture, 39, 65

Totalitarianism, 107

Trajan, 59

Truth, 12, 77, 85, 103, 105, 115, 202n2

Turkish, 42, 52

Tyranny, 56, 68, 75, 87, 89, 103–104, 106, 127, 185n95

Unamuno, Miguel de, 92

United States, ix-x, 4, 11–12, 15, 17, 21, 24, 58, 78–79, 84, 95, 97, 99–100, 102, 105, 114, 116, 127, 136, 139, 142, 155, 162–164, 165n7, 166n12, 169nn79, 80, 180n9, 182n47, 188n177, 192n77, 193n106, 202n15, 204n56

Universalism, 17–19, 22, 28, 42, 92, 113, 147, 149, 160, 200n99

Uruguay, 140

Utilitarianism, 9, 72, 160, 186n137

Utopian, 19, 22, 30, 52, 80–81, 87, 92, 116–117, 129, 135, 155

Utopianism, 7

Vacher de Lapouge, Georges, 96

Vallenilla Lanz, Laureano:
　Bolívar, 82, 85, 94, 103
　caudillismo, 85, 98, 102
　democratic Caesarism, 87, 89, 101, 103
　dictatorship, 87, 89, 108

Vallenilla Lanz, Laureano: *(continued)*
  gendarme, 87–88, 105
  Laboulaye, 86–87, 90
  Machiavelli, 83–84, 87, 101, 103
  modernization, 87, 107–110
  nation, 85–86, 95, 107–110
  Positivism, 89–91
  race, 84, 86, 93, 96–100, 105
  sociology, 90, 96, 111
  Taine, 86–87, 90
  tyranny, 103, 104, 106
Values, 33, 37, 72, 96, 104, 119, 123–126, 130, 133,
  139, 153, 161, 176n96, 198n47, 203n31
Vasconcelos, José:
  aesthetics, 113, 120–124, 135
  agonism, 118, 128
  art, 115, 118, 120–122, 126, 131
  beauty, 133–137
  cosmopolitan, 117, 132
  harmony, 127–128, 134–135
  miscegenation, 129, 134
  music, 121, 133–134
  Nietzsche, 119–125, 130–134
  race, 113, 117–119
  rhythm, 128, 134–135
  synthesis, 113, 120–121
  taste, 128–129
  teleology, 131–132

Violence, 27, 36, 42–43, 59, 72, 86, 98, 146, 152,
  158, 193n110
Viroli, Maurizio, xi, 183nn65, 67, 184n78,
  185nn96, 98, 100
Virtù, 72, 105, 133, 159, 176n96, 186n121,
  188n196, 189n9, 194n126, 136, 195nn151,
  161, 202n6
Virtue, 8, 34, 44–46, 53–55, 61, 64, 66, 68,
  71–74, 77, 80, 82, 135, 142, 148, 179n184,
  185n105
Vitoria, Francisco de, 36, 38, 149, 172n17, 174n51,
  175n77
Vultu, 37, 48

Wagner, Richard, 121–124, 197n32
Walzer, Michael, xi, 171n106, 202n5
War, 41, 52, 68, 69, 77, 106–107, 148, 181n20,
  185n98, 188n188
Washington, Booker T., 14, 169n75
Weber, Max, 22, 107–110, 156, 185n113, 195nn163,
  175, 196n182
Will to Power, 120–122, 200n95
Winant, Howard, 11, 168n63, 198n51
Women, 9, 26, 41, 57, 59, 90, 159, 175n87, 192n84
Worms, René, 86, 191n56

Zarathustra, 120, 125, 133, 134, 198n50, 200n101
Zea, Leopoldo, 202n18